Guide to Software Development

Arthur M. Langer

Guide to Software Development

Designing and Managing the Life Cycle

Second Edition

 Springer

Arthur M. Langer
Center for Technology Management
Columbia University Arts & Sciences
New York, NY, USA

School of Professional Studies
Columbia University
New York, NY, USA

ISBN 978-1-4471-7394-6 ISBN 978-1-4471-6799-0 (eBook)
DOI 10.1007/978-1-4471-6799-0

Printed on acid-free paper

This Springer imprint is published by Springer Nature
The registered company is Springer-Verlag London Ltd.

Preface

How to improve the quality and process of implementing enterprise software remains a most challenging topic at conferences on information development and business process reengineering. Over the past few decades, the question of how to do this has only become more complex, especially with the growth of sophisticated packaged software products in the market such as SAP and Oracle Financials. These products, called Enterprise Resource Planning (ERP), claim to provide a quicker and more cost-effective way to fully integrate software applications in all parts of the business. Yet so many of them fail to be either chaeaper or faster by the time they are put into production. Furthermore, the decision to make or buy software is not simple, and in many cases, organizations now need to consider some combination of both. Therefore, the problem that this book addresses is to how best determine to make such decisions and what effect such decisions have on the Software Development Life Cycle (SDLC). Although there are many different SDLC methodologies, this book offers an integrated approach that includes the management and decision practices that are critical for success. Accordingly, the roles of the analyst and the project manager need to be linked throughout the SDLC. The objective, however, continues to be how information technology professionals can create automated solutions that fit user and customer needs. By suggesting that professionals may find success in mixing methodologies, this book breaks important new ground.

Many books written on this subject tend to focus too much on the mechanics of how to do analysis or how to do project management, rather than on the art of performing both functions successfully. As I have stated in previous books, the most successful implementers are not necessarily the best technicians, but rather are gifted individuals who have the ability and insight to extract information from users and transfer their knowledge into logical solutions. But today even accurate requirements do not ensure success without quality management. The field of information technology is no longer new, and the time has come for education to focus on producing quality products faster and cheaper. Thus, this book seeks to develop the skills and insights that distinguish successful software implementations.

This new edition identifies many new alternatives for how to manage and model a system using sophisticated analysis tools and advanced management practices. It emphasizes how and when professionals can best apply them and what benefits can be derived from their application. The book's approach is to recommend that

analysts and managers must be agile, adopt risks in the analysis and design process, and not overcommit to using any one methodology but rather learn to deal within the constraints of the political and cultural realities of their organizations. It may come as a surprise to many lay readers to learn that this approach is unique among many textbooks. Yet the fact is that most books teach only a single method and advocate the use of that method alone in all projects.

Most important in this second edition are a number of new topics that are integral to the software development process including such areas as cybersecurity, big data, and digital transformation, as well as the importance of interfacing directly with the consumers of the business. Indeed, we are now in the age of "digital consumerization," where all application design decisions will inevitably be determined by the buyer, not the internal user. The challenge that this book addresses is how analysts need to forecast or predict what consumers will need in the future. As such analysts will need to take risks and understand that the predictive requirements they develop will have a relatively short life, before new consumer needs make them obsolete. Unfortunately, there are no magic bullets to successful predictions and failures will occur. As a result, organizations must develop multiple initiatives to ultimately succeed. This can only happen when analysts can "sense" what consumers will need and then design applications that "respond" quickly before these needs become realities.

The Aim of This Book

The risks involved when making decisions about enterprise software solutions are substaintial: those projects that involve reengineering activities have a failure rate of over 50 %. Obviously, then, the stakes are very high, and identifying the sources of failure can be invaluable. In general, I have found that project failures can be attributed to two major issues: (1) those that have difficulty defining accurate business requirements, and (2) those that have problems with managing change. Both of these major challenges can be overcome by following many of the steps I have outlined in this book. This book is therefore meant to be a "how-to" guide taking theory and applying it to the realities of practice. These reengineering failure rates should not be confused with the failures of prediction discussed above.

The book recognizes that there are few off-the-shelf products that can provide a complete solution for any organization. Thus, most enterprise-level solutions will be a combination of package and custom developed software. This "hybrid" realism has changed the way professionals undertake the SDLC particularly as it relates to selection of third-party vendors and the legal ramifications of working with outside consultants. For this reason, the book includes subjects like build vs. buy, searching for vendor solutions, and vendor contract considerations.

My enthusiasm for writing this book was supported by many of my students at Columbia University who found that existing books on software development to be:

- *Very hypothetical.* Although they explain the methodologies and management concepts, they do not provide enough concrete examples.
- *Too technical.* They do not deal with the political and cultural realities of how things get done in organizations. Indeed, the objective of providing software solutions is to service business units in organizations. The management side of developing software solutions is as important as the technical side.
- *Lacking modest but effective cases.* The examples do not provide an understanding of the technical and management concepts effectively or are too simplistic for practice implementation.

The Intended Audience for This Book

This book assumes a reasonable understanding of computer and business concepts. The material is presented to be used for an introductorary project management class or analysis and design course in a university program. In addition, it can be used by practicing information technology professionals or executives who are managing software projects and need an in-depth understanding of the principles of the analysis and design and project management processes. Furthermore, many business managers who are also responsible for ERP-type projects may find this book as a way of developing a useful understanding of the requirements process as well as the entire SDLC.

New York, NY, USA Arthur M. Langer

Acknowledgments

I want to acknowledge my students at Columbia University in the Executive Masters in Technology Management program for their dedication and inspiration, and certainly for keeping me current in the evolving digital world. A special thanks is given to the executive mentors who give their time to support our students so that we have a next generation of IT leaders.

A special recognition is owed to Cali and Shane Caprio, my two grandchildren who bring me joy every day.

New York City, NY, USA Arthur M. Langer
September 2016

Contents

Part III How to Implement

Introduction

After decades of writing about the field of analysis and design, I write this book to focus on the evolution of software in the world. We have seen over the past 50 years, the continual expansion of the library of software applications that are used in common workplace as well as in the personal lives of people throughout the world. Indeed, software applications continue to change the world, and as a result the challenge of managing the advent of huge application libraries has become of paramount importance. In addition, the advent of social networking has also had a salient impact on the uses and effects of applications over the Internet, and the expansion of open source has now created an environment of applications that can be used on demand and across multiple platforms. We are also facing a new generation of software users who behave as consumers in that they want applications that are personalized and operate across multiple devices. Furthermore, we are experiencing what we are now calling digital transformation, the era in which organizations must provide products and services that meet the demands of a digital economy.

The purpose of this book is to provide professionals and academics with a guide to managing the life cycle of placing software applications into production. This book breaks new ground because of this narrow focus, which is more on implementation than on engineering per se. This book provides guidance on how to determine whether to make or buy and allows readers to determine sections that are fitting for their use. Technical readers, that is, those engaged in analysis and design, will find chapters that provide the approach and tools on how to create an architecture of system needs. Business users can become more educated in the system development life cycle for both packaged software or customized applications. Business and IT people will also get a better understanding of project management methods and contract consideration in the relationships they have with vendors and independent consultants. Furthermore, this new edition addresses the evolving role of the analyst in the age of digital transformation, the impact of predictive analytics in the way we use big data, how projects need to be managed in virtual settings, and why cyber security must be a fundamental part of the way applications are architecture. Most

© Springer-Verlag London Limited 2016
A.M. Langer, *Guide to Software Development*,
DOI 10.1007/978-1-4471-6799-0_1

important is the need to reduce risks in the types of applications we release into the market. We can no longer take the position that our users ultimately understand the needs and behaviors of the consumer market.

What Is, Is

Over 50 years of developing requirements for systems have taught us that the only successful approach to developing software applications is to accept what exists in the user's environment, however far from ideal those conditions may be, and work within those limitations. It may be very tempting to use analysis time to try to refocus how the user does business. Yet efforts to redesign or reengineer, unless specifically requested by the user, will typically be a waste. Although your assessment may be correct and your suggestions potentially useful, being correct is less important in this situation than being wise and understanding the ability of your users to successfully implement and utilize what they need. Analysts tend to ignore this simple wisdom, much to their own distress and that of their clients.

Looking at a typical example of an analysis situation will help to illustrate this point. Let us assume that an enterprise needs a relational database model to gather information about a subject area of the business. There are 200 offices that will need to connect into a nationally provided service. Users disagree on the mission of the applications and cannot determine what reports or query information they want. Some offices are automated, but they do not have the same software and hardware. There is little expertise in the user community to determine the data requirements and file layouts (identifying elements in each file). Management has requested that the analyst establish a specification, which identifies the requirements of the system as well as the necessary hardware and software.

Faced with so unwieldy a task, many analysts will adopt the following approach in an attempt to impose order on a disorderly situation:

1. Force users to define all requirements. Since they are unable to do so, this insistence will probably result in their guessing or providing incomplete information.
2. Determine the hardware and software configuration, despite having inaccurate or incomplete requirements and ignore security.
3. Ignore the political environment.
4. Establish a project plan that everyone knows will fail, but push ahead with it anyway.

It should be clear that this approach is the wrong one, on a number of different counts. Yet such an approach is all too typical for analysts confronted with a less-than-ideal working environment. Happily, there is a better approach for all concerned, one that recognizes and responds to the conditions actually present at the users' site. In this case it is evident that the users are not positioned to provide the requirements for a system, largely because they do not fully understand their own

needs and because they do not agree among themselves. What the analyst needs to understand in such a situation is that because of this lack of knowledge and organization, user needs will tend to change during the process of product analysis and design. Such changes are to be expected; they are simply part of the life cycle for this particular implementation. To ignore the situation and try to implement a system is to invite failure. Put simply then, what is, is. The task of the analyst is to work with what is, rather than trying to change it or—even worse—simply denying it. Once you as an analyst understand that reality, you understand that your solution must accommodate what will inevitably occur.

Here is a more sensible approach to the situation described above:

1. Focus on designing a model that can provide the users and consumers with the capability they want. Create a project plan that assumes that the database will be incomplete during Phase I because of the users' inability to define the correct information. The process will therefore be an iterative one and thus will be finalized during the later parts of the development life cycle.
2. Do not try to identify hardware before it is clear what the usage requirements are, such as peak time processing, number of users, etc. It will be more beneficial to establish the operating system or architectural environment that you want to support, pending the results of the analysis.
3. Utilize a software system or tool that will allow users to generate new scenarios such that they can see how these scenarios relate to the entire system.
4. Set up a pilot program. This will require that certain offices agree to be test-sites for the early versions of the software. The function of the pilot is to provide feedback on the effectiveness and shortfalls of the product. It is important to state clearly the objectives of the pilot and the format of the feedback in order to ensure the success of the exercise.
5. Formulate a plan that depicts a schedule for getting the entire enterprise implemented and live on the new system. Be sensitive to the politics of the situation and use a realistic approach that will not require a cultural change in order to implement software in the existing environment.

The essence of this approach is to develop a strategy that fits the reality of the environment, rather than force the environment to change. Throughout this book, we will explore this simple but crucial concept. No two system development projects are identical, and the more familiar the analyst is with the environment, the more successful the project will be. This book will also argue against the conventional wisdom that suggests using an approach based on only a single methodology (e.g., Yourdon, Martin, Booch, etc.). The mixing of methodologies allows the analyst a wider range of tools. Hands-on experience shows that this kind of mixing of methodologies can be done quite successfully and that it is appropriate in a large number of analysis situations.

Most important to the purpose of this book is the evolution of the application development world over the last 30 years. We have gone from solely an in-house build-it-yourself focus to what is commonly known as "commercially off-the-shelf

(COTS)" solutions. This book will integrate the classic approaches of developing applications to specifically meet user needs with the unique conditions of going with the "best-fit" approach of COTS. But the decisions today are not at all binary—build versus buy, etc. With the expansion of software modules, programs that provide specific tasks and pieces of code can be brought together to build applications, but yet are bought. Furthermore, there is the impact of open source and outsourcing alternatives, which have changed the way organizations pursue application decisions.

Finally, what I feel sets this book apart from others is its commitment to an IT and User integration. Too many books still discuss how IT can save the day or lead the implementation. Leadership is a tricky thing, and it certainly does not suggest control as a solution. IT must become better leaders by displaying the ability to influence management and users, not to tell them what needs to be done. Thus, this book speaks to both IT and non-IT personnel and hopefully provides a provocative approach to ensuring better success when determining the why, what, and how of providing application solutions.

Just What Is a Complex Project?

Most analysts, project team members, and users worry about the complexity of their projects. Their requirements seem entirely unique to them, and therefore a very special approach seems to be required. How many times have you heard: "the tools and approaches used elsewhere just won't work in this environment"?

The truth, however, is very different: the only truly complex projects are those that people make so! It is important for the analyst to recognize that the procedures utilized, regardless of the size of the project, should remain fundamentally the same. As we have discussed above, the analyst's approach to the implementation of each project should be tailored individually; however, the procedures for this implementation should remain constant. Very often the organization of interviews, the utilization of techniques such as Joint Application Development, (discussed later in this chapter), or the simple addition of more analysts to the project can solve what appear to be insurmountable problems.

In fact, most of the myriad problems that arise in product development can be traced to two fundamental issues:

1. People are trying to solve the wrong problem, i.e., the identified problem is not really what is wrong.
2. The solution to the real problem is often much simpler than it first appears to be.

Because we have failed to recognize these issues, the industry's frustration with developing appropriate software solutions has been chronic, and this situation has not really improved over the last 25 years! The question is why?

To put it bluntly, analysts often fail to do their jobs properly! We tend to put together plans and schedules that are doomed from the start to fail, an issue treated

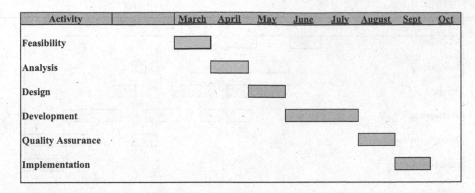

Activity		March	April	May	June	July	August	Sept	Oct
Feasibility									
Analysis									
Design									
Development									
Quality Assurance									
Implementation									

Fig. 1.1 Sample Gantt chart

in more detail later. The ultimate goal of the analyst must take into account the reality of the environment in which the work is occurring. Remember, work within the environment. Let users decide what degree of change is appropriate for their own operation; do not take it upon yourself to demand that they change.

For example, how many times have you seen a Gantt chart[1] for a project schedule that resembles the one in Fig. 1.1.

It looks nice, but in reality the plan it depicts could never happen. Focus in particular on the intersection of development and quality assurance, QA activities. The plan shows that once development is finished, the materials are forwarded to QA for testing. The sequence assumes, however, that QA will never find an error and that therefore the materials will never be returned to development! Any analyst knows that this scenario is very unlikely to occur. Such poor planning results in deficient allocation of resources to the project. Should the development schedule be met, programming resources most probably will be allocated to other projects. Thus, if QA finds errors, (which they undoubtedly will), reallocating these programming resources becomes difficult and problematic. And remember: programmers do not like returning to an "old" program to do maintenance or error fixing.

Figure 1.2 reflects a more realistic view of the life cycle of the project.

The difference in approach is striking. The question is, as sensible as this plan appears to be, why don't we always do it this way? Quite frankly, this plan does not look as nice—as neat and tidy—as the previous plan. But of course simply denying the pain of reality—the inevitable inconveniences and delays—does not make that reality go away. In defense of the previous configuration, some developers might suggest that the iterations of efforts between testing and fixing the software are assumed to be included in the QA time. Maybe, but don't count on it! Just look at the second schedule and you will see how the results of this proper allocation added to the delivery time of the project. It is clear that the original plan was simply incorrect.

[1]A Gantt chart is a tool that depicts progress of tasks against time. It was developed by Henry L. Gantt in 1917.

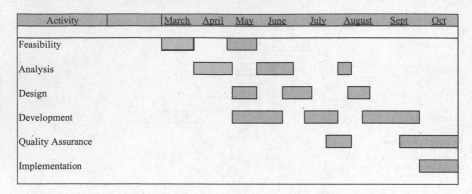

Fig. 1.2 Modified Gantt chart reflecting realistic project activity behavior

There is absolutely no reason why a schedule should not reflect the reality of what will most probably occur. The results are clear: realistic planning provides a more reliable schedule. Among the many benefits of such a schedule are the confidence and respect gained by both the users and the development staff. There is nothing like producing a schedule that reflects what everyone is confident will occur.

At this point, experienced analysts are no doubt wondering: what happens when management dictates to us how much time we have and shows no flexibility about running behind schedule? This problem is unfortunately not uncommon and typically fits into one of three scenarios:

1. Management is ignorant about the analysis and construction of systems and simply has no idea how much time is required to complete the project. In this case the analyst will need to develop a convincing presentation for management about the details of how systems are designed and developed. The presentation should be carefully documented to refer to the industry statistics for similar projects in similar companies. This kind of documentation adds much credibility to the discussion. You can also consider having an independent source, such as a respected consulting firm, support your position.
2. Management has little confidence in development. They feel that picking a date and sticking to it is the best method of getting the project finished. Yes, this is the bully technique! It usually results from bad experiences, probably from looking at those unrealistic Gantt charts. In this situation, the analyst must take steps to gain management's confidence. Using the suggestions above would be a good start. In addition, you will need to research and to understand the history of what your predecessors did to encourage this type of distrusting and dictatorial attitude on the part of management and find a tactful way to address those issues.
3. Unfortunately, bad management does exist. If you cannot win any concessions or understanding from management, you may have reached what is known as the "no-win scenario"; management is simply unwilling to allot adequate time for the completion of the project and they are unwilling to be persuaded otherwise. When this situation exists in the workplace, the advice is straightforward: you

can leave or you can find some way to deal with this constraint. In either case, be aware that under the no-win scenario, there is little hope that the project will result in the development of quality software. This perspective is not cynical, but rather realistic: some projects are doomed to fail before they begin. What is important is that the analyst recognizes as early in the life cycle as possible that the project cannot be successful.

Because this book represents more about selection and management of software applications, it is necessary to modify the systems development life cycle (SDLC). The *traditional SDLC* is the most commonly used to design products in three major parts:

1. Requirements analysis
2. Data modeling
3. Normalization

During the first phase, requirements analysis, the development and design team conduct interviews in order to capture all the business needs as related to the proposed system. The data modeling phase consists of the creation of the logical data model that will later be used to define the physical data model or database structures. After the database has been modeled and designed, the normalization phase is implemented to help eliminate or reduce as much as possible any redundant data. All of the specifics of how this is accomplished will be detailed in the tools of analysis chapters. Below is a more specific description of what activities are included in the development, testing, and production cycles of the SDLC.

Development

The development life cycle includes four overall components. Using this perspective, "development" would consist of all the necessary steps to accomplish the creation of the application. This includes feasibility, analysis, design, and the actual coding. Feasibility represents the tasks necessary to determine whether the software project makes business sense. Most organizations would integrate the process of return-on-investment (ROI) during this step. ROI consists of the financial steps that determine mathematically whether the project will provide the necessary monetary returns to the business. Focusing solely on monetary returns can be a serious pitfall, since there are many benefits that can be realized via nonmonetary returns (Langer 2011). Feasibility often contains what is known as a high-level forecast or budget. The "high" would represent the "worst case" scenario on cost and the "low" the best case or lowest cost. The hope of course is that the actual cost and timetable would fall somewhere in between the high and the low. But feasibility goes beyond just the budget; it also represents whether the business feels that the project is attainable within a specific timetable as well. So, feasibility is statement of both financial and business objectives and an overall belief that the cost is worth the payback.

Analysis is the ultimate step of creating the detailed logical requirements or the architecture of the applications and database. Ultimately, the analyst creates a requirements document that outlines all of the needs for the coders to work from, without going back to the users directly for clarification. Analysis, as an architectural responsibility, is very much based on a mathematical progression of predictable steps. These steps are quite iterative in nature, which requires practitioners to understand the gradual nature of completion of this vital step in development. Another aspect of the mathematics of analysis is decomposition. Decomposition as we will see establishes the creation of the smaller components that make up the whole. It is like the bones, blood, and muscles of the human body that ultimately make up what we physically see in a person. Once a system is decomposed, the analyst can be confident that the "parts" that comprise the whole are identified and can be reused throughout the system as necessary. These decomposed parts are called "objects" and comprise the study and application of object-oriented analysis and design. So the basis of working with users ultimately leads to the creation of parts known as objects that act as interchangeable components that can be used whenever needed. One should think of objects like interchangeable parts of a car. They sometimes are called "standard" parts that can be reused in multiple models. The benefits are obvious. Such is the same objective with software: the more reusable, the more efficient and cost-effective.

Design is far less logical than analysis but a far more creative step. Design is the phase that requires the physical decisions about the system, from what programming language to use, which vendor database to select (e.g., Oracle, Sybase, DB2), to how screens and reports will be identified. The design phase can also include decisions about hardware and network communications or the *topology*. Unlike analysis, design requires less of a mathematical and engineering focus, to one that actually serves the user view. The design process is perhaps the most iterative, which could require multiple sessions with users using a trial and error approach until the correct user interface and product selection has been completed. Design often requires "experts" in database design, screen architecture experts as well as those professionals that understand performance needs of network servers, and other hardware components required by the system.

Coding represents another architectural as well as mathematical approach. However, I would suggest that mathematics is not the most accurate description of a coding structure, rather it's about understanding how logic operates. This component of mathematics is known as "Boolean" algebra or the mathematics of logic. Boolean algebra is the basis of how software communicates with the real machine. Software is the physical abstraction that allows us to talk with the hardware machine. Coding then is the best way to actually develop the structure of the program. Much has been written about coding styles and formats. The best known is called "structured" programming. Structured programming was originally developed so that programmers would create code that would be cohesive, that is, would be self-reliant. Self-reliance in coding means that the program is self-contained because all of the logic relating to its tasks is within the program. The opposite of cohesion is coupling. Coupling is the logic of programs that are reliant on each other, meaning that

a change to one program necessitates a change in another program. Coupling is viewed as being dangerous from a maintenance and quality perspective simply because changes cause problems in other reliant or "coupled" systems. The relationship of coding to analysis can be critical given that the decision on what code will comprise a module may be determined during analysis as opposed to coding.

Testing

Testing can have a number of components. The first form of testing is called program debugging. Debugging is the process of a programmer ensuring that his/her code in a program executes as designed. Debugging, therefore, should be carried out by the programmer, as opposed to a separate quality assurance group. However, it is important to recognize that debugging does not ensure that the program is performing as required by end users, rather only confirms that the code executes and does not abort during program execution. What does this mean? Simply that a programmer should never pass a program to quality assurance that does not execute, at least showing that it does perform under all conditions. Once again, this process does not ensure that the results produced by the program are correct or meet the original requirements set forth by users.

Once a program has been "debugged" it should then be sent through the quality assurance process. Today, most large organizations recognize that quality assurance needs to be performed by non-programming individuals. As a result organizations create separate quality assurance organizations that do nothing but test the correctness and accuracy of programs. Quality assurance organizations typically accomplish this by designing what is known as acceptance test planning. Acceptance test plans are designed from the original requirements, which allow quality assurance personnel to develop assurance testing based on the user's original requirements as opposed to what might have been interpreted. For this reason acceptance test planning is typically implemented during the analysis and design phases of the life cycle but executed during the testing phase. Acceptance test planning also includes system type testing activities such as stress and load checking (ensuring that the application can handle larger demands or users) or integration testing (whether the application communicates and operates appropriately with other programs in the system), as well as compatibility testing, such as ensuring that applications operate on types of browsers or computer systems. Testing, by its very nature is an iterative process that can often create "loops" of redesign and programming. It is important to recognize that acceptance testing has two distinct components: first, the design of the test plans, and second, the execution of those acceptance plans.

Production

Production is synonymous with the "going-live" phases. Ultimately, production must ensure the successful execution of all aspects of a systems performance.

During production, there is the need to establish how problems will be serviced, what support staff will be available, and when and how inquiries will be responded to and scheduled for fixing. This component of production may initiate new development and testing cycles because of redesign needs (or misinterpreted user needs). This means that the original requirements were not properly translated into system realities.

On the other hand, production as a life cycle includes other complex issues:

- Backup, recovery, and archival
- Change control
- Performance fine-tuning and statistics
- Audit and new requirements

Backup, Recovery, and Archiving

Operational backup should be defined during the development phases; however, there are inevitably backup requirements that need to be modified during production. This occurs because the time it takes to complete data backup is difficult to predict. The speed in which data can be placed on another media is not an exact science and is based on the complexity of how data is selected and the method of placement to another location and/or media. The speed also heavily relies on factors such as disk input/output speed, network throughput (speed of communication network), database backup algorithms, and the actual intervals between backup cycles. Why does this matter? It matters because backups require systems to be "off-line" until they complete, meaning that the system is in-effect not operational. Thus, the longer the backup process, the longer the system is off-line. The most popular example of the potential backup dilemma is the overnight processes that must be completed by the beginning of the next morning. If the process of backup will take longer than the allowed time, then analysts/designers need to determine a way that can condense the time line. The alternatives might typically include limiting the actual data used to back up, multiple devices to increase throughput, etc.

Recovery, on the other hand, is more about testing the quality of the backed up data and to determine whether the data stored can be recovered in the operational system. So, the first aspect is to see whether the necessary data needed to bring the system "back" can be accomplished. One hopes that recovery will never be necessary, but the most glaring exposure on quality assurance is to not really know whether the data we think we have can actually be restored back to operational forms. For example, it is one thing to backup a complex database; it's another to restore that data so that the key fields and indexes are working appropriately after restoration. The only assurance for this is to actually perform a restore in a simulation. Simulations take analysis and design talent and need to be conducted on some intervals that ensure that backup data integrity is preserved.

Restoration and backup become even more comprehensive when portions are what is called "archived." Archived data is data that is deemed no longer necessary in the "live" system, but data that may be required under some circumstances. So, data that is determined to be ready for archival needs to be backed up in such a way

that it can be restored, not to the live system, but rather a special system that will allow for the data to be queried and accessed as if it was live. The most relevant example that I can provide here is accounting data from past periods that are no longer needed in the operations system, but may need to be accessed for audit purposes. In this example it might be necessary to restore a prior year's accounting data to a special system that simulates a prior year in question, but that has no effect on the current system.

This traditional SDLC is no longer applicable to most development projects that start might with an existing package—especially a third-party vendor developed product. Thus a modified SDLC is required for packaged software development that comprises 12 complex steps:

1. Assessing business requirements
2. Build vs. buy issues
3. Establishing requirements (RFI, RFP)
4. Searching for solutions
5. Controlling costs and realistic budgeting
6. Creating requirement documents using analysis tools
7. The data
8. Legacy systems and data conversion
9. Business process reengineering
10. Data analytics and data warehouses
11. Documentation and acceptance testing
12. Going live and conclusions

Figure 1.3 graphically shows the flow from one stage of the SDLC to another.

It is interesting to note that the *integrated* SDLC for pre-developed software applications are actually far more complex than that of the traditional SDLC for undeveloped products. This can be attributed to the fact that packaged software products require both development-related activities and project management—management that covers both internal activities and vendor management. Each step of this modified SDLC is defined below and forms the basis of the chapters to follow—each chapter defining the details of how each step can ensure a higher rate of success. Furthermore there are generic things that need to be done while the SDLC is occurring, including analysis tools to be used, project management, standards, and vendor contract considerations. These subjects are often addressed outside the SDLC rather be parallel concepts that can derail the success of the project if not integrated properly. To avoid this pitfall, these four other components are embedded in the forthcoming chapters. A brief description of each chapter follows.

Chapter 2: Assessing Business Requirements

The first and most critical step in providing a software solution is to understand what users really want. The word "user" has actually been replaced over the years with the word "business." Indeed, the target for most application solutions need to be geared to solving a business issue, rather than the user's personal needs. This

Fig. 1.3 Diagram of chapter flow

point is very relevant to the large-scale implementations of ERP (enterprise resource planning) solutions. ERP are large organizational products that essentially link all aspects of the business to an integrated system—certainly a complex application. Historically, almost half of ERP implementations fail as succeed. ERP project failures are typically associated with the inability of the user community to accept the way the system works in comparison to their personal business preferences. That is, the user community is not willing to change its procedures to meet the more generic business operations that are designed into package software products. Thus heavy modifications to the existing product inevitably cause project delays and potential failures.

Chapter 3: Build Versus Buy

The classic question that has challenged business organizations is whether to build applications in-house or to buy them as prepackaged software. This chapter will provide guidance on the appropriate steps to determine the right choice. Obviously the decisions can be complex and vary depending on the application, the generic nature of the application itself, and the time requirements to have a functional application to meet business needs. Build decisions are further complex in that they can be developed in-house or an outsource provider. Buying can also come with choices on the amount of custom modifications that are necessary—the general rule being that over 20 % modifications tend to be a bad choice for the buy equation.

Chapter 4: Establishing Requirements Using a Request for Proposal (RFP) and a Request for Information (RFI)

Once decisions have been made for build vs. buy and appropriate specifications have been completed, organizations need to create a document that can be examined by third-party vendors or product suppliers so that an estimate of "fit" can be assessed—fit meaning the amount of customization required or development time necessary. Two such documents can be used: request for information (RFI) or a request for proposal (RFP).

This chapter seeks to define the similarities and differences between the two types of documents and when one type might be preferred over the other. In either situation, the main focus of the documents is to provide potential vendors or developers with enough information so that they can determine the scope of the effort and the associated costs for providing a solution. The documents also provide the selection group to be able to compare bids because the requirements are consistent—that is, the document itself requires a standard format of response, thus allowing each solution to be compared, as they say, apples-to-apples.

Chapter 5: Searching for Solutions

This chapter sets forth the strategy for obtaining bids from the best sources that match the requirements. There are challenges to determine what types of vendor and/or consulting firms need to be selected and what preliminary steps firms should exercise before asking for a formal bid. This section also addresses the types of searches that can be done, from hiring a third-party consulting firm, an independent

contractor, to a more public forum. Levels of searches are also addressed, including having decision points where certain vendors get eliminated and narrowed to a final group of acceptable solutions. The section also covers the ways to contact potential solution firms and the procedures for doing the necessary due diligence of not only the product but also the firm itself. That is, too many firms may not be as dependable as its marketing materials suggest. Solutions also include hybrid approaches where both third-party and internally developed software can be integrated.

Chapter 6: Controlling Costs and Realistic Budgeting

Costs are always a huge factor when undertaking major application projects. We know from experience that application projects typically are late and over budget. The question is why? The problem often relates to underestimating the complexity of the project and the time it takes to get organizations to properly define what they need. And let's not forget the role of politics, which inevitably affects the way things get done. It is also very difficult to define what you need and to obtain consensus across departments and organizations. Today, any software application will likely touch multiple parts of the organization and require retrofitting of other "legacy" applications. This section will address ways in which costs can be properly forecasted and how to develop realistic budgets that are attainable during the life of the project.

Chapter 7: Analysis Methods and Tools

This chapter provides an overview of the tools or core concepts that analysts use to create specifications, or the logical equivalences of what the system needs to do to provide answers for users. The chapter defines each type of structured diagramming technique and what each diagramming method provides to completing the logical architecture of the system. Regardless of whether a package software system is required or the system is to be developed internally, the organization must create logical analysis before it can truly understand the needs of the business.

Chapter 8: Creating Requirements Documents Using Analysis Tools

This chapter builds on Chap. 7 and outlines a step-by-step procedure for designing and developing specifications that reflect the engineering requirements for building systems. This portion of the book provides the necessary tools that analysts and designers need to provide program developers with detailed, yet creative technical specifications toward the *processing* portion of the requirements document including data flow diagrams, process flow diagrams, building a data dictionary, writing algorithms, state transition diagrams, and an introduction to entity relational diagrams. Validating that an application meets requirements is a most difficult process. This chapter discusses alternative ways of accomplishing this task, including creating checklists, quality assurance procedures, group review sessions, and product simulations. The approach is to focus more on what the software does not do, as opposed to its features and functions. The chapter also emphasizes a review of mathematical calculations, that is, the way in which the system handles formulas

and produces results. Results also encompass analysis alternatives, types of outputs, and open systems compatibilities.

Chapter 9: The Data

This chapter covers how the back-end database engine is designed. The process of logic data modeling to produce a complete entity relational diagram is covered, as well as methods of transferring data to multiple data storage facilities. Creation of data repositories is also discussed. The chapter effectively completes the data portion of the requirements document.

Chapter 10: Legacy Systems and Integration

This chapter outlines the process of interfacing the new system with preexisting applications called *legacies*. Issues of product fulfillment, connectivity of legacy databases and processes, and integration of multiple systems architecture are covered. This chapter combines many of the suggested approaches to user interface and application specifications development that are covered in previous chapters.

Chapter 11: Business Process Reengineering

This chapter identifies a way of *changing* rather than interfacing with legacy systems using a technique called business process reengineering (BPR). BPR examines the entire ways in which data is used and processed and takes a holistic approach to how a packaged solution can replace many of the preexisting applications. In other words, BPR seeks to replace rather than interface which requires organizations to rethink how this would change their processes to meet the ways a packaged software would make the business more efficient.

Chapter 12: Digital Transformation and Consumer Requirements

This chapter explores the effects of the digital global economy on the ways in which software requirements are constructed. From this perspective, digital transformation involves a type of reengineering, but one that is not limited to rethinking just how systems work together, rather the entire business itself. Digital transformation also affects the risks that organizations must take and has established a shrinking s-curve. Ultimately, this chapter emphasizes the need to engineer software without users and without traditional input sources.

Chapter 13: Data Analytics and Data Warehouses

In this chapter the process of engineering data query and reporting options are discussed, especially to allow organizations to effectively report and analyze the operation. The chapter shows alternative data storage methods to enhance reporting performance and covers the recording, storage, and analysis of transactions that occur across enterprise systems. There is particular focus on decision support systems development, use of big data, end user query development, predictive analytics, and reconciliation of reporting through data warehousing.

Chapter 14: Documentation and Acceptance Testing

New systems must be documented and tested to ensure they comply with the requirements document. Thus, this chapter addresses the role of documentation and how acceptance test plans are developed and put into operation before the system is deemed usable and ready for implementation. The approach is to focus more on what the software does not do, as opposed to its features and functions. The chapter also emphasizes a review of mathematical calculations, that is, the way in which the system handles formulas and produces results. When changes are made to any application package, there are also a series of steps that must be undertaken to ensure that the quality of the package is maintained. This process can be very convoluted, since the customizations could affect other aspects of the original package. The approach to solving this dilemma usually requires a close partnership among the stakeholders, including the software vendor, the vendor who made the modifications, and the internal organization.

Chapter 15: Project Management

This chapter presents a definition and description of the duties and responsibilities of the project manager. The project manager is the most important individual in the application software process. Overall, the project manager must have both soft skills and hard skills. Hard skills are defined as the technical skills necessary to converse with development personnel, and soft skills cover such management abilities as leadership, integrity, intuition, mentoring, creativity, and compassion. The chapter also provides the necessary processes, recommended procedures, and reporting techniques that tend to support higher rates of project success. Furthermore, many projects have suffered because the management was not able to appropriately manage the contracted vendors. Organizations make the mistake of assuming that outsourced development and management is a safeguard for successful project completion. Organizations must understand that third-party vendors are not a panacea for comfort and that rigorous management processes must be in place in order to ensure a successful project. The "squeaky wheel gets oiled" phrase is very applicable when managing your vendors. This chapter offers best practices that keep vendors on their toes!

Chapter 16: Virtual Teams and Outsourcing

The main purpose of this chapter is to provide formidable solutions to a growing dilemma of how teams work in a virtual and global environment. The advent of virtual teams creates another level of complexity for designing and maintaining project teams. It also furthers the value proposition of why project management, in general, is required for successful transformation into a virtual community of workers and supports further justifications for outsourcing application development and product support services.

Chapter 17: Cyber Security, ISO 9000, and the Software Development Life Cycle

New software systems need to comply with general standards for them to be useful, especially if they are integrating with legacy applications or part of a complete redesign using BPR. ISO 9000 is an international concept of standardization of quality that should be adopted in any major software development or implementation of a packaged software solution. Furthermore this chapter shows how cyber security architecture requires integration with a firm's SDLC, particularly within steps that include strategic analysis and design, engineering, and operations.

Chapter 18: Vendor Contract Considerations

Once vendors have been selected, organizations need to have contracts that protect their corporate interests, while at the same time are fair to the vendors. Vendors typically have standard contracts or skeleton agreements for organizations to work from, but there are significant issues that must be covered such as indemnity, access to source code, process of communication if there are problems, warrantees and guarantees, and support.

Chapter 19: Going Live and Conclusions

User training usually requires a phased approach paralleling the life cycle of the new product. Some parts of training can take place early, but a huge portion will likely occur as the system approaches the go live phase. Training may also need to be repetitive and completed among different management and staff users. Training can be shared, that is, some being done by internal users and others by the third-party vendors or by the product company. There is also the concept of "train-the-trainer," where third-party trainers train internal users to take on the major parts of training among the user staffs. The chapter also covers the documentation, often considered part of the training process. The contribution of the organization's IT department is always one of debate. Many organizations consider the IT department as the "owner" of the effort and expect that IT personnel will act as the main department handling every aspect of the implementation. Other organizations adapt a user-controlled effort, where the IT department is essentially used to accomplish specific tasks. The latter approach has a major advantage in that the business becomes the owner and effectively should be since they are the beneficiaries of the application software product. In yet another approach, the IT executive takes on a leadership role, where IT is responsible from an executive level, but the business department still owns the responsibility to get the product implemented and absorbed by the organization. This chapter represents the pinnacle of the project completion. Sections cover key issues to be coordinated among the stakeholders, business partners, and vendors to ensure that everything is ready for production. The go live step should also consider the handling of problems, including application bugs that need to be fixed or worked around (finding an alternative way of doing something in the system). The go live phase must also address final sign-off with vendors and stakeholders.

Reference

Langer, A. M. (2011). *Information technology and organizational learning: Managing behavioral change through technology and education* (2nd ed.). New York: CRC Press.

Part I

Determining Needs

Assessing Business Requirements

So how does one assess the needs of a system before seeking a solution in the market? The most valuable step is to create a requirements document that depicts the needs of the system you are seeking. It also provides a platform for the businesses affected by the software solution to agree to agree before starting the process of selection. The first aspect of understanding business requirements are the Tiers of Software Development.

The Tiers of Software Development

The life cycle of software development continues to evolve, particularly with the advent of the object paradigm. The life cycle of development inevitably affects the way analysis and design are accomplished. Indeed, it only seems natural that the rapid changes in software methodologies would be accompanied by parallel development in analysis and design. Unfortunately, such is not the case, and the advances in software development continue to overshadow the importance of analysis and design.

As the software industry focuses on integrated software solutions through robust Web-based packaged software, it becomes vitally important for the analyst to use the appropriate sequence of tiers to arrive at requirements. Developers cannot expect good results from taking shortcuts, tempting as it may be to do so. The recommended sequence of tiers is outlined below:

User Interface

Regardless of the type of software applications being developed, systems cannot be effectively designed without an appropriate user interface. The user-interface tier acts as the foundation for the project: without a solid foundation at this level, the project is at risk of collapsing at some point during development. Despite its

© Springer-Verlag London Limited 2016
A.M. Langer, *Guide to Software Development*,
DOI 10.1007/978-1-4471-6799-0_2

importance, the user-interface tier is often overlooked: many software projects today move too quickly into development without the effort having been spent to determine what is really needed from the user community. Successful analysts are aware of the critical importance of the user-interface phase of any project. Chapter 1 focuses on methods of formulating user interfaces that can significantly improve software development.

Tools

Software systems require that analysts have the appropriate tools to do their job. Furthermore, and an even more significant challenge, is understanding which of the many available tools to use at any given point. Software development tools are often designed for specialized use rather than for general application, and using the wrong tool can potentially cause significant damage. Finally, the sequence of use for each specialized tool is also critical to success. Indeed, the order of operation, as well as the relationship among specialized analysis tools, must be mastered to ensure success.

Productivity Through Automation

Having the appropriate tools and knowing how and when to use them are only part of the formula for success. Analysts must also be productive—and productivity can be accomplished only through the use of automation. Automation is implemented using integrated computer-aided software engineering (CASE) products. These products provide the analyst with an automated and integrated toolbox of features that are centralized through a core data dictionary and repository.

Object Orientation

Successful projects employ the concepts of object orientation (OO). Whether or not software systems are OO compliant, analyzing systems using the object method builds better systems that are more cohesive, reusable, and maintainable. More cohesive code is "tighter" code and is more easily fixed and maintained. It is also the foundation of the reusable components that can be incorporated into other applications later. Without the OO construct, systems tend to have pieces that are re-coded and hard to maintain. With the advent of the enterprise solutions and e-commerce transactions that will be vital to the survival of corporate business strategy, building object-based systems has become more of a requirement than an option. However, as this book will show, businesses and organizations cannot just jump into OO, but rather they must create the foundations first through the previous tiers of development. Put another way, it is more important to understand the concepts of OO during analysis and design than it is to have the OO scheme actually programmed.

Client/Server

Today's software is still governed by the concept of client/server processing. While client/server has become more widespread, it has not necessarily become better understood. As with the OO paradigm, client/server software development is often confused with network hardware strategy. While client/server hardware topology is an important issue in itself, it has little to do with the process of deciding how software modules should interact across the network and where such modules should be placed. Such decisions will be driven by issues that arise during the process of analysis. Client/server software processing, in its true implementation, involves the interaction of objects and defining the way in which they will communicate with each other. Thus, analysts must first be versed in the laws governing OO if they are to pursue the client/server model. Incidentally, almost all Web-based applications that use JAVA, Active-X, and other controls are designed essentially under the guidelines of interaction objects in a client/server environment.

Internet/Intranet

The advent of Web-based technology, sometimes known as Internet/intranet processing, has led the industry to the use of a new breed of software applications. This new breed requires more robust processing and involves careful design and placement of pictures that provide users with a true "cafeteria" style of operation. These new applications bring new challenges to analysts and designers. Increasingly, it is not programmers who are designing the interface; rather, analysts themselves are beginning to work with commercial advertisers and marketing departments to create a "look and feel" that will be critical to the survival of many businesses. Web-based systems, a result of the Internet/intranet boom, represent another level of analysis. I believe that in the future, e-business will exert the strongest shaping influence on the analyst's profession—a profession destined to become tomorrow's integrators of systems development. Indeed, programming tools will continue to become easier to develop and more abundant in precoded forms. There will, undoubtedly, be less distribution of development teams, that is, companies will find more and more outsourced solutions to fill their needs. Notwithstanding the "automation" of code, the need for integrators who can communicate with executives, line management, and operations personnel will ultimately be the most significant forces in the development of strategic-based systems over the Internet.

Internet/intranet processing requires that analysts have mastered the client/server paradigm. Indeed, many professionals have dubbed Internet development as "client/server grown-up." While this may or may not be the best definition of Internet/intranet development, it is another statement that supports the tier concept, the concept that underlies the approach of this book.

The Tiers of Software Development is focused on presenting the steps necessary to be successful as a professional analyst. I call each of these steps tiers because of their building-block nature and their dependencies on each other. I believe, therefore, that to learn to become an effective analyst, the specifics within each of these

Tier	Analyst Application
6	Internet/Intranet – Web based transaction processing, media, and graphics
5	Client/Server – breaking down objects to their client and server applications
4	Object orientation – selection of objects and classes
3	CASE – automation and productivity of Tier 2
2	Structured Tools – DFD, PFD, ERD, STD, process specification, data repository
1	User Interface – interviewing skills, JAD, RAD

Fig. 2.1 Tiers of analysis and software application development

tiers must be mastered and must pass critical information to the next level. Rather than look at analysis sequentially, I would present the steps as levels as depicted in Fig. 2.1.

The table graphically shows how each tier must be dependent on the other. There is a profound message in this diagram which suggests that no tier can be developed or exist without the previous one. To ensure success on a project, everyone involved in the design and development of application software must fully understand the interdependent nature of these tiers. Analysts must be able to convey to their colleagues how to develop Internet/intranet applications. Organizations must have excellent user interfaces, mastery of a structured toolset, a vehicle for automation so that the process will be productive, an understanding of the concept of objects, and a way to deploy these objects in a client/server environment. It all sounds so simple, and in many ways it is. The question answered by this new edition is *how?*|

The following sections provide a step-by-step process of gathering the data that you need to create a requirements document.

Establishing User Interfaces

The success factors in analysis start with the established interfaces from day one. What does this mean? You must start the process by meeting with the right people in the organization. In the best projects, the process is as follows:

1. Executive interface: There needs to be an executive-level supporter of the project. Without such a supporter, you risk not being able to keep the project on schedule. Most important, you need a supporter for the political issues that you may need to handle during the project (discussed in detail later). The executive supporter, sometimes known as a sponsor, should provide a preliminary schedule advising the organization of what is expected and the objectives of the project. The executive supporter should attach a letter to the preliminary schedule and send it to the project team members. The letter must put the importance of the project into perspective. Therefore, it is strongly recommended that you draft this letter yourself or at least have influence over its content, since doing so can ensure that the message is delivered appropriately. The executive supporter

Fig. 2.2 Established interface layers

should also establish regular reviews with the analyst and the user community to ensure that objectives are being met.

2. Department head or line manager interface: If appropriate, the department head should provide guidance about which individuals should represent the department needs. If there are several people involved, the analyst should consider a JAD-like approach. Depending on the size of the organization, the department head might also establish review sessions to ensure compliance.

3. Functional user interface: Perhaps the most important people are the ones who can provide the step-by-step needs of the system. Figure 2.2 shows a typical organization interface structure.

Forming an Interview Approach

The primary mission of an analyst or systems designer is to extract the physical requirements of the users and convert each to its logical equivalent. The most critical step in this mission is the actual interview, in which you must establish a rapport with the user(s) that will facilitate in obtaining the information you need. Your approach will dramatically change based on the level and category of the individual being interviewed. Therefore, prior to meeting with any user, it is critical to understand the culture of the company, its past experiences with automation, and most importantly its organization structure.

The following five-step procedure will help guide you more smoothly through the interview process:

Step 1—get the Organization Chart:

There are few things that are more useful in understanding the chain of command and areas of responsibility. Depending on the size of the enterprise and the scope of the project, the Organization Chart should start at the executive supporter level and work down to the operational users.

Step 2—understand everyone's role in the Organization Chart:

If there are any individuals not involved in the project (who should be given their position in the organization), first ask why and then make a notation for yourself that they are not to be included. Management may assume an individual or role should not be included and may often overlook their importance. Do not be afraid to ask why a person is not deemed necessary for the analysis of the system, and determine if you are satisfied with the reasons for their exclusion. Remember, you can still control and change the approach at this point, and management will probably respect you for doing so.

Step 3—assume the situation is political:

Be sure you understand the personalities that you will have to deal with. In almost any implementation, politics among people becomes part of the process. To ignore its existence—and the constraints it is likely to impose—is to invite failure. The question is how to obtain information about internal politics. The best approach is to start as high up in the organization as possible, typically at the executive supporter level. You might be surprised at the amount of information they have. Of course, you should not ask explicitly about the politics, but rather phrase your question as follows: "Can you give me some perspective on potential department and personnel conflicts that may occur during the interview cycle and that I should be aware of?" You may not always get the answer you need, but if you keep asking the question during every interview, you will discover a great deal about the way the organization functions. And remember, only people make projects complex!

Step 4—obtain information about user skill sets:

To start an interview without knowledge of the user's technical skills puts the analyst at a huge disadvantage. Having this information will allow you to formulate a plan of questions and to determine the best approach to the interview. If the user has no knowledge, the questions should be tailored to include a minimum of technical content. The following guidelines for preparing for interviews reflect a common-sense approach, yet it is amazing how many analysts fail even to consider such strategies:

1. Gather information before the session to allow the user—as well as yourself—to be prepared and to give you both a much clearer understanding of what will be covered during the interview.
2. Develop a questionnaire. Technical questions should be phrased differently depending on the level of knowledge possessed by the user.
3. Determine whether the interview will provide enough input to obtain the necessary information. This is not always the case; however, it happens more often than you might think. Understanding user capabilities before the interview may change not only the scope of the meeting, but may also suggest who, in addition to the user, may need to be in attendance at the interview.

Step 5—arrange for a pre-meeting with the user:

A pre-meeting may not always be possible, and in any case it must be a short meeting, perhaps half an hour. The session should be designed to be high level and provide a general idea of what will be covered during the actual interview. But more importantly, it will allow you to get a snapshot of the user. You might say you are obtaining a "comfort level" (or "discomfort level") for that user, and such meetings can provide you with an idea of what to expect and how to finalize your approach. What do you look for? Here are some directions:

1. The pre-meeting should give you enough feedback to place or confirm the user's technical level.
2. Look at everything in the user's office or their environment. Is it sloppy? Is it tidy and organized? The state of the user's environment will often be consistent with the way they provide information. The insight you gain from observing the environment should give you guidance about the types of questions to ask this individual.
3. Look for signs of attitude. The user's level of interest should be evident. Do they view the upcoming session as a waste of time or are they excited about the meeting?
4. The information gleaned in the pre-meeting can provide you with helpful hints about what to expect from the interview and from the user in general.

Dealing with Political Factions

The importance of internal politics at the user's site should never be underestimated. Perhaps the most common question raised by both professionals and student analysts is how to provide quality analysis when office politics get in the way. Here are some guidelines:

1. First, assess whether you are in the No-Win Scenario. Many of us hate to admit that the No-Win Scenario does indeed exist in many environments, but you should be on the lookout for the signs. If your manager will not support you, if the company is underpaying you, if the users hate you, if there are no automated tools to do the analysis, and if the upper management doesn't care, then you are in a difficult position. If you cannot change the situation, you must inform management that the results of your analysis will be significantly impaired by the lack of support and tools to complete the project properly. The techniques offered in this book assume that all parties are interested in providing the best solution possible, not in providing a system that is barely adequate.
2. On the other hand, do not be too quick to assume that you are in the No-Win Scenario. Most politically hampered projects need some strategy to get them on course, and most problems can be overcome if you know how to approach them.

Here is a typical example of such a problem and some ideas you can apply to solve it:

Problem:

The users who currently operate the system won't talk to me. They are afraid either that the new system might replace them or that their jobs will significantly change. In short, they fear change.

Recommended Solution:

Most operational users are managed by a supervisor or "in charge." Sometimes even a line manager can be directly responsible for production workers. In any event, you must determine who is responsible and meet with that person. The purpose of the meeting is to gain their support. This support is significant since you might find that the supervisor was once in operations and will be able to understand the problems you may encounter. If the meeting is successful, the supervisor may be able to offer a strategy. This strategy can vary from a general meeting with the users, to individual discipline, to escalation to the upper management. Whatever you do, do not allow such a situation to continue and do not accept abuse; to do so will ultimately reflect on you and your abilities.

Obviously, if the supervisor is also a problem, then you have no choice but to go to the upper management. However, this option is not a desirable one from the analyst's viewpoint. The upper management's reaction may not be helpful, and it could be damaging. For example, they might be indifferent to your problem and instruct you to deal with it yourself, or they might simply send the supervisor a letter. In some cases you may be fortunate and the supervisor's responsibilities regarding the system will be given to another manager. Consider, though, how unpleasant the consequences may be if you appeal to the upper management and get no support: you may be left working with an already unhelpful supervisor who has been made even more so by your complaint. It is important to remember that once you go to the upper management, the line has been drawn. Supervisors typically are responsible for the day-to-day operation. They usually know more about the entire operation than anyone else, and therefore you are well advised to find a way to get them on your side. A supportive supervisor can be invaluable in helping you overcome problems, as long as you are not shy about suggesting ways to get the users comfortable.

Categories and Levels of Users

Establishing user interfaces represents the vehicle to formulate much of the interview approach. It is necessary, however, to go further into the characteristics of the people particularly with respect to the *category* and *level* they have within the organization. Figure 2.2 established the three general categories, called executive, department head or line manager, or functional. It is important to explore their characteristics. In order that we better understand each category, I have always asked the following question: *What would be their interest in the success of the project, that*

is, what would make them happy with the new system? Let's apply this question for each user category:

1. *Executive users*: individuals at this layer are most interested in the concept of return on investment (ROI). ROI basically focuses on whether an investment will provide a financial return that makes the effort worthwhile to the organization. While there are many comprehensive formulas that are often applied to the study of ROI, our context pertains to the short- and long-term benefits of investing in building new software. There are generally five reasons why executives agree to fund software development. They are listed in order of significance to the investor:

 (a) *Monetary return*: simply put this means that the software will generate dol-lar revenue. An example might be the Internet software that supports online ordering systems such as Amazon has for book shipments. Their system not only provides the functionality to handle shipments, but provides a Web interface that can be directly associated with revenues provided by book orders through the Internet.

 (b) *Increased productivity*: many software systems are unable to demonstrate direct monetary benefits; however, many of them are developed to increase productivity. This means that the system will allow organizations to actually produce and deliver more. Thus, the system allows the organization to derive higher revenues through increased productivity of its resources.

 (c) *Reducing costs*: software projects are approved so that organizations can reduce their existing overhead costs. This typically relates to the replace-ment of manual activities with computer ones. While reducing costs appears to be similar in nature to increasing productivity, they are often implemented for different reasons. Increased productivity usually relates to organizations that are growing and are looking for ways to improve output because of very high demand. Reducing costs, on the other hand, can represent a defensive measure, where an organization is seeking to find ways to cut costs because of a shrinking market.

 (d) *Competition*: software systems are created because the competition has done so. Therefore, competitive reasons for producing software are a defensive measure against someone else who has demonstrated its value. An example of this is in the banking sector. Citibank was one of the first banks to intro-duce automated teller machines (ATM). Other banks soon followed because of the success that Citibank had with proliferating ATMs throughout New York State. This does not imply, however, that competitive systems are always defense mechanisms; indeed, many commercial websites are being introduced based simply on market forecasts for their potential to increase business.

 (e) *For the sake of technology*: while not the most popular, some organizations will invest in new systems because they think its time to do so or they are concerned that their technology is getting old. This way of supporting new systems development is rare, as it suggests the spending of money without a clear understanding of its benefits.

Therefore, the executive category of users is one that is interested in the value of the investment. These users have a global view of needs as opposed to the details. In fact, they may know little of how things are really done. The value of the executive interface is to provide the scope and objectives of the project against their perceived value they intend to get from the software. Another popular phrase for this is called the *domain* of the system. Domain often refers to *boundaries*. Ultimately, what makes them happy is a system that delivers what was promised or the expected ROI.

2. *Department head or line manager users*: these users represent two main areas of user input. First they are responsible for the day-to-day productivity of their respective departments. Thus, they understand the importance of meeting the objectives of the organization as set forth by the executives. Indeed, they often report the executives. On the other hand, department heads and line managers are responsible to their staff. They must deal with the functional users and prescribe ways to improve both their output and their job satisfaction. These users perhaps provide what I call *the best bang for the buck*, a phrase that usually means that for the time, you get the most. One can see that the department heads and line managers are responsible for most of what happens every day in an organization. Another phrase that can be used to describe them is your *Most Valuable Players (MVPs)*. However, beware, MVPs are the hardest to find and get for the interviews. What makes department heads and line managers happy is the most complex. They want a system that produces the output that they are expected to provide and they need a system that makes and keeps their staff happy and productive.
3. *Functional users*: also known as the users in the trenches, these people essentially do the operational activities. While they know a lot about their processes, they usually care little about the productivity and expected ROI. I often see these users as people who want little pain and just want to work the hours they need to. Thus, fancy systems are of little interest to them unless they provide no pain— and no pain derives to a system that makes their job easier.

The next area to understand about users is their level. By level, I mean their understanding of computers. There are three levels of users:
 1. *Knowledgeable*: the determination of knowledge can be tricky and certainly based on someone's opinion. I define knowledge in reference to experience. An experienced user can be defined as a person who "has been through it before." A user who has been through the development of a new system can therefore be defined as "knowledgeable" within this context.
 2. *Amateur*: the definition of an amateur is based not so much on experience, but rather to the type of experience the user has. Amateurs can be thought of as hobbyists who enjoy working with computers at home, but have no professional experience in developing software in an organization. In this perspective, I believe in the global definition of an amateur as one who does not get paid for the work.

3. *Novice*: these users have no experience with computers. While there are fewer of such users than 10 years ago, they still exist. A better way of perceiving a novice user is to relate to my definition of knowledgeable. In this context, a novice user is one that has never been part of the implementation of a new system in a professional environment.

Perhaps the most problematic of the above levels is the amateur. I have found that users who are knowledgeable provide benefit to projects. They, in many ways, act as a checkpoint for the analyst in that they can ask good questions and particularly remember historical problems that actually can help the development process. Novice users add little value and also add few problems. They tend to do what you ask of them. Amateurs, on the other hand, tend to know enough to be dangerous. They also tend to have a profound interest in the topic that they often get off on tangents about the technology as opposed to concentrating on the particulars of the project.

What is most important is the mapping of these categories and levels. An analyst might interview a knowledgeable executive or a novice functional user. Each permutation can affect the way interviews are conducted. For example, an interview with a group of amateurs would focus the analyst on ensuring that the agenda is very specific; otherwise, discussions could easily get off track. Therefore, the understanding about user levels and categories can only assist in the development of effective interview approaches.

Joint Application Development (JAD)

JAD is a process that was originally developed for designing computer-based systems. JAD centers on a 3- to 5-day workshop that brings together business area people (users) and IS (information systems) professionals. Under the direction of a facilitator, these people define anything from high-level strategic plans to detailed system specifications. The products of the workshop can include definitions of business processes, prototypes, data models, and so on.

Simply put, JAD is a method for holding group sessions with users, instead of individually. You may have no choice but to use JAD when there are simply too many users to interview. JAD is also an excellent tool for use in highly political situations where obtaining consensus among users is difficult. JAD significantly differs from standard analysis in that it requires an up-front commitment from the user community. Specifically, the users must ultimately run the sessions themselves and make commitments to provide the requirements of the system. Finally, if prototypes are used, JAD is an excellent means of applying rapid application development (RAD). Both prototyping and RAD will be discussed in greater detail later.

The most important part of implementing JAD is the management of the process and the determination of the appropriate individuals to be involved. The standard roles used in JAD are:

- Executive sponsor: This is an individual who plays effectively the same role as the executive supporter introduced earlier in this chapter. This person is typically at the vice president level and ultimately has the responsibility for the business area. The ideal person for this role is someone to whom a user will have to report if they plan to miss a session and who can reprimand them if they do. This thinking may seem harsh or cynical, but the risk is high that users may find more important things to do when the sessions begin. Such absenteeism can entirely undermine the process, and IS should not be called upon to police users.
- Facilitator: In the best situations, the facilitator should not come from either the user community or IS, but rather an independent area or consulting firm. This arrangement allows the session to be independent. That is, the facilitator of the JAD must be impartial and have overall responsibility for controlling the flow of the sessions. In the ideal scenario, the facilitator should report to the executive sponsor.
- Scribe: A person who is designated to record minutes and decisions and who in many cases actually produces the models using a computer-aided software engineering (CASE) tool. A good scribe has knowledge of the business area, good analytical skills, and knowledge of CASE software. For these reasons, scribes often come from IS.
- IS representatives: IS should not be in the meetings to provide requirements, but should rather be available to answer questions about the existing hardware and software. This information can be critical when discussing physical constraints of the existing systems and what data is currently available.

Below is an example of an 11-phase implementation outline for a JAD session with approximately 60 users in ten different business areas:

Phase I: Dfine JAD Project Goals
The purpose of these sessions will be to meet with senior management and other key organization people in order to:
- Get a clear understanding of the history of the project.
- Finalize the scope and time frame requirements of the existing plan.
- Understand the current organization and whether political or other constraints exist.
- Jointly determine the number and size of JAD sessions to be held.
- Determine the best role of information systems in the JAD.
- Define which key users and other managers should be interviewed individually prior to the JAD.

Produce a Management Guide after Phase I. Its purpose will be to define management's purpose, scope, and objectives of the project. That is, it communicates management's direction and commitment. The Management Guide will be approved and issued by the upper management to the participating users and information system personnel.

Phase II: Meet with Key Users and Managers

Estimate that you may need to interview about 20 people from key organizations prior to the JAD. These key users and managers should typically represent three levels of the organization. The purpose of these meetings will be to:

- Get familiar with the existing systems.
- Validate the number of sessions and specific participants needed.
- Assess the technical expertise of the participating users.
- Determine what specific information can be gathered by the users prior to the JAD sessions.
- Gather previous analysis and design materials and documents that may exist and explain user requirements.
- Discuss types of agendas and length of sessions.
- Focus on specific requirements of certain users.

Schedule interviews to last about 60–90 min, and prepare an agenda that will put the purpose and scope of the interview into perspective.

Phase III: Meet with Information Systems

Get a technical overview of the existing analysis performed and state of all working documents. Gather information on:

- Project history
- Potential problems envisioned in implementing the new system
- Proposed hardware to support the new system (if relevant)
- IS representatives to participate in the JAD sessions
- Models and information that can be used in the JAD sessions

Phase IV: Prepare JAD Approach

Prepare a complete JAD program that will outline recommendations for the number and types of sessions to be held. The JAD approach will also consider the modeling tools to be used and the methods for getting user sign-off. You should focus on the following specific issues:

- The number and type of preparation sessions necessary to get users familiar with the modeling terminology.
- What business processes have already been previously modeled and can be reviewed during the sessions. This is done to avoid discussing processes that users feel have already been defined from previous analysis sessions.
- The number and types of sessions along with specific users in attendance at each session.
- A work document of the proposed agendas for each type of session.
- Overview of materials to be used such as overheads, flip charts, and room requirements
- Proposed format of the user sign-off documents.

You should meet with the upper management to review the proposed approach for implementation.

Phase V: Finalize JAD Organization Structure

Assign JAD facilitators to specific sessions along with information systems support personnel (Scribes, analysts, facilitators, etc.). Determine the number of JAD facilitators required. You may need one JAD project leader to take overall responsibility for the entire engagement. A detailed timeline of specific deliverables and reviews should be produced for the entire project, including reports to the upper management on the JAD session progress.

Phase VI: Hold Overview Training Sessions

Depending on the results of Phase IV, hold any necessary sessions to get users familiar with the methods that will be used during the JAD. This is typically a 1-day course on analysis and includes an overview of modeling lingo and tools such as:

- Business Area Analysis
- Process Flow Diagrams (data flows)
- Entity Relational Diagrams and normalized data modeling
- Process specifications
- Activity matrices
- State Transition Diagrams
- Decomposition models
- Object-oriented techniques
- Prototyping

Phase VII: Hold JAD Workshop Sessions

Prior to these sessions, participants will be asked to come prepared with certain information that they will need to assist in the process. This information may typically include sample forms and reports that they use or need. The workshop sessions will be held with a set time frame and an agenda of items typically including:

- Assumptions: these will be reviewed with the users and opened for discussion. An assumption will either:
 - Stay as it is.
 - Be revised.
 - Become an open issue (if consensus cannot be reached).
- Design business processes: review the collection of activities relating to the business and the system.
- Data requirements: data is defined to support the business process. Data models are used, developed, and reviewed as necessary.
- Design screens: the screens will typically use a series of menus or other branching techniques to define how users need to access the various functions. This is usually accomplished by identifying main menu and submenu selections.

- Design reports: report names are collected and completed with detailed report descriptions. This normally includes:
 - Report name
 - Description
 - Frequency
 - Number of copies
 - Distribution list
 - Selection criteria
 - Sort criteria
 - Data elements
- Open issues: these issues are added throughout the sessions. Open issues are those that are not resolved after a period of discussion. These are kept on a separate chart.

Throughout the above processes, the scribe will be tracking minutes of the meeting as well as the open issues and new diagramming requirements.

Phase VIII: Resolve Open Issues

Prior to subsequent sessions, all open issues must be resolved, either by smaller work groups or if necessary by the upper management. In any event, it is critical that this is managed by both the facilitator and upper management prior to moving to the next level sessions.

Phase IX: Prepare Materials for Workshop Review Sessions

The facilitator should produce a sign-off level document for review. Process and data models and process specifications will be reviewed and finalized. These sessions can also include prototype screens and reports.

Phase X: Hold Sign-Off Workshops

These workshops will be designed to review the results of the initial JAD sessions. The process and data models will be reviewed. If prototypes are used, the sessions will utilize screen walkthroughs as a method of gaining user acceptance. The exact number of review sessions will depend on the complexity of the system as well as the number of screens and reports to be prototyped.

During these sessions, user acceptance test plan may also be discussed and outlined for eventual submission to the responsible QA organization. This will typically involve a discussion of the minimum acceptance testing to be validated against the product and the mechanism for testing in the field.

Phase XI: Finalize Specification Document

After review sessions are completed, the facilitator will prepare the final document to be submitted for approval and eventual implementation. If prototypes are used, the screens and reports can be moved into the software development (construction) phase. There should also be post-JAD reviews with the development

teams to clarify information supplied in the final system specification document.

JAD is introduced and discussed in this chapter because of its generic inclusion in the user-interface phase of analysis. However, it should be noted that the above outline can be integrated with many of the subjects contained in later chapters of this text. The analyst may, therefore, wish to review this outline again after completing the book in order to determine how the other concepts of analysis can be used in a JAD session.

Problems and Exercises

1. Why is it so critical for the analyst to understand the "culture" of the organization?
2. What is a Gantt Chart? How are Gantt Charts used and why is it important that they be realistic estimates of how the project will occur?
3. Management support is a key component of the success of any project. Sometimes management may unfairly dictate the terms and deadlines of projects. Provide examples of different possible management opinions and how analysts can prepare effective responses to them.
4. What are the benefits of obtaining an Organization Chart prior to conducting interviews with users?
5. How does politics affect the role of the analyst and his/her approach to the information-gathering function of the interviews?
6. Why does understanding user skills provide the analyst with an advantage during interviews?
7. Explain how meeting a user in their office or place of work can assist the analyst in developing a better approach prior to the interview.
8. What is the purpose of JAD sessions? How do they compare to individual interviewing? Discuss the advantages and disadvantages of JAD.
9. Define each of the roles necessary for effective JAD sessions.
10. What is the purpose of a Management Guide?
11. Develop a proforma JAD outline for a project of 20 users in three business locations.

Build Versus Buy

This chapter addresses a difficult and controversial decision that is made every time an organization seeks a software solution to meet its needs: do we make it to our specific needs, or do we buy something that is made to order but may not do everything we want? Often the build decision is called the "make" alternative and suggests that the product will be made in-house versus the buy concept that can be referred to as outsourcing. I do not believe these simple labels are accurate or appropriate. Whether something is build or bought has little to do with whether the process is outsourced, so we need to be careful in the way we label these two alternatives.

Inman et al. (2011) suggests that build and buy decisions need to be made at both the strategic and operational levels. Burt et al (2003) provided some direction on the strategic reasons for buying and tied it into a definition of outsourcing, providing three concrete categories of reasons not to outsource:

1. The item is critical to the success of the overall product and is perceived so by the company's clientele.
2. The item requires specialized design and skills and such skills are limited in the organization.
3. The item fits into the firm's core competencies but needs to be developed in the future.

Historically, most organizations selected the buy option because their assumption was that it lowered costs. Indeed, over 70 % of product ownership usually occurs after implementation. So where is this cost? It occurs in maintenance, where in-house teams must continually alter and develop. The off-the-shelf concept tends to keep costs lower because in theory the sum of all the clients will create better software for all. Others suggest that a company should always first seek a package because of common business challenges including:

- Cost
- Time to market

© Springer-Verlag London Limited 2016
A.M. Langer, *Guide to Software Development*,
DOI 10.1007/978-1-4471-6799-0_3

- Political situation in the environment
- Architectural differences
- Skill sets of existing staff

However, the Gartner Group in 2003 published a report that suggested this trend was changing and that there were a growing number of firms that were returning to building applications internally. Gartner cited the following reasons for the change of heart:

- Rising competitive advantages of using emerging technologies
- Increased availability of talented software developers
- Poor reputation of prior uses of package software—that it is not agile enough and difficult for departments to use
- Increased needs to adapt to unique and changing business needs

Ledeen's (2011) and Moore's (2002) analysis of how to approach make vs. buy is quite useful. He established a step-by-step criterion to help organizations to make the best decision. This criterion included the following:

- Core vs. context
- Coverage
- Direction
- TCO
- Scale
- Timing
- Standards

Core vs Context
This decision point relates to the strategic importance of the application. The more strategic the application, the more likely that the organization develop software internally (also see Langer 2011, below). The concept is simple: if the application relates to basic functions in accounting, HR, or payroll, then it is not a core. However, software used by Walmart, although accounting related is used as a supply chain management that drives every aspect of their competitive advantage as a company. The result of course is that Walmart developed their supply chain as a core and unique application. Moore's chart shown in Fig. 3.1 provides an interesting matrix of how core can be determined:

	Core Engage	Context Disengage
Mission Critical (Control)	MAKE	OUTSOURCE
Supporting (Entrust)	PARTNER	CONTRACT

Fig. 3.1 Build vs. buy chart

The chart shown in Fig. 3.1 reflects that mission critical application should be developed in-house and context-oriented applications may be modified to meet package requirements.

Coverage

The coverage assesses the extent of the match of the packaged product with the business requirements. The general rule is that a package should have at least 80 % of the features and functions needed by the organization. However, Ledeen states that this could be a trap, suggesting that a package's capabilities outside of the immediate needs of the business are equally as important. This is relevant, given that business needs are continually evolving; organizations must be cognizant of having applications that cannot only handle what is but also what may be the future needs of the business. In addition, a certain feature in a packaged solution may actually offer a better business alternative than currently used by the business—so it's a complex issue as they say.

Direction

The keywords relating to direction is flexibility, maintainability, and extendibility of the software throughout its life. Ultimately, direction relates to how much control the organization has over the product, especially those products that may need to change—that is, the volatility of what the software does. For example, if the product is a basic accounting system, it is likely not to change substantially over its life. However, if it is a healthcare product that is regulated by government requirements in a highly fragile market, then direction is a key decision factor. Much of this relates to the design and architecture of the product itself. Can it be easily modified? What is the extent of changes that can be controlled via user input? All of these factors are significant to whether a package is the wise choice.

Total Cost of Ownership (TCO)

The TCO represents the entire cost. Components of this cost include license fees for the product, maintenance, product customizations, and support. The major variable in TCO is custom modifications. Vendors will often provide an estimate but managers need to be careful of "scope creep" where original requirements for customizations become greatly expanded during the design phase of the project. A good approach that can help this decision is to determine the number of features and functions in the package that the organization does *not* need. A packaged solution that has many features and functions that are not needed might suggest that the application is not a great match and is likely designed for a different audience. It is important to note that many application packages were developed first as a custom application for a specific client and then tailored for others. This process was a typical evolution of how many software packages evolved in the market. Therefore, understanding the history of how the application package was developed might provide a hint as to the TOC and the fit in general—the two tend to go together.

Scale

The size of the package is a factor, especially when it has many modules. This is very relevant in large Enterprise Resource Planning (ERP) products where a high degree of scaled interoperability is important. These modular products also allow clients to purchase business components at later periods and easily retrofit them. However, if it is *not* the intention of the organization to scale, then a large integrated package may be overkill.

Timing

There are many who would believe that a packaged solution will be faster to implement—but be careful, because often this is not the case. Packaged solutions may add steps to the SDLC and as a result could actually prolong the timing of going live on the product. Ledeen suggests that while COTS provides greater predictability, it could be a reflection on the limits of flexibility and imposed restrictions. Either case I would strongly recommend that the decision whether to have a make vs. buy be not contended solely based on speed to completion—the organization may be in for a big surprise. The more an organization can accept the base package, the faster the implementation will be, for sure. However, accepting the package as is does not necessarily mean that it is the best thing for the business.

Standards

Ledeen defines standards as the consistency across systems of the way things get done. I see this issue more in terms of consistency of architecture of the organization. This means that the hardware platforms and software architecture (middleware, office products, etc.) should be consistent for packaged software to maximize its benefits. If this is not the case, that is, where you have multiple architectures across the organization, then the value of a package becomes less evident. This is especially true if the package requires a specific architecture for all of the systems. This is why open systems are so attractive to organizations. Unfortunately in multinational firms, having many architectures is not unusual. Much of this may have occurred due to corporate acquisitions of other firms—when you acquire a new business, you often acquire a new systems architecture—both hardware and software!

Other evaluation criteria

The above issues are important, but there are other contextual things to consider when making the decision:

- *Complexity of product*: The more intricate the software application, the harder for COTS to work. Complex products also tend to shorten the life cycle and have more evolving needs.
- *State of the art*: Users who seek packaged solutions often require the latest and greatest up-to-date product. They may be disappointed to learn that package software has some unique limitations in this area. First, vendors of packages have

user bases to take care of—who ultimately have older versions and hardware that they must support. This results in difficulties with downward compatibilities of their user base. Just look at Microsoft's problems when they upgrade operating systems and software. IBM used to issue "no support" edicts to its customers who failed to upgrade their products over time. The better vendors force their users to upgrade but it is always messy.

• *Maintenance*: COTS often involves product upgrades and new maintenance releases. Sometimes maintenance releases include bug fixes and workarounds for packaged discovered problems. Maintenance can also be very tricky—how do organizations load new versions from the vendors when there are customizations, for example? It gets to be a challenge especially when the updates are regulatory in nature. COTS that have customizations inevitably need to go through a retrofit, where the customized portions have to be "re-customized" to deal with packaged software upgrades. This certainly adds to the cost equation over the life of the package.

While the above suggestions offer guides on what to think about and measure, the process is still complex without a real scientific methodology to determine ultimately whether to make or buy or both. However, Langer (2011) provides yet another concept called Driver/Supporter theory in which "buy" decisions would only be made for applications that were considered "supporters." Figure 3.2 depicts a supporter item as something that has reached the stage of commodity notated in the circle labeled as "economies of scale."

The diagram shows that all technology needs to start out as drivers but eventually become supporters, thus losing their uniqueness in the marketplace. It is as if you

Fig. 3.2 Langer's Driver/Supporter life cycle

were creating a strategic advantage by implementing a new email system—this would not really provide the organization with a competitive advantage—rather as an enabler to compete a very different concept. The point I am making here is that a new email system would likely be "bought" and possibly implemented using an outsource vendor. In accordance with Burt et al. then, this would be a case for buying as opposed to making.

Drivers and Supporters

I think the concept of Driver/Supporter is essential to understanding make/buy decisions. This section provides further details on this theory and practice as a vehicle for better determination of make vs. buy.

To summarize Driver/Supporter, there are essentially two types of generic functions performed by departments in organizations: driver functions and supporter functions. These functions relate to the essential behavior and nature of what a department contributes to the goals of the organization. I first encountered the concept of drivers and supporters at Coopers & Lybrand, which was at that time a Big 8[1] accounting firm. I studied the formulation of driver vs. supporter as it related to the role of our EDP (Electronic Data Processing) department. The firm was attempting to categorize the EDP department as either a driver or supporter.

Drivers are defined as those units that engaged in frontline or direct revenue generating activities. Supporters are units that did not generate obvious direct revenues but, rather, were designed to support frontline activities. For example, operations such as internal accounting, purchasing, or office management were all classified as supporter departments. Supporter departments, due to their very nature, were evaluated on their effectiveness and efficiency or economies of scale. In contrast, driver organizations are expected to generate direct revenues and other ROI value for the firm. What was also interesting to me at the time was that drivers were expected to be more daring—since they must inevitably generate returns for the business. As such, drivers engage in what Bradley and Nolan (1998) coined "sense and respond" behaviors and activities. Let me explain.

Marketing departments often generate new business by investing or "sensing" an opportunity, quickly—because of competitive forces in the marketplace. Thus, they must sense an opportunity and be allowed to respond to it in timely fashion. The process of sensing opportunity and responding with competitive products or services is a stage in the cycle that organizations need to support. Failures in the cycles of sense and respond are expected. Take, for example, the launching of new fall television shows. Each of the major stations goes through a process of "sensing" what shows might be interesting to the viewing audience. They "respond" after research and review with a number of new shows. Inevitably, only a few of these selected

[1] The original "Big 8" consisted of the eight large accounting and management consulting firms: Coopers & Lybrand, Arthur Anderson, Touche Ross, Delloite. Haskins & Sells, Arthur Young, Price Waterhouse, Pete Marwick Mitchell and Ernst and Whinney, up until the late 1980s, when these firms began to merge. Today there are four: Price Waterhouse Coopers, Delloit & Touche, Ernst and Young, and KPMG (Pete Marwick and others).

shows are actually successful; some fail almost immediately. While relatively few shows succeed, the process is acceptable and is seen by management as the consequence of an appropriate set of steps for competing effectively—even though the percentage of successful new shows is very low. Therefore, it is safe to say that driver organizations are expected to engage in high-risk-oriented operations, of which many will fail for the sake of creating ultimately successful products or services.

The preceding example raises two questions: (1) How does "sense and respond" relate to the world of information technology, and (2) why is it important? Information technology is unique in that it is both a driver and a supporter, the latter being the generally accepted norm in most firms. Indeed, most IT functions are established to support a myriad of internal functions such as:

- Accounting and finance
- Data-center infrastructure (email, desktop, etc.)
- Enterprise-level application (ERP)
- Customer support (CRM)
- Web and e-commerce activities

As one would expect, these IT functions are viewed as overhead related, as somewhat of a commodity, and, thus, constantly managed on an economy-of-scale basis—that is, how can we make this operation more efficient, with a particular focus on cost containment?

So what then are IT driver functions? By definition, they are those that engage in direct revenues and identifiable return-on-investment (ROI). How do we define such functions in IT, as most activities are sheltered under the umbrella of marketing organization domains (excluding, of course, software application development firms that engage in marketing for their actual application products)? I define IT driver functions as those projects that, if delivered, would change the relationship between the organization and its customers, that is, those activities that directly affect the classic definition of a market: forces of supply and demand, which are governed by the customer (demand) and the vendor (supplier) relationship.

The conclusion of this section, therefore, is that no driver application product should be implemented using complete outsourcing, rather made in-house and owned by the firm. This does not, however, suggest that certain services and components be subcontracted out as long as the ownership remains within the company.

The Supporter Side of Buying

Based on the definition of a driver, the supporter side may indeed represent the need to buy a packaged solution. Since supporter functions are "operational" by definition, they are considered to be a commodity and thus able to be implemented using more standardized application software. Thus, all of the advantages of using packaged software apply. In addition there should be less need for customization. For example, think of the choice to build an email system—you would only build it in-house if you required unique capabilities that provided a competitive advantage. That is, the email system would be a driver application because it would change the

relationship between the buyer and seller. This is exactly the situation that occurred with Walmart, where what would ordinarily have been considered a commodity accounting system became an application of great strategic advantage. On the other hand, an email system that could provide such advantage would be unlikely for most organizations, and therefore they would seek a product that does what most organizations need in any email system—as a supporter solution.

Open-Source Paradigm

Open-source software can be defined as free source code developed among a community that believes strongly in a free software movement. Initial examples of successful open-source products are Linux and Netscape Communicator. The open-source movement is supported under the auspices of the Open Source Initiative (OSI) that was formed in 1998 to provide guidance and standards of application.

As I previously mentioned, the evolution of open source as an alternative to developing software has grown enormously in the software industry. Open source can also represent an option with make vs. buy. Choices of whether to make or buy do not necessarily need to be binary, that is, one or the other, but rather could end up as a hybrid decision. For example, an organization can develop its own application using open source within its application development strategy or it can license a third-party product that also contains open source. Finally, packages may be licensed that can be bridged or integrated with various open-source modules. In any case, open source broadens the range of choices when determining the best application solution.

Open-source users must, however, agree to the following conditions of use as well as provide conditions of use to others:

- Free distribution.
- Inclusion of source code.
- License must allow modifications and derived works.
- Allowed redistribution of modifications under the same license of the original software. License may require the derived work to carry a different name or version to protect the integrity of the original author.
- No discriminations against any specific groups or fields of endeavors.
- License cannot be restrictive to any software and be technology platform neutral.

To a certain extent, open source provides organizations with the option to use package software that is free to modify and then offer their changes back to those that need it in the user base—so it can be a forum where organizations can share needs. The negative aspect to sharing is if the modification contains proprietary algorithms that represent a competitive advantage for the firm. The software must also be hardware neutral which presents challenges for those applications that run on proprietary systems. Still, open-source applications are growing in popularity especially as a cloud computing option.

Furthermore, open source might present some unexpected legal issues particularly as it relates to ownership of the software. Suppose you use an open-source routine or module in your proprietary application and then the company is acquired by another entity. The question then is who owns the product? Legally the portion that is open source cannot be owned, which creates a dilemma that was likely not foreseen by the organization's IT management. This dilemma is particularly relevant to vendor software products.

Cloud Computing Options

Cloud computing is the ultimate server-based paradigm. Simply put, the host (cloud) has all of the hardware, software, services, and databases to support your business or enterprise. The organization essentially has the terminals and printers to do the work. Figure 3.3 depicts a cloud configuration.

Cloud is about reduction of cost and perhaps using products that are shared by others. This does not mean that clouds cannot have proprietary products, rather that they have the ability to mix and match what is available in the cloud to meet specific needs of the organization. Because many of these applications can be shared in the cloud, the cost of ownership is very much lowered. Perhaps the largest benefit for using a cloud is in the savings for infrastructure and operations staff who would otherwise need to support the operation internally.

Fig. 3.3 Cloud configuration

Deployment Models

There are essentially five different deployable models for cloud computing:

1. *Public/external*: this is the basic model that allows users to access a network via the Internet and typically pay on a usage or application access basis. It resembles the 1970 concept of timesharing.
2. *Private/internal*: a private cloud in many ways resembles an intranet concept in that it is an internally developed shared service for the organization. As in an intranet, a private cloud requires organizations to design the network and support it as if it were public –of course with less complexity.
3. *Community*: this configuration represents a group of organizations that share resources. In effect it is a restricted public cloud—only certain organizations can use it. Community clouds are attractive for specific industries that have similar needs or associations.
4. *Hybrid*: a hybrid cloud really relates to providing specific administrative IT functions like backup, performance, and security for both public and private cloud deployments. So it is more of a utility type of cloud service often provided by internal IT services or vendors like Oracle, etc.
5. *Combined*: this is the application of multiple types of clouds that allow organizations to enjoy the best provisions that it provides to each business.

Figure 3.4 depicts the graphical representations of these cloud-type deployments.

Fig. 3.4 Cloud deployment types (Source: Wikipedia)

Obviously cloud computing has its drawbacks—it is essentially outsourcing major parts of your operation to a third party—for which is always a risk, so these should be measured as follows:

- *Security*: while all third parties promise security, history has shown that they can be pierced from the outside. So security remains a concern for private and important data. For example, having healthcare information and other personal information in a cloud could be very dangerous.
- *Governmental and political issues*: if stored data is kept in other locations under the auspices and control of other countries, it could be restricted, taken, or kept from those that need it. The data could also be compromised because of different legal systems and changes in government policies. We see such problems in multinational firms quite often.
- *Downtime*: how much can any vendor guarantee ongoing service without outage, and to what extent can clouds have fail over abilities and at what cost?
- *Conversions*: if you should need to move from one cloud provider to another, what are the risks and problems with moving applications and what compatibility problems will occur especially with data conversion?

Summary

This chapter examined the complexities of whether to make or buy an application solution. Hybrid solutions, which involve both a third-party package and internally developed applications, are very realistic alternatives. The evolution of open source and cloud computing offers new opportunities to design and create hybrid systems that provide broader alternatives that historically were available. Furthermore, the concept of Driver/Supporter provides a more scientific way of determining whether to make or buy software solutions.

Problems and Exercises

1. Explain what is meant about core vs. content
2. Why is TOC so important?
3. Describe Langer's theory of Driver/Supporter.
4. Define open source. How can open source change the decision process on make vs. buy?
5. What is cloud computer? Explain the different types of clouds.

References

Bradley, S. P., & Nolan, R. L. (1998). *Sense and respond: Capturing value in the network era.* Boston: Harvard Business School Press.

Burt, D. N., Dobler, D. W., & Starling, S. L. (2003). *World class supply management: The key to supply chain management* (7th ed.). Boston: McGraw-Hill/Irwin.

Inman, R. A., Sale, R. S., Green, K. W., & Whitten, D. (2011). Agile manufacturing: Relation to JIT, operational performance and firm performance. *Journal of Operations Management, 29,* 343–355.

Langer, A. M. (2011). *Information technology and organizational learning: Managing behavioral change through technology and education* (2nd ed.). New York: CRC Press.

Ledeen, K. S. (2011). *Make v. buy: A decision paradigm for information technology applications.* Nevo Press.

Moore, G. (2002). *Living on the fault line: Managing for shareholder value in any economy.* New York: HarperCollins.

Establishing Requirements Using a Request for Proposal (RFP) and a Request for Information (RFI)

4

Organizations may need to create formal documents that articulate the needs they have for a software solution. These formal documents or requirements could be either for a package solution or customized development or both. There are of course intricacies to creating these documents which also need to address related needs such as project management, ownership, quality assurance, indemnifications, and delivery schedules. There are two common methods of communicating these formal requirements: a Request for Information (RFI) or a Request for Proposal (RFP). An RFI is usually seen as a subset for an RFP, so an RFI might precede a more detailed RFP. Therefore, the purpose of this chapter is to provide the details of what should be included in each document, when one might be more advantageous than the other, and the process for obtaining responses from vendors.

RFI

An RFI is a document that can obtain feedback from prospective vendors who can provide a solution to the request. An RFI (as well as an RFP) should always state the problem—which is typically the need to address a business issue that needs an application software solution. However, the major focus of the RFI is to collect information about potential vendors so that the organization can do comparative analysis on what is available in the market and to some extent the costs associated with various application solutions. Another way then of looking at an RFI is a way of surveying the marketplace before presenting a full-blown RFP, which typically requires a cost proposal from a vendor. Another advantage of an RFI is that it is relatively quick to put together. Of course this is relative to the complexity of the project. A typical RFI consists of the following sections and content:

- Introduction
- Background of the company
- Information about the project

© Springer-Verlag London Limited 2016
A.M. Langer, *Guide to Software Development*,
DOI 10.1007/978-1-4471-6799-0_4

- Reasons for the RFI—purpose and scope
- Specific requests—what is the requestor asking vendors to provide
- Due date for the response
- Confidentiality requirements
- Vendor qualifications
- Appendices of detailed information pertinent for the responding vendor

A sample RFI (Source: sourcing4oem.com) is presented in Fig. 4.1:

Request for Information

[Sample]

Company name
Date:

Contents

Fig. 4.1 Sample RFI

Confidentiality & Non Disclosure

All information included in this RFI is confidential and only for the recipient knowledge. No information included in this document or in discussions connected to it may be disclosed to any other party.

Introduction

This RFI is a request for information regarding your company and your products/services. The same information will be gathered from different companies and will be used to evaluate what vendors we will follow up the sourcing process with a RFP.

Scope

Specific information is requested according to the form below.

Abbreviation and terminology

[Special Terms specific to the industry]

RFI Process

Please fill in all information on the attached form.

Response

Vendor responses must be forwarded hardcopy and via email [company email account]

Contacts

For questions regarding this RFI, you are welcome to contact:
[Name of Individual Responsible]
[your title]
[Company Name]
[your phone number]
[your email address]

Timeframe

This is the timeframe for the RFI responses
9/28/2011 – The RFI is sent out
[MM]/[DD]/[YY] – Last date for questions by Vendors
[MM]/[DD]/[YY] – Last date for submission of RFI response
[MM]/[DD]/[YY] – Results from the evaluation
[MM]/[DD]/[YY] – RFP sent to select vendors who are deemed appropriate by requestor

Fig. 4.1 (continued)

Background description of what is requested

Of [your company]

[Your company] was established [XXXX] is a company listed on [XX], and produces [XX]. Our production is located at [XX] and [XX]. Our main products are [XX]. Our annual turnover is about [XX]. Our mission is [XX].

More information can be found on [www.xxxxxx.zzz].

Context of the product or service

[Describe what kind of information is being requested regarding the vendor's product and/or service.]

Statement of Need

[Describe the solution being requested.]

Requirements

[Describe the requirements, such as technical needs that the product or service must address and fulfill.]

Qualifications

[Description of what qualifies a vendor for delivering the products and/or services.]

Other Important Information

Payment term: XX days

Delivery term: EXW/FCA/etc

Delivery address(es):

Quality requirements (such as PPM):

Other requirements:

Fig. 4.1 (continued)

Form to fill in as answer to the RFI

Question	Answer
Company name	
Company address	
Company web page	
Main products/services	
Main market/customers	
Ownership structure	
Structure of parent corporation, joint ventures, subsidiaries, partnerships or other relevant relations	
Number of years in business	
Company location(s)	
Employees	
Production	
R&D	
Marketing and sales	
Quality department	
Most Recent Financial information (FYE MM/YY)	
Gross Sales	
Gross margin	
Profit/Loss	
Stock markets where your company is listed	
Contact person responsible for answering this RFI	
Telephone	
Email	
Products/Services listed in RFI not available	
Reference customers using comparable products or services (including contact information)	
Reference customers using your products or services today, although they are not comparable with what is requested in this RFI (including contact information)	
Locations available for implementation, if not worldwide.	
Availability of support worldwide	

Fig. 4.1 (continued)

The RFI sample in Fig. 4.1 reflects a relatively simple request for vendor information. The RFI should be used to obtain information about the number of potential vendors that can offer a solution and who are interested in bidding. Another alternative for producing an RFI is to hire an outside consulting firm that can manage the process for the organization. Such firms typically have a list of preferred vendors, so that the RFI step can be eliminated and the consulting firm can just send the RFP out to their list of potential solutions. Such consulting firms can also produce the RFP so that the entire step is somewhat outsourced. There are obvious benefits to outsourcing this task to a third party:

1. Existing IT staff does not have the expertise or time.
2. An outside view can be very advantageous.
3. Existing list of preferred solution providers.
4. Overall savings.
5. Faster solution.
6. Less politics.

RFP

As discussed the RFP represents the more detailed requirements document that allows prospective bidders (vendors) to provide a cost proposal and solution for the reported needs of the organization. RFPs must be specific to the needs of the application to ensure that a vendor has enough information to provide an accurate quote. Figure 4.2 provides a sample RFP for a Web solution.

The sample (Fig. 4.2) serves as a template for creating an RFP. While this template provides information about the company and some high-level requirements, an RFP process also requires a detailed requirements document that vendors can review in order to determine the best price for the requested services.

Requirements Document

The requirements document is an adjunct specification often called a business specification. The purpose of the business specification is to provide a document that provides readers with a functional understanding of the needs of a software application. The specification should be written in prose format so that vendors can easily understand its meaning and intent. The business specification is not technically complete, rather enough that lets vendors to determine the architectural needs and inputs and outputs required by the applications. Good business

PREFACE

This RFP has been prepared to meet the unique requirements of XYZ. This investment banking corporation is headquartered in New York City and provides financial services in the US well as interfacing with its Global counterparts globally.

XYZ requires services to support a number of initiatives relating to the development of internal and external websites:

1. Integrated Intranet to support various components of each business segment
2. Internet applications to support outside markets and recruitment
3. Integration and consistency of database applications
4. Support systems such as maintainable content-based management systems that are developed specifically to support XYZ applications.
5. Branding and creative design

XYZ Commitment

XYZ is committed to:

- providing user requirements specifications and supporting documentation (see Appendix I).
- purchasing necessary hardware and software for the websites.
- providing analysis of data.
- providing internal project management and interfaces with vendors.

I-COMPANY INFORMATION

XYZ is a major force in global investment banking. Its clients around the world include major corporations and governments. As the investment banking division of the XYZ Group it adds value by combining the global resources of one of the USs largest banks with market-leading international expertise.

Fig. 4.2 Sample RFP

XYZ has over 1800 employees in North America, and will shortly merge with other firms to form a larger and more diverse entity. The major components of its operation today include:

1. Equity business
2. Corporate Finance
3. Global Finance/Private Equity
4. Loans and Structured Finance
5. Consulting services

While XYZ North America is a self-sustaining member of XYZ global, there are a number of joint interfaces that require the coordination of resources particularly with the London office. These interfaces typically relate to branding, image, logo, and integrated global services that affect multiple entities. There are also cases where economies of scale and common clientele dictate a level of partnering within groups.

Each business area's activities are more often treated and operated as separate businesses within the bank. As such, there are multiple liaisons that are necessary to ensure that each unit specific needs are met, particularly in the information services area. Many of the internal departments are seeking to enhance their image at XYZ, and therefore are seeking to establish or enhance their presence by providing more access to information through a corporate Intranet. Furthermore, there are certain departments that need to provide external initiatives through the firm's Internet site. Specifically this includes college recruitment as well as constant new initiatives in a dynamic business. While XYZ has a large IT infrastructure, there was no formal organization to provide e-business solutions to these units. An e-consulting organization was formed to address these needs. This group, called e-Solutions reports to the Corporate Affairs department (CA). Part of the mission of CEA is to ensure a consistent corporate brand image, thus providing this Intranet and marketing web services through CEA was the appropriate department to provide the service.

II-e-COMMUNICATIONS Department

The purpose of the e-Communications Lab is to establish and launch e-business service for XYZ in North America. This service unit will implement Intranet and Internet solutions to provide added value to various entities at XYZ. Its initial business plan is to establish credibility within the company by providing a central service organization that can understand the needs of business units and create quality, cost effective, and state-of-the-art e-commerce systems. Specifically e-Communications Lab will:

2. Develop an Internet mini-site highlighting specific products and services.
3. Develop intranet sites for business lines and service companies enabling them to raise their profiles within the company.
4. Maintain Internet/Intranet content ensuring the company's presence as being on the cutting-edge of contemporary e-commerce technology.

Fig. 4.2 (continued)

The diagram below provides a pictorial of the e-Communications Lab business
functions and interfaces to provide these services:

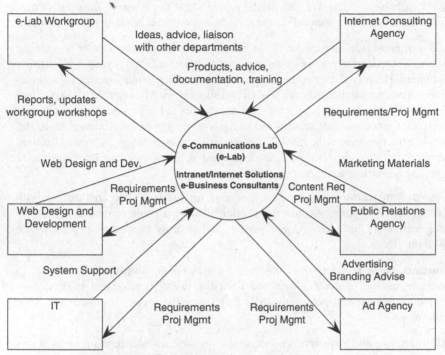

III Web Design and Development Projects

The focus of these projects is to implement more centralized Intranet applications
that can provide consistency, credibility, and quality within the company, yet at
the same time provide a consistent vision of the companies resources. The Internet
projects are limited to North American products and services at this time, but cer-
tain projects may span into the global international community, as well as focus on
external Internet products and services. Most of the projects in the short term, how-
ever, will relate to the development of Intranet sites for business lines that need to
raise their profiles within the company. Projects will vary in size and cost—some
requiring the storing of data and content in databases; others simply requiring the
movement of content among well-designed and thought-out screens. XYZ seeks a
business partner that can provide the following services:

Identity and Branding: this involves helping XYZ form a vision of their business
units over the Web. XYZ seeks firms that have established a number of methods to
assist clients in re-defining themselves in the Internet network era, particularly in the
financial community. It is expected that this will involve the translation of XYZ's
existing and forthcoming brand to the on-line world via the Web.

Fig. 4.2 (continued)

Creative Design: this requires vendors to provide creative and artistic web designs that are consistent with the firm's business themes, yet provide attractive and intuitively useable systems. We seek to find partners that can integrate the creative process and at the same time provide the technical vision and implementation as well.

e-Commerce: it is our expectation, as stated above, to have one vendor provide the entire life-cycle of web and e-commerce systems. The selected partner must provide the internal technical development team that is necessary to integrate legacy applications, provide complete database design and support for Microsoft SQL_Server and possibly Oracle. Furthermore, we expect our partner to have a systems-development cycle that reflects a well thought out analysis-to-design-to development foresight, that in effect convinces the XYZ of the vendor's ability to bring projects to fruition. Vendors are also expected to have development teams that can implement user tracking, reporting, traffic analysis, and security.

System Integration: this involves the need to interface new applications with existing XYZ systems. As such our vendor must be capable of providing systems architecture support, conversion expertise, and security experts to help formulate Web interfaces.

Intranet Tools Development: this area focuses on the ability of the Intranet to improve internal communication and workflow using flexible and tailored content management and publishing tools that foster the specific needs of the XYZ community.

Maintenance and Support: vendors need to provide maintenance and support services to assist in the ongoing relationship with XYZ. This can involve the need to get timely changes or enhancements made to a particular site, or providing documentation and training to a complimentary internal staff of XYZ Web developers. Help-line support should also be provided at both peak and off-peak times.

Existing System Issues

There have been a few year-end projects that have been completed to establish the presence of e-Lab. This consists of a new central Intranet home site, a Risk Management Reporting site, a Loans organization site, and a Human Resources central forms and handbook site. It is important that the image of the these sites be consistent with the new firm.

IV SPECIFICATION REQUIREMENTS

Vendors will be provided with technical specifications that are prepared by XYZ. Specifications will consist of an overview business specification, followed by detailed specifications that outline each site's functions, data needs, and reporting requirements. Flow diagrams showing the options of page selections are also included. A sample specification is shown on the following pages.

Fig. 4.2 (continued)

(Note: Attach Sample Specification)

V SERVICE PROPOSAL REQUIREMENTS

The submitted proposals should be organized according to the basic outline set forth below:

GENERAL COMMENTS

Provide a brief description and history of your firm and its current size. This should be in the format of a statement of qualifications and should include a brief financial history. If your proposal represents a joint effort between your company and another vendor, detail the relationship between your firm and the other involved. In addition, the specific responsibilities of each participating vendor in the joint effort should be described.

Vendors should also include a summary of the major benefits of working with their company.

Database And Application Software

Provide a list and explanation of the types of development environments supported. This should include program languages, databases supported, and third-party tools used, including content management products supported or developed.

Vendors are required to include as part of their bids costs for project management, testing and post implementation activities. Additional requirements include:

1. Methodology of creative design to development process (Life-cycle).
2. Delivery Schedule - provide the lead-time required for each application to be delivered and installed.
3. Software Support - indicate the manner in which database application software support will be provided and the pricing arrangement for each support.
4. Maintenance - describe maintenance provided, including warranty period, the availability and location of service and expected delivery time.
5. Security - describe the types and levels of system and software security. Specify how security is set-up and maintained and whether security can be controlled at the screen level.

Vendor Assistance And Training

Any assistance to be provided by the vendor should be described. Vendor assistance should be clearly defined, including whether the assistance is chargeable or supplied at no additional charge. Areas to be addressed should include, but not limited to:

1. Training - include description, location, and frequency of available training.
2. Installation Support - describe the recommended approach for installing your proposed system including a sample time-phased schedule of vendor and company manpower requirements, in detail and summarized form.

Fig. 4.2 (continued)

3. On-Going Support - describe the support provided such as "help lines", etc. In addition, explain your software upgrade procedures including frequency of new releases/upgrades.

Cost Summary

All cost considerations should be included in this section of the proposal.

1. Web Application software (including source and object code) by application:

 - *Hourly/daily rates*
 - *One time charges to develop and quality assure*
 - *Warranty and Maintenance fees*
 - *Tiered pricing structure alternatives and fixed fee basis*

2. Project Management
3. Maintenance and Support

Other Requirements

Please provide the following information:

1. List of users with installations similar to the proposed number of database applications and scope of the CG requirements, including company name, address, telephone number, contact person, and length of time the system has been installed. Vendors must also complete the Client Reference questionnaire.
2. Financial Statements Last two fiscal years.
3. Sample contract.

Examples of summary and detailed implementation

Responding To The Questionnaires

A comprehensive listing of company and web system requirements stated in the form of questionnaires can be found in subsequent sections. Some questions require a written response while others may be answered using codes listed below. To the right of each desired requirement a space provided for code responses. The following codes may be used:

Y Capability can be provided
N Capability cannot be provided
N/A Not Applicable (state reason)

Many of the questions will require an in-depth response typically needing an attachment. In these situations, Vendors should provide the appropriate attachment identification in the response area.

Confidentiality

This request contains information about XYZ that is confidential. We ask that you respect this confidence and not disclose this information to any third parties. XYZ, in turn, will treat the information you submit as confidential.

Fig. 4.2 (continued)

VENDOR REQUIREMENTS

01	General Information	Response
1	How many years have you been in the software business?	
2	When did your business start ?	
3	Have you developed software in a similar industry ?	
4	How long is the Warranty Period ?	
5	What are your typical terms and conditions of doing business?	
6	Are references available ?	
7	Do you have assigned Account Representatives ?	
8	Are user sites available for visitations ?	

02	Financial Evaluation		Response
1	Does the Firm have annual audited financial statements?		
2	Will prior fiscal year statements be available ?		
3	What is the Firm's fiscal year end ?		
4	List statistics for prior fiscal year end: ?		
	4a	Total Gross Revenues	
	4b	Total Net Revenues	
	4c	Total Net Income	
	4d	Total Assets	
	4e	Percent of Gross Sales related to Software Development	
	4f	R&D Budget	
	4g	Number of Customers	
5	How many consecutive years have been profitable ?		
6	Are Revenues by Product Division Available ?		

03	Employee Analysis		Response
1	Number of full-time Employees		
	1a	Sales	
	1b	Advertising/Creative Design	
	1c	Web Design	
	1d	Project Management/Consulting	
	1e	Development/Programming	
	1f	Middleware and XML	
	1g	Database/Backend	
	1h	Customer Support/Training	

Fig. 4.2 (continued)

	1i	Maintenance	
	1j	R&D	
	1k	Administration	
2		Number of full-time Employees last year	
3		Percent of turnover in last three (3) years	

04		Development and Flexibility Evaluation	Response
1		What is your internal procedure for Revision Control ?	
2		What is your procedure for informing clients of new versions?	
3		Is Custom Programming always available ?	
	3a	What is the hourly rate ?	
4		Do you supply your own:	
	4a	Content Management Software ?	
	4b	Value Added Resseller (VAR) relationships ?	
5		Does your contract assure clients the receipt of:	
	5a	New Release information and Documentation ?	
	5b	Source and Object code and all development routines ?	
6		Do you provide on-site support ?	
	6a	Toll-Free Help-line available ?	
	6b	24-hour Hot-line available ?	
7		When is support available (M, T, W, Th,..F,..Sa,..Su.)	
8		Is Support available 5 pm to 8 am ?	
	8a	weekdays ?	
04		Development and Flexibility Evaluation (cont'd)	Response
	8b	weekends	
9		Where are your software support offices ?	
	9a	Which location(s) will support Dresdner ?	
	9b	How many employees will be available to support Dresdner's software ?	
10		Enclose a copy of policies regarding application software support	
11		Enclose a copy of programming standards	
12		How are web enhancements distributed ?	
13		Are new manuals/documentation provided with each version released ?	
14		Do you support old releases of any proprietary package software ?	

Fig. 4.2 (continued)

15	Are you involved with any Web Industry Groups ?	
15a	How often does the Group meet (per year)	
15b	Who conducts the meetings (Users or Vendor)	
15c	Where do they meet ?	
15d	Is there a membership fee ?	
15e	Is there a Newsletter ?	
15f	Are user recommendations implemented ?	

06	Project Management/Implementation	Response
1	Do you provide project management services ?	
2	Do you assist in determining personnel resources required on the project?	
3	Do you define the roles and responsibilities for:	
3a	vendor ?	
3b	user ?	
3c	IT department ?	
4	Do you conduct kick-off meeting to introduce project ?	
5	Do you prepare weekly and monthly status reports ?	
6	Do you provide requirements documentation for:	
6a	hardware ?	
6b	software ?	
6c	necessary network configurations ?	
7	Do you prepare a Server capacity plan ?	
8	Do you prepare a site planning document ?	
9	Do you implement a methodology for migrationg from test to production ?	
10	Do you provide user security ?	

06	Branding/Design (cont'd)	Response
11	Do you provide branding services?	
12	Do you integrate branding and web site design to do:	
12a	logos ?	
12b	Interactive video?	
12c	Content design?	

Fig. 4.2 (continued)

13	Relating to design:	
13a	Provide content design images ?	
13b	define data requirements ?	
13c	identify update strategies ?	
13d	develop the interface methodology ?	
13e	design all required interfaces ?	
13f	document interface designs ?	
13g	test all developed interfaces ?	
13h	install all interface programs ?	

06	Testing and Quality Assurance	Response
14	Relating to testing, do you:	
14a	provide a test plan ?	
14b	identify additions to the production system ?	
14c	identify deletions to the production system ?	
14d	create test input data ?	
14e	list steps and procedures to create or extract test data ?	
14f	identify valid test results prior to testing ?	
14g	run tests with valid data ?	
14h	run tests with invalid data ?	
14i	be responsible for unit test plans ?	
14j	be responsible for system and volume testing ?	
14k	base acceptance for payment on client supplied test results ?	
15	Relating to conversion of existing data, will you:	
15a	identify data to be converted ?	
15b	develop conversion methodology ?	
15c	prepare conversion specifications ?	

Fig. 4.2 (continued)

06	Testing and Quality Assurance	Response
15d	design necessary file formats ?	
15e	test file conversion programs ?	
15f	install conversion programs in production ?	
16	Relating to implementation, will you:	
16a	prepare a complete workplan to get into production ?	
16b	develop alternative procedures should implementation plan fail ?	
16c	be responsible for problems encountered with software ?	
16d	be responsible for problems encountered with hardware ?	
16e	provide operations procedures for application software ?	
16f	provide operations procedures for recommended operating system ?	
16g	provide operations procedures for recommended hardware ?	
17	Supply an implementation workplan with activities and time frames.	

07	Documentation	Response
1	Will the system come with the following Documentation:	
1a	Operator Manuals ?	
1b	Technical Manuals ?	
1c	Programmer Manuals ?	
1d	User Manuals ?	
1e	System Flowcharts and/or Data Flow Diagrams ?	
1f	System Narratives ?	
1g	Table and File Layouts ?	
1h	Data Element Descriptions ?	
1i	Screen Formats ?	
1j	Data Validation Routines ?	
1k	Utility Programs ?	
1l	Backup and Recovery Programs ?	
1m	Security Routines ?	
1n	Logic Design (Data Flow Diagrams, Entity Relations, etc.) ?	
1o	Program Flowcharts ?	

Fig. 4.2 (continued)

07	Documentation (cont'd)	Response
1p	Program Narratives ?	
1q	Audit and Control descriptions ?	
1r	Quality Assurance Testing Scripts ?	
2	Will the system contain documentation for configuring the software:	
2a	Required Library Names ?	
2b	Required file or database names ?	
2c	File allocation and initialization ?	
2d	File distribution and directory placement ?	
3	Will the system contain documentation for product administration:	
3a	Database file system ?	
3b	End-User Security/Function Security Access ?	
3c	Master File Maintenance ?	
3d	Updating Applications Software ?	
4	Will the system contain the documentation for operations procedures:	
4a	User procedures at the screen level ?	
4b	Daily Operations ?	
4c	Evening/End of day operations ?	
07	Documentation (cont'd)	Response
4d	Recovery/Restart ?	
4e	Error handling and exceptions processing ?	
4f	Requesting Vendor Support ?	
5	Will the system contain documentation for data input and output control:	
5a	Input forms and how to use ?	
5b	Data Entry procedures ?	
5c	Balancing and reconciliation ?	
5d	Report verification ?	
6	Will the following documentation be provided periodically:	
6a	Features contained in new releases ?	
6b	Software bug fixes and operating system patches/new versions ?	

Fig. 4.2 (continued)

08	Training	Response
1	Is implementation training provided ?	
2	Is User Training provided ?	
2a	On-Site training ?	
2b	Off-site training ?	

09	Security	Response
1	Can you provide applications that have:	
1a	Field level security ?	
1b	Program security ?	
1c	Screen security ?	
1d	Menu level security ?	
1e	Application level security ?	
1f	Logged transactions (change, delete, etc.) ?	
2	Is security defined in a:	
2a	Master table ?	
2b	Data dictionary format ?	
3	On-line security is maintained by:	
3a	Batch update ?	
3b	On-line entry-batch update ?	
3c	On-line real-time ?	
4	Will there be the ability to create access profiles:	
4a	Attach and relate user to profile real-time ?	

10	Editing and Error Handling	Response
1	Will the Screen be capable of:	
1a	Providing on-line editing after individual fields are entered ?	
1b	Providing a means of changing field edits ?	
1c	Displaying standard error message and codes ?	
1d	Providing on-line help feature ?	
2	Provide an overriding key/command to cancel a transactions ?	
3	Database capabilities:	
3a	Logging of errors and dumps ?	
3b	To provide system failure recovery programs ?	

Fig. 4.2 (continued)

VII CLIENT REFERENCE QUESTIONS

Complete a separate questionnaire for at least three users who can be contacted for reference. References used should be able to demonstrate a similar implementation requirement and in particular, any companies involved in financial operations.

Reference

1. Company Information

 Company Name: _____

 Street Address: _____

 City: _____ State: _____ Zip: ____

 Phone: _____

 Website: _____

 e-mail Address: _____

 Contact's Name: _____ Position: _____

2. Website Design

 Number of Site Pages _____

 Number of Database Interface _____

 Hits per Month _____

 Number of Users _____

 Highest number of simultaneous access _____

3. Hardware/Software Installed

 System Platform (model) _____

 Browsers _____

 Middleware _____

 Database _____

 Operating System _____

4. Application Software Installed

 Security Access _____

 Encryption/Decryption _____

 Application Development Language _____

 Screen Software _____

 Report/Writer _____

 Communications Package _____

 3GL Software Interfaces _____

 Others: List _____

Fig. 4.2 (continued)

Client: XYZ Corporation	Date: 9/5/11
Application: Operations Database	Supersedes:
Subject: Contact Management	Author: A. Langer
Process: Overview - Business Spec	Page: 1 of 2

Overview

The Contact Management Process will allow users to add, modify or delete specific contacts. Contacts will be linked to various tables including Company. A Contact refers to a person who is related to XYZ for business reasons. It can be a Client, a Vendor, a consultant, a person involved in a negotiation, etc.

Contact General Information:

The Database must allow for the centralization of all the contacts handled by all the departments in XYZ.
The database and screens will be focused on the following information component groupings:

Basic Information

This is the minimum data requirement and includes such elements as Name, Title, Organization, Phone, Fax, Address, Country, etc.

Contact Profile Information

Further qualification and related elements. Relations include:

* department
* type of client
* nature of client (primary, technical)
* interest of prospect
* importance of client
* memberships (FTUG)
* FT employee

> *This is a Business Specification which reflects the overall requirements in prose format. Its focus is to provide the user who is not technical with a document that they can authorize.*

Fig. 4.3 Sample business specification

specifications include forms that articulate the logical requirements as shown in Figs. 4.3 and 4.4.

Chapters 7, 8, and 9 provide more details on how to create formal requirements documents with both business and technical specifications.

Problems and Exercises

1. What is an RFI?
2. What is an RFP?
3. Compare the differences between an RFI and an RFP.
4. What is the purpose of having a confidentiality and nondisclosure clause?
5. Explain why an RFP needs to be associated with a requirements document.
6. What is meant by logical requirements?

Client: XYZ Company	Date: 9/15/11
Application: Contact Management	Supersedes: 9/5/11
Subject: Program Specification Detail	Author: A. Langer
Spec-ID FTCM01 - Add/Modify Screen Processing	Page: 1 of 1

Process Flow Description:

The user will input information in the top form. At a minimum, at least the Last Name or Contact ID will be entered. The system must check a Security indicator prior to allowing a user to modify a Contact. The Security will be by Department or Everyone. Therefore, if the Modify button is selected and the user is restricted by a different department, Display:

" Access Denied, not eligible to modify, Department Restriction"

If Security authorized, the Add/Modify Button will activate the following business rules:

 If Contact-ID (cntid) not blank
 Find match and replace entered data into record
 If no match display "Invalid Contact-ID" and refresh cursor

 If Contact-ID (cntid) Blank and Last-Name (cntlname) Blank then
 Display "Contact-ID or Last-Name must be entered"
 Place Cursor at Contact-ID (cntid) entry.

 If Contact-ID (cntid) Blank and Last-Name (cntlname) + First-Name (cntfname) is Duplicate
 Display Window to show matches so that user can determine if contact already in
 system
 If user selects the Add Anyway button
 assume new contact with same name and assign new Contact-ID (cntid)
 Else
 upon selection bring in existing data and close window.
 Else
 Create new record with all new information fields and assign Contact-ID (cntid)

 If Company button activated
 Prompt user for Company-ID (cmpcd) and/or Company-Name (cmpna)
 If duplicate
 link foreign-key pointer to matched company
 Else
 Add Company-Name (cntcmpna) to Contact Table only
 Display "You must use Company Screen to Link, Company Master File Not
 Updated"

Fig. 4.4 Business specifications

Searching for Solutions

<div style="text-align:right">5</div>

The purpose of this chapter is to provide guidelines on the process of finding possible solutions for application needs. Thus far the preceding chapters have provided the structure and build vs. buy alternatives. It is now important to define the steps necessary to find the solution and prospective partners that meet the RFP needs.

Selecting the Management Team

Searching for the right solutions starts with forming an internal team responsible for managing the process through selection decision. The following roles and responsibilities should be considered:

- *Team Director/Lead*: this individual should be at a senior level, perhaps director or above, and have responsibility over the project selection team process and any other members that are needed. This individual could either be from IT or from a business unit. I suggest that this individual come from the business with assistance from IT management; in this way it allows the business to feel that they "own" the project.
- *Business/Functional Members*: these individuals should provide representation from all of the affected parties, including business unit personnel and administrative organizations such as accounting and human resources. These representatives should be at a line manager level, that is, knowledgeable about day-to-day needs and familiar with current systems in place.
- *Experts*: these are individuals who have specific knowledge in areas as opposed to specific business lines—they usually are technical experts in their fields and are needed at certain times during the evaluation process.
- *IT Manager*: this individual should be a senior representative from the IT department who essentially provides facilitation and direction from an architectural perspective, that is, providing information about the technical capabilities of

© Springer-Verlag London Limited 2016
A.M. Langer, *Guide to Software Development*,
DOI 10.1007/978-1-4471-6799-0_5

possible solutions as well as upholding certain architectural standards necessary to maintain capabilities among other systems.

- *Outside Consultants*: depending on the size of the project, some firms get outsiders involved to provide objective input that is free of the cultural and political constraints of the company. Outsiders can be from two areas: (1) from industry and are familiar with the applications or (2) have technical and project experience.

The question is who makes these individual choices? Smart firms select an executive to make some of these decisions. Often this will likely be the chief information officer (CIO) along with an operations executive. Sometimes it falls under the auspices of the chief financial officer (CFO) or chief operating officer (COO).

In terms of the actual participant choices, Tayntor (2006) suggests focusing on diversity of composition. She breaks composition into two major components:

1. *Functionality*: these individuals are focused on the operational aspects of the solution—that is, does it get the functions done so that the day-to-day business can run. To this extent, Tayntor recommends that there be multiple levels of operational personnel involved, so that varying perspectives on needs of the business are considered. Remember, levels of user views, as previously discussed, vary by responsibility because it affects what is valued.
2. *Technical*: the necessary expertise that can determine the automation considerations of any possible solution. Again, this includes architecture and product software issues. Product software issues can include systems software, application software, and productivity software (databases, spreadsheets, etc.).

There are, of course, generic factors that should be considered when forming the evaluation team. This includes selecting people that are group thinkers, can cooperate with others, are respected by employees, and are politically astute. Further, the evaluation team could become too large, resulting in a team that is difficult to manage and may not be able to reach consensus.

The Process of Due Diligence

Whether or not an RFP is used or not or whether an organization uses a consulting firm to assist them, it is important that the company engage in due diligence practices before selecting any vendor—for package development of specific application development. Due diligence is defined as a process of investigation before making a contractual decision. Effectively, it ensures that you know as much as possible about the vendor you are selecting. There are a number of components to the due diligence process: .

- Reference checks.
- Review vendor financial statements

- Bank references
- On-site and client site reviews
- Training
- Upgrade process
- General questions to ask
- Understand the company ownership

Performing Reference Checks

Vendors need to provide a list of clients that can be used as a positive reference. Most vendors will provide the names and contact information of their selection. Obviously these clients represent a positive experience. Organizations are better off asking vendors for a list of all their clients and then select from that list. This process will provide a more accurate depiction of satisfaction. Furthermore, I would suggest knowing about how a vendor deals with crisis—you want to know more about how a vendor will support you during problems than when things are going smoothly. Almost all vendors have problem accounts.

Reviewing Financial Statements

This is a very important process. I suggest that the vendor provide 3 years of historical financial statements. Public companies must have a certified audit, but if the vendor is privately held, they are not required to do so, which means that the statements may be prepared by someone internally—so they may not be accurate. In any case they must be able to provide them. The next question is what to look for? I would get your CFO or controller involved with the review because financial statements can be very tricky to read. However, here are some critical things to look for in the vendor's financial statements:

- *Cash on Hand*: this simply tells you how much actual cash the company has available.
- *Accounts Receivable*: how much is outstanding from their clients and to be collected.
- *Accounts Payable*: this represents the size of the company's debt—that is, money they owe.
- *Accrued Expenses*: this usually represents the amount of accrued payroll due to the vendor's employees—it is another form of cash debt.
- *Retained Earnings*: provides a perspective of previous earnings from profits. This should be matched against the company profit/loss statements.

So what do you look for in the above data? Here are some "red flags!":

1. If the cash on hand is less than accounts payable, it may mean that the company has exposure if they do not collect their accounts receivable. I would also require an aged accounts receivable so that your organization can determine how much of the accounts receivable are within 30 or 60 days—meaning that it will likely be collected. If the accounts receivable shows a lot of cash due over 60 days, it might mean that the vendor is having problems collecting, or cannot finish the work to get paid, or they have unhappy clients who do not want to pay them!
2. Ask for an aged accounts payable schedule as this will show how soon the debt is to be paid. If most of the debt is due within 60 days, it further allows you to determine the solvency of the vendor.
3. Ask for a detailed schedule of the accrued expenses as this will let you know how much is due for payroll and payroll taxes. Payroll must be paid timely.
4. If the accounts payable and accrued expenses are larger than the combined cash on hand and the accounts receivable, then the vendor may not be very solvent.
5. If retained earning is negative, it means that the vendor has not yet reached a profit stage in the company—that is, the vendor has not yet reached a profit cumulatively since its inception.

The financial statements do not always paint the complete picture financially. The organization or its attorney should do a search to ensure that there are no outstanding lawsuits against the vendor, or past ones, as well as liens from third parties. Further, a Dun & Bradstreet (D&B) search should be done which will provide a rating on payment ability of the vendor—specifically if they pay their bills late.

Doing Bank References

The organization should obtain authorization to contact the vendor's banks to verify cash on hand and to verify that the vendor has a good standing with the bank. This is a simple process and one that every vendor will likely agree to do. Unfortunately it is often overlooked or considered unnecessary. The organization should request a complete list of financial institutions and types of accounts maintained by the vendor.

Scheduling On-Site Demonstrations

Organizations should arrange for prospective vendor solutions to come on-site and demonstrate the capabilities of their product. This demonstration should be accomplished by first having meetings with the vendor and providing them with test data. In this way the demonstrations actually show company information and how it can be accessed by the users of the product. This can be very effective, especially for the general business user who may be challenged to imagine how the software will actually operate on the data of his/her business unit. Having on-site demonstrations

also allows the vendor to get a better grasp for the politics of the company and how they can compliment the operating team.

Scheduling On-Site Review at Vendor Site(s)

Organizations should visit the vendor's corporate or local office. You want to see the organization at work and meet the administrative people who you might be dealing with in the future. Doing a vendor site visit is extremely important for nonpublic companies and for very small vendors. Today, websites make companies that are very small look very big, although size is not always an indicator of corporate solvency. Doing actual client site reviews is also very constructive. While calling a vendor client is productive, actually seeing the implementation and meeting more than one person can tell a lot about the how the vendor operates.

Reviewing Vendor Training Capabilities

A number of packaged products require significant training of staff to be successful. The vendor may have an excellent product but lousy support and training. Organizations should review the training philosophy of the vendor, review the materials, and cover how their clients rate training. Initial training, however, is only one aspect of training. As organization lose and add employees, there may be needs for continual support or sporadic training based on new versions of the product. Interviewing some of the vendor trainers is another effective way of determining the strength of their staff. Some large vendors can also make training available through third-party firms that specialize in supporting them. This may or may not be an effective solution. Problems occur when a training company is out of sync with the software company especially when there are product bugs for which the training company cannot fix or offer a temporary "work-around."

Understanding the Product Upgrade Process

Software enhancements are realities. It is important to understand the vendor's approach to handling this process. Due diligence should cover the number of upgrades historically provided to clients, how the process works, and how upgrades are retrofitted to software that has been customized (this process addresses the problem of software enhancements that overlay customized code from an earlier version). Organizations should also understand the costs associated with receiving upgrades. This often is included as part of the annual maintenance fee but sometimes such costs are not included and must be paid each time there are maintenance releases. If customizations are involved, organizations should understand the costs for retrofitting upgrades with the customized changes. Maintenance fees usually are 15% of the then-going software license fees. Maintenance and upgrade costs

become more complex when the applications are developed specifically for the client. In these cases the method of upgrade and associated costs must be carefully reviewed during due diligence.

General Questions to Ask

Perhaps the most important part of the due diligence process is knowing what questions to ask and how to ask them. For example, when checking client satisfaction, do not ask the vendor's client if they are happy. Ask them how the vendor supported them when they had difficulties. This type of phrasing gets the right answers—you want to know how the vendor will treat you when you disagree, not when you agree. This is also true when asking about implementation schedules—do not ask how they keep on schedule; ask them what they do when they are behind!

Understanding the Vendor Ownership

One can never be sure what represents a comfort zone when dealing with a vendor's ownership. If it is a private firm, ask whether a venture firm owns the controlling shares. Venture and private equity firms invest in companies for one reason—to flip them and make money. This means they will either sell the company at some point or help the entity to go public. The latter is a good thing in most cases, but the former—selling the company could mean lots of changes, both in the firm's philosophy and in its personnel. So the only answer, to a large degree, is to understand the vendor's timetable—are they in a growth period? When might the investors want to get out? Also, who are the original founders? Do they want to sell or expand the company. You might not get an honest answer, but why not ask!!

Reviewing the Product's Architecture and Design

The type of software and systems required by the vendor and the overall architecture of the solution are extremely important issues not to be overlooked. Therefore, organizations should do a complete "platform" review to ensure that the product will operate properly across all of their systems. Organizations should be particularly sensitive when considering software that has not demonstrated that it can successfully execute on a new or different architecture. Although we believe that we live in a world of open systems, there are still products that are very dependent on specific versions of operating systems and specific systems environments. An example of this problem can be related to the Cone Mills case against Systems Software Associates (SSA) Enterprise Resource Planning (ERP) product called BPCS (Business Processing and Control System). The product was originally designed to operate under the IBM midrange product lines (Systems 36, 38, and AS400), which are very proprietary platforms. When the software industry began to

transition to open systems particularly Windows and UNIX, SSA attempted to convert its product and advertise that its product could run under the HP-UX architecture. Cone Mills selected the HP-UX environment, and although SSA stated it would operate, there were problems. Apparently BPCS could only operate on HP-UX if the entire system was installed. Unfortunately, Cone Mills only selected certain modules. The product was significantly delayed by over a year and eventually SSA declared bankruptcy in 2002. These types of results do not favor anyone—all sides tend to lose. So the message is that organization should be very wary of being the first to implement any package on a platform that the vendor cannot physically show success.

Another complication discussed earlier in this book is the use of open source. While this might be very attractive, organizations need to be sure that the open source contained in any vendor license does not restrict or prohibit certain uses, and if there are any proprietary modifications made to a portion of the package using open source, what are the restrictions in use that affect the organization? Certainly open source in this situation might preclude the organization from selecting the vendor's product.

Another factor in selection is product scalability. Should the organization grow and need to expand its use of the package or customized solution, will the software be able to run across multiple platforms or on a larger system? This again becomes a question of architecture, so at some point, the IT organization must review this information with the vendor carefully. It might also be a good idea to consider engaging a third-party reviewer, similar to an independent engineer's report before one buys a house.

Finding Vendors

This section provides input on alternatives for finding available vendors that meet the needs of the RFP. We have already discussed the use of an outside consulting firm. There are significant advantages to bringing in a large firm to help:

1. Already have a list of acceptable vendors.
2. Prior relationships with many of the vendors.
3. Leverage with vendors because they represent future opportunities if the vendor does a good job.
4. Leverage against the large consulting firm. A third-party consulting firm that has liability insurance that can support any type of malpractice activities. Simply put, because of their size, they can be sued.
5. Experience of the consulting firm with RFPs and selections of vendors.

If the organization elects to not use an outside consultant, then the following are alternative methods to find prospective vendors to bid:

- *Use the Internet*: searching for vendors can be very effective using the modern search engines available to the general user. Furthermore, the Internet allows the organization to easily find out information about the company, its clients, and in some cases its financial performance (if they are a public company, they have their financials posted on the Internet). In addition, the Internet allows the organization to uncover any issues with the vendor's clients, e.g., articles written about problems, or legal suites that are posted, etc.
- *Facebook and Chat Rooms*: using today's social media, most vendors have active "Facebook" and chat rooms. Many also have user groups that can be contacted to receive information about the satisfaction with the vendor's clients and products overall.
- *Industry Groups*: there are a number of groups that provide information about suggested solutions across different product lines. Subscribing or becoming a member of such groups can be very beneficial. Industry contacts can also be used as networks, and such networks can provide informal information that can be very valuable.
- *Conferences*: many professional IT organizations exist as well as industry groups that hold regular conferences. This is another network that can provide important information from those organizations that have implemented similar solutions.
- *Research Organizations*: companies like Gartner Group provide certain research services for a fee. A number of such firms also allow subscriptions to their databases that have information about solutions, vendors, and current clients. Another research partner can be universities, who typically have faculty that will provide research services for lower costs and for the general education of their students. Using research universities is one of the most underutilized assets available to organizations.

Paying for a Plan

Another clever approach to finding the right vendor is to ask prospective vendors to provide a project management plan showing how they would actually implement their solution for your company. This may seem like a typical project plan, but these efforts should be set up as a prelude to evaluating the effectiveness of the vendor and their ability to deliver requested tasks. The downside of this approach is that it will likely cost the organization money: you may need to pay the vendor to do this extra work. However, it may be well worth the expense to become familiar with how the vendor supports you. In many cases you can negotiate an option with the vendor which credits the payment should they win the bid—that is, the steps being taken would need to be done by the selected vendor anyway. Another downside could be that the cost and effort do not necessarily allow the organization to determine the quality of the software and the ultimate value of the solution, but it is yet another option to consider.

Summary

It is important to note that the search for a vendor is a complex step that depends heavily on whether you wish to make or buy the solution or as previously discussed both. We should not see the vendor selection as a binary one, that is, there may be a need for more than one vendor, who may represent one phase or area of the solution. While this may sound like an obvious alternative, it is not without danger. Anytime you have more than one vendor partnering to deliver one solution, you run the risk of one blaming the other and no one really responsible for the entire contract. Even getting a consulting firm to manage the effort does not ensure that they can really ensure that there will not be problems. That is why many organizations like to have a one-stop solution where the vendor is responsible for every aspect of the implementation. The benefits are obvious should the vendor actually be capable of doing all of the needed activities from programing to product delivery to training and implementation.

Another alternative is to have a firm that monitors the vendor's activities but is not really responsible for any deliveries. Once again the large consulting firms provide this project management service. Although this seems worth the investment, you are also taking on yet another vendor to manage. Perhaps the best solution is to have an effective management team that helps ensure that the project remains on time and on budget, assuming of course that the right vendor has been selected.

Problems and Exercises

1. Explain the purpose of due diligence. Discuss three components that affect the due diligence process.
2. What is the importance of the architecture review? Who in the organization should be responsible for this task?
3. What are the alternative ways to find qualified vendors? Which of them do you prefer? Support your opinion.
4. What is the role and responsibility of an outside consultant?
5. Provide three positive aspects of retaining an outside consultant and three negatives.
6. What are the advantages and disadvantages of having someone outside the organization develop and perhaps manage the plan?

Reference

Tayntor, C. B. (2006). *Successful packaged software implementation*. New York: Auerbach Publications.

Controlling Costs and Realistic Budgeting

<div style="text-align:right">**6**</div>

A critical step is setting a budget before starting the process. Once the budget is set, then overriding estimates is difficult and tends to feed the stereotype view of IT projects as being expensive and full of project overruns. The purpose of this chapter is to provide some guidelines on how to determine a viable budget and focus on controlling runaway costs because of inappropriate management as well as project scope creep.

The most important aspect of cost analysis is to prepare a budget. The first part of creating any budget is to determine the categories of cost. Costs usually belong to categories that relate to project activities. It is suggested then that you start the budget by sequentially thinking about the steps necessary to complete the project, from the selection process through implementation and go live (post-implementation):

- Kickoff and Selection
- Implementation
- Post-Implementation

Within each of these processes are categories of costs as follows:

Kickoff and Selection
- *Internal Staff Costs*: this includes all of the internal staff resource needs throughout the project, including the selection team. The cost for these resources is usually determined based on an internal rate, that is, the company determines the internal charge for use of its staff on special projects. Essentially internal staff costs are a form of "funny money" or an allocation, but they usually are a correct way of measuring staff costs of the project. The individuals engaged in this allocation should consist of IT personnel, user department staff, and administrative people.
- *Travel and Expenses*: this includes out-of-pocket expenses incurred during the search and decisions for selecting vendors.

© Springer-Verlag London Limited 2016
A.M. Langer, *Guide to Software Development*,
DOI 10.1007/978-1-4471-6799-0_6

- *Software Costs*: this relates to any special software tools that are needed for the evaluation such as a package to assist with the assessment.
- *Consultant and Legal*: these are associated professional costs for special assistance during the selection period, especially outside help with the selection process and any legal costs associated with license agreements, customized development, and project management arrangements.

Implementation
- *Software Costs*: these costs include software license fees, custom modifications, utility products (e.g., EDI), databases, operating systems, and security.
- *Hardware Costs*: these costs consist of servers, PCs, memory, cloud computing, printers, scanners, backup devices, and disk space.
- *Network Costs*: this includes infrastructure costs for cabling, racks, routers, switches, modems, leased or dedicated lines, communications software, and Internet charges.
- *Project Team Costs*: these are labor costs for the project manager/team leader, systems analyst, programmers, testers, and outside consultants.
- *User Team Costs*: includes the team leaders, user managers, and support personnel.
- *Support Team Costs*: this includes general IT utility expenses for IS support, database analysts, and networking staff.
- *Miscellaneous Project Team Costs*: these include costs for furniture, telephone, project management software tools, administrative support, communications, videoconferencing charges, user manuals, and special education.
- *Training Costs*: these costs cover user training of the various user teams, the materials associated with the training, and should also cover any travel to and from training locations.
- *Data Costs*: this relates to costs associated with cleaning up legacy data before conversion as well as archiving costs to protect the data from previous systems.
- *Miscellaneous or Other Costs:* these costs include quality assurance, internal audit, steering groups, conferences, and general networking of personnel during the implementation.
- *Allocation Overhead Costs*: these costs are allocations usually for using organizational resources from central services like office space and utility expenses. Since there is no direct way of calculating these expenses, they are typically done through an accounting charge method. Not all organizations use this, but many have this as part of the budget process. The CFO can usually provide this information.
- *Contingency*: this represents an old method of having a cost allocated to unforeseen expenses. Some organizations allow it; others do not. Again, the CFO usually dictates the company policy.

Post-implementation
- *Maintenance Costs*: these are usually annual costs for license fees and support for guaranteed upgrades, hardware coverage, and database support. These expenses can also include data disaster and recovery costs.

A sample budget format is shown on Fig. 6.1.

Sample Budget	Year:	Rate $ per Unit/Day	0 Quantity Units/Days	0 $	1 Quantity Units/Days	1 $	2 Quantity Units/Days	2 $	3 Quantity Units/Days	3 $	Total $
Ref	Project Expenditures										
1	Selection process										
1.1	Internal resources / staff costs:										
1.1.1	- Information Systems (IS) department	325	10	3250							3250
1.1.2	- user departments	250	20	5000							5000
1.1.3	- procurement department	325	2	650							650
1.2	Travel and expenses	225	12	2700							2700
1.3	Specification / RFP tools and programs	550	2	1100							1100
1.4	Consultancy assistance	0	0	0							0
1.5	Legal assistance	0	0	0							0
	Total selection costs			12700		0		0		0	12700
	Implementation process										
2	Software costs										
2.1	Application software user licenses	1025	0	0	55	56375	35	35875	0	0	92250
2.2	Software modifications	0	0	0	0	0	0	0	0	0	0
2.3	Additional licenses e.g. Citrix, EDI software	1025	0	0	5	5125	0	0	0	0	5125
2.4	Database user licenses	5200	0	0	1	5200	0	0	0	0	5200
2.5	Operating system	0	0	0	0	0	0	0	0	0	0
2.6	Additional security applications	0	0	0	0	0	0	0	0	0	0
	Sub total			0		66700		35875		0	102575

Fig. 6.1 Sample budget format

3	Hardware costs							
3.1	Servers (new or upgraded; dedicated or shared)	22000	0	2	44000	0	0	44000
3.2	PC's (new or upgrades)	1200	0	25	30000	0	0	30000
3.3	Additional memory	0	0	0	0	0	0	0
3.4	Additional CPU	0	0	0	0	0	0	0
3.5	Additional processing services (temporary or permanent) e.g. via cloud services or other internal resource	0	0	0	0	0	0	0
3.6	Printers	1100	0	5	5500	0	0	5500
3.7	Scanners	0	0	0	0	0	0	0
3.8	UPS	0	0	0	0	0	0	0
3.9	Back up devices	0	0	0	0	0	0	0
3.10	Disk storage	0	0	0	0	0	0	0
	Sub total	0	0		79500	0	0	79500

4	Network costs							
4.1	Cabling or wireless LAN, WAN or other network	5500	0	1	5500	0	0	5500
4.2	Racks	0	0	0	0	0	0	0
4.3	Routers	0	0	0	0	0	0	0
4.4	Switching devices	0	0	0	0	0	0	0
4.5	Modems	0	0	0	0	0	0	0
4.6	Leased or dedicated lines	5150	0	1	5150	0	0	5150
4.7	Communications software	0	0	0	0	0	0	0
4.8	Internet access broadband, satellite	0	0	0	0	0	0	0
	Sub total	0	0		10650	0	0	10650

Fig. 6.1 (continued)

No.	Item								
5	**Labor costs**								
	For implementation tasks e.g.: system installation, integration, tailoring, interface development, process re-engineering, report writing, functional and user testing, data conversion and documentation								
5.1	**Project team**								
5.1.1	Project manager	600	0	10	6000	10	6000	0	12000
5.1.2	Project leader	450	0	20	9000	20	9000	0	18000
5.1.3	Systems analysts	350	0	10	3500	0	0	0	3500
5.1.4	Programmers	275	0	20	5500	20	5500	0	11000
5.1.5	Systems testers	250	0	20	5000	30	7500	0	12500
5.1.6	Vendor consultants	800	0	3	2400	3	2400	0	4800
5.1.7	Additional team resources e.g. contractors, temporary staff, other consultants	0	0	0	0	0	0	0	0
5.1.8	Travel and expenses	0	0	0	0	0	0	0	0
	Sub total		0		31400		30400	0	61800
5.2	**User team**								
5.2.1	User team leader	0	0	0	0	0	0	0	0
5.2.2	User team members	0	0	0	0	0	0	0	0
5.2.3	User team managers	0	0	0	0	0	0	0	0
	Sub total		0		0		0	0	0
5.3	**Support costs**								
5.3.1	Client manager	450	0	4	1800	4	1800	0	3600
5.3.2	IS support	325	0	6	1950	6	1950	0	3900

Fig. 6.1 (continued)

Item	Description	Unit cost	no.	£	no.	£	no.	£	no.	£
5.3.3	DB analyst	250	0	0	2	500	2	500	4	1000
5.3.4	Networking support	0	0	0	0	0	0	0	0	0
	Sub total			0		4250		4250		8500
5.4	**Project team and office costs**									
5.4.1	Temporary office accommodation	0	0	0	0	0	0	0	0	0
5.4.2	Furniture, stationery and supplies	0	0	0	0	0	0	0	0	0
5.4.3	Additional telephones and lines	0	0	0	0	0	0	0	0	0
5.4.4	Project tools e.g. project management software, testing programs	0	0	0	0	0	0	0	0	0
5.4.5	Project website set up and maintenance	0	0	0	0	0	0	0	0	0
5.4.6	Administrative support	0	0	0	0	0	0	0	0	0
5.4.7	Communications costs	0	0	0	0	0	0	0	0	0
5.4.8	Video teleconferencing	0	0	0	0	0	0	0	0	0
5.4.9	Printing e.g. user manuals	0	0	0	0	0	0	0	0	0
5.4.10	Project information / education / marketing materials	0	0	0	0	0	0	0	0	0
	Sub total			0		0		0		0
6	**Training**									
6.1	Technical training for implementation team (by vendor)	900	0	0	10	9000	10	9000	10	9000
6.2	Training key users (by vendor)	900	0	0	4	3600	10	9000	10	12600
6.3	Temporary internal training facilities	0	0	0	0	0	0	0	0	0
6.4	Training remainder of users (internally or by vendor)	0	0	0	0	0	0	0	0	0
6.5	Training materials	125	0	0	10	1250	50	6250	50	7500
6.6	Travel and expenses to attend training	0	0	0	0	0	0	0	0	0
	Sub total			0		13850		15250		29100

Fig. 6.1 (continued)

7	**Data costs**	
7.1	Data clean-up / de-duplication	
7.2	Data archiving	Sub total
8	**Other costs**	
8.1	Quality Assurance	
8.2	Internal audit review(s) of new system(s)	
8.3	Project steering group	
8.4	Decommissioning of legacy systems	
8.5	Networking with other organizations, who are using / implementing the same system(s) - travel and expenses costs	
8.6	Attending conferences, software vendor user groups, networking, meetings - fees, travel and expenses costs	Sub total
9	**Allocated Costs**	
9.1	Additional heat, air conditioning, light, power for project implementation and ongoing live running	
9.2	Other allocated business costs	Sub total

Fig. 6.1 (continued)

No.	Item	Unit cost					Total
10	**Contingency**						
10.1	Estimated 10% of total implementation costs	0	0	20000	10000	0	30000
	Total implementation costs		0	226350	95775	0	322125
11	**Post Implementation Process**						
11	**Maintenance costs**						
11.1	Annual vendor maintenance / service charges for:						
11.1.1	- software	12500	0	0 / 0	1 / 12500	1 / 12500	25000
11.1.2	- hardware	14600	0	0 / 0	0 / 0	0 / 0	0
11.1.3	- database	1200	0	0 / 0	1 / 1200	1 / 1200	2400
11.2	Internal IS support	0	0	0 / 0	0 / 0	0 / 0	0
11.3	Disaster recovery for systems and data (internally or outsource to remote location)	1100	0	5 / 5500	2 / 2200	2 / 2200	9900
	Total ongoing costs		0	5500	15900	15900	37300
	Project cost calculations						
	Total project cost						372125
	Number of users (software licenses)						90
	Total project cost per user						4135

Fig. 6.1 (continued)

Controlling Costs

While the budget shown in Fig. 6.1 reflects the items to be included in a budget forecast, it does not address what might be deemed appropriate spending within these categories of expenses. As such, this section aims to provide some guidelines as to what might be considered realistic amounts and pitfalls to be wary about as the project moves from selection to implementation to post-implementation. Unfortunately, IT organizations lack financial efficiencies and may not alone be able to formulate the total costs effectively (Ryan and Raducha-Grace 2010). Thus, it is important to get all of the business management and accounting involved to ensure the right budget amount is carefully formulated.

Hardware and Infrastructure

The most immediate issues for these expenses relate to company direction, first for infrastructure. I have already discussed the implications of whether or not to use a cloud solution. Obviously going to a cloud architecture is much cheaper and avoids the whole issue of designing, creating, and maintaining a data center. So I would recommend comparing the actual costs of owning a data center versus an outsourced cloud. It is also important to recognize the difference in accounting, not withstanding actual cash outlay. To be specific, most data center costs, including hardware, networking, and installation, fall under the accounting of capital expenditures. Capital expenditures are recognized in accounting standards as long-term assets, for which the actual expense is depreciated over a number of years, depending on the type of asset. The number of years that can be depreciated on the books of the company is published in various standard organizations like FASB (Financial Accounting Standards Board) and is part of what is known as GAAP (generally accepted accounting principles) and GAAS (generally accepted accounting standards). To go further into accounting concepts would be beyond the scope of this book, but essentially, if you have hardware costs totaling $150,000, the company would likely depreciate that expense over 3 years, recording in the first year only $50,000 of the total expense. That is, each year for 3 years, the organization would only record $50,000 per year. The concept behind this allocation of cost is that the organization is actually prepaying for the value of the hardware, so it takes only a portion of the useful life each year, in this case 3 years. So the question becomes: what do you put in the first year budget? Likely only $50,000, however the project cost is still $150,000. However, allocating a cost across 3 years may have more value to the business than let's say a hardware alternative that would be $125,000 expensed in the first year for a cloud!! To say the least, this can be tricky!

Going with a cloud, on the other hand, would mean a rental expense for the use of the equipment and services, so the total cost per month is the total cost—there is no depreciation because there is no ownership of the asset. Whether the hardware cost can be allocated to other benefits is also questionable, but in reality it could be very important. So let's say the data center can be shared or leveraged for another

system. It appears that the trend suggests that companies should avoid owning and operating their own data centers, so the cloud could be the answer.

Software

Software falls into two categories: package and developed. For the purposes of this section, I focus on the package software price or license fee. Software is licensed because vendors typically do not sell the rights to the code, but rather the "right to use the package" under the rights and limitations granted by the license agreement. So you basically rent the right to use the software package so long as the organization abides by the terms and conditions of the license agreement.

More important is understanding the cost of the license. The license fee can be complex. Certainly there will be an initial license to use the product—the price if you will of the initial purchase. Then there are certain license costs that may relate to third-party utilities that the software package requires—like a database product (Oracle, for instance) that may have separate license requirements or what is known as "run-time" software, which can be programs owned by others or needed in a specific operating system for the product to run. Often such products also carry a "per user" cost, so the more concurrent users on the system, the higher the cost. The last component of cost is the software maintenance fee. While this is usually presented by the vendor as optional, it may very well not be—in the sense that if your organization does not have the maintenance, you will not receive automatic upgrades, bug fixes, and general vendor support.

In terms of pricing, software packages, like any product in the market, are priced on two factors: (1) what the market will bear and (2) the competitive landscape. The market price is very vague at times, but is usually set by the "best of breed" in the industry. This tends to work in the same way that top luxury cars set the price. Certainly what organizations are willing to pay is a factor, but the leader in a category of software typically leads the acceptable price. So the recommendation when budgeting the cost for the package is to survey the market and review the feature/functions of the software in the marketplace and what tends to be the price.

The competitive landscape also relates to the market but yet it is different. The competition can upset the leaders pricing, in the same way that a new car undersells what was perceived as the standard price within a class of car. We even see this at the top class, where Lexus and Acura invaded the luxury class car price which was previously dominated by the German manufacturers. The prices were lower and yet the quality was high. Such is sometimes true in the software industry as well. New technologies or open source can provide pressure on the industry leaders to lower prices—hardware does the same as we saw when the PCs began to take market share away from the midrange computer industry. The technology industry has also been regulated by Moore's Law, which predicts a doubling of processing capabilities—which again drive prices down as we saw in the PC chip market.

Other prices, like per user fees and maintenance, are more predictable. For example, the market price for maintenance is usually 15% of the "then going" license

fees—meaning that your maintenance can increase over the years! Per user fees often hover in the $50–$100 range per user. There are also more cost options here. For example, many software vendors offer multiple-year maintenance plans. This means if you prepay 3 years of maintenance at the time of purchase, organizations typically receive a huge discount. You can also reduce per unit costs by buying more users than you might need at the time of purchase.

So the general recommendations are to budget consistent with the leading market vendor's license prices, but also look for newcomers if there is a willingness in the organization to take more risk. The other components of package costs are more predictable, but decisions on multiyear maintenance or packaged deals should be discussed during budget time with the selection committee.

Consulting Fees

Consulting fees are usually very predictable and very much regulated by the marketplace. They are driven by the laws of supply and demand and also by the type of consultation needed. For example, when SAP implementations were very much in demand and talent availability was low, hourly rates for SAP consultants were high—almost $2000 per day at the height of demand. Today they are much lower, say $800 per day or even lower. Consulting rates for training are also lower, perhaps $300 per day, depending on the type of training needed. However, consulting rates can be purchased in blocks; by committing to a number of days, up-front organizations can expect reasonable discounts from vendors. So the suggestion here is to check the market prices for comparison. This can be accomplished by calling vendors, searching the Internet, or simply working with Gartner or other research firms.

Customization Costs

There are two types of budgeting here. Vendors like to get an hourly or daily rate for their development staff. Prices vary by level with a senior programmer going for $125–$150 per hour and QA people perhaps at $75–100 per hour. Budgeting for customizations on an hourly basis is bad business and can become an exposure to exceeding your budget. Organizations should negotiate fixed prices or "not to exceed" costs for custom modifications. Unfortunately, organizations may not know the extent of the custom modifications required until the analysis and design is completed. There are two choices then: (1) create a budget to do the analysis and design before determining the budget for package customizations or (2) budget based on a limit—perhaps an upper limit amount that the organization is willing to spend. This may not be a bad option as it sets expectations for the selection team and user community. It might also suggest that if the package exceeds this budget amount, then perhaps it is not the right fit.

The Balanced Scorecard as a Budget Tool

Another method that can be used to validate budget versus user needs is a management tool called the Balanced Scorecard. The Balanced Scorecard was introduced by Robert Kaplan and David Norton in the early 1990s as a tool to solve measurement problems. An organization's ability to develop and operationalize its intangible assets has become more and more a critical component for success. The Balanced Scorecard can also be used as a solution for measuring IT outcomes that do not always have obvious financial costs associated with them. Furthermore, the Balanced Scorecard is a "living" document that can be modified as certain objectives or measurements require change. This is a critical advantage because as I have demonstrated, technology projects often change in scope and in objectives as a result of internal and external factions.

The ultimate value then of the Balanced Scorecard in this context is to provide a means for evaluating cost versus need, not only for measuring completion against set targets but also for defining how expected transformations map onto the strategic objectives of the organization. In effect it is the ability of the organization to execute its strategy toward implementing an application software solution. Before explaining the details of how a Balanced Scorecard can be applied, I offer Fig. 6.2 that shows exactly where the scorecard fits into the overall picture of implementing packaged software solutions into concrete costs versus benefits.

The generic objectives of a Balanced Scorecard are designed to create a strategy-focused organization. Thus, all of the objectives and measurements should be derived from the organization's vision and strategy (Kaplan and Norton 2001).

Fig. 6.2 Balanced Scorecard (Source: Kaplan and Norton (2001))

Mobilize Change through Executive Leadership

Translate the Strategy to Operational Terms

Balanced

Strategy

Scorecard

Make Strategy a Continual Process

Align Organizational to the Strategy

Make Startegy Everyone's Job

These measurements are based on the fundamental principles of any strategically focused organization and on alignment and focus. Kaplan and Norton defined these principles as the core of the Balanced Scorecard:

1. *Translate the Strategy to Operational Terms*: this principle includes two major components that allow an organization to define its strategy from a cause-and-effect perspective using a strategy map and scorecard. Thus the strategy map and its corresponding Balanced Scorecard provide the basic measurement system.
2. *Align the Organization to the Strategy*: Kaplan and Norton defined this principle as favoring synergies among organizational departments that allow communities of practice to have a shared view and common understanding of their roles.
3. *Make Strategy Everyone's Everyday Job*: this principle supports the notion of a learning organization that requires everyone's participation, from the CEO to clerical levels. To accomplish this mission, the members of the organization must be aware of business strategy and individuals may need "personal" scorecards and a matching reward system for accomplishing the strategy.
4. *Make Strategy a Continual Process*: this process requires the linking of important yet fundamental components including organizational learning, budgeting, management reviews, and a process of adaptation. Much of this principle falls into the areas of learning organization theories that link learning and strategy in ongoing perpetual cycles.
5. *Mobilize Change through Executive Leadership*: this principle stresses the need for a strategy-focused organization that incorporates the involvement of senior management and can mobilize the organization and provide sponsorship to the overall process.

Using the core Balanced Scorecard schematic, I have modified it to operate with packaged software implementations as shown in Fig. 6.3:

1. *Evaluation of Technology*: the first step is to have an infrastructure that can determine how technology fits into a specific strategy. Once this is targeted, the evaluation team needs to define it in operational terms.
2. *Align Technology with Business Strategy*: once technology is evaluated, it must be integrated into the business strategy. This involves ascertaining whether the addition of technology will change the current business strategy.
3. *Make Technology Projects Part of Communities of Practice*: affected communities need to be strategically aware of the project. Organizational structures must determine how they distribute rewards and objectives across departments.
4. *Phased-In Technology Implementation*: short- and long-term project objectives are based on Driver and Supporter life cycles. This will allow organizational transformation phases to be linked to implementation milestones.
5. *Executive Interface*: CEO and senior managers act as executive sponsors and project champions. This can also be related to the team leaders across the business lines.

Fig. 6.3 Modified
scorecard for the SDLC

The Balanced Scorecard ultimately provides a framework to view strategy from four different measures:

1. *Financial*: ROI and risk continue to be important components of strategic evaluation.
2. *Customer*: this involves the strategic part of how to create value for the organization's customers.
3. *Internal Business Processes*: this relates to the business processes that provide both customer satisfaction and operational efficiency.
4. *Learning and Growth*: this encompasses the priorities and infrastructure to support organizational transformation through the implementation of the application software package.

The generic Balanced Scorecard framework shown in Fig. 6.3 needs to be extended to address the needs of software implementations. I propose the following adjustments:

1. *Financial*: requires the inclusion of indirect benefits from technology, particularly as Lucas (1999) specified, in nonmonetary methods of evaluating ROI. Risk must also be factored in based on specific issues for each technology project.
2. *Customer*: technology-based products are integrated with customer needs and provide direct customer package interfaces. Further, Web systems that use the Internet are very dependent on consumer use. As such, technology can modify organizational strategy because of its direct effect on the customer interface.
3. *Internal Business Processes*: technology requires business process reengineering (BPR), which is the process of reevaluating existing internal norms and behaviors before designing a new system. This new evaluation process will addresses customers, operational efficiencies, and cost.

4. *Learning and Growth*: organizational learning techniques, under the umbrella of ROD, need to be applied on an ongoing and evolutionary basis.

The major portion of the Balanced Scorecard strategy is in its initial design, that is, in translating the strategy or, as in the Packaged Software Scorecard, the evaluation of technology. During this phase a strategy map and an actual Balanced Scorecard are created. This process should begin by designing a Balanced Scorecard that articulates the business strategy. Remember that every organization needs to build a strategy that is unique and based on its evaluation of the external and internal situation (Olve et al. 2003). To clarify the definition of this strategy, it is easier to consider drawing the scorecard initially in the form of a strategy map. A generic strategy map essentially defines the components of each perspective, showing specific strategies within each one, as shown in Fig. 6.4.

Balanced Scorecard, particularly using a strategy map, allows practitioners to reconcile how changes will affect the entire plan.

Another important component of the Balanced Scorecard, and the reason why I choose to use it as the measurement model for budgeting, is its applicability to the SDLC. In particular, the learning and growth perspective shows how the Balanced Scorecard ensures that learning and strategy are linked in organizational development efforts and ultimately link back to costs vs. benefits.

Implementing Balanced Scorecards can be a critical part of the project, specifically in who does the work, what the roles are, and who has the responsibility for operating the scorecards. While many companies use consultants to guide them, it is important to recognize that Balanced Scorecards reflect the unique features and

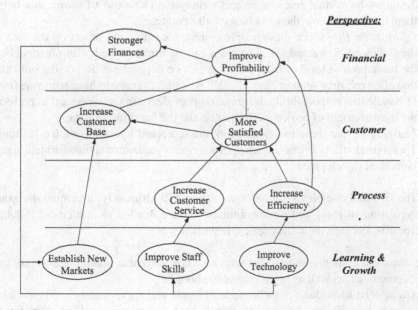

Fig. 6.4 Strategy map

functions of the company. As such, the rank and file need to be involved with the design and support of Balanced Scorecards.

Every business unit that has a scorecard needs to have someone assigned to it, someone accountable for it. A special task force may often be required to launch the training for staff and to agree on how the scorecard should be designed and supported. It is advisable that the scorecard be implemented using some application software and made available on an Internet network. This provides a number of benefits:

- Reduces paper and/or local files that might get lost or not be secured.
- Allows for easy "role-up" of multiple scorecards to a summary level.
- Access via the Internet (using an external secured hookup); allows the scorecard to be maintained from multiple locations. This is particularly attractive for staff members and management who travel.

According to Olve et al. (2003), there are five primary responsibilities that can support Balanced Scorecards:

1. *Business Stakeholders*: this is typically a senior manager who is responsible for the group that is using the scorecard. This individual is an advocate of using scorecards and requires compliance where deemed necessary. Stakeholders use scorecards to help them manage the life cycle of a technology implementation.
2. *Scorecard Designers*: these individuals are responsible for the look and feel of the scorecard, as well as its content. To some extent the designers set standards for "look and feel," text, and terminology. In certain situations the scorecard designers have dual roles as project managers. Their use of scorecards helps them understand how the technology will operate.
3. *Information Providers*: these people collect, measure, and report on the data in the Balanced Scorecard. This function can be implemented with personnel on the business unit level or from a central service department. Reporting information often requires support from IT staff, so it makes sense to have someone from IT handle this responsibility. Information providers use the scorecard to perform the measurement of project performance and the handling of data.
4. *Learning Pilots*: these individuals link the scorecard to organizational learning. This is particularly important when measuring organizational transformation and individual development.

The size and complexity of an organization will ultimately determine the exact configuration of roles and responsibilities that are needed to implement Balance Scorecards. Perhaps the most applicable variables are:

- *Competence*: having individuals who are knowledgeable about the business and its processes, as well as knowledgeable about IT.
- *Availability*: individuals must be made available and appropriately accommodated in the budget. Balanced Scorecards that do not have sufficient staffing will fail.

- *Executive Management Support*: as with most technology projects, there needs to be a project advocate at the executive level.
- *Enthusiasm*: implementing Balance Scorecards requires a certain energy and excitement level from the staff and their management. This is one of those intangible, yet invaluable variables.

The balanced scorecard can ultimately become the tools that allow the management team to (1) better determine how much the budget will be and associate that with expected business benefits and (2) a method to measure progress and fight off scope creep.

Problems and Exercises

1. What is the purpose of a budget? Be specific.
2. What is post-implementation?
3. Explain the difference between a regular expense and a capital expense.
4. What is the Balanced Scorecard? How can it assist in developing a budget?
5. How does a strategy map contribute to the understanding of everyone's role in a proposed new system?
6. What is scope creep? How does the Balanced Scorecard address the problem?
7. What is ROI? How does it relate to a controlled budget?

References

Kaplan, R. S., & Norton, D. P. (2001). *The strategy-focused organization*. Cambridge, MA: Harvard University Press.

Lucas, H. C. (1999). *Information technology and the productivity paradox*. New York: Oxford University Press.

Olve, N., Petri, C., Roy, J., & Roy, S. (2003). *Making scorecards actionable: Balancing strategy and control*. New York: Wiley.

Ryan, R., & Raducha-Grace, T. (2010). *The business of IT: How to improve service and lower cost*. Boston: IBM Press.

Analysis Methods and Tools

The Concept of the Logical Equivalent

The primary mission of an analyst or systems designer is to extract the physical requirements of the users and convert them to software. All software can trace its roots to a physical act or a physical requirement. A physical act can be defined as something that occurs in the interaction of people, that is, people create the root requirements of most systems, especially those in business. For example, when Mary tells us that she receives invoices from vendors and pays them 30 days later, she is explaining her physical activities during the process of receiving and paying invoices. When the analyst creates a technical specification, which represents Mary's physical requirements, the specification is designed to allow for the translation of her physical needs into an automated environment. We know that software must operate within the confines of a computer, and such systems must function on the basis of logic. The logical solution does not always treat the process using the same procedures employed in the physical world. In other words, the software system implemented to provide the functions, which Mary does physically, will probably work differently and more efficiently than Mary herself. Software, therefore, can be thought of as a logical equivalent of the physical world. This abstraction, which I call the concept of the logical equivalent, is a process that analysts must use to create effective requirements of the needs of a system. The LE can be compared to a schematic of a plan or a diagram of how a technical device works. At the heart of any SDLC, success is the ability to understand the user's needs.

The success ratio for creating a concise and accurate schematic of the system, whether for packaged software or developed in-house, will be directly proportional to how well you master the concept of the logical equivalent. Very often requirements are developed by analysts using various methods that do not always contain a basis for consistency, reconciliation, and maintenance. There is usually far too much prose used as opposed to specific diagramming standards that are employed by engineers. After all, we are engineering a system through the development of software applications. The most critical step in obtaining the LE is the

© Springer-Verlag London Limited 2016
A.M. Langer, *Guide to Software Development*,
DOI 10.1007/978-1-4471-6799-0_7

understanding of the process of functional decomposition. Functional decomposition is the process for finding the most basic parts of a system, like defining all the parts of a car so that it can be built. It would be possible not from looking at a picture of the car, but rather at a schematic of all the functionally decomposed parts. Developing and engineering software is not different.

Below is an example of an analogous process using functional decomposition with its application to the LE.

In obtaining the physical information from the user, there are a number of modeling tools that can be used. Each tool provides a specific function to derive the LE. The word "derive" has special meaning here. It relates to the process of long division, or the process or formula we apply when dividing one number by another. Consider the following example:

$$
\begin{array}{r}
256 \quad \text{remainder } 4 \quad \} \text{ Result or Answer} \\
5 \overline{\smash{\big)}\ 1284} \qquad\qquad\quad\ \} \text{ Problem to Solve} \\
\underline{10} \\
284 \\
\underline{25} \qquad\qquad\qquad\quad\ \} \text{ Formula applied to produce result or answer} \\
34 \\
\underline{30} \\
4
\end{array}
$$

The above example shows the formula that is applied to a division problem. We call this formula long division. It provides the answer, and if we change any portion of the problem, we simply reapply the formula and generate a new result. Most important, once we have obtained the answer, the value of the formula steps is only one of documentation. That is, if someone questioned the validity of the result, we could show them the formula to prove that the answer was correct (based on the input).

Now let us apply long division to obtaining the LE via functional decomposition. The following is a result of an interview with Joe, a bookkeeper, about his physical procedure for handling bounced checks.

> Joe the bookkeeper receives bounced checks from the bank. He fills out a Balance Correction Form and forwards it to the Correction Department so that the outstanding balance can be corrected. Joe sends a bounced check letter to the customer requesting a replacement check plus a $15.00 penalty (this is now included as part of the outstanding balance). Bounced checks are never re-deposited.

The appropriate modeling tool to use in this situation is a data flow diagram (DFD). A DFD is a tool that shows how data enters and leaves a particular process. The process we are looking at with Joe is the handling of the bounced check. A DFD has four possible components:

	Process	This denotes the name of the actual function being performed. A valid process is one in which data is transformed from one form to another
	Data flow	This represents data entering or leaving a process, external, or data store. The arrow denotes direction of the flow. A data flow is sometimes called "data in motion"
	Data store	Stored data usually kept in a file. It represents data that can be accessed from a specific area. A data store is sometimes called "data at rest"
	External	A provider or user of the data that is not part of the system. It therefore represents a boundary

Now let us draw the LE of Joe's procedure using DFD tools (Fig. 7.1).

The DFD in Fig. 7.1 shows that bounced checks arrive from the bank, the Account Master file is updated, the Correction Department is informed, and customers receive a letter. The bank, Correction Department, and customers are considered "outside" the system and are therefore represented logically as externals. This diagram is considered to be at the first level or "Level 1" of functional decomposition. You will find that all modeling tools employ a method to functionally decompose. DFDs use a method called "leveling."

The question is whether we have reached the most basic parts of this process or should we level further. Many analysts suggest that a fully decomposed DFD should have only one data flow input and one data flow output. Our diagram currently has many inputs and outputs and therefore it can be leveled further. The result of functionally decomposing to the second level (Level 2) is as follows (Fig. 7.2).

Notice that the functional decomposition shows us that Process 1: Handling Bounced Checks is really made up of two subprocesses called 1.1 Update Balance and 1.2 Send Letter. The box surrounding the two processes within the externals

Fig. 7.1 Data flow diagram for handling bounced checks

Fig. 7.2 Level 2 data flow diagram for handling bounced checks

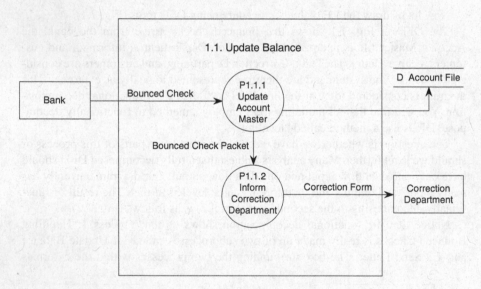

Fig. 7.3 Level 3 data flow diagram for handling bounced checks

reflects them as components of the previous or parent level. The double-sided arrow in Level 1 is now broken down to two separate arrows going in different directions because it is used to connect Processes 1.1 and 1.2. The new level is more functionally decomposed and a better representation of the LE.

Once again we must ask ourselves whether Level 2 can be further decomposed. The answer is yes. Process 1.1 has two outputs to one input. On the other hand, Process 1.2 has one input and one output and is therefore complete. 1.2 is said to be at the functional primitive, a DFD that cannot be decomposed further. Therefore, only 1.1 will be decomposed.

Let us decompose 1.1 as follows (Fig. 7.3).

Fig. 7.4 Functionally decomposed Level 3 data flow diagram for handling bounced checks

Process 1.1 is now broken down into two subprocesses: 1.1.1 Update Account Master and 1.1.2 Inform Correction Department. Process 1.1.2 is a functional primitive since it has one input and one output. Process 1.1.1 is also considered a functional primitive because the "Bounced Check Packet" flow is between the two processes and is used to show connectivity only. Functional decomposition is at Level 3 and is now complete.

The result of functional decomposition is the DFD shown in Fig. 7.4.

As in long division, only the complete result, represented in Fig. 7.4, is used as the answer. The preceding steps are formulas that we use to get to the lowest, simplest representation of the logical equivalent. Levels 1, 2, and 3 are used only for documentation of how the final DFD was determined.

The logical equivalent is an excellent method that allows analysts and systems designers to organize information obtained from users and to systematically derive the most fundamental representation of their process. It also alleviates unnecessary pressure to immediately understand the detailed flows and provides documentation of how the final schematic was developed.

Tools of Structured Analysis

Now that we have established the importance and goals of the logical equivalent, we can turn to a discussion of the methods available to assist the analyst. These methods serve as the tools to create the best models in any given situation and thus the most exact logical equivalent. The tools of the analyst are something like those of a surgeon, who uses only the most appropriate instruments during an operation. It is important to understand that the surgeon is sometimes faced with choices about which surgical instruments to use; particularly with new procedures, there is sometimes disagreement among surgeons about which instruments are the most effective. The choice of tools for analysis and data processing is no different; indeed, it can vary more and be more confusing. The medical profession, like many others, is

governed by its own ruling bodies. The American Medical Association and the American College of Physicians and Surgeons, as well as state and federal regulators, represent a source of standards for surgeons. Such a controlling body does not exist in the data processing industry, nor does it appear likely that one will arise in the near future. Thus, the industry has tried to standardize among its own leaders. The result of such efforts has usually been that the most dominant companies and organizations create standards to which others are forced to comply. For example, Microsoft has established itself as an industry leader by virtue of its software domination. Here, might is right!

Since there are no real formal standards in the industry, the analysis tools discussed here will be presented on the basis of both their advantages and their shortcomings. It is important then to recognize that no analysis tool (or methodology for that matter) can do the entire job, nor is any perfect at what it does. To determine the appropriate tool, analysts must fully understand the environment, the technical expertise of users, and the time constraints imposed on the project. By "environment" we mean the existing system and technology, computer operations, and the logistics—both technically and geographically—of the new system. The treatment of the user interface should remain consistent with the guidelines discussed in Chap. 2.

The problem of time constraints is perhaps the most critical of all. The tools you would ideally like to apply to a project may not fit the time frame allotted. What happens, then, if there is not enough time? The analyst is now faced with selecting a second-choice tool that undoubtedly will not be as effective as the first one would have been. There is also the question of how tools are implemented, that is, can a hybrid of a tool be used when time constraints prevent full implementation of the desired tool.

Making Changes and Modifications

Within the subject of analysis tools is the component of maintenance modeling, or how to apply modeling tools when making changes or enhancements to an existing product. Maintenance modeling falls into two categories:

1. Pre-modeled: where the existing system already has models that can be used to effect the new changes to the software.
2. Legacy system: where the existing system has never been modeled; any new modeling will therefore be incorporating analysis tools for the first time.

Pre-Modeled

Simply put, a pre-modeled product is already in a structured format. A structured format is one that employs a specific format and methodology such as the data flow diagram.

The most challenging aspects of changing pre-modeled tools are:

1. Keeping them consistent with their prior versions
2. Implementing a version control system that provides an audit trail of the analysis changes and how they differ from the previous versions. Many professionals in the industry call this version control; however, care should be taken in specifying whether the version control is used for the maintenance of analysis tools. Unfortunately, version control can be used in other contexts, most notably in the tracking of program versions and software documentation. For these cases, special products exist in the market which provides special automated "version control" features. We are not concerned here with these products but rather with the procedures and processes that allow us to incorporate changes without losing the prior analysis documentation. This kind of procedure can be considered consistent with the long division example in which each time the values change, we simply reapply the formula (methodology) to calculate the new answer. Analysis version control must therefore have the ability to take the modifications made to the software and integrate them with all the existing models as necessary.

Being Consistent

It is difficult to change modeling methods and/or CASE tools in the middle of the life cycle of a software product. One of our main objectives then is to try to avoid doing so. How? Of course, the simple answer is to select the right tools and CASE software for the first time. However, we all make mistakes and, more importantly, there are new developments in systems architecture that may make a new CASE product attractive. You would be wise to foresee this possibility and prepare for inconsistent tool implementation. The best offense here is to:

- Ensure that your CASE product has the ability to transport models through a ASCII file or cut/paste method. Many have interfaces via an "export" function. Here, at least, the analyst can possibly convert the diagrams and data elements to another product.
- Keep a set of diagrams and elements that can be used to establish a link going forward, that is, a set of manual information that can be re-input to another tool. This may be accomplished by simply having printed documentation of the diagrams; however, experience has shown that it is difficult to keep such information up to date. Therefore, the analyst should ensure that there is a procedure for printing the most current diagrams and data elements.

Should the organization decide to use different tools, e.g., process-dependency diagrams, instead of data flow diagrams, or a different methodology such as Crow's foot method in entity relationship diagramming, then the analyst must implement a certain amount of reengineering. This means mapping the new modeling tools to the existing ones to ensure consistency and accuracy. This is no easy task, and it is strongly suggested that you document the diagrams so you can reconcile them.

Version Control

This book is not intended to focus on the generic aspects of version control; however, structured methods must have audit trail. When a new process is changed, a directory should be created for the previous version. The directory name typically consists of the version and date such as xyz1.21295, where xyz is the name of the product or program, 1.2 the version, and 1295 the version date. In this way previous versions can be easily recreated or viewed. Of course, saving a complete set of each version may not be feasible or may be too expensive (in terms of disk space, backup systems, etc.). In these situations, it is advisable to back up the previous version in such a manner as to allow for easy restoration. In any case, a process must exist, and it is crucial that there be a procedure to do backups periodically.

Legacy Systems

Legacy systems usually reside on mainframe computers and were developed using 3GL[1] software applications, the most typical being COBOL. Unfortunately, few of these systems were developed using structured tools. Without question, these are the most common systems undergoing change today in many organizations. All software is comprised of two fundamental components: processes and data. Processes are the actual logic and algorithms required by the system. Data, on the other hand, represent the information that is stored and used by the processes. The question for the analyst is how to obtain the equivalent processes and data from the legacy system. Short of considering a complete rewrite, there are two basic approaches:

The Data Approach

Conversion of legacy systems for purposes of structured changes requires the modeling of the existing programs to allow for the use of analysis tools. The first step in this endeavor is the modeling of the existing files and their related data structures. Many 3GL applications may not exist in a relational or other database format. In either case, it is necessary to collect all of the data elements that exist in the system. To accomplish this, the analyst will typically need a conversion program that will collect the elements and import them into a CASE tool. If the data is stored in a relational or database system, this can be handled through many CASE products via a process known as reverse engineering. Here, the CASE product will allow the analyst to select the incoming database, and the product will then automatically import the data elements. It is important to note that these reverse-engineering features require that the incoming database is SQL (Structured Query Language)

[1] 3GL refers to third-generation language. These programming languages belong to a family of design that typically uses compilers to transform a higher-level language into assembly code for the target computer.

Fig. 7.5 Reverse engineering using a CASE product

compatible. Should the incoming data file be of a non-database format, i.e., a flat file,[2] then a conversion program will need to be used. Once again, most CASE tools will have features that will list the required input data format.

Figure 7.5 is a sample of the reengineering capabilities of a CASE tool:

Once the data has been loaded into the CASE product, the various data models can be constructed. This process will be discussed further in Chap. 8.

Although we have shown in Fig. 7.5 a tool for loading the data, the question still remains: how do we find all the data elements? Using COBOL as an example, one could take the following steps:

1. Identify all of the File Description (FD) tables in the COBOL application programs. Should they exist in an external software product like the librarian, the analyst can import the tables from that source. Otherwise the actual file tables will need to be extracted and converted from the COBOL application program source. This procedure is not difficult; it is simply another step that typically requires conversion utilities.

[2]A file consisting of records of a single record type, in which there is no embedded structure information governing relationships between records. Microsoft Press, Computer Dictionary, Second Edition, pg 169.

Fig. 7.6 Working storage
section of a COBOL
program

```
WORKING-STORAGE SECTION.
01 PAYROLL-RECORD.
     05     NAME.
            10     INITIAL-1                    PIC X.
            10     LAST-NAME                    PIC X(20).
     05     DATE-OF-HIRE.
            10     MONTH-OF-HIRE                PIC 99.
            10     DAY-OF-HIRE                  PIC 99.
            10     YEAR-OF-HIRE                 PIC 99.
     05     PAY-NUMBER                          PIC 9(6).
```

2. Scan all Working Storage sections (see Fig. 7.6) for data elements that are not defined in the File Description section. This occurs very often when COBOL programmers do not define the actual elements until they are read into a Working Storage section of the program. This situation, of course, requires further research, but it can be detected by scanning the code.
3. Look for other data elements that have been defined in Working Storage that should be stored as permanent data. Although this can be a difficult task, the worst case scenario would involve the storing of redundant data.
4. Once the candidate elements have been discovered, ensure that appropriate descriptions are added. This process allows the analyst to actually start defining elements so that decisions can be made during logical data modeling.

The Process Approach

The most effective way to model existing programs is the most direct way, that is, the old-fashioned way: start reading and analyzing the code. Although this approach may seem very crude, it is actually tremendously effective and productive. Almost all programming languages contain enough structure to allow for identification of input and output of files and reports. By identifying the data and reports, the analyst can establish a good data flow diagram as shown in Fig. 7.7.

The example in Fig. 7.7 shows two File Description (FD) tables that are defined in a COBOL program. The first table defines the input file layout of a payroll record and the second is the layout of the output payroll report. This is translated into a DFD as shown in Fig. 7.8.

In addition, depending on the program language, many input and output data and reports must be defined in the application code in specific sections of the program. Such is true in COBOL and many other 3GL products. Furthermore, many 4GL products force input and output verbs to be used when manipulating databases. This is very relevant to any products that use Embedded SQL to do Input/Output. The main point here is that you can produce various utility programs ("quick & dirty," as they call them) to enhance the accuracy and speed of identifying an existing program's input and output processing.

Once the flows in the data flow diagram are complete, the next step is to define the actual program logic, or what is typically called the process specifications

```
DATA DIVISION.
FILE SECTION.
FD      PAYROLL-FILE
        LABEL RECORDS ARE OMITTED.
01      PAYROLL-RECORD.
        05      I-PAYROLL-NUMBER              PIC X(5).
        05      I-NAME                        PIC X(20).
        05      I-HOURS-WORKED                PIC 99V9.
        05      FILLER                        PIC XXX.
        05      I-PAYRATE                     PIC 99V999.
        05      I-DEPENDENTS                  PIC 99.
        05      FILLER                        PIC X(20).

FD      REPORT-FILE
        LABEL RECORDS ARE OMITTED.
01      REPORT-RECORD.
        05      O-PAYROLL-NUMBER              PIC X(5).
        05      FILLER                        PIC XX.
        05      O-NAME                        PIC X(20).
        05      FILLER                        PIC XX.
        05      O-HOURS-WORKED                PIC 99.9.
        05      FILLER                        PIC XX.
        05      O-PAYRATE                     PIC 99.999.
        05      FILLER                        PIC XX.
        05      O-DEPENDENTS                  PIC 99.
        05      FILLER                        PIC XX.
        05      O-GROSS-PAY                   PIC 999.99.
        05      FILLER                        PIC XX.
        05      O-TAX                         PIC 999.99.
        05      FILLER                        PIC XX.
        05      O-NET-PAY                     PIC 999.99.
```

Fig. 7.7 Input data and report layouts of a COBOL program

Fig. 7.8 Translated
COBOL File Descriptions
into a data flow diagram

(discussed later in this chapter). Once again there is no shortcut to save you from going through the code program by program. There are some third-party software tools on the market that can provide assistance, but these tend to be very programming-language specific. Although the manual method may seem overwhelming, it can be accomplished successfully and will often provide great long-term benefits. Many companies will bring in part-time college interns and other clerical assistance to get this done. It should be noted that a CASE tool is almost

always required to provide a place to document logic. This is especially important if the CASE tool will be used to generate actual program code. Further specifics regarding analyzing legacy systems are discussed in Chap. 9.

Specification Formats

An ongoing challenge for many IS and software firms is the question: What is a good specification? Many books written about analysis tools tend to avoid answering this question directly. When addressing the quality of a process specification, we must ultimately accept the inevitable prognosis that we can no longer be exclusively graphical. Although Yourdon and DeMarco[3] argued that structured tools needed to be graphical, the essence of a specification is in its ability to define the algorithms of the application program itself. It is therefore impossible to avoid writing a form of pseudocode. Pseudocode is essentially a generic representation of how the real code must execute. Ultimately, the analyst must be capable of developing clear and technically correct algorithms. The methods and styles of process specifications are outlined on the following pages. The level of technical complexity of these specifications varies based on a number of issues:

1. The technical competence of the analyst. Ultimately, the analyst must have the ability to write algorithms to be most effective.
2. The complexity of the specification itself. The size and scope of specifications will vary and as a result so will the organization of the requirements.
3. The type of the specifications required. There are really two levels of specifications: business and programming. The business specification is very prose oriented and is targeted for review by a nontechnical user. Its main purpose is to gain confirmation from the user community prior to investing in the more specific and technical programming specification. The programming specification, on the other hand, needs to contain the technical definition of the algorithms and is targeted for technical designers and programmers.
4. The competence of the programming staff as well as the confidence that the analyst has in that staff. The size and capabilities of the programming resources will usually be directly proportional to the emphasis that the analyst will need to · place on the specifics and quality needed for a process specification.

Although the alternative techniques for developing a process specification are further discussed in Chap. 3, Fig. 7.9 should put into perspective the approach to deciding the best format and style of communication. It is important to understand that overlooking the process specification and its significance to the success of the project can have catastrophic effects on the entire development effort. Figure 7.9 thus reflects the type of specification suggested based on the technical skills of the users.

[3] Yourdon, Ed (1989), Modern Structured Analysis and DeMarco, Tom (1979), Structured Analysis and System Specification focused on the importance of using graphic diagrams wherever possible.

High-Level Non-Technical Users	Technically Literate Users	Very Technical Users or MIS Personnel
Business Specification in Prose	Business Specification in Prose	No need for separate Business Specification
Do not show Programming Specification	Show and review Programming Specification	Incorporate Business Spec with Programming Specification

Fig. 7.9 Types of process specifications based on user computer literacy

Client: XYZ Corporation	Date: 9/5/11
Application: Operations Database	Supersedes:
Subject: Contact Management	Author: A. Langer
Process: Overview - Business Spec	Page: 1 of 2

Overview

The Contact Management Process will allow users to add, modify or delete specific contacts. Contacts will be linked to various tables including Company. A Contact refers to a person who is related to XYZ for business reasons. It can be a Client, a Vendor, a consultant, a person involved in a negotiation, etc.

Contact General Information:

The Database must allow for the centralization of all the contacts handled by all the departments in XYZ.
The database and screens will be focused on the following information component groupings:

Basic Information
This is the minimum data requirement and includes such elements as Name, Title, Organization, Phone, Fax, Address, Country, etc.

Contact Profile Information
Further qualification and related elements. Relations include:

- department
- type of client
- nature of client (primary, technical)
- interest of prospect
- importance of client
- memberships (FTUG)
- FT employee

This is a Business Specification which reflects the overall requirements in prose format. Its focus is to provide the user who is not technical with a document that they can authorize. This Business Specification should then point to the detailed programming logic that is shown below.

Fig. 7.10 Sample business specification

Client: XYZ Company	Date: 9/15/11
Application: Contact Management	Supersedes: 9/5/11
Subject: Program Specification Detail	Author: A. Langer
Spec-ID FTCM01 - Add/Modify Screen Processing	Page: 1 of 1

Process Flow Description:
The user will input information in the top form. At a minimum, at least the Last Name or Contact ID will be entered. The system must check a Security indicator prior to allowing a user to modify a Contact. The Security will be by Department or Everyone. Therefore, if the Modify button is selected and the user is restricted by a different department, Display:
 " Access Denied, not eligible to modify, Department Restriction"

If Security authorized, the Add/Modify Button will activate the following business rules:

 If Contact-ID (cntid) not blank *This area actually states*
 Find match and replace entered data into record *the algorithm required by*
 If no match display "Invalid Contact-ID" and refresh cursor *the program. It is in a*
 format called Pseudocode"
 If Contact-ID (cntid) Blank and Last-Name (cntlname) Blank then *meaning "false code."*
 Display " Contact-ID or Last-Name must be entered" *This type of logic resembles*
 Place Cursor at Contact-ID (cntid) entry. *Cobol format.*

 If Contact-ID (cntid) Blank and Last-Name (cntlname) + First-Name (cntfname) is Duplicate
 Display Window to show matches so that user can determine if contact already in
 system
 If user selects the Add Anyway button
 assume new contact with same name and assign new Contact-ID (cntid)
 else
 upon selection bring in existing data and close window.
 Else
 Create new record with all new information fields and assign Contact-ID (cntid)

 If Company button activated
 Prompt user for Company-ID (cmpcd) and/or Company-Name (cmpna)
 If duplicate
 link foreign-key pointer to matched company
 else
 add Company-Name (cntcmpna) to Contact Table only
 Display "You must use Company Screen to Link, Company Master File Not
 Updated"

Fig. 7.11 Sample programming specification

Figures 7.10 and 7.11 are sample business and programming specifications, respectively, that depict the flow from a user specification to the detailed program logic.

Problems and Exercises

1. Describe the concept of the logical equivalent as it relates to defining the requirements of a system.
2. What is the purpose of functional decomposition? How is the leveling of a DFD consistent with this concept?

3. How does long division depict the procedures of decomposition? Explain.
4. What is a legacy system?
5. Processes and data represent the two components of any software application. Explain the alternative approaches to obtaining process and data information from a legacy system.
6. What is reverse engineering? How can it be used to build a new system?
7. Why is analysis version control important?
8. Explain the procedures for developing a DFD from an existing program.
9. What is the purpose of a process specification? Explain.
10. Outline the differences between a business specification and a programming specification. What is their relationship, if any?

Part II

Development Architecture

Creating Requirements Documents Using Analysis Tools

<div style="text-align:right">8</div>

Chapter 7 discussed the concept of the logical equivalent, justifying and defining it by showing a functional decomposition example using data flow diagrams. In this section, we will expand upon the capabilities of the DFD by explaining its purpose, advantages, and disadvantages (described later as the Good, the Bad, and the Ugly) and most importantly, how to draw and use it.

Purpose

Yourdon's original concept of the DFD was that it was a way to represent a process graphically. A process can be defined as a vehicle that changes or transforms data. The DFD therefore becomes a method of showing users strictly from a logical perspective how data travels through their function and is transformed. The DFD should be used in lieu of a descriptive prose representation of a user's process. Indeed, many analysts are familiar with the frustrations of the meeting where users attend to provide feedback on a specification prepared in prose. These specifications are often long descriptions of the processes. We ask users to review it, but most will not have had the chance to do so before the meeting, and those who have may not recollect all the issues. The result? Users and analysts are not in a position to properly address the needs of the system, and the meeting is less productive than planned. This typically leads to more meetings and delays. More important, the analyst has never provided an environment in which the user can be walked through the processes. Conventional wisdom says that people remember 100% of what they see, but only 50% of what they read. The graphical representation of the DFD can provide users with an easily understood view of the system.[1]

The DFD also establishes the boundary of a process. This is accomplished with two symbols: the terminator (external) and the data store. As we will see, both represent data that originate or end at a particular point.

[1]Yourdon, Ed (1989), Modern Structured Analysis, pp. 134–35.

© Springer-Verlag London Limited 2016
A.M. Langer, *Guide to Software Development*,
DOI 10.1007/978-1-4471-6799-0_8

Designing the House

Drawing Architect Blueprint

Fig. 8.1 The interfaces required to design and build a house

The DFD also serves as the first step toward the design of the system blueprint. What do we mean by a blueprint? Let us consider the steps taken to build a house. When we want to build a house, the first step is to contact a professional who knows how to do design. We call this individual an architect. The architect is responsible for listening to the homebuilder and drawing a conceptual view of the house that the homebuilder wants. The result is typically two drawings. The first is a prototype drawing of the house, representing how the house will appear to the homebuilder. The second is the blueprint which represents the engineering requirements. Although the homebuilder may look at the blueprint, it is meant primarily for the builder or contractor who will actually construct the house. What has the architect accomplished? The homebuyer has a view of the house to verify the design, and the builder has the specifications for construction.

Let us now translate this process to that of designing software. In this scenario, the analyst is the architect and the user is the homebuyer. The meeting between the architect and the homebuyer translates into the requirements session which will render two types of output: a business requirements outline and prototype of the way the system will function and a schematic represented by modeling tools for programmers. The former represents the picture of the house and the latter the blueprint for the builder. Designing and building systems, then, is no different conceptually from building a house. The DFD is one of the first—if not the first—tools that the analyst will use for drawing graphical representations of the user's requirements. It is typically used very early in the design process when the user requirements are not clearly and logically defined.

Figures 8.1 and 8.2 show the similarities between the functions of an architect and those of an analyst.

How do we begin to construct the DFD for a given process? The following five steps serve as a guideline:

1. Draw a bubble to represent the process you are about to define.

Designing the System

Prototype Analyst DFD

Fig. 8.2 The interfaces required to design and build a system

2. Ask yourself what thing(s) initiate the process: what is coming in? You will find it advantageous to be consistent in where you show process inputs. Try to model them to the left of the process. You will later be able to immediately define your process inputs when looking back at your DFD, especially when using them for system enhancements.

3. Determine the process outputs, or what things are coming out, and model them to the right of the process as best as you can.

4. Establish all files, forms, or other components that the process needs to complete its transformation. These are usually data stores that are utilized during processing. Model these items above or below the process.

5. Name and number the process by its result. For example, if a process produces invoices, label it "Create Invoices." If the process accomplishes more than one event, label it by using the "and" conjunction. This method will allow you to determine whether the process is a functional primitive. Ultimately, the name of the process should be one that most closely associates the DFD with what the user does. Therefore, name it what the user calls it! The number of the process simply allows the analyst to identify it to the system and most importantly to establish the link to its children levels during functional decomposition.

Let us now apply this procedure to the example below:

Vendors send Mary invoices for payment. Mary stamps on the invoice the date received and matches the invoice with the original purchase order request. Invoices are placed in the Accounts Payable folder. Invoices that exceed thirty days are paid by check in two-week intervals.

Step 1: Draw the bubble (Fig. 8.3).

Step 2: Determine the inputs. In this example we are receiving an invoice from a vendor. The vendor is considered a terminator since it is a boundary of the input and the user cannot control when and how the invoice will arrive. The invoice itself is represented as a data flow coming from the vendor terminator into the process (Fig. 8.4).

Fig. 8.3 A process bubble

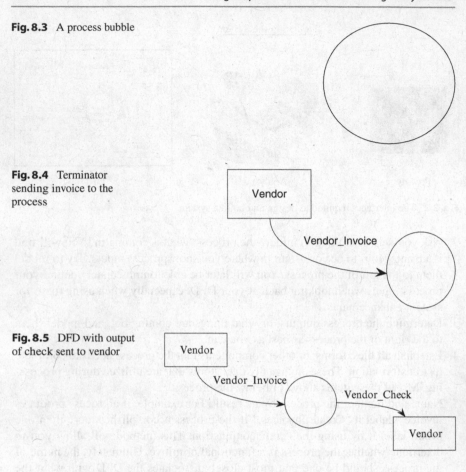

Fig. 8.4 Terminator
sending invoice to the
process

Fig. 8.5 DFD with output
of check sent to vendor

Step 3: Determine the outputs of the process. In this case the result of the process is
that the vendor receives a check for payment (Fig. 8.5).

Step 4: Determine the "processing" items required to complete the process. In this
example, the user needs to.

 • Match the invoice to the original Purchase Order.
 • Create a new account payable for the invoice in a file.
 • Eventually retrieve the invoice from the account payable file for payment.

Note that the Purchase Order file is accessed for input (or retrieval) and therefore is
modeled with the arrow coming into the process. The Accounts Payable file, on the
other hand, shows a two-sided arrow because entries are created (inserted) and
retrieved (read). In addition, arrows to and from data stores may or may not contain
data flow names. For reasons that will be explained later in the chapter, the inclusion
of such names is not recommended (Fig. 8.6).

Step 5: Name and number the process based on its output or its user definition
(Fig. 8.7).

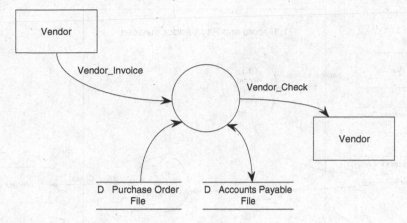

Fig. 8.6 DFD with interfacing data stores

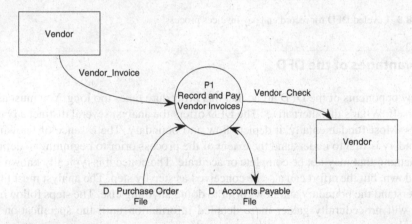

Fig. 8.7 Final named DFD

The process shown in Fig. 8.7 is now a complete DFD that describes the event of the user. You may notice that the procedures for stamping the invoice with the receipt date and the specifics of retrieving Purchase Orders and Accounts Payable information are not explained. These other components will be defined using other modeling tools. Once again, the DFD reflects only data flow and boundary information of a process.

The DFD shown in Fig. 8.7 can be leveled further to its functional primitive. The conjunction in the name of the process can sometimes help analysts to discover that there is actually more than one process within the event they are modeling. Based on the procedure outlined in Chap. 7, the event really consists of two processes: recording vendor invoices and paying vendor invoices. Therefore, P1 can be leveled as in Fig. 8.8.

Fig. 8.8 Leveled DFD for record and pay invoices process

Advantages of the DFD

Many opponents of the DFD argue that this procedure takes too long. You must ask yourself: What's the alternative? The DFD offers the analyst several distinct advantages. Most fundamentally, it depicts flow and boundary. The essence of knowing boundary is first to understand the extent of the process prior to beginning to define something that may not be complete or accurate. The concept is typically known as top down, but the effort can also be conceived as step by step. The analyst must first understand the boundary and flows prior to doing anything else. The steps following this will procedurally gather more detailed information until the specification is complete.

Another important aspect of the DFD is that it represents a graphical display of the process and is therefore a usable document that can be shown to both users and programmers, serving the former as a process verification and the latter as the schematic (blueprint) of the system from a technical perspective. It can be used in JAD sessions and as part of the business specification documentation. Most importantly, it can be used for maintaining and enhancing a process.

Disadvantages of the DFD

The biggest drawback of the DFD is that it simply takes a long time to create: so long that the analyst may not receive support from management to complete it. This can be especially true when there is a lot of leveling to be performed. Therefore, many firms shy away from the DFD on the basis that it is not practical. The other disadvantage of the DFD is that it does not model time-dependent behavior well,

that is, the DFD is based on very finite processes that typically have a very definable start and finish. This, of course, is not true of all processes, especially those that are event driven. Event-driven systems will be treated more thoroughly when we discuss state transition diagrams later in this chapter.

The best solution to the time-consuming leveling dilemma is to avoid it as much as possible. That is, you should avoid starting at too high a summary level and try to get to the functional primitive as soon as you can. If in our example, for instance, the analyst had initially seen that the DFD had two processes instead of one, then the parent process could have been eliminated altogether. This would have resulted in an initial functional primitive DFD at Level 1. The only way to achieve this efficiency on a consistent basis is through practice. Practice will eventually result in the development of your own analysis style or approach. The one-in, one-out principle of the logical equivalent is an excellent way of setting up each process. Using this method, every event description that satisfies one-in, one-out will become a separate functional primitive process. Using this procedure virtually eliminates leveling. Sometimes users will request to see a summary-level DFD. In these cases the functional primitives can be easily combined or "leveled up."

Process Flow Diagrams

While the data flow diagram provides the analyst with the LE of a process, it does not provide for the sequentiality of the processes themselves. The sequential steps of a process and the dependencies can provide an important facility to analyzing the completeness of a system. This can be particularly relevant when the information gathered from users is suspect or may be inaccurate. A process flow diagram (PFD) can illuminate new processes and steps that could have been missed because it requires users to go through each phase of their system as it occurs or in the actual sequence. Having users go through their process as it actually occurs can allow them to remember things that they might otherwise miss or forget. Therefore, using process flows provides another tool that can test the completeness of the interview and LE.

Many methodologies, such as the James Martin technique, suggest that analysts should use PFDs instead of DFDs; however, it is my opinion that both models can coexist and actually complement each other. This section will focus on how a process model is implemented and balanced against a DFD.

Components of a PFD

Historically, PFDs were called flowcharts. Flowcharts, while still valuable for certain diagramming tasks, are too clumsy and detailed to be an effective and structured modeling tool. The PFD suggested here is similar to a DFD, in that it contains processes, externals, and data flows. However, PFDs focus more on how externals, flows, and processes occur in relation to sequence and time. DFDs, on the other

Fig. 8.9 Sample process
flow diagram

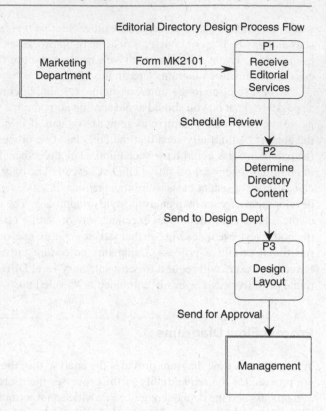

hand, are only focused on the net inputs and outputs of flows and the disposition of data at rest. Figure 8.9 is an example of a process flow.

Figure 8.9 shows how a PFD flows from one task to another. As with a DFD, externals are depicted by a rectangle. Flows are labeled and represent information in transition. Unlike DFDs, process flows do not necessarily require labeling of the flow arrows, and the processes themselves reflect descriptively what the step in the system is attempting to accomplish, as opposed to necessarily defining an algorithm.

DFD-PFD Compared

Perhaps the most significant difference between a DFD and a process flow is in its integration as a structured tool within the data repository. For example, a labeled data flow from a DFD must create an entry into the data dictionary or repository. Flow arrows from process flows do not. Furthermore, a functional primitive data flow points to a process specification; no such requirement exists in a process flow. Figure 8.10 represents a comparison of the Editorial Design Process Flow in DFD format.

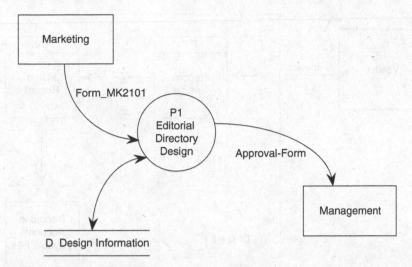

Fig. 8.10 PFD in DFD format

The DFD similarity relates to the same boundaries of externals (i.e., marketing and management). The DFD flows, while similar, must be defined in the data diction-ary or repository and therefore contain integrated formulas. The other notable differ-ence is the interface of the data store "Design Information" which will eventually be defined as an entity and decomposed using logical data modeling techniques.

The question must be asked: what are the benefit of using a PFD and DFD? The answer lies in the correspondence between a process rectangle and a DFD process bubble. Process rectangles actually represent sequential steps within the DFD. It could be related to an IF statement in pseudocode or just a statement to produce a report or write information to a file. The PFD, in a sense, can provide a visual depic-tion of how the process specification needs to be detailed. One functional primitive DFD can thus be related to many process rectangles.

Based on the above analysis, therefore, a PFD can be justified as a tool in support of validating process specifications from within a DFD. In addition, the PFD might discover a missing link in logic that could result in the creation of a new DFD. Based on this argument, the process flow can be balanced against a DFD and its functional primitives. Finally, it represents the potential for providing a graphic display of certain levels of logic code. The balancing of the PFD to the DFD shown in Fig. 8.8 is shown in Fig. 8.11.

This example provides a view of how a DFD may contain multiple process flows. However, DFD 1.2 has a one-to-one relationship with P4 of the PFD. While P4 might be considered the same as DFD 1.2, its purpose is to describe, at a basic level, the specific order of events that take place within the event itself. There can be an argument made that every PFD component should represent a functional primitive DFD. This simply is not the case and the analyst must remember that the PFD often reflects just a graphic view of the steps (or specification) *within* a DFD functional primitive. In this way the PFD serves to validate the completeness of the

Fig. 8.11 PFD and DFD cross-referenced

DFD. Analysts should also relate each process in the PFD to a specific portion of logic in the process specification component of the structured specification.

Sequence of Implementation

The question of whether the DFD should be created before or after a PFD must be discussed. In many ways, it can be left to the preference of the analyst. However, it is my preference to do the DFD first. My reason for following this sequence lies in the efficiency of creating the DFD, as well as the ability to compare the DFD

children against the sequential flow of the PFD. Creating the DFD first also supports the concept of decomposition, since the PFD will inevitably relate to the process specification of a functional primitive DFD. While this approach seems to be easier, there is certainly justification to do the PFD first, especially if an overview flow diagram provides a means of scoping the boundaries of an engineering process.

Data Dictionary

The data dictionary (DD) is quite simply a dictionary that defines data. We have seen that the data flow diagram represents a picture of how information flows to and from a process. As we pick up data elements during the modeling design, we effectively "throw" them into the data dictionary. Remember, all systems are comprised of two components: data and processes. The DD represents the data portion.

There is a generic format followed by analysts, called DD notation. The conventional notations are listed below:

=	Equivalence
+	Concatenation
[]	Either/or boundary
/ .	Either/or separator
()	Optional
{ }	Iterations of
**	Comment

Equivalence (=)

The notion of equivalence does not express mathematical equality but rather indicates that the values on the right side of the equal sign represent all the possible components of the element on the left.

Concatenation (+)

This should not be confused with or compared to "plus"; it is rather the joining of two or more components. For example, Last_Name + First_Name means that these two data elements are being pieced together sequentially.

Either/Or with Option Separator ([/])

It means "one of the following" and therefore represents a finite list of possible values. An example would include the definition of Country = [USA/Canada/United Kingdom/etc.].

Optional ()

The value is not required in the definition. A very common example is middle initial: Name = Last_Name + First_Name + (Middle_Init).

Iterations of { }

The value between the separators occurs in a specific or infinite number of times. Examples include:

1{X}5 The element "X" occurs from one to five times
1{X} The element "X" occurs from one to infinity
3{X}3 The element "X" must occur three times

Comments (**)

They are used to describe the element or point the definition to the appropriate process specification should the data element not be definable in the DD. We will explain this case later in this section.

Now that we have defined the components of the DD, it is important to expand on its interface with other modeling tools, especially the DFD. If we recall the example used earlier to describe drawing a DFD, the input data flow was labeled "Vendor_Invoice" (see Fig. 8.4). The first DD rule to establish is that all labeled data flow names must be defined in the DD. Therefore, the DFD interfaces with the DD by establishing data element definitions from its labeled flows. To define Vendor_Invoice, we look at the physical invoices and ascertain from the user the required information needed by the system. It might typically be defined as follows:

Vendor _ Invoice = Invoice _ Number + Vendor _ Invoice _ Date +
Vendor _ Invoice _ Name + Vendor _ Invoice _ Address _ Line _ 1 +
Vendor _ Invoice _ Address _ Line _ 2 +
Vendor _ Invoice _ Address _ Line _ 3 + Vendor _ State + Vendor _ City +
Vendor _ Zip _ Code + Vendor _ Salesperson + PO _ Number +
Vendor _ Date _ Shipped + Vendor _ Shipped _ Via +
Vendor _ Required _ Date + Vendor _ Terms + 1{Item Quantity +
Item _ Description + Item _ Unit _ Price + Item _ Amount} + Subtotal
Sales _ Tax + Shipping / Handling + Invoice _ Total _ Due

The above example illustrates what a vendor invoice would usually contain and what is needed to be captured by the system. Note that Vendor_Invoice is made up of component data elements which in turn need to be defined in the DD. In addition, there is a repeating group of elements { Item – Quantity + Item_Description + Item_ Unit_Price + Item_Amount } which represents each line item that is a component of the total invoice. Since there is no limit to the number of items that could make up one invoice, the upper limit of the iterations clause is left blank and therefore

represents infinity. A sample of how the physical invoice would appear is shown in Fig. 8.12.

It should be noted that many of the DD names have a qualifier of "Vendor" before the field name. This is done to ensure uniqueness in the DD as well as to document where the data element emanated from the DFD. To ensure that all data elements have been captured into the DD, we again apply functional decomposition, only this time we are searching for the functional primitive of the DD entry. We will call this functionally decomposed data element an Elementary Data Element. An Elementary Data Element is therefore an element that cannot be broken down any further. Let us functionally decompose Vendor_Invoice by looking to the right of the definition and picking up the data elements that have not already been defined in the DD. These elements are:

Vendor_Invoice_Number	=	1 { Numeric} 5
Vendor_Invoice_Date	=	8 { Numeric }8
Vendor_Invoice_Name	=	1 { Alphanumeric } 35
Vendor_Invoice_Address_Line_1	=	1 { Alphanumeric } 25
Vendor_Invoice_Address_Line_1	=	1 { Alphanumeric } 25
Vendor_Invoice_Address_Line_1	=	1 { Alphanumeric } 25
Vendor_State	=	** All States in USA, Self-Defining
Vendor_City	=	1 { Alphanumeric } 30
Vendor_Zip	=	5 { Numeric } 5+(4 {Numeric} 4)
Vendor_Salesperson	=	1 { Alphanumeric } 20
PO_Number	=	4 { Alphanumeric } 4
Vendor_Date_Shipped	=	8 { Numeric } 8
Vendor_Shipped_Via	=	1 { Alphanumeric } 10
Vendor_Required_Date	=	8 { Numeric } 8
Vendor_Terms	=	1 { Numeric } 3
Item_Quantity	=	1 { Numeric } 5
Item_Description	=	1 { Alphanumeric } 30
Item_Unit_Price	=	** Dollars Self-Defining
Item_Amount	=	** See Process Spec xxx
Subtotal	=	** See Process Spec yyy
Sales_Tax	=	1 {Numeric }3 ** Assumed Percentage
Shipping/Handling	=	** Dollars Self-Defining
Invoice_Total_Due	=	** See Process Spec zzz

Precision Products
1456 Emerson St
Parsippany, NJ 07055-1254

INVOICE

INVOICE NO:
DATE: August 15, 2011

To: :

SALESPERSON	P.O. NUMBER	DATE SHIPPED	SHIPPED VIA	REQUIRED DATE	TERMS
				10/5/95	

QUANTITY	DESCRIPTION	UNIT PRICE	AMOUNT
			$0.00
			$0.00
			$0.00
			$0.00
			$0.00
			$0.00
			$0.00

SUBTOTAL	$0.00
SALES TAX	
SHIPPING & HANDLING	
TOTAL DUE	$0.00

Fig. 8.12 Sample invoice form

The following rules and notations apply:

1. A Self-Defining definition is allowed if the data definition is obvious to the firm or if it is defined in some general documentation (e.g., Standards & Reference Manual). In the case of Vendor_State, an alternative would be

$$Vendor_State = [AL / NY / NJ / CA.......etc.] \text{ for each state value.}$$

2. Data elements that are derived as a result of a calculation cannot be defined in the DD, but rather point to a process specification where it can be properly identified. This also provides consistency in that all calculations and algorithms can be found in the process specification section.

3. Typically values such as numeric, alphanumeric, and alphabetic do not require further breakdown unless the firm allows for special characters. In that case, having the exact values defined is appropriate.
4. An iteration definition, where the minimum and maximum limit are the same (e.g., 8 {Numeric} 8), means that the data element is fixed (i.e., must be 8 in length).

The significance of this example is that the DD itself, through a form of functional decomposition, creates new entries into the DD while finding the Elementary Data Element. A good rule to follow is that any data element used in defining another data element must also be defined in the DD. The DD serves as the center for storing these entries and will eventually provide the data necessary to produce the stored data model.

Process Specifications

Many analysts define a process specification as everything else about the process not already included in the other modeling tools. Indeed, it must contain the remaining information that normally consists of business rules and application logic. DeMarco suggested that every functional primitive DFD points to a "Minispec" which would contain that process' application logic.[2] We will follow this rule and expand on the importance of writing good application logic. There are, of course, different styles and few textbooks that explain the importance to the analyst of understanding how these need to be developed and presented. Like other modeling tools, each process specification style has its good, bad, and ugly.

Pseudocode

The most detailed and regimented process specification is pseudocode or "Structured English." Its format is designed to require the analysts to have a solid understanding of how to write algorithms. The format is very "COBOL-like" and was initially designed as a way of writing functional COBOL programming specifications. The rules governing pseudocode are as follows:

- Use the Do While with an Enddo to show iteration.
- Use If-Then-Else to show conditions and ensure each If has an End-If.
- Be specific about initializing variables and other detail processing requirements.

Pseudocode is designed to give the analyst tremendous control over the design of the code. Take the following example:

[2] DeMarco, Tom (1979), Structured Analysis and System Specification, pp. 85–86

There is a requirement to calculate a 5 % bonus for employees who work on the 1st shift and a 10 % bonus for workers on the 2nd or 3rd shift. Management is interested in a report listing the number of employees who receive a 10 % bonus. The process also produces the bonus checks.

The pseudocode would be:

```
Initialize 10% counter=0
Open Employee Master File
DoWhile more records
    If Shift="1" then
        Bonus=Gross_Pay * .05
    Else
        If Shift="2" or "3" then
            Bonus=Gross_Pay * .10
            Add 1 to Counter
        Else
            Error Condition
    Endif
        Endif
Enddo
Print Report of 10% Bonus Employees
Print Bonus Checks
End
```

The above algorithm gives the analyst great control over how the program should be designed. For example, note that the pseudocode requires that the programmer has an error condition should a situation occur where a record does not contain a first, second, or third shift employee. This might occur should there be a new shift that was not communicated to the information systems department. Many programmers might have omitted the last "If" check as follows:

```
Initialize 10% counter=0
Open Employee Master File
DoWhile more records
    If Shift="1" then
        Bonus=Gross_Pay * .05
    Else
        Bonus=Gross_Pay * .10
        Add 1 to Counter
    Endif
Enddo
Print Report of 10% Bonus Employees
Print Bonus Checks
End
```

This algorithm simply assumes that if the employee is not on the first shift, then they must be either a second or third shift employee. Without this being specified by the analyst, the programmer may have omitted this critical logic which could have resulted in a fourth shift worker receiving a 10% bonus! As mentioned earlier, each style of process specification has its advantages and disadvantages, in other words, the good, the bad, and the ugly.

The Good

The analyst who uses this approach has practically written the program, and thus the programmer will have very little to do with regard to figuring out the logic design.

The Bad

The algorithm is very detailed and could take a long time for the analyst to develop. Many professionals raise an interesting point: do we need analysts to be writing process specifications to this level of detail? In addition, many programmers may be insulted and feel that an analyst does not possess the skill set to design such logic.

The Ugly

The analyst spends the time, the programmers are not supportive, and the logic is incorrect. The result here will be the *I told you so* remarks from programmers, and hostilities may grow over time.

Case

"Case"[3] is another method of communicating application logic. Although the technique does not require as much technical format as pseudocode, it still requires the analyst to provide a detailed structure to the algorithm. Using the same example as in the pseudocode discussion, we can see the differences in format:

```
Case 1st Shift
    Bonus=Gross_Pay * .05
Case 2nd or 3rd Shift
    Bonus=Gross_Pay * .10
    Add 1 to 10% Bonus Employees
Case Neither 1st, 2nd or 3rd Shift
    Error Routine
EndCase
Print Report of 10% Bonus Employees
Print Bonus Checks
End
```

[3]The case method should not be confused with CASE (computer-aided software engineering) products, which is a software used to automate and implement modeling tools and data repositories.

This format provides control as it still allows the analyst to specify the need for error checking; however, the exact format and order of the logic is more in the hands of the programmer. Let's now see the good, bad, and ugly of this approach:

The Good

The analyst has provided a detailed description of the algorithm without having to know the format of logic in programming. Because of this advantage, CASE takes less time than pseudocode.

The Bad

Although this may be difficult to imagine, the analyst may miss some of the possible conditions in the algorithm, such as forgetting a shift! This happens because the analyst is just listing conditions as opposed to writing a specification. Without formulating the logic as we did in pseudocode, the likelihood of forgetting or overlooking a condition check is increased.

The Ugly

Case logic can be designed without concern for the sequence of the logic, that is, the actual progression of the logic as opposed to just the possibilities. Thus the logic can become more confusing because it lacks actual progressive structure. As stated previously, the possibility of missing a condition is greater because the analyst is not actually following the progression of the testing of each condition. There is thus a higher risk of the specification being incomplete.

Pre-post Conditions

Pre-post is based on the belief that analysts should not be responsible for the details of the logic, but rather for the overall highlights of what is needed. Therefore, the pre-post method lacks detail and expects that the programmers will provide the necessary details when developing the application software. The method has two components: preconditions and post-conditions. Preconditions represent things that are assumed true or that must exist for the algorithm to work. For example, a precondition might specify that the user must input the value of the variable X. On the other hand, the post-condition must define the required outputs as well as the relationships between calculated output values and their mathematical components. Suppose the algorithm calculated an output value called Total_Amount. The post-condition would state that Total_Amount is produced by multiplying Quantity times Price. Below is the pre-post equivalent of the bonus algorithm:

```
Pre-Condition 1:
    Access Employee Master file and where 1st shift="1"
Post-Condition 1:
    Bonus is set to Gross_Pay * .05.
    Produce Bonus check.
```

```
Pre-Condition 2:
     Access Employee Master file and where 2nd shift="2" or 3rd
     shift="3"
Post-Condition 2:
     Bonus is set to Gross_Pay * .10
     Add 1 to 10% Bonus count.
     Produce Bonus check and Report of all employees who receive
     10% bonuses.

Pre-Condition 3:
     Employee records does not contain a shift code equal to "1",
     "2", or "3"
Post-Condition 3:
     Error Message for employees without shifts="1", "2", or "3"
```

As we can see, the above specification does not show how the actual algorithm should be designed or written. It requires the programmer or development team to find these details and implement the appropriate logic to handle it. Therefore, the analyst has no real input into the way the application will be designed or the way it functions.

The Good

The analyst need not have technical knowledge to write an algorithm and does not need to spend an inordinate amount of time to develop what is deemed a programming responsibility. Therefore, less technically oriented analysts can be involved in specification development.

The Bad

There is no control over the design of the logic, and thus the opportunity for misunderstandings and errors is much greater. The analyst and the project are much more dependent on the talent of the development staff.

The Ugly

Perhaps we misunderstand the specification. Since the format of pre-post conditions is less specific, there is more room for ambiguity.

Matrix

A matrix or table approach is one that shows the application logic in tabular form. Each row reflects a result of a condition, with each column representing the components of the condition to be tested. The best way to explain a matrix specification is to show an example (Fig. 8.13).

Bonus Percent	Shift to be tested
5% Bonus	1st Shift
10% Bonus	2nd Shift
10% Bonus	3rd Shift

Fig. 8.13 Sample matrix specification

Although this is a simple example that uses the same algorithm as the other specification styles, it does show how a matrix can describe the requirements of an application without the use of sentences and pseudocode.

The Good
The analyst can use a matrix to show complex conditions in a tabular format. The tabular format is preferred by many programmers because it is easy to read, organize, and often maintain. Very often the matrix resembles the array and table formats used by many programming languages.

The Bad
It is difficult, if not impossible, to show a complete specification in matrices. The example in Fig. 8.13 supports this, in that the remaining logic of the bonus application is not shown. Therefore, the analyst must integrate one of the other specification styles to complete the specification.

The Ugly
Matrices are used to describe complex condition levels, where there are many "If" conditions to be tested. These complex conditions often require much more detailed analysis than shown in a matrix. The problem occurs when the analyst, feeling the matrix may suffice, does not provide enough detail. The result is that conditions may be misunderstood by the programmer during development.

Conclusion
The question must be asked again: What is a good specification? We will continue to explore this question. In this chapter we have examined the logic alternatives. Which logic method is best? It depends! We have seen from the examples that each method has its advantages and shortcomings. The best approach is to be able to use them all and to select the most appropriate one for the task at hand. To do this effectively means clearly recognizing which style provides the best benefit for the component of the system being analyzed. Figure 8.14 attempts to put the advantages and shortcomings into perspective.

Pseudocode	Case	Pre-Post	Matrix
Complex and detailed algorithms that need significant clarification.	The application logic is detailed but it is not necessary to develop the complete flow of the process.	Tremendous level of confidence in development staff to get the necessary application logic detail.	Large number of conditions (If statements) with an emphasis on lots of conditions before the answer is reached (i.e., complex If statements.
The analyst is also having difficulty with defining the logic.	There is more confidence in the programming staff.	The application logic is very simple and does not need further clarification.	No need for error condition checking.
Should be used when the analyst is very concerned about the aptitude of the programming staff.	The analyst wants to define all error handling conditions, but not to design them.	Few conditions ("If" statements)	Little application logic that needs to be further explained.
The analyst is very sensitive to error handling.	There are a reasonable number of "If " statements.	No need or limited error handling requirements.	

Fig. 8.14 Process specification comparisons

State Transition Diagrams

State transition diagrams (STD) were designed to model events that are time dependent in behavior. Another definition of the STD is that it models the application alternatives for event-driven activities. An event-driven activity can be defined as any activity that depends directly on the behavior of a precondition which makes that event either possible or attractive. Before going any further, let's use an example to explain this definition further:

> Mary leaves her office to go home for the day. Mary lives 20 minutes walking distance from the office. When departing from the office building, she realizes that it is raining very hard. Typically, Mary would walk home; however, due to the rain, she needs to make a decision at that moment about how she will go home. Therefore, an event has occurred during the application of Mary walking home which may change her decision and thus change the execution of this application.

As shown above, we have defined an event that, depending on the conditions during its execution, may have different results. To complete the example, we must examine or define what Mary's alternatives are for getting home (Fig. 8.15).

The matrix in Fig. 8.15 shows us the alternative activities that Mary can choose. Two of them require a certain amount of money. All of the alternatives have positive and negative potentials that cannot be determined until executed; therefore, the decision to go with an alternative may depend on a calculation of probability. We sometimes call this a calculated risk or our "gut" feeling. Is it not true that Mary will not know whether she will be able to find a taxi until she tries? However, if Mary

Alternative	Pre-Condition	Positive Result	Negative Result
1. Walk Home	None	Mary gets home and does not spend money	Mary gets very wet
2. Take Subway train	Must have $1.50 for Subway	Mary gets home without getting too wet.	Mary spends money and must be careful for her safety when going into the Subway
3. Take a Taxi	Must have $15.00 for the Taxi ride	Mary gets home faster and without getting wet.	It's expensive and it may be difficult to find a Taxi. There could also be a lot of traffic, resulting in delays.

Fig. 8.15 Mary's event alternatives

Fig. 8.16 State transition diagram for going home

sees a lot of traffic in the street and not many taxis, she may determine that it is not such a good idea to take a taxi.

Much of the duplication of the scenario shown in Fig. 8.15 falls into the study of Artificial Intelligence (AI) software. Therefore, AI modeling may require the use of STDs. The word "state" in STD means that an event must be in a given precondition before we can consider moving to another condition. In our example, Mary is in a state called "Going Home From the Office." Walking, taking a train, or taking a taxi is an alternative way of getting home. Once Mary is home, she has entered into a new state called "Home." We can now derive that walking, taking a train, or taking a taxi is a condition that can effect a change in state, in this example leaving the office and getting home. Figure 8.16 shows the STD for "going home."

This STD simply reflects that two states exist and that there is a condition that causes the application to move to the "Home" state. When using STDs, the analyst should:

1. Identify all states that exist in the system. In other words, all possible permutations of events must be defined.
2. Ensure that there is at least one condition to enter every state.
3. Ensure that there is at least one condition to leave every state.

The reasons for and approach to an STD differ greatly from those of a DFD. A DFD should be used when modeling finite, sequential processes that have a definitive beginning and end. We saw this situation in the previous examples in this chapter. The STD, on the other hand, is needed when the system effectively never ends, that is, when it simply moves from one state to another. Therefore, the question is

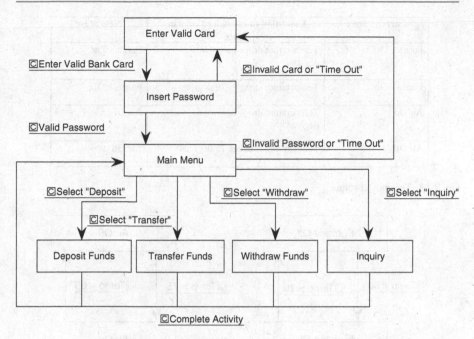

Fig. 8.17 Bank teller state transition diagram

never whether we are at the beginning or end of the process, but rather the current state of the system. Another example, one similar to that used by Yourdon in "Modern Structured Analysis," is the Bank Teller state diagram (Fig. 8.17).

Although you may assume that "Enter Valid Card" is the start state, an experienced analyst would know better. At any time, the automated teller is in a particular state of operation (unless it has abnormally terminated). The "Enter Valid Card" state is in the "sleep" state. It will remain in this mode until someone creates the condition to cause a change, which is actually to input a valid card. Notice that every state can be reached and every state can be left. This rule establishes perhaps the most significant difference between the DFD and STD. Therefore, a DFD should be used for finite processes and a STD where there is ongoing processing, moving from one status to another.

Let us now show a more complex example which emphasizes how the STD can uncover conditions that are not obvious or were never experienced by the user. Take the matrix of states for a thermostat shown in Fig. 8.18.

Figure 8.19 shows the STD for the states and conditions given in Fig. 8.18.

Upon review, we notice that there are really two systems and that they do not interface with each other. Why? Suppose, for example, that the temperature went above 70 and that the system therefore went into the Furnace Off state, but that the temperature nevertheless continued to increase unexpectedly. Users expect that whenever the Furnace Off state is reached, it must be winter. In the event of a winter heat wave, everyone would get very hot. We have therefore discovered that we must

Current State	Condition to cause a change in State	New State
Furnace Off	Temperature drops below 60 degrees	Furnace On
Furnace On	Temperature exceeds 70 degrees	Furnace Off
Air On	Temperature drops below 65 degrees	Air Off
Air Off	Temperature exceeds 75 degrees	Air On

Fig. 8.18 Thermostat states

Fig. 8.19 State transition diagram based on the user-defined states

Current State	Condition to cause a change in State	New State
Furnace Off	Temperature exceeds 75 degrees	Air On
Air Off	Temperature drops below 65 degrees	Furnace On

Fig. 8.20 Additional possible states of the thermostat

have a condition to put the air on even if a heat wave had never occurred before in winter. The same situation exists for the Air Off where we expect the temperature to rise instead of falling. We will thus add two new conditions as shown in Fig. 8.20.

The STD is then modified to show how the Furnace and Air subsystems interface (Fig. 8.21).

Using STDs to discover missing processes (that would otherwise be omitted or added later) is very important. This advantage is why STDs are considered very effective in artificial intelligence and object-oriented analysis, where the analyst is constantly modeling event-driven, never ending processes. We will see further application of STDs in Chap. 5: Object-Oriented Techniques.

Fig. 8.21 Modified state transition diagram based on modified events

Entity Relationship Diagrams

The model that depicts the relationships among the stored data is known as an entity relationship diagram (ERD). The ERD is the most widely used of all modeling tools and is really the only method to reflect the system's stored data.

An entity in database design is an object of interest about which data can be collected. In a retail database application, customers, products, and suppliers might be entities. An entity can subsume a number of attributes: product attributes might be color, size, and price; customer attributes might include name, address, and credit rating.[4]

The first step to understanding an entity is to establish its roots. Since DFDs have been used to model the processes, their data stores (which may represent data files) will act as the initial entities prior to implementing logical data modeling.

It is believed, for purposes of data modeling, that an entity can be simply defined as a logical file which will reflect the data elements or fields that are components of each occurrence or record in the entity. The ERD, therefore, shows how multiple entities will interact with each other. We call this interaction the "relationship." In most instances, a relationship between two or more entities can exist only if they have at least one common data element among them. Sometimes we must force a relationship by placing a common data element between entities, just so they can communicate with each other. An ERD typically shows each entity and its connections as shown in Fig. 8.22.

The example in Fig. 8.22 shows two entities: Orders and Customers. They have a relationship because both entities contain a common data element called Customer#. Customer# is depicted as "key data" in the Customer entity because it must be unique for every occurrence of a customer record. It is notated as "PK1" because it is defined as a primary key, meaning that Customer# uniquely identifies a particular customer. In Orders, we see that Customer# is a primary key but it is concatenated with Order#. By "concatenation," we mean that the two elements are

[4] Microsoft Press, Computer Dictionary, Second Edition, pg. 149.

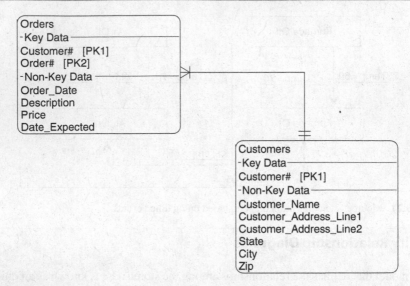

Fig. 8.22 Entity relationship diagram showing the relationship between the Order and Customer entities

combined to form a primary key. Nevertheless, Customer# still has its separate identity. The line that joins the entities is known as the relationship identifier. It is modeled using the "Crow's foot" method, meaning that the many relationships are shown as a Crow's foot, pictured above going to the Order entity. The double vertical lines near the Customer entity signify "One and only One." What does this really mean? The proper relationship is stated:

> One and only One Customer can have One to Many Orders

In English it means that customers must have placed at least one order, but can also have placed more than one. "One and only One" really indicates that when a customer is found in the Order entity, the customer must also exist in the Customer entity. In addition, although a customer may exist multiple times in the Order entity, it can exist in the Customer master entity only once. This relationship is also know as the association between entities and effectively identifies the common data elements and the constraints associated with their relationship. This kind of relationship between entities can be difficult to grasp, especially without benefit of a practical application. Chapter 4 will provide a step-by-step approach to developing an ERD using the process of logical data modeling.

Problems and Exercises

1. What is a functional primitive?
2. What are the advantages and disadvantages of a data flow diagram?

3. What is meant by "leveling up"?
4. What is the purpose of the data dictionary?
5. Define each of the following data dictionary notation symbols: =, +, [],/, (), { }, **.
6. What is an Elementary Data Element? How does it compare with a functional primitive?
7. Define the functions of a process specification. How does the process specification interface with the DFD and the DD?
8. Compare the advantages and disadvantages of each of the following process specification formats:
 - Pseudocode
 - Case
 - Pre-Post Condition
 - Matrix
9. What is an event-driven system? How does the program manager in Windows applications represent the behavior of an event-driven system?
10. When using an STD, what three basic things must be defined?
11. What is an entity? How does it relate to a data store of a DFD?
12. Explain the concept of an entity relationship diagram.
13. What establishes a relationship between two entities?
14. Define the term "association."

Mini-Project

You have been asked to automate the Accounts Payable process. During your interviews with users, you identify four major events as follows:

I. Purchase Order Flow

1. The Marketing Department sends a Purchase Order (P.O.) form for books to the Accounts Payable System (APS).
2. APS assigns a P.O. number and sends the P.O.-White copy to the vendor and files the P.O.-Pink copy in a file cabinet in P.O.#.sequence.

II. Invoice Receipt

1. A vendor sends an invoice for payment for books purchased by APS.
2. APS sends invoice to the Marketing Department for authorization.
3. Marketing either returns invoice to APS approved or back to the vendor if not authorized.

4. If the invoice is returned to APS, it is matched up against the original P.O.-Pink. The PO and vendor invoice are then combined into a packet and prepared for the voucher process.

III. Voucher Initiation

1. APS receives the packet for vouchering. It begins this process by assigning a voucher number.
2. The chief accountant must approve vouchers > $5000.
3. APS prepares another packet from the approved vouchers. This packet includes the P.O.-Pink, authorized invoice, and approved voucher.

IV. Check Preparation

1. Typist receives the approved voucher packet and retrieves a numbered blank check to pay the vendor.
2. Typist types a two-part check (blue, green) using data from the approved voucher and enters invoice number on the check stub.
3. APS files the approved packet with the check green in the permanent paid file.
4. The check is either picked up or mailed directly to the vendor.

Assignment

1. Provide the DFDs for the four events. Each event should be shown as a single DFD on a separate piece of paper.
2. Level each event to its functional primitives.
3. Develop the process specifications for each functional primitive DFD.

References

DeMarco, T. (1979). *Structured analysis and system specification*. Englewood Cliffs: Prentice Hall.
Yourdon, E. (1989). *Modern structured analysis*. Englewood Cliffs: Prentice Hall.

The Data

Introduction to Databases

Chapter 8 focused on application specifications as they relate to process. Using DFDs, PDFs, State Diagrams, etc., I showed how data elements are defined in the DD. However, the process of completing the DD and building complex relational databases has further steps. This chapter focuses on how to design databases for use with e-commerce Web applications. The completion of the DD and the creation of the database schematic, called the Entity Relational Diagram, provide developers with the data architecture component of the system. We call the process of creating this architecture logic data modeling. The process of logic data modeling not only defines the architecture; it also provides the construct for the actual database, often called the physical database. The physical database differs from its logical counterpart in that it is subject to the rules and formats of the database product that will be used to implement the system. This means that if Oracle is used to implement the logical schema, the database must conform to the specific proprietary formats that Oracle requires. Thus, the logical model provides the first step in planning for the physical implementation. First we will examine the process of building the appropriate schematic. Even if a packaged software product is selected, the chances are that it will need to use a database product like Oracle. Thus, many of the analysis and design below will be extremely important in determining the best fit for a package.

Logic Data Modeling

Logic data modeling (LDM) is a method that examines a particular data entity and determines what data elements need to be associated with it. There are a number of procedures, some mathematically based, to determine how and what the analyst needs to do. Therefore, LDM only focuses on the stored data with the intent to design what can be defined as the "engine" of the system. Often this "engine" is

© Springer-Verlag London Limited 2016
A.M. Langer, *Guide to Software Development*,
DOI 10.1007/978-1-4471-6799-0_9

called the "backend." The design of the engine must be independent from the process and must be based on the rules of data definition theory. Listed below are the eight suggested steps to build the database blueprint. This blueprint is typically called the schema, which is defined as a logical view of the database:

1. Identify data entities.
2. Select primary and alternate keys.
3. Determine key business rules.
4. Apply normalization to third normal form.
5. Combine user views.
6. Integrate with existing data models (e.g., legacy interfaces).
7. Determine domains and triggering operations.
8. De-normalize as appropriate.

Prior to providing concrete examples, it is necessary to define the database terms used in this chapter. Below are the key concepts and definitions:

- *Entity*: an object of interest about which data can be collected. Whitten & Bentley (2007) define an entity as "a class of persons, places, objects, events, or concepts about which we need to capture or store data (p. 728)." For example, in an e-commerce application, customers, products, and suppliers might be entities. The chapter will provide a method of determining entities from the DFD. An entity can have many data elements associated with it, called attributes.
- *Attribute*: data elements are typically called attributes when they are associated with an entity. These attributes, or cells of an entity, belong to or "depend on" the entity.
- *Key*: a key is an attribute of an entity that uniquely identifies a row. A row is defined as a specific record in the database. Therefore, a key is an attribute that has a unique value that no other row or record can have. Typical key attributes are "Social Security number," "Order Number," etc.
- *Business Rule*: this is a rule that is assumed to be true as defined by the business. Business rules govern the way keys and other processes behave within the database.
- *Normalization*: a process that eliminates data redundancy and ensures data integrity in a database.
- *User View*: the definition of the data from the perspective of the user. This means that how a data element is used, what is its business rules, and whether it is a key or not depend largely on the user's definition. It is important that analysts understand that data definitions are not universal.
- *Domains*: this relates to a set of values or limits of occurrences within a data element or attribute of an entity. An example of a domain would be STATE, where there is a domain of 50 acceptable values (i.e., NY, NJ, CA, etc.).
- *Triggers*: these are stored procedures or programs that are activated or *triggered* as a result of an event at the database level. In other words, an event (insert, delete, update) may require that other elements or records be changed. This

change would occur by having a program stored by the database product (such as Oracle) automatically execute and update the data.

- *Cardinality*: this concept defines the relationship between two entities. This relationship is constructed based on the number of occurrences or associations that one entity has with another. For example, one customer record could have many order records. In this example, both customer and orders are separate entities.
- *Legacy Systems*: these are existing applications that are in operation. Legacy applications sometimes refer to older and less sophisticated applications that need to be interfaced with newer systems or replaced completely (see Chap. 10).
- *Entity Relational Diagram*: a schematic of all the entities and their relationships using cardinal format. An Entity Relational Diagram provides the blueprint of the data or the diagram of the data engine.

Logic Data Modeling Procedures

The first step in LDM is to select the entities that will be used to start the normalization process. If DFDs have been completed in accordance with the procedures outlined in Chap. 3, then all data stores that represent data files become transformed into data entities. This approach offers the major advantage of modeling process before data. If DFDs or some comparable process tool is not used, then analysts must rely on the information they can obtain from the legacy systems, such as existing data files, screens, and reports. The example shown in Fig. 9.1 depicts how a data store from a DFD becomes an entity. The data contained in the data store called "Orders" is represented as an actual form containing many data elements. Thus, this example represents a physical form translated into an LE called a data store, which then is transformed again into an entity (Figs. 9.1 and 9.2).

Key Attributes

The next step in LDM is to select the primary and alternate keys. A primary key is defined as an attribute that will be used to identify a record or occurrence in an entity. The primary key, like any key attribute, contains a unique value. Often there is more than one attribute in an entity that contains unique values. We call an attribute that can be a primary key a *candidate* key attribute. This simply means that this attribute can serve in the role of the primary key. If there is only one candidate, then there is no issue: that candidate becomes the primary key. In the event that there is more than one candidate attribute, then one must be selected the primary key, and the others will be called *alternate* or *secondary* key attributes. These alternate key attributes provide benefit in the physical database only. This means that they can be used to identify records in the database as an *alternative* should the primary key not be known. Take the example shown in Fig. 9.3. Suppose that an employee entity has two candidate keys: Social Security number and employee ID. Employee ID is selected as the primary key, so Social Security number becomes an alternate key. In the logical entity,

John's Parts, Inc ORDER

1818 West Way

New York, NY 10027

ORDER NO: 12345

DATE: August 15, 2011

To: :
 A. Langer & Assoc., Inc.
 John St
 Third Floor
 White Plains, NY, 10963

P.O. NUMBER	DATE SHIPPED	SHIPPED VIA	REQUIRED DATE	TERMS
4R32	3/28/2001	UPS	4/1/2001	30 days

QUANTITY	ITEM ID	ITEM NAME	UNIT PRICE	AMOUNT
6	31	Wires	6.50	39.00
2	27	Wheel Covers	25.00	50.00
				$ 0.00
				$ 0.00
				$ 0.00
				$ 0.00
				$ 0.00
		SUBTOTAL		$ 89.00
		SALES TAX		
		SHIPPING & HANDLING		$ 5.50
		TOTAL DUE		$ 99.50

Fig. 9.1 Sample customer order form

Social Security number is treated as any other non-key attribute; however, in the physical database, it can be used (or indexed) to find a record. This could occur when an employee calls to ask someone in human resources about accrued vacation time. The human resources staff would ask the employee for their employee ID. If the employee did not know his/her employee ID, the human resources staff could ask them for their Social Security number and use that information as an alternative way

Fig. 9.2 Transition of the
order data store into an
entity

Fig. 9.3 Primary key and
alternate key attributes

to locate that individual's information. It is important to note that the search on the primary key will be substantially faster, because primary key searches use a method called direct access, as opposed to index methods, which are significantly slower. This raises the question: When there are multiple candidate key attributes, which key attribute should be selected as the primary key? The answer is the attribute that will be used most often to find the record. This means that employee ID was selected the primary key attribute because the users determined that it was the field most often used to locate employee information. Therefore, e-commerce analysts must ensure that they ask users this question during the interview process. Figure 9.3 provides a graphic depiction of the employee entity showing employee ID as the primary key attribute and Social Security number as a non-key attribute.

There is another type of key attribute called *foreign* keys. Foreign keys provide a way to link tables and create relationships between them. Since foreign keys are created during the process of normalization, I will defer discussion about them to the section on normalization in this chapter.

Normalization

While the next step in LDM is to determine key business rules, it is easier to explain the process of normalization first. That is, normalization occurs after defining key

business rules in practice, but not when introducing the topic for educational purposes. Therefore, key business rules will be discussed after normalization.

Normalization, without question, is the most important aspect of LDM. As mentioned above, normalization is defined as the elimination of redundancies in an entity and ensures data integrity. It is the latter point that is critical in understanding the value of normalization in the design of e-commerce database systems. Understanding of the LDM process depends largely on understanding how to implement the normalization process.

Normalization is constructed in a number of "normal forms." While there are five published normal forms, normal forms 4 and 5 are difficult to implement and most professionals avoid them. Therefore, this book omits normal forms 4 and 5. The three normal forms of normalization are listed below. Note that a normal form is notated as "NF."

First NF: No repeating non-key attributes or group of non-key attributes.
Second NF: No partial dependencies on a part of a concatenated key attribute.
Third NF: No dependencies of a non-key attribute on another non-key attribute.

Each normal form is dependent on the one before it, that is, the process of completing normalization is predicated on the sequential satisfaction of the normal form preceding it. Normalization can be best explained by providing a detailed example. Using the Order form provided in Fig. 9.1, we can start the process of normalization. Fig. 9.4 shows the logical equivalent of the Order form in entity format. In this example, the primary key is Order number (signified by the "PK" notation), which requires that every order has a unique Order number associated with it. It should also be noted that a repeating group made up of five attributes is shown in a separate box. This repeating group of attributes correlates to an area on the Order form, which often is referred to as an order line item. This means that each item associated with the order appears in its own group, namely, the item identification, its name, unit price, quantity, and amount. The customer order in Fig. 9.1 shows two items associated with the Order number 12345.

The process of determining compliance with normalization is to evaluate whether each normal form or NF has been satisfied. This can be accomplished by testing each NF in turn. Thus, the first question to ask is: Are we in first NF? The answer is no because of the existence of the repeating attributes: Item ID, Item Name, Quantity, Unit Price, and Amount or as specified above an "order line item." In showing this box, the example exposes the repeating group of items that can be associated with a customer order. Another way of looking at this phenomenon is to see that within the Order, there really is another entity, which has its own key identification. Since there is a repeating group of attributes, there is a first NF failure. *Anytime an NF fails or is violated, it results in the creation of another entity.* Whenever there is a first NF failure, the new entity will always have as its primary key a concatenated "group" of attributes. This concatenation, or joining of multiple attributes to form a specific value, is composed of the primary key from the original entity (Orders) attached with a new key attribute from the repeating group of

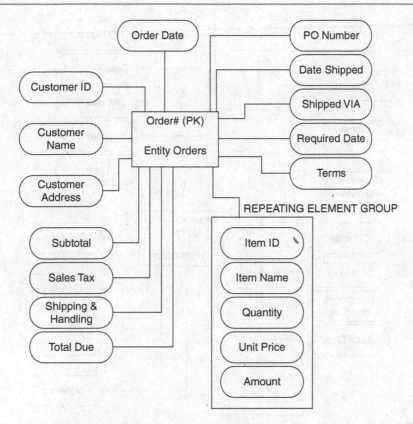

Fig. 9.4 Order entity and its associated attributes

elements. The new key must be an attribute that controls the other group of attributes. In this example, the controlling attribute is Item ID. After the new "key attribute" is determined, it is concatenated with the original key attribute from the Order entity. The remaining non-key attributes will be removed from the original entity to become non-key attributes of the new entity. This new entity is shown in Fig. 9.5.

The new entity, called Order Items, has a primary key that reflects the concatenation of the original key Order number from the entity Orders, combined with Item ID, which represents the controlling attribute for the repeating group. All of the other repeating attributes have now been transferred to the new entity. The new entity Order Item allows the system to store multiple order line items as required. The original entity left without this modification would have limited the number of occurrences of items artificially. For example, if the analyst/designer had defaulted to five groups of order line items, the database would always have five occurrences of the five attributes. If most orders, in reality, had fewer than five items, then significant space would be wasted. More significant is the case where the order has more than five items. In this case, a user would need to split the order into two physical orders so that the extra items could be captured. These two issues are the salient benefits of attaining entities in their first NF. Therefore, leaving the entity Order as is would in effect create an integrity problem.

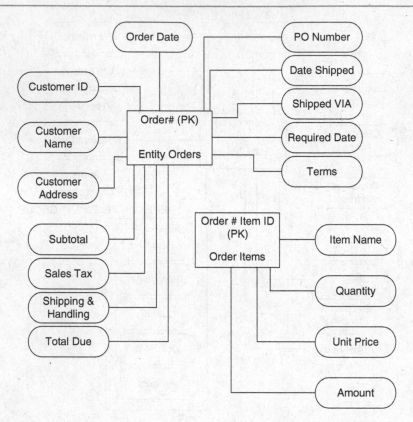

Fig. 9.5 Orders in the first NF

Once the changes to the entity Orders have been completed and the new entity Order Item has been completed, the system is said to be a database in first NF. It is important to note that the new primary key of the entity Order Items is the combination of two attributes. While the two attributes maintain their independence as separate fields of data, they are utilized as one combined value for purposes of their role as a key attribute. For example, based on the data in the Order form from Fig. 9.1, the entity Order Items would have two records. The first record would have the primary key of 1234531, which would be the concatenation of Order number (12345) with Item ID (31). The second record would be 1234527, which is the same Order number, but concatenated with the second Item ID (27). From an SQL feature perspective, while the key attribute concatenates each attribute into one address, it can be searched as separate fields. So a user could search for all the items associated with Order 12345, by simply searching on Order Items that contain an Order number = "12345." This exemplifies the power of versatility in the relational model. Once first NF has been reached, the next test must ensue, that is, testing for compliance with second NF.

Second NF testing applies *only* to entities that have concatenated keys. Therefore, any entity that is in the first NF and does not have a concatenated primary key must already be in the second NF. In our example, then, the entity "Orders" is already in the second NF because it is in the first NF and does not have a concatenated primary key. The entity Order Items, however, is in a different category: Order Items has a concatenated primary key attribute and must be tested for compliance with the second NF. The second NF requires the analyst to ensure that every non-key attribute in the entity is totally dependent on all components of the primary key or all of its concatenated attributes. When we apply the test, we find that the attribute "Item Name" is dependent only on the key attribute "Item ID." That is, the Order number has no effect or control over the name of the item. This condition is considered a second NF failure. Once again, a new entity must be created. The primary key of the new entity is the portion of the concatenated key that controlled the attribute that caused the failure. In other words, Item ID is the primary key of the new entity, because "Item Name" was wholly dependent on the attribute "Item ID." It is worthwhile at this time to explain further the concept of attribute dependency. For one attribute to be dependent on another infers that the controlling attribute's value can change the value of the dependent attribute. Another way of explaining this is to say that the controlling attribute, which must be a key, controls the record. That is, if the Item ID changes, then we are looking at a different Item Name, because we are looking at a different Item record.

To complete the creation of the new entity, Items, each non-key attribute in the original entity Order Items must be tested for the second NF violation. Note that as a result of this testing, "Quantity" and "Amount" stay in the Order Item entity because they are dependent on both Order number and Item ID. That is, the quantity associated with any given Order Items occurrence is dependent not only on the Item itself, but also the particular order it is associated with. We call this being wholly dependent on the concatenated primary key attribute. Thus, the movement of non-key attributes is predicated on the testing of each non-key attribute against the concatenated primary key. The result of this test establishes the three entities shown in Fig. 9.6.

The results of implementing the second NF reflect that without it, a new Item (or Item ID) could not have been added to the database without an order. This obviously would have caused major problems. Indeed, the addition of a new Item would have to precede the creation of that Item with a new Order. Therefore, the new entity represents the creation of a separate Item master file.

Figure 9.6 represents Orders in the second NF. Once again, we must apply the next test—the third NF—to complete normalization. Third NF tests the relationship between two non-key attributes to ensure that there are no dependencies between them. Indeed, if this dependency were to exist, it would mean that one of the non-key attributes would, in effect, be a key attribute. Should this occur, the controlling non-key attribute would become the primary key of the new entity. Testing this against the sample entity reflects that Customer name and Customer address[1] are

[1] Customer address would normally be composed of three address lines and the existence of State, city, and zip code. It has been omitted from this example for simplicity.

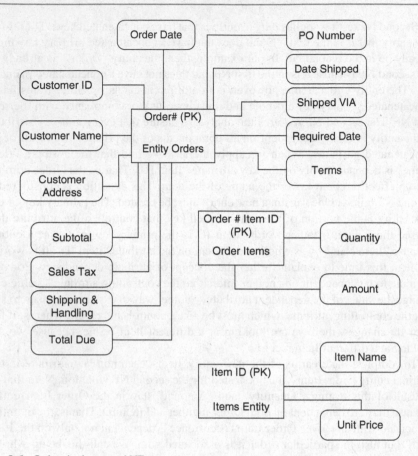

Fig. 9.6 Orders in the second NF

dependent on Customer ID. Therefore, the entity Orders fails the third NF and a new entity must be created. The primary key of the new entity is the non-key attribute that controlled the other non-key attributes, in this case Customer ID. The new entity is called Customers, and all of the non-key attributes that depend on Customer ID are moved to that entity as shown in Fig. 9.7.

What is unique about the third NF failures is that the new key attribute remains as a non-key attribute in the original entity (in this case, Orders). The copy of the non-key attribute Customer ID is called a foreign key and is created to allow the Order entity and the new Customer entity to have a relationship. A relationship between two entities can exist only if there is at least one common keyed attribute between them. Understanding this concept is crucial to what normalization is intended to accomplish. Looking at Fig. 9.7, one can see that the entity Order and Order Items have a relationship because both entities have a common keyed attribute: Order ID. The same is true in the creation of the Item entity, which resulted in the second NF failure. The relationship here is between the Order Item entity

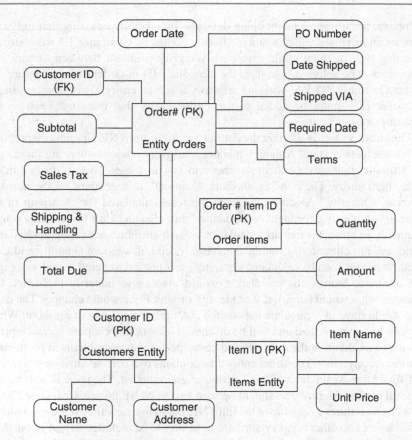

Fig. 9.7 Orders in preliminary third NF

and the Item entity, where both entities contain the common key attribute Item ID. Both of these relationships resulted in the *propagation* of a key attribute from the original entity to the newly formed entity during the normalization process. By propagation, we mean that a pointer or copy of the key attribute is placed in the new entity. Propagation is implemented using foreign keys and is a natural result of the process. Note that the "PK" is followed by an "FK" signifying that the keyed attribute is the result of a propagation of the original key attribute. Such is not the case in the third NF. If Customer ID were to be removed from the Order entity, then the relationship between Orders and Customers would not exist because there would be no common keyed attribute between the two entities. Therefore, in the third NF, it is necessary to force the relationship because a natural propagation has not occurred. This is accomplished by creating a pointer from a non-keyed attribute to the primary keyed copy, in this case Customer ID. The concept of a pointer is important. Foreign key structures are typically implemented internally in physical databases using indexes. Indexes, or indirect

addresses, are a way of maintaining database integrity by ensuring that only one copy of an attribute value is stored. If two copies of Customer ID were stored, changing one of them could create an integrity problem between Orders and Customers. The solution is to have the Customer ID in Orders "point" indirectly to the Customer ID key attribute in the Customer entity. This ensures that a Customer ID cannot be added to the Order entity that does not exist in the Customer master entity.

The question now is whether the entities are in the third NF. Upon further review, we see the answer is no! Although it is not intuitively obvious, there are three non-key attributes that are dependent on other non-key attributes. This occurs first in the Order Item entity. The non-key attribute "Amount" is dependent on the non-key attribute "Quantity." Amount represents the total calculated for each item in the order. It is not only dependent on "Quantity" but also on "Unit Price." This occurs frequently in attributes that are calculations. Such attributes are called *derived* elements and are eliminated from the database. Indeed, if we store Quantity and Unit Price, "Amount" can be calculated separately as opposed to being stored as a separate attribute. Storing the calculation would also cause integrity problems. For example, what would happen if the Quantity or Unit Price would change? The database would have to recalculate the change and update the Amount attribute. While this can be accomplished and will be discussed later in this chapter, it can be problematic to maintain in the database and cause performance problems in production e-commerce systems. The Order entity also contains two derived attributes: Subtotal and Total Due. Again, both of these attributes are removed. The issue is whether the removal of derived attributes should be seen as a third NF failure. C. J. Date (2000) views these failures as outside of the third NF, but in my view they represent indirect dependencies on other non-key attributes and should be included as part of the third NF test. In any case, we all agree that derived elements should be removed in the process of LDM. The third NF LDM is modified to reflect the removal of these three attributes as shown in Fig. 9.8.

Once the third NF is reached, the analyst should create the Entity Relational Diagram (ERD), which will show the relationships or connections among the entities. The relationship between entities is established through associations. Associations define the cardinality of the relationship using what is known as the Crow's foot method as shown in Fig. 9.9.

The Crow's foot method is only one of many formats. The method contains three key symbols:

\leqslant Denotes the cardinality of many occurrences.
O denotes zero occurrence.
|
Denotes one occurrence.

Therefore, the ERD in Fig. 9.9 depicts the relationships of all the entities as follows:

Fig. 9.8 Orders in the second phase of the third NF

1. One and only one (signified by the double lines) Order record can have one to many Order Item records. It also shows that any Order in the Order Item entity must exist in the Order entity.
2. One and only one Item record can have zero to many Order Item records. The difference in this relationship and the one established between Orders and Order Items is that Items may not have a relationship with Order items, signified by the zero in the Crow's foot. This would often occur when there is a new item that has not yet received any orders.
3. The Order Item entity has a primary key, which is a concatenation of two other primary keys: Order ID from the Order entity and Item ID from the Item entity. This type of relationship is said to be an "associative" relationship because the entity has been created as a result of a relational problem. This relational problem exists because the Order entity has a "many-to-many" relationship with

Fig. 9.9 The entities in ERD format using Crow's feet

the Item entity. Thus the first NF failure, which created the associative entity Order Items, is really the result of a "many-to-many" situation. A many-to-many relationship violates normalization because it causes significant problems with SQL coding. Therefore, whenever a many-to-many relationship occurs between two entities, an associative entity is created which will have as its primary key the concatenation of the two primary keys from each entity. Thus, associative entities make many-to-many relationships into two one-to-many relationships so that SQL can work properly during search routines. Associative entities are usually represented with a diamond box.

4. One and only one customer can have zero to many Orders, also showing that a customer may exist who has never placed an order. As an example, this would be critical if the business were credit cards, where consumers can obtain a credit card even though they have not made a purchase. Note that the Customer ID is linked with Orders through the use of a non-key foreign key attribute.

Limitations of Normalization

Although the third NF has been attained, there is a major problem with the model. The problem relates to the attribute Unit Price in the Item entity. Should the Unit Price of any Item change, then the calculation of historical Order Item purchases would be incorrect. Remember that the attribute "Amount" was eliminated because it was a derived element. This might suggest that normalization does not work properly! Such is not the case. First we need to evaluate whether putting "Amount" back in the ERD

Fig. 9.10 Final ERD with order item unit price

would solve the problem. If the Unit Price were to change, then Amount would need to be recalculated *before* it was done. While this might seem reasonable, it really does not offer a *solution* to the problem, just a way around it. The actual problem has little to do with the attribute "Amount," but more to do with a missing attribute. The missing attribute is Order Item Unit Price, which would represent the price at the time of the order. Order Item Unit Price is dependent on both the Order and the Item and therefore would become a non-key attribute in the Order Item entity (i.e., it is wholly dependent on the entire concatenated primary key). The only relationship between Unit Price and Order Item Unit Price is at the time the order is entered into the system. In this situation, an application program would move the value or amount of the Unit Price attribute into the Order Item Unit Price attribute. Thereafter, there is no relationship between the two attributes. Because this is a new data element that has been discovered during normalization, it must be entered into the data dictionary. Thus, a limitation of normalization is that it cannot normalize what it does not have; it can normalize only the attributes that are presented to the formula. However, the limitation of normalization is also an advantage: the process can help the analyst recognize that a data element is missing. Therefore, normalization is a "data-based" tool that the analyst can use to reach the logical equivalent. Figure 9.10 shows the final ERD with the addition of Order Item Unit Price.

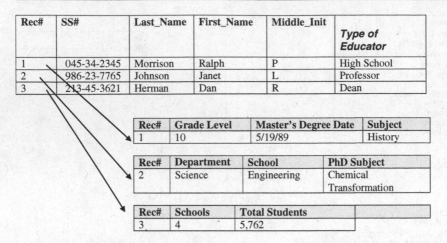

Rec#	SS#	Last_Name	First_Name	Middle_Init	Type of Educator
1	045-34-2345	Morrison	Ralph	P	High School
2	986-23-7765	Johnson	Janet	L	Professor
3	213-45-3621	Herman	Dan	R	Dean

Rec#	Grade Level	Master's Degree Date	Subject
1	10	5/19/89	History

Rec#	Department	School	PhD Subject
2	Science	Engineering	Chemical Transformation

Rec#	Schools	Total Students	
3	4	5,762	

Fig. 9.11 Supertype/subtype relationship

The Supertype/Subtype Model

A troublesome database issue occurs in the LDM when there are records within an entity that can take on different characteristics or have many "types" of attributes. "Type" means that a portion of the attributes in a specific record can vary depending on the characteristic or identification of the row within that entity. Another way of defining type is to describe it as a group of attributes within a given record that are different from other records of the same entity depending on the *type* of record it represents. This type is referred to as a "subtype" of the record. A subtype, therefore, is the portion of the record that deviates from the standard or "supertype" part of the record. The "supertype" portion is always the same among all the records in the entity. In other words, the "supertype" represents the global part of the attributes in an entity. The diagram in Fig. 9.11 depicts the supertype/subtype relationship.

The difference between a subtype and an ordinary type identifier (using a foreign key) is the occurrence of at least one non-key attribute that exists only in that subtype record. The major reason to create a supertype/subtype relationship is the occurrence of multiple permutations of these unique attributes that exist in just certain subtype records. Limiting these permutations of attributes within one record format can be problematic. First, it can waste storage, especially if each subtype has significant numbers of unique attributes. Second, it can create significant performance problems particularly with the querying of data. Using Fig. 9.11, we can see two ways to store this data. The first (Fig. 9.12) is a basic representation where all the permutations exist in one entity called "Educators." The "type" of row is identified by using a foreign key pointer to a validation entity called "Educator Type."

Fig. 9.12 Educator ERD using foreign key identifier

Fig. 9.13 Educator entity supertype/subtype model

Although this representation of the data uses only one entity, it wastes storage space because *all* of the attributes of the entity are never needed by any one "type" of record. Furthermore, a user must know which attributes need to be entered for a particular type of record. This method of logic data modeling violates the concepts of normalization and entrusts the integrity of values of elements in an entity to either an application program's control (stored procedure) or to the memory of the user. Neither of these choices is particularly dependable or has proven to be a reliable method of data integrity.

On the other hand, Fig. 9.13 provides a different solution using the supertype/ subtype model.

This model constructs a separate entity for each type of educator, linked via a special notation in the relational model, known as the supertype/subtype relation. The relationship is mutually exclusive, meaning that the supertype entity Educator can have only one of the three subtypes for any given supertype occurrence. Therefore, the relationship of one record in a supertype must be one to one with only one subtype. The supertype/subtype model creates a separate subtype entity to carry only the specific attributes unique to its subtype.

There are two major benefits to this entity structure. First, the construct saves storage because it stores only the attributes it needs in each entity. Second, the subtype information can be directly addressed without accessing its related super-type. This is possible because each subtype entity contains the same primary key as its parent. This capability is significant because a user can automatically obtain the unique information from any subtype without having to search first through the supertype entity. This is particularly beneficial when the number of records in each subtype varies significantly. Suppose, for example, there are six million educators in the database. The Educator database would therefore contain six million rows. Let's say that five million of the educators are high school teachers, and as such, the High School subtype entity has five million records. Eight hundred thousand educators are professors, and the remaining 200,000 educators are deans; there-fore, the Professor database and Dean database have 800,000 and 200,000 records, respectively. Using the supertype/subtype model applications could access each subtype without searching through every record in the database. Furthermore, because access to one subtype does not affect the other, performance is greatly improved.

It is important to note that the supertype/subtype model is not limited to mutual exclusivity, that is, it can support multiple subtype permutations. For example,

Fig. 9.14 Supertype/subtype model without mutual exclusivity

Fig. 9.15 Cascading subtypes

suppose an educator could be a high school teacher, college professor, and a dean, at the same time, or any permutation of the three types. The sample model would then be modified to show separate one-to-one relationships as opposed to the "T" relationship shown in Fig. 9.13. The alternative model is represented in Fig. 9.14.

Supertype/subtypes can cascade, that is, they can continue to iterate or decompose within each subtype. This is represented in Fig. 9.15.

Notice that in the example shown in Fig. 9.15, the same primary key continues to link the "one-to-one" relationships between the entities. In addition, the figure also shows another possibility in the supertype/subtype model. This possibility reflects that a subtype can exist without containing any non-key attributes. This occurs in the example in the subtype entity *Adjunct Prof*. The "empty" entity serves only to identify the existence of the subtype, without having a dedicated non-key attribute associated with it. The *Adjunct Prof entity*, therefore, is created only to allow the other two subtypes (*Tenured Prof* and *Contract Prof*) to store their unique attributes. This example shows how supertype/subtype models can be

Fig. 9.16 Cascading subtypes with alternating exclusivities

constructed and how they often have subtypes that are created for the sole purpose of identification.

Cascading subtypes can mix methods, that is, some levels may not be mutually exclusive, while other cascade levels can be mutually exclusive as shown in Fig. 9.16.

There is a controversial issue among database developers. The controversy relates to whether it is necessary to create a special attribute that identifies which entity contains the subtype entry for any given supertype. In other words, how does the database know which subtype has the continuation information? This dilemma is especially relevant when mutually exclusive relationships exist in the supertype/ subtype. The question is ultimately whether the supertype/subtype model needs to contain an identifier attribute that knows which subtype holds the continuation record, or is the issue resolved by the physical database product? Fleming and von Halle (1989) addressed this issue in the *Handbook of Database Design*, where they suggest that the "attribute is at least partially redundant because its meaning already is conveyed by the existence of category or subtype relationships" (p. 162). Still, the issue of redundancy may vary among physical database products. Therefore, I

Fig. 9.17 Supertype/subtype with subtype identifier element

suggest that the logical model contain a subtype identifier for mutually exclusive supertype/subtype relationships as shown in Fig. 9.17.

Note that the example in Fig. 9.17 has the subtype identifier, Professor Types, as a validation entity in the third normal form.

Supertype/subtypes must also be normalized following the rules of normalization. For example, the subtype Educator Types contains elements that are not in the third NF. Attributes Grade_Level and Subject in the subtype entity High School Teacher can be validated using a look-up table. Department, School, and PhD_Subject can also be validated. The resulting third NF ERD is shown in Fig. 9.18.

Key Business Rules

Key business rules are the rules that govern the behavior between entities when a row is inserted or deleted. These business rules are programmed at the database

Fig. 9.18 Supertype/subtype in third NF

level using stored procedures and triggers (see Step 7: determine domains and triggering operations). These procedures are typically notated as constraints. Constraints enforce the key business rules that will be defined by the analysts and are the basis of what is meant by referential integrity, that is, the integrity based on the relations between tables. The process of insertion and deletion focuses on the relationship between the parent entity and the child entity. A child entity is always the entity that has the Crow's foot pointing to it. Based on the ERD in Fig. 9.10, the parent-child entity relationships are as follows:

- Order entity is the parent of Order Item entity (child).
- Customer entity is the parent of Order entity (child).
- Item entity is the parent of Order Item entity (child).

When discussing insertion of a row, it is always from the perspective of the child entity. That is, key business rules governing the insertion of a child record concern what should be done when attempting to insert a child record that does not have a corresponding parent record. There are six alternatives:

1. *Not Allowed*: this means that the constraint is to disallow the transaction. For example, in Fig. 9.10, a user could not insert an Order Item (child) for an Order number that did not exist in the Order entity (parent). Essentially, the integrity of the reference would be upheld, until the Order number in the Order entity was inserted first.
2. *Add Parent*: this means that if the parent key does not exist, it will be added at the same time. Using Fig. 9.10, this would mean that the user would be prompted to add the Order number to the Order entity before the child Item would be inserted. The difference between Not Allowed and Add Parent is that the user can enter the parent information during the insertion of the child transaction. Using this rule still enforces referential integrity.
3. *Default Value*: the use of a default value allows a "dummy" row to be inserted into the parent. An example of the use of a default occurs when collection agencies receive payments from an unknown person. The parent entity is "Account" and the child entity is "Payments." The Account entity would have a key value called "Unapplied" which would be used whenever an unidentified payment was collected. In this scenario, it is appropriate to have the dummy record because the child transaction is really unknown, but at the same time needs to be recorded in the database. It is also useful because the user can quickly get a list of "unapplied" payments and it upholds referential integrity.
4. *Algorithm*: an algorithm is an "intelligent" default value. Using the same example as (3), suppose the user wanted to track unapplied payments by State. For example, if an unapplied payment were received in New York, the parent (Account entity) would have a record inserted with a value "Unapplied—New York." Therefore, each State would have its own default. There are also default keys that are based on sophisticated algorithms to ensure that there is an understanding to the selection of the parent's key attribute value. Again, this selection ensures referential integrity because a record is inserted at both the parent and child entities.
5. *Null*: assigning a null means that the parent does not exist. Most database products such as Oracle allow such selection, and while it is maintained within the product, it violates referential integrity because the parent is unknown.
6. *Don't Care*: this essentially says that the user is willing to accept that referential integrity does not exist in the database. The user will tell you that they never wish to balance the records in the child with those in the parent. While this happens, it should be avoided, because it creates a system without integrity.

When discussing deletion of a row, it is always from the perspective of the parent entity. That is, key business rules governing the deletion of a parent record concern what should be done when attempting to delete a parent record that has corresponding child records. There are similarly six alternatives:

1. *Not Allowed*: this means that the constraint is to disallow the deletion of the parent record. In other words if there are children records, the user cannot delete the parent. For example, in Fig. 9.10, a user could not delete an Order (parent) if there were corresponding records in the Order Item entity (child). This action would require the user first to delete all of the Order Items or children records before allowing the parent Order to be deleted.
2. *Delete All*: this is also known as *cascading*, because the system would automatically delete all child associations with the parent entity. Using the same example as (1), the children records in Order Items would automatically be deleted. While this option ensures referential integrity, it can be dangerous because it might delete records that are otherwise important to keep.
3. *Default Value*: the use of a default value is the same as in insertion, that is, it allows a "dummy" row to be inserted into the parent. This means that the original parent is deleted, and the child records are redirected to some default value row in the parent entity. This is sometimes useful when there are many old parent records, such as old part-numbers, which are cluttering up the parent database. If keeping the child records is still important, they can be redirected to a default parent row, such as "Old Part-Number."
4. *Algorithm*: the use of the algorithm is the same as with an insertion. As in the case of (3) above, the default value might be based on the type of product or year it became obsolete.
5. *Null*: as in the case of insertion, the assigning of a null means that the parent does not exist. This creates a situation where the child records become "orphans." Referential integrity is lost.
6. *Don't Care*: same as in insertion. The database allows parent records to be deleted without checking to see if there are corresponding child records in another entity. This also results in losing referential integrity and creates "orphans."

In summary, key business rules are concerned with the behavior of primary keys during insert and delete operations. There are six alternative options within each operation (insert and delete). Four of the options uphold referential integrity, which is defined as the dependability of the relationships between items of data. Data integrity is an issue any time there is change to data, which in e-commerce systems will be frequent. Thus, the e-commerce analyst must ensure that once primary keys have been determined, it is of vital importance that users are interviewed regarding their referential integrity needs. Analysts should not make these decisions in a vacuum and need to present the advantages of referential integrity appropriately to users so that they can make intelligent and well-informed decisions.

Fig. 9.19 The Client
entity

```
Clients
-Key Data ──────────
Client_Id  [PK1]
-Non-Key Data ──────────
Client_Name
Client_Address
Client_Age
Client_Quality_Indicator
```

Fig. 9.20 The Customer
entity

```
Customers
-Key Data ──────────
Customer_Id  [PK1]
-Non-Key Data──────────
Customer_Name
Customer_Address
Customer_Buyer_Indicator
Customer_Credit_Rating
```

This discussion of key business rules was predicated on using examples derived from the discussion on normalization. As discussed earlier in this section, the application of normalization occurs after the determination of key business rules, especially since it may indeed affect the design of the ERD, and in the programming of stored procedures. This will be discussed further in the Determine Domains and Triggering Operations' section of this chapter.

Combining User Views

The application of normalization focused on breaking up or decomposing entities to include the correct placement of data. Each NF failure resulted in creating a new entity; however, there are situations where certain entities may need to be combined. This section is labeled "Combining User Views" because the meaning of data is strongly dependent on how the user defines a data element. Unfortunately, there are circumstances where data elements are called different things and defined differently by different users in different departments. The word "different" is critical to the example. In cases where we think we have two entities, we may, in fact, have only one. Therefore, the process of combining user views typically results in joining two or more entities as opposed to decomposing them as done with normalization. The best way to understand this concept is to recall the earlier discussion on logical equivalents. This interpretation of the logical equivalent will focus on the data rather than the process. Suppose there are two entities created from two different departments. The first department defines the elements for an entity called "Clients" as shown in Fig. 9.19.

The second department defines an entity called "Customers" as shown in Fig. 9.20.

Fig. 9.21 Combined client
and customer entity

```
Customers
- Key Data ─────────────────────
Customer_Id   [PK1]
- Non-Key Data ──────────────────
Customer_Name
Customer_Address
Customer_Buyer_Indicator
Customer_Credit_Rating
Customer_Age
Customer_Quality_Indicator
```

Upon a closer analysis and review of the data element definitions, it becomes apparent that the two departments are looking at the same object. Notwithstanding whether the entity is named Client or Customer, these entities must be combined. The process of combining two or more entities is not as simple as it might sound. In the two examples, there are data elements that are the same with different names, and there are unique data elements in each entity. Each department is unaware of the other's view of the same data, and by applying logical equivalencies, the following single-entity results are shown in Fig. 9.21.

The example in Fig. 9.21 uses names that made it easier for an analyst to know they were the same data elements. In reality, such may not be the case, especially when working with legacy systems. In legacy systems, names and definitions of elements can vary significantly among departments and applications. Furthermore, the data definitions can vary significantly. Suppose Client is defined as VARCHAR2(35) and Customer as VARCHAR2(20). The solution is to take the larger definition. Instilling other scenarios, one element could be defined as alphanumeric and the other numeric. In these circumstances the decisions become more involved with user conversations. In either situation, it is important that the data elements do get combined and that users agree to agree. In cases where user agreement is difficult, then analysts can take advantage of a data dictionary feature called Alias. An Alias is defined as an alternate name for a data element. Multiple Aliases can point to the same data dictionary entry. Therefore, screens can display names that are Aliases for another element. This alternative can solve many problems when using different names is necessary.

Another important issue in combining user views is performance. While analysts should not be overly concerned about performance issues during LDM, it should not be ignored either. Simply put, the fewer entities, the faster the performance; therefore, the least number of entities that can be designed in the ERD, the better.

Integration with Existing Data Models

The purpose of this section is to discuss specific analysis and design issues relating to how to integrate with existing database applications. The connectivity with other database systems is difficult. Indeed, many firms approach the situation by phasing each business area over time into a new redeveloped operation. In these circumstances, each phased area needs a "legacy link" which allows the "old" applications to work with the new phased-in software. Chapter 10 will focus on the procedures for integration of both the data and application components of packaged software systems. This section is limited to only those issues that affect the design of entities during LDM.

Linking entities with existing databases may force e-commerce analysts to rethink how to preserve integrity while still maintaining the physical link to other corporate data. This occurrence is a certainty with e-commerce systems given that certain portions of the data are used inside and outside the business. The following example shows how this problem occurs:

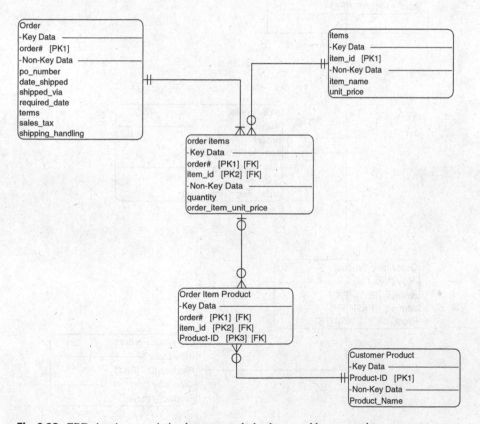

Fig. 9.22 ERD showing association between web databases and legacy employee master

The analyst is

> designing a website that utilizes the company's Orders Master database. The website needs this information to allow customers to see information about their past orders for items so they can match it to a product database supplied by the e-commerce system. This feature is provided to customers to allow them to understand how items have been utilized to make their products. Unfortunately, the master Order Item database holds only orders for the past year and then stores them off-line. There is no desire by the Order department to create a historical tracking system. The ERD in Fig. 9.22 shows the relationships with the corporate Order Item database file.

Note that the Order Item Product entity has a one or zero relationship with the Order Item Master entity. This means that there can be an Order Item in the Order

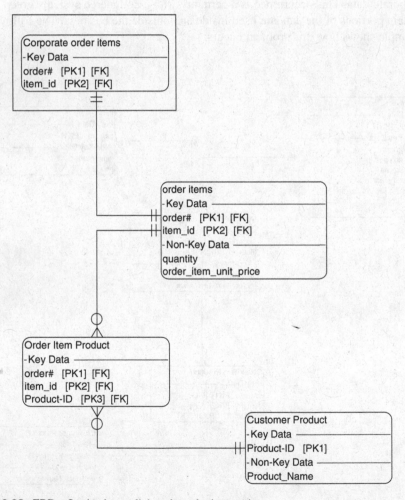

Fig. 9.23 ERD reflecting legacy link to the order item entity

Item Product entity that does not exist in the Order Item entity. Not only does this violate normalization; it also presents a serious integrity problem. For example, if the customer wanted to display information about their products and each component Item, all Items that do not exist in the Order Item entity will display blanks, since there is no corresponding name information in the Order Item file. Obviously this is a flaw in the database design that needs to be corrected. The remedy is to build a subsystem database that will capture all of the Order items without purging them. This would entail a system that accesses the Order Item database and merges it with the Web version of the file. The merge conversion would compare the two files and update or add new Order items without deleting the old ones. That is, the master Order Items would be searched daily to pick up new Order Items to add to the Web version. Although this is an extra step, it maintains integrity, normalization, and, most importantly, the requirement not to modify the original Order Item database. The drawback to this solution is that the Web version may not have up-to-date Order Item information. This will depend on how often records are moved to the Web database. This can be remedied by having a replication feature, where the Web Order Item would be created at the same time as the master version. The ERD would be reconstructed as shown in Fig. 9.23.

In the diagram shown in Fig. 9.23 the Order Item master and its relation to the Web Order Item entity are shown for informational purposes only. The master Order Item becomes more of an application requirement rather than a permanent part of the ERD. In order to "operationalize" this system, the analyst must first have to reconstruct the history data from the purged files or simply offer the historical data as of a certain date.

Determining Domains and Triggering Operations

The growth of the relational database model has established processes for storing certain application logic at the database level. We have already defined key business rules as the vehicle to create constraints at the key attribute level. However, there are other constraints and procedures that can occur depending on the behavior of non-key attributes. Ultimately, business rules are application logic that is coded in the database language, for example, PL_SQL for Oracle. These non-key attribute rules could enforce such actions as: If CITY is entered, the STATE must also be entered. This type of logic rule used to be enforced at the application level. Unfortunately, using application logic to enforce business rules is inefficient because it requires the code to be replicated in each application program. This process also limits control, in that the relational model allows users to "query" the database directly. Thus, business rules at the database level need to be written only once, and they govern all types of applications, including programs and queries.

As stated earlier, business rules are implemented at the database level via stored procedures. Stored procedures are offered by most database manufacturers, and although they are similar, they are not implemented using the same coding schemes.

Therefore, moving stored procedures from one database to another is not trivial. In Chap. 8, the importance of having portable stored procedures and their relationship to partitioning databases across the Internet, intranets, and wide area networks (WANs) will be discussed further. It is important to note that distributed network systems are being built under the auspices of client/server computing and may require communication among many different database vendor systems. If business rules are to be implemented at the database level, the compatibility and transportability of such code become a challenge.

Business rule implementations fall into three categories: keys, domains, and triggers. Key business rules have already been discussed as part of the normalization process. Domains represent the constraints related to an attribute's range of values. If an attribute (key or non-key) can have a range of values from one to nine, we say that range is the domain value of the attribute. This is very important information to be included and enforced at the database level through a stored procedure for the same reasons as discussed above. The third and most powerful business rule is triggers.

Triggers are defined as stored procedures that when activated "trigger" one or a set of other stored procedures to be executed. Triggers act on other entities, although in many database products, triggers are becoming powerful programming tools to provide significant capabilities at the database level rather than at the application level. Triggers resemble batch-type files which when invoked execute a "script" or set of logical statements as shown below:

```
/* Within D. B.. only authorized users can mark  */
  /* ecommerce corporation as confidential '*/
  if user not in ('L','M') then
  :new.corpConfidential := 'N';
  end if;
end if;
/* Ensure user has right to make a specific users private */
if exec= 'N' then
  :new.corpexec:= 'N';
end if;
```

This trigger was implemented in a contact management e-commerce system. The trigger is designed to allow corporate information to be marked as confidential only by specific executives. This means that an appointed executive of the corporation can enter information that is private. The second component of the trigger is programmed to automatically ensure that the executive's contacts are stored as private or confidential. These two stored procedures show how application logic executes via Oracle triggers. It is important to remember that these business rules are enforced by the database regardless of how the information is accessed.

Triggers, however, can cause problems. Because triggers can initiate activity among database files, designers must be careful that they do not impair performance. For example, suppose a trigger is written that affects 15 different database

files. Should the trigger be initiated during the processing of other critical applications, it could cause significant degradation in processing and thus affect critical production systems.

The subject of business rules is very broad yet must be specific to the actual database product to be used. Since analysts may not know which database will ultimately be used, specifications for stored procedures should be developed using the specification formats presented in Chap. 3. This is even more salient in e-commerce systems given the possibility that different databases can be used across the entire system. This dilemma will be discussed in Chap. 8 as part of the integration issues facing e-commerce analysts and designers.

De-Normalization

Third NF databases can often have difficulty with performance. Specifically, significant numbers of look-up tables, which are actual third NF failures, create too many index links. As a result, while we have reached the integrity needed, performance becomes an unavoidable dilemma. In fact, the more integrity, the less performance. There are a number of ways to deal with the downsides of normalized databases. One is to develop data warehouses and other off-line copies of the database. Data warehousing will be discussed in Chap. 12: Database Query, Report, and Transaction Processing. Another alternative is to de-normalize. There are many bad ways to de-normalize. Indeed, any de-normalization hurts integrity. But there are two types of de-normalization that can be implemented without significantly hurting the integrity of the data.

The first type of de-normalization is to revisit third NF failures to see if all of the validations are necessary. Third NF failures usually create tables that ensure that entered values are validated against a master list. For example, in Fig. 9.10, the Customer entity, created as a result of a third NF failure, provides a validation to all customers associated with an Order. This means that the user cannot assign any customer, but rather only those residents in the Customer entity. The screen to select a Customer would most likely use a "drop-down" menu, which would show all of the valid Customers for selection to the Order. However, there may be look-up tables that are not as critical. For example, zip codes may or may not be validated. Whether zip codes need to be validated depends on the use of zip codes by the users. If they are just used to record a Customer address, then it may not be necessary or worthwhile to have the zip code validated. If, on the other hand, they are used for certain types of geographic analysis or mailing, then, indeed, validation is necessary. This process—the process of reviewing the use and need for a validation table—should occur during the interview process. If this step is left out, then there is a high probability that too many non-key attributes will contain validation look-up entities that are unnecessary and hurt performance.

The second type of de-normalization is to add back "derived" attributes. While this is not the preferred method, it can be implemented without sacrificing integrity. This can be accomplished by creating triggers that automatically launch a stored

procedure to recalculate a derived value when a dependent attribute has been altered. For example, if Amount is calculated based on Quantity * Unit Price, then two triggers must be developed (one for Quantity and one for Unit Price) which would recalculate Amount if either Quantity or Unit Price were changed. While this solves the integrity issue, analysts must be cognizant over the performance conflict should the trigger be initiated during peak processing times. Therefore, there must be a balance between the trigger and when it is allowed to occur.

Summary

This chapter has provided the logical equivalent to the data component of the e-commerce system. The process of decomposing data is accomplished using LDM, which has eight major steps that need to be applied in order to functionally decompose the data. Data flow diagrams (DFDs) are a powerful tool to use during process analysis because they provide direct input into the LDM method. Specifically, data flows provide data definitions into the data dictionary, which is necessary to complete LDM. Furthermore, data stores in the DFD represent the major entities, which is the first step in LDM. The output of LDM is an ERD, which represents the schematic or blueprint of the database. The ERD shows the relationships among entities and the cardinality of those relationships.

The LDM also makes provisions to develop stored procedures, which are programs developed at the database level. These procedures allow "referential integrity" to be enforced without developing application programs that operate outside the data. Stored procedures can be used to enforce key business rules, domain rules, and triggers. Triggers are batch-oriented programs that automatically execute when a particular condition has occurred at the database level, typically, when an attribute has been altered in some way.

The process of LDM also allows for the de-normalization at the logical design level. This is allowed so that analysts can avoid significant known performance problems before the physical database is completed. De-normalization should occur at the user-interface time, as many of the issues will depend on the user's needs.

Problems and Exercises

1. What is logical data modeling trying to accomplish?
2. Define normalization. What are the three normal forms?
3. What does normalization not do?
4. What is meant by the term "derived" data element?
5. Describe the concept of combining user views. What are the political ramifications of doing this in many organizations?
6. What are legacy links ? Describe how they can be used to enforce data integrity.
7. Name and define the three types of business rules.

8. Why are stored procedures in some ways a contradiction to the rule that data and processes need to be separated?
9. What are the disadvantages of database triggers?
10. What is meant by de-normalization? Is this a responsibility of the analyst?

Mini-Project

The Physician Master File from a DFD contains the following data elements:

Data element	Description
Social Security #	Primary Key
Physician ID	Alternate Key
Last_Name	Last Name
First_Name	First Name
Mid_Init	Middle Initial
Hospital_Resident_ID	Hospital Identification
Hospital_Resident_Name	Name of Hospital
Hospital_Addr_Line1	Hospital Address
Hospital_Addr_Line2	Hospital Address
Hospital_Addr_Line3	Hospital Address
Hospital_State	Hospital's State
Hospital_City	Hospital's City
Hospital_Zip	Hospital's Zip Code
Specialty_Type	The Physician's specialty
Specialty_Name	Description of specialty
Specialty_College	College where received degree
Specialty_Degree	Degree Name
Date_Graduated	Graduation Date for specialty
DOB	Physician's Date of Birth
Year_First_Practiced	First year in practice
Year's_Pract_Exp	Practice Experience Years
Annual_Earnings	Annual Income

Assumptions:
a. A physician can be associated with many hospitals, but must be associated with at least one.
b. A physician can have many specialties or have no specialty. Assignment: Normalize to third normal form.

References

Date, C. J. (2000). *An introduction to database systems* (7th ed.). New York: Addison-Wesley.

Fleming, C., & von Halle, B. (1989). *Handbook of relational database design*. Menlo Park: Addison-Wesley.

Whitten, J. L., & Bentley, L. D. (2007). *Systems analysis and design methods* (7th ed.). New York: Mc Graw Hill.

Legacy Systems and Integration

10

Introduction

A legacy system is an existing application system in operation. While this is an accurate definition, there is a perception that legacy systems are old and antiquated applications operating on mainframe computers. Indeed, Brodie and Stonebraker (1995) state that "a legacy information system is any information system that significantly resists modification and evolution" (p. 3). They define typical legacy systems as:

- Large application with millions of lines of code.
- Usually more than 10 years old.
- Written in legacy languages like COBOL.
- They are built around a legacy database service (such as IBM's IMS) and some do not use a database management system. Instead they use older flat-file systems such as ISAM and VSAM.
- The applications are very autonomous. Legacy applications tend to operate independently from other applications, which means that there is very limited interface among application programs. When interfaces among applications are available, they are usually based on export and import models of data, and these interfaces lack data consistency.

While many legacy systems do fit these scenarios, many do not. Those that do not can, however, be considered legacies under my original definition, that is, any application in operation. What this simply means is that there are what I call "generations" of legacy systems that can exist in any organization. Thus, the definitions of what constitutes a legacy system are much broader than Brodie and Stonebraker's descriptions. The more important issue to address is the relationship of legacy systems with packaged software systems. In Chap. 1, I defined a packaged software systems as one that encompassed both internal and external applications. Thus, existing internal production systems, including third-party outsourced products,

© Springer-Verlag London Limited 2016
A.M. Langer, *Guide to Software Development*,
DOI 10.1007/978-1-4471-6799-0_10

must be part of any application strategy. Furthermore, there are many legacy systems that perform external functions as well, albeit not in an Internet interface.

This chapter defines the type of legacy systems that exist and provides guidelines on how to approach their integration with packaged software applications. The project manager or analyst must determine whether a legacy system should be replaced, be enhanced, or remain as is. This chapter also provides the procedures for dealing with each of these three choices and its effect on the overall architecture of the decision whether to make or buy a system.

Types of Legacy Systems

The types of legacy systems tend to mirror the life cycle of software development. Software development is usually defined within a framework called "generations." Most professionals agree that there are five generations of programming languages:

1. *First generation*: the first generation was known as machine language. Machine language is considered a low-level language because it uses binary symbols to communicate instructions to the hardware. These binary symbols form a one-to-one relationship between a machine language command and a machine activity, that is, one machine language command performs one machine instruction. It is rare that any legacy systems have first-generation software.
2. *Second generation*: this generation was comprised of assembler programming languages. Assembler languages are proprietary software that translates a higher-level coding scheme into more than one machine language instruction. Therefore, it was necessary to design an assembler, which would translate the symbolic codes into machine instructions. Mainframe shops still may have a considerable amount of assembly code that exists, particularly with applications that perform intricate algorithms and calculations.
3. *Third generation*: these languages continued the growth of high-level symbolic languages that had translators into machine code. Examples of third-generation languages are COBOL, FORTRAN, BASIC, RPG, and C. These languages use more English-like commands and have a higher ratio of machine language produced from one instruction. Third-generation languages tend to be more specialized. For example, FORTRAN is better suited for mathematical and scientific calculations. Therefore, many insurance companies have FORTRAN because of the high concentration on actuarial mathematic calculations. COBOL, on the other hand, was designed as the business language and has special features to allow it to manipulate file and database information. There are more COBOL applications that exist than any other programming language. Most mainframe legacy systems still have COBOL applications. RPG is yet another specialized language that was designed for use on IBM's midrange machines. These machines include the System 36, System 38, and AS/400 computers.

4. *Fourth generation (4GL)*: these programming languages are less procedural than third-generation languages. In addition, the symbols are more English-like and emphasize more about desired output results than how the programming statements need to be written. As a result of this feature, many less technical programmers have learned how to program using 4GLs. The most powerful features of 4GLs include query of databases, code generation, and graphic screen generation abilities. Such languages include Visual Basic, C++, Visual Basic, PowerBuilder, Delphi, and many others. Furthermore, 4GL languages also include what is known as *query languages* because they contain English-like questions that are used to directly produce results by directly accessing relational databases. The most popular 4GL query language is Structured Query Language (SQL).

5. *Fifth generation*: these programming languages combine what is known as rule-based code generation, component management, and visual programming techniques. The rule-based code generation became popular in the late 1980s with the creation of artificial intelligence software. This software uses an approach called knowledge-based programming, which means that the developer does not tell the computer how to solve problems, but rather the problem (Stair and Reynolds 1999). The program figures out how to solve the problem. While knowledge-based programming has become popular in specialized applications, such as in the medical industry, it has not been as popular in business.

Most legacy applications will either be third- or fourth-generation language systems; therefore, analysts need to have a process and methodology to determine how to integrate packaged software technology with these applications.

Third-Generation Language Legacy System Integration

As previously discussed, most third-generation language legacy systems were developed using COBOL. COBOL was developed to provide a method of forcing programmers to self-document their code so that other programmers could maintain it. Unfortunately, COBOL requires what is known as a File Description table (FD). The FD defines the record layout for every file used by the COBOL program. In other words, every file is described within the program and must match the format of the actual physical data file. This means that any change to a file structure must be synchronized with every COBOL program that uses that data file. Thus, COBOL is somewhat eclectic: there is no real separation of the data description and the program logic. In COBOL programs then, a change in data format could necessitate a change in the program code. That is why COBOL programs suffer from large degrees of coupling of code. Coupling is defined as the reliance of one piece of the code on another.

COBOL programs may or may not use a relational database as its source of data. I earlier defined two other common formats called ISAM and VSAM, which are flat-file formats, meaning that all data elements are contained in one record as

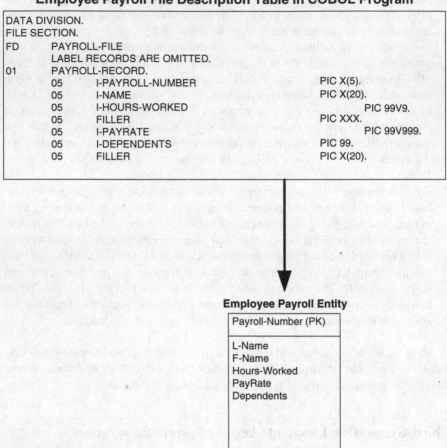

Fig. 10.1 COBOL File Description interface with database manager

opposed to multiple files as is the case in the relational database model. However, many COBOL legacy systems have been converted to work with relational databases such as IBM's DB2. In this situation the FD tables interface with the database's file manager so that the two entities can communicate with each other. Figure 10.1 depicts the interface between program and database.

Notwithstanding whether the COBOL legacy is using a database interface or flat files, the analyst needs to determine whether to replace the application, enhance it, or leave it as is.

```
FD      REPORT-FILE
        LABEL RECORDS ARE OMITTED.
01      REPORT-RECORD.
        05      O-PAYROLL-NUMBER                    PIC X(5).
        05      FILLER                              PIC XX.
        05      O-NAME                              PIC X(20).
        05      FILLER                              PIC XX.
        05      O-HOURS-WORKED                      PIC 99.9.
        05      FILLER                              PIC XX.
        05      O-PAYRATE                           PIC 99.999.
        05      FILLER                              PIC XX.
        05      O-DEPENDENTS                        PIC 99.
        05      FILLER                              PIC XX.
        05      O-GROSS-PAY                         PIC 999.99.
        05      FILLER                              PIC XX.
        05      O-TAX                               PIC 999.99.
        05      FILLER                              PIC XX.
        05      O-NET-PAY                           PIC 999.99.
```

Fig. 10.2 COBOL File Description tables

Replacing Third-Generation Legacy Systems

When replacing third-generation legacies, analysts must focus on both the data and processes. Because of the age of these systems, it is likely that there will be little documentation available, and the amount available will most likely be outdated. Indeed, the lack of proper documentation is the major reason why legacy systems are slow to be replaced: rewriting code without documentation can be an overwhelming and time-consuming task. Unfortunately, all things must eventually be replaced. Delaying replacement leads to legacy systems that keep businesses from remaining competitive. The following sections provide a step-by-step approach to COBOL-based legacies.

Approaches to Logic Reconstruction

The best way to reconstruct the logic in COBOL applications is to separate the data from the processes. This can be accomplished by creating data flow diagrams (DFD) for each program. Having a DFD will result in defining all of the inputs and outputs of the application. This is accomplished by following the tasks below:

1. Print the source code (actual COBOL written code) from each application. Each application will contain an "FD" section that defines all of the inputs and outputs of the program. These will represent the data stores of the data flow diagrams (Fig. 10.2).
2. DFDs should be decomposed so that they are at the functional primitive level (one-in and one-out, preferred). This provides functional decomposition for the

old application and sets the framing for how it will be decomposed into an object-oriented solution.

3. By reviewing the code, write the process specifications for each functional primitive.

4. Follow the steps as outlined in Chap. 8 to determine which functional primitive DFDs become methods of a particular class.

5. Capture all of the data elements or attributes required by each functional primitive DFD. These attributes are added to the data dictionary (DD).

6. Take each major data store and create an entity. Do normalization and logic data modeling in accordance with the procedures in Chap. 4, combining these elements with the packaged software system as appropriate.

7. Data stores that represent reports should be compared against sample outputs. These reports will need to be redeveloped using a report writer such as Crystal's report writer or a data warehouse product.

8. Examine all existing data files and/or databases in the legacy system. Compare these elements against those discovered during the Logic Reconstruction. In third-generation products, there will be many data elements or fields that are redundant or used as logic "flags." Logic flags consist of fields used to store a value that depicts a certain state of the data. For example, suppose a record has been updated by a particular program. One method of knowing that this occurred is to have the application program set a certain field with a code that identifies that it has been updated. This method would not be necessary in a relational database product because file managers automatically keep logs on the last time a record has been updated. This example illustrates how different third-generation legacy technology differs from more contemporary technologies.

There is no question that replacing third-generation legacies is time consuming. However, the procedures outlined above will prove to be accurate and effective. In many situations, users will decide that it makes sense to reexamine their legacy processes, especially when the decision has been made to rewrite the program and integrate it with packaged software system. We call this business process reengineering. Business process reengineering is therefore synonymous with enhancing the legacy system (see Chap. 11).

Enhancing Third-Generation Legacy Systems

Business process reengineering (BPR) is one of the more popular methodologies used to enhance third-generation applications. A more formal definition of BPR is "a requirement to study fundamental business processes, independent of organization units and information systems support, to determine if the underlying business processes can be significantly streamlined and improved."[1] BPR is not just

[1] Whitten, Jeffrey, Bentley, Lonnie, Barlow, Victor, Systems Analysis & Design Methods, Third Edition, pg. 238.

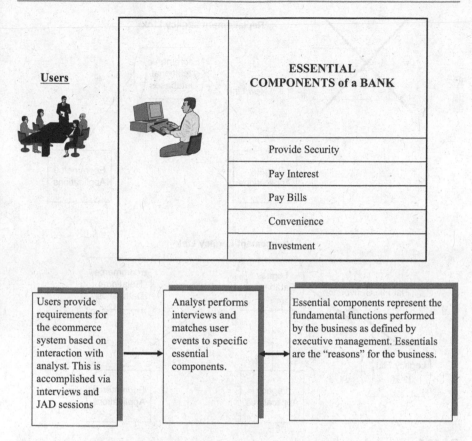

Fig. 10.3 Essential components of a bank

rebuilding the existing applications for the sake of applying new technology to older systems but also an event that allows for the application of new procedures designed around the object-oriented systems paradigm. In this scenario, however, BPR is used to enhance existing applications without rewriting them in another generation language. Instead, the analyst needs to make changes to the system that will make it function more like an object component even though it is written in a third-generation language. In order to accomplish this task, it is necessary for the analyst to create the essential components of the legacy operation. Essential components represent the core business requirements of a unit. Another way of defining core business requirements is to view essential components as the reasons why the unit exists—what does it do—and for what reasons. For example, Fig. 10.3 depicts the essential components of a bank.

Once the essential components have been created, then the legacy applications need to be placed in the appropriate component so that it can be linked with its related packaged software applications.

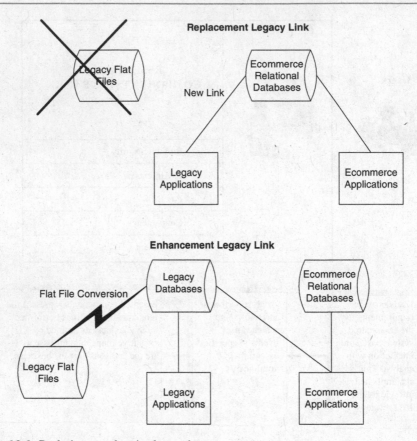

Fig. 10.4 Replacing vs. enhancing legacy data

The first step to applying successful BPR to legacy applications is to develop an approach to defining the existing system and extracting its data elements and applications. Once again, this is similar to the process described in Fig. 10.3 when replacing third-generation legacy applications in that the data needs to be captured into the data repository, and the applications need to be defined and compared to a new model based on essential components.

Data Element Enhancements

The analyst will need to design conversion programs that will access the data files that are not in relational database format and place them in a data repository. The ultimate focus is to replace all of the existing data files in the legacy with relational databases that can be linked with packaged software databases. This methodology differs from replacing legacies. In replacement engineering, data files are integrated directly into a packaged software system. This means that the legacy data will often

be used to enhance the packaged software databases. However, the process of enhancing legacy systems means that the legacy data will remain separate but converted into the relational model. For legacies that already have relational databases, there is no restructuring required beyond setting up links with the packaged software database. Figure 10.4 reflects the difference between replacing legacy data and enhancing it.

Another interesting difference between the two approaches is that enhanced legacies will likely have intentional data redundancy. This means that the same element may indeed exist in multiple databases, a violation of third-normal form. However, the redundancy must exist for the sake of maintaining separate identities of the systems. Duplicate elements may take on different formats. The most obvious is where a data element has alias, meaning that an element has many different names, but the same attributes. Another type is the same element name, but with different attributes. The third type, and the most challenging, is the duplicate elements that have different names and different attributes. While duplicate data elements may exist in enhanced legacy applications that are integrated with the packaged software product, it is still important to identify duplicate data relationships. This can be accomplished by documenting data relationships in a CASE tool and in the database's physical data dictionary where aliases can exist.

Application Enhancements

BPR typically involves a methodology called Business Area Analysis (BAA). The purpose of BAA is to:

- Establish the various legacy business areas that will be linked with the packaged software system.
- Reengineer the new and old requirements of each business area.
- Develop requirements that provide an OO perspective of each legacy business area, meaning that there is no need to map its requirements to the existing physical organization structure.
- Define the links that create relationships among all the legacy business areas and the packaged software business areas.

This is accomplished by mapping business areas to specific essential component. Applications designed for the packaged software system must also be mapped to an essential component. Once this has occurred, the legacy applications and packaged software applications must be designed to share common processes and databases as shown in Fig. 10.5. BPR is discussed further in Chap. 11.

Once the legacy and packaged software applications have been placed in their appropriate essential component, they will need to be linked, that is, communicate with each other to complete the integration of the internal and external systems. Linking occurs in two ways: parameter messaging and database. Parameter messaging requires that the legacy programs be modified to receive data in the form of

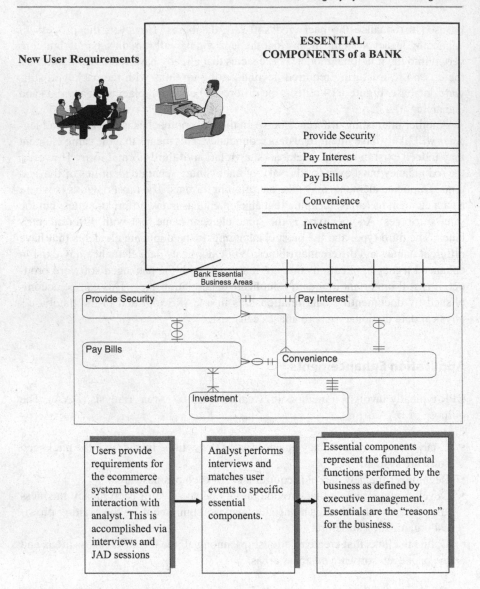

Fig. 10.5 BPR legacy modeling using essential components

parameters. This allows the application system to deliver information directly to the legacy program. Conversely, the legacy program may need to return information back to the packaged software system. Therefore, legacy applications need to be enhanced so they can actually format and send a data message to the packaged software system. A database interface is essentially the same concept except that it occurs differently. Instead of the application sending the data directly to another

Fig. 10.6 Linking data between legacy and packaged software systems

Legacy Link Using a Parameter

Data as a Parameter

Legacy Applications

New Applications

Legacy Link using a Database

Legacy Link Databases

Legacy Applications

New Applications

program, it forwards it as a record in a database file. The legacy program that returns the data also needs to be modified to forward messages to a database.

There are advantages and disadvantages of using either method. First, parameters use little overhead and are easy to program. They do not provide reusable data, that is, once a message has been received, it is no longer available to another program. Parameters are also limited in size. Databases, on the other hand, allow programs to send the information to multiple destinations because it can be read many times. Unfortunately, it is difficult to control what applications or queries can access the data, which does raise questions about how secure the data is. Furthermore, applications must remember to delete a record in the database if it is no longer required. Figure 10.6 reflects the two methods of transferring data between legacy systems and packaged software applications.

Once the legacy and the new packaged software applications have all been mapped to the essential components, analysts can use a CRUD diagram to assist them in reconciling whether all of the data and processes have been found. The importance of the CRUD diagram is that it ensures:

• That an essential component has complete control over its data
• That all of the entities are accessible by at least one process
• That processes are accessing data (Fig. 10.7)

While CRUD is not 100 % accurate, it certainly uncovers potential problems. Even if BPR is not used, the CRUD diagram is an excellent tool to use to determine the processes and data needed for an essential component or an object. Once the

Processes or Business Function / Data Subject or Entity	Process Orders	Validate Products	Shipping	Commission
Customers	R		R,U	
Orders	C,U		U	R
Items	R	C,U,D	R	R
Inventory	R,U	C,U	U	
Expense Section				
Market Person	R			U

Fig. 10.7 Sample CRUD diagram

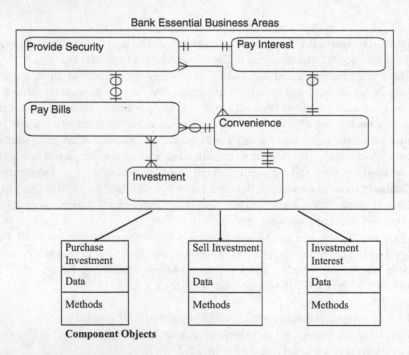

Fig. 10.8 Essential component object diagrams

CRUD diagram is finalized, the objects and classes would then be created as shown in Fig. 10.8; some of these objects are still in the form of a third-generation COBOL program, while others might be in a JAVA-based packaged software format. CRUD is discussed in more detail in Chap. 11.

"Leaving As Is":Third-Generation Legacy Systems

Moving to an object-oriented and client/server paradigm from a third-generation product like COBOL may not be feasible. The language design of third-generation procedural programs may result in conceptual gaps between procedural and object-oriented philosophies. For example, distributed object-oriented programs require more detailed technical infrastructure knowledge, and graphics manipulation then was required in older legacy systems. Native object-oriented features such as inheritance, polymorphism, and encapsulation do not apply in traditional third-generation procedural design. It is difficult, if not impossible, to introduce new object concepts and philosophies during a direct COBOL to JAVA migration. If the translation is attempted without significant restructuring (as discussed earlier in this chapter), then the resulting product will likely contain slower code that is more difficult to maintain.

There can also be a cultural divide that occurs. Veteran COBOL programmers and newer JAVA developers do not understand each other's technologies. This scenario will often create bias during any conversion effort. Furthermore, COBOL programmers learning new technology can present them with self-specified threats to their cultural status. Furthermore, COBOL and RPG applications have benefited from the more lengthy testing, debugging, and overall refinement than newer programming generations. While JAVA is more dynamic, it is less stable, and the procedure of debugging and fixing problems is very different than for COBOL or RPG. Therefore, the analyst will leave the legacy "as is" and create only packaged software links for passing information that is required between the two systems. While this is similar to the "linking" proposed for enhancing legacy systems, it is different because legacy programs are not enhanced, except for the external links needed to pass information. This is graphically shown in Fig. 10.9.

Using parameters or databases to link connecting information is still relevant, but analysts must be cognizant that legacy data formats will not be changed. This means that the legacy applications will continue to use their original file formats. Another concept used to describe "links" is called "bridges." The word suggests that the link serves to connect a gap between the packaged software system and the legacy applications. Bridging can also imply temporary link. Very often "as is" can be seen as a temporary condition because legacy conversions cannot occur all at once, so it is typically planned in phases. However, while parts of the system are being converted, some portions may need temporary bridges until it is time to actually enhance them. One can visualize this as a temporary "road block" or detour that occurs when there is construction on a highway.

Fig. 10.9 "As is" legacy links

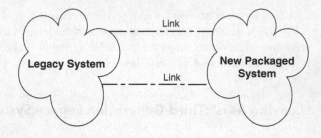

```
Select   IdNo, Last-Name, First-Name
from     employee
where    IDNo = "054475643"
```

Fig. 10.10 SELECT statements in a fourth-generation language application

Fourth-Generation Language Legacy System Integration

Integrating fourth-generation legacy systems with packaged software technology is much easier than third-generation languages. The reasons are twofold. First, most fourth-generation implementations are already using a relational database, so conversion of data to the packaged software system is less complex. Second, fourth-generation language applications typically use SQL-based code, so conversion to an object-oriented system is also less involved.

Replacing Fourth-Generation Legacy Systems

As stated above, replacement of fourth-generation language systems is less complex than third-generation languages with respect to the packaged software conversion. As with any systems replacement, separating data and process is the suggested approach. Fortunately, in fourth-generation language systems, process and data are likely to already be separate, because of the nature of its architecture. Specifically, fourth-generation languages typically use relational databases, which architecturally separate data and process. Therefore, replacing the legacy is more about examining the existing processes and determining where the applications need to be reengineered.

Approaches to Logic Reconstruction

The best approach to logic analysis is to print out the source code of the programs. If the source is written in SQL, then the analyst should search for all SELECT statements. SQL SELECT FROM statements define the databases that the program is using as shown in Fig. 10.10.

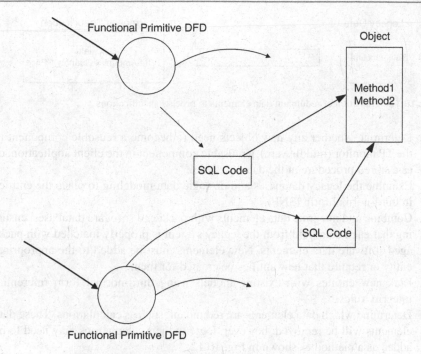

Fig. 10.11 SQL code transition to object method

As in third-generation languages Logic Reconstruction, the analyst should produce a DFD for every program as follows:

1. SELECT statements define all inputs and outputs that a program uses. Each SELECT statement file will be represented by a DFD data store. Reviewing the logic of the application program will reveal whether the data is being created, read, updated, or deleted (CRUD).
2. DFDs should be decomposed to the functional primitive level so that the framework to an object-oriented system is established.
3. For each DFD copy the relevant SQL code, making modifications where necessary to provide more object-oriented functionality to the program. This means that the decomposition of the code will likely require that some new logic be added to transform it to a method. This is shown in Fig. 10.11.
4. Examine existing systems objects and determine if functional primitive DFDs belong to an existing class as a new method or whether it truly represents a new object in the packaged software system.
5. Capture all of the data elements required by the new methods and add them to their respective object. Ensure that the packaged software DD is updated appropriately.

Fig. 10.12 Transition of redundant data elements to process specifications

6. Determine whether any new objects need to become a reusable component in the TP monitor (middleware), a reusable component in the client application, or as a stored procedure at the database level.
7. Examine the legacy databases and do logic data modeling to place the entities in third-normal form (3NF).
8. Combine and integrate data elements with packaged software databases, ensuring that each data field from the legacy system is properly matched with packaged software data elements. New elements must be added to the appropriate entity or require that new entities be created for them.
9. Link new entities with existing models using third-normal form referential integrity rules.
10. Determine which data elements are redundant, such as calculations. These data elements will be removed; however, logic to their calculations may need to be added as a method as shown in Fig. 10.12.

Enhancing Fourth-Generation Legacy Systems

Enhancing fourth-generation language legacy systems is really the process of converting it to an object-oriented client/server system. BPR (business process reengineering) is also used on fourth-generation language legacy systems to accomplish this transition. The process, as one might expect, is much easier than for third-generation languages; however, the process of determining essential components is the same in both types of systems. Once essential components are established, the existing applications need to be decomposed and realigned as appropriate. This is accomplished by using BAA, as it was used for third-generation legacy applications. The fact that fourth-generation languages are less procedural than third-generation languages greatly assists this transition. Fourth-generation language systems, by simply looking at the SQL SELECT statements, can identify which data files are used by the application. Using logic modularity rules, an analyst can establish cohesive classes based on applications that use the same data. This can be accomplished without using DFDs, although reengineering using DFDs is always a more thorough method for analysts to follow.

Linkage of fourth-generation language legacy and packaged software applications needs to be accomplished after application reengineering is completed. As with third-generation language systems, this can either be accomplished using a data parameter or the creation of a special database. However, with

Fig. 10.13 Fourth-generation language legacy-shared database architecture

fourth-generation languages, it is likely that application integration will occur using databases, since both systems use them in their native architectures. An analyst will most likely find that application communication with fourth-generation languages will not always require separate databases to be designed solely for the purpose of systems linkage. The more attractive solution to integration is to identify the data elements that are common between the two systems so it can be shared in a central database available to all applications as shown in Fig. 10.13.

The use of CRUD in fourth-generation languages is used less, but is certainly applicable and should be implemented by the analyst if he/she feels that the code is too procedural. In other words, the code architecture resembles third generation as opposed to fourth generation.

"Leaving As Is": Fourth-Generation Legacy Systems

The process of limiting integration to just the sharing of data is similar to the design architecture that I used for third-generation language systems. Indeed, the architecture of linking separate and distinct software systems can only be accomplished by sharing common data. Once again this data can be shared either using a data parameter or data file.

Because many fourth-generation language systems utilize the same architecture as a packaged software system (three-tier client/server using Windows NT/2000 or UNIX/LINUX), it is sometimes advantageous to make use of certain operating system-level communication facilities. For example, UNIX allows applications to pass data using an operating system facility called a "pipe." A pipe resembles a parameter, in that it allows an application to pass a message or data to another application without creating an actual new data structure, like a database. Furthermore, a pipe uses an access method called "FIFO" (first-in, first-out), which is the same access criteria used by parameters. FIFO also requires that once the data is read, it cannot be read again. The major advantage of using a pipe is that the message/data can be stored long after the application that created the message has terminated in memory. Thus linkage of information among packaged software and

Fig. 10.14 Intra-application communication using a UNIX pipe

fourth-generation language applications can be accomplished in RAM at execution time, which is called "intra-application communication." This capability reduces overhead as well as the need for separate modules to be designed that would just handle data communication as shown in Fig. 10.14.

Hybrid Methods: The Gateway Approach

Thus far in this chapter, I have focused on the interface between a specific type of legacy and a packaged software system. Each type was defined with respect to its "generation" type. In reality, however, legacy systems are not that self-defined. Many large organizations have "legacy layers," meaning that multiple generations exist throughout the enterprise. In this case, attempting to integrate each generation with a central packaged software system is difficult and time consuming. Indeed, migrating and integrating legacy systems are difficult enough. In these complex models, another method used for migration of legacy applications is a "hybrid" approach called "gateway." The gateway approach means that there will be a software module that mediates requests between the packaged software system and the legacy applications. In many ways, a gateway performs similar tasks as a TP system. Thus, the gateway acts as a broker between applications. Specifically gateways:

- Separate yet integrate components from different generation languages. It allows for the linkages among multiple generation language systems.
- Translates requests and data between multiple components.
- Coordinates between multiple components to ensure update consistency. This means that the gateway will ensure that redundant data elements are synchronized.

Typical gateway architectures would be designed as shown in Fig. 10.15.

The most beneficial role of the gateway is that it allows for the phasing of legacy components. The infrastructure provides for an incremental approach to conversion by establishing a consistent update process for both data and applications.

Fig. 10.15 Gateway architecture for Legacy Integration

Incremental Application Integration

A gateway establishes a transparency for graphical user interfaces (GUI), character-based interfaces, and automated interfaces (batch updates) to appear the same to the packaged software system. Hence, the gateway insulates the legacy system so that its interface with the packaged software systems seems seamless. This is accomplished through an interface that translates requests for process functions and routes them to their appropriate application, regardless of the generation of the software and its particular phase in the packaged software migration. Figure 10.16 depicts the process functions of the gateway system.

The most salient benefit of the gateway approach is its consistency with the object-oriented paradigm and the concept of application reusability. Specifically, it allows any module to behave "like" a reusable component notwithstanding its technical design. Under this architectural philosophy, a particular program, let's say, a third-generation language system, may eventually be replaced and placed into the gateway, with temporary bridges built until the overall migration is completed. This procedure also supports a more "global" view of the enterprise as opposed to just focusing on a particular subsystem. Figure 10.17 depicts the concept of process integration using the gateway architecture.

Fig. 10.16 Application functions of legacy gateways

Incremental Data Integration

Incremental data integration focuses on the challenge of keeping multiple sets of data coordinated throughout a packaged software system.

The two primary issues relating to data integration focus on queries and updates. Queries involve the access of complete information about a data set (collection of related data elements) across multiple systems. Much of the query challenges can be addressed by using a data warehouse or data mining architecture. This will be discussed in detail in Chap. 12. The gateway would serve as the infrastructure that would determine how many copies of the data exist and its location.

The more difficult and more important concept of data integration is the ability of the gateway to coordinate multiple updates across databases and flat-file systems. This means that the changing of a data element in one component would "trigger" an automatic update to the other components. There are four scenarios that could exist regarding the different definitions of data elements:

1. The data elements in each system have the same name. This at least allows analysts to identify how many copies of the element exist in the system.

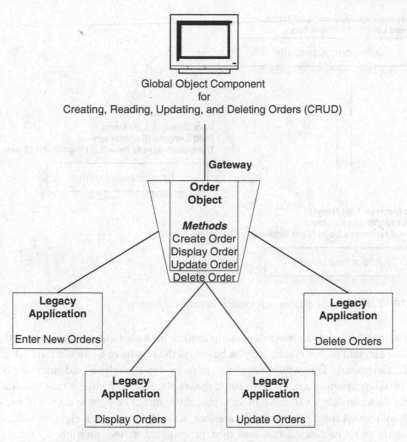

Fig. 10.17 Process integration and migration using gateway architecture

2. The data elements do not match up by name. This requires that the analyst design a "mapping" algorithm that tracks the corresponding name of each alias.
3. Data elements match by name but not by attribute. In this case the analyst must propagate updates to the data element by tracking the different attribute definitions it has across systems. These differences can vary dramatically. The most obvious is element length. If the length of the data element is shorter than the one that has been updated, then there is the problem of field truncation. This means that either the beginning value of ending value of the string will be lost when the value is propagated to the system with the shorter length definition. On the other hand, if the target is longer, then the process must populate either the beginning or end of the string so that the element has a complete value. This is graphically depicted in Fig. 10.18.

Furthermore, the same data element might have different data types, meaning that one is alphanumeric and the other numeric. In this case, analysts need to know that certain values (e.g., a leading zero) will not be stored in the same way depending on its data type classification.

Legacy Data Element: Last Name
Field Length: 17 characters

Johnsonhousesmith

Data Element: Last Name
Field Length: 15 characters
Truncation occurs from Left Significant Characters

hnsonhousesmith

Data Element: Last Name
Field Length: 15 characters
Truncation occurs from Right Significant Characters

johnsonhousesmi

Fig. 10.18 Propagating data elements with different field lengths

4. There is not a one-to-one relationship among data elements. This suggests that a data element in one system may be based on the results of a calculation (a derived data element). This would require a more in-depth analysis and mapping often solved by creating a stored procedure that replicates the business rule to calculate the data element's value. So in this case, there might be simple copies of the element moved from one system to another, as well as one data element value that needs to be calculated first and then propagated across multiple systems. For example, if the data element "Total-Amount" is entered in one system but calculated as Quantity times Price in another, the propagation of the values is very complex. First, the analyst must know whether the calculated value is performed first before the resultant value; in this case, Total-Amount is reentered in another system. If this is true, then the propagation is much easier; once the calculation is made, then the result is copied to the "entered" element. The converse is much more complex. If the Total-Amount was entered, but the values of Quantity and Price were not, then it would be very difficult to propagate until both Quantity and Price were entered. The example is further complicated if adjustments are made to the Quantity, Price, or Total-Amount. For any change, the systems would need to automatically be "triggered" to recalculate the values to ensure they are in synchronization. Figure 10.19 graphically shows this process.

Fig. 10.19 Propagation of
calculated data elements

**System Calculates Total Amount as
Quantity * Price and does not Store Total
Amount as an Element**

Quantity	Price

Program "Triggers" stored
procedure to update Derived
Data Element stored in
Legacy System

Legacy Data Element Total-Amount

Total-Amount

	Bill of Lading Container		Screen 1 of 4
B/L:____ SCAC: _____ VESSEL: _____			Total: ____
	VOYAGE: _____		CTN: _____
	PO Information		
Contract/PO: _____		Tot Unit: _____	
Item: _____		GWT: _____	
Style: _____		CBM: _____	
Stat: _____		O/F Chrg: _____	
Orig Country: _____		Con Rate: _____	
	Activities		
Activity	Descr	Date	Location

Fig. 10.20 Character-based user screen

Fig. 10.21 Transformed character-based to GUI screen

Converting Legacy Character-Based Screens

It would be naïve to assume that most legacy systems do not have character-based screens. Character-based screens are those that do not make use of the GUI. While most character-based screens in existence emanate from third-generation language mainframe implementations, there are also many early fourth-generation language systems that preceded the GUI paradigm. Unfortunately, character-based screens often do not map easily to its GUI counterparts. The analyst must be especially careful not to attempt to simply duplicate the screens in the legacy software. Figure 10.20 shows a typical character-based legacy screen. Note that there can be up to four Contract/POs as shown in the upper right-hand corner. The user is required to enter each Contract/PO on a separate screen.

On the other hand, the replacement GUI screen in Fig. 10.21 takes advantage of the view bar that allows for scrolling in a window. Therefore, the GUI version requires only one physical screen, as opposed to four.

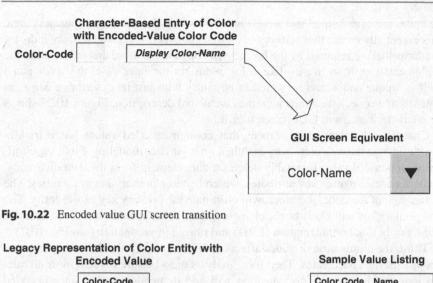

Fig. 10.22 Encoded value GUI screen transition

Fig. 10.23 Transition to encoded databases

The Challenge with Encoded Legacy Screen Values

In most legacy character-based screens, a common practice was used to create codes that represented another more meaningful data value. For example, numeric codes (1, 2, 3, 4, etc.) might be used to represent product colors such as blue, green, dark red, etc. Legacy applications used codes because they reduced the number of characters needed to type in the value on a screen. The technology to implement common GUI features such as drop-down menus and pop-up windows was not available. Indeed, many people used codes just from habit or had to use them in order to implement computer systems. When transitioning to a GUI system, especially on the Web, it is wise to phase out any data elements that are in an encoded form unless

the codes are user defined and are meaningful within the industry or business area. This essentially means that certain codes, like state (NY, CT, CA, etc.), are industry standards that are required by the business, as opposed to those created to aid in the implementation of software—like color codes. In the later case, the color name itself is unique and would be stored in an entity with just its descriptive name, as opposed to a code, which then identifies the actual description. Figure 10.22 shows the character-based and GUI screen transition.

Changing character-based screens that contain encoded values has a trickle-down effect on the data dictionary and then on logic data modeling. First, the elimination of a coded value inevitably deletes a data element from the data dictionary. Second, codes are often key attributes, which become primary keys of entities. The elimination of the code, therefore, will eliminate the primary key of the entity. The new primary key will likely be the element name. These changes must then be made to the Entity Relational Diagram (ERD) and placed in production (see Fig. 10.23).

Third, the elimination of codes affects previous stored procedures that use queries against the coded vales. Therefore, analysts must be sure to reengineer all queries that use the codes. This transition will add tremendous value since encoded elements typically add unnecessary overhead and time delays to queries. Finally, the elimination of encoded values will free up considerable space and index overhead. This will result in an increase in performance of the legacy system.

Legacy Migration Methodology

As stated earlier, all legacy systems inevitably must reach the end of their original life cycle. Therefore, notwithstanding whether certain components will remain "as is" or enhanced, eventually IT management must plan for migration to another system. The issue that this section addresses is how to establish a migration life cycle that takes into consideration an incremental approach to the replacement of various legacy components within an enterprise computer system. The previous sections provided a framework of what can be done with legacy systems and their integration with other systems. This section provides a step-by-step template of procedures to follow that can assist the analysts on the schedule of legacy migration including temporary and permanent integration. This approach is an incremental one, so analysts can use it as a checklist of the progression they have made in the legacy migration life cycle. In all there are 12 steps as follows:

1. Analyze the existing legacy systems.
2. Decompose legacy systems to determine schedules of migration and linkage strategies.
3. Design "as is" links.
4. Design legacy enhancements.
5. Design legacy replacements.
6. Design and integrate new databases.
7. Determine new infrastructure and environment, including gateways.

Fig. 10.24 Legacy
migration life cycle

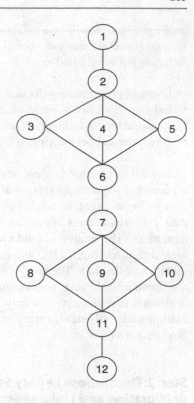

8. Implement enhancements.
9. Implement links.
10. Migrate legacy databases.
11. Migrate replacement legacy applications.
12. Incrementally cut over to new systems.

The above steps are graphically depicted in Fig. 10.24.

Note that there are two streams of steps, that is, steps 3–5 and 8–10 that can occur in parallel. These steps encompass the three types of legacy migration choices that can be made: replacement, enhancement, and "as is." While this life cycle seems simple, in reality it is a significant challenge for most migrations to plan, manage, and modify these steps and their interactions. Indeed, creating a migration plan and adequately coordinating the incremental and parallel steps are a difficult project. The subsequent sections will provide more details for each of these 12 steps.

Step 1: Analyze the Existing Legacy Systems

It is obviously important that analysts fully understand all of the existing legacy components that exist in the system. The objective is to provide the requirements of each system and how it relates to the system. Analysts must remember that little to

no documentation will be available to fully represent the architecture of the legacy system. However, analysts should compile as much information that is available including but not limited to:

- User and programming documentation
- Existing users, software developers, and managers
- Required inputs and outputs and known services of the legacy system
- Any historical perspective on the history of the system itself

Regardless of what existing information and documentation is available, certain aspects of reverse engineering must be used. Various CASE (computer-aided software engineering) tools should be used that allows analysts to create a repository of data and certain levels of code analysis, particularly for third-generation language migrations. The analyst should create DFDs and PFDs for process analysis and logic data modeling (LDM) and Entity Relational Diagramming (ERD) for representation of the data. The analyst should also determine which legacy components are decomposable and non-decomposable. Inevitably, regardless of whether the decision is to replace immediately, enhance, or leave "as is," ultimately little of the existing code will survive the ultimate migration of a legacy system (Brodie and Stonebraker 1995).

Step 2: Decompose Legacy Systems to Determine Schedules of Migration and Linkage Strategies

The gradual migration of legacy systems is easiest accomplished when analysts utilize decomposition engineering. Previous chapters have outlined the process of functional decomposition, which is based on the breaking down of a system into its functional components. Decomposition, which results in components, also allows for reusability of code. Since the fundamental premises of a packaged system are reusability, the process of decomposition is a mandatory part of the life cycle of any legacy migration. Thus, analysts should decompose all DFDs to functional primitives. Process analysis continues with the writing of process specifications for each functional primitive. These functional primitives will either be rewritten from the existing code or documentation or recreated from analyzing the functionality of the program. Analysts need to remove all dependency logic that links modules from the legacy code because it represents coupling among the programs. Module dependencies can typically be identified by finding *procedure calls* from within the legacy code. Ultimately, each of these process specifications will become methods. Eventually all methods will be mapped to classes and identify the attributes that each class needs. While this sounds simple, there will be a number of processes for which decomposition will be problematic. This will typically occur for legacy code that is too eclectic and needs to simply be reengineered. In these cases, analysts may want to interview users to understand the functionality that is required, as opposed to relying solely on the written legacy code.

From a data perspective, Entity Relational Diagrams (ERD) need to undergo normalization. Remember that the DD and ERD produced in Step 1 are a mirror of the existing system, which most likely will not be in third-normal form. Thus this step will result in the propagation of new entities and even new data elements. Furthermore, data redundancies will be discovered as well as derived elements that should be removed from the logic model. However, while these steps are taking place, analysts need to be cognizant that the process of normalization represents the total new blueprint of how the data should have been originally engineered. The actual removal of elements or reconstruction of the physical database needs to be a phased plan in accordance with the overall legacy migration effort. Thus Step 2 provides the decomposed framework, but not the schedule of implementation.

Finally analysts must always be aware of the challenges of decomposition, particularly over-decomposition, meaning that too many classes have been formed that will ultimately hurt systems performance. There needs to be a mix of decomposed levels, which will serve as the basis of the new migration architecture.

Step 3: Design "As Is" Links

This step involves determining and designing what components will remain untouched except for linkages that are necessary with other package software components. These modules are determined not to be part of the initial migration plans; however, they need to function *within* the packaged software system infrastructure and are therefore part of its architecture. Part of the decision needs to include how data will be migrated into the packaged software framework. In most cases, "as is" components continue to use their legacy data sources. Consideration must be given to how legacy data will be communicated to other components in the packaged software system. Analysts need to consider either a parameter-based communication systems or a centrally shared database repository as outlined earlier.

Step 4: Design Legacy Enhancements

This step determines which modules will be enhanced. BPR (business process reengineering) will be used to design new features and functions in each business area. Analysts should identify essential components and determine what changes need to be employed to make the existing system behave more like an object-oriented system. Common processes and databases also need to be mapped so that shared resources can be designed between legacy and packaged software systems. New linkages will also be needed and the analyst must determine whether to use parameters or databases or both to implement the communication among application systems.

User screens may also need to be updated as necessary, especially to remove encoded values or moving certain character-based screens to GUI. Many of the enhancements to a legacy application are implemented based on the analysis

performed in Step 1. Any modifications will need to eventually operate on newer platforms once the total migration of legacy systems is completed. Analysts need to be cognizant that additional requirements mean increasing risk, which should be avoided when possible. However, during enhancement consideration, it is almost impossible to ignore new requirements. Therefore, analysts need to focus on risk assessment as part of the life cycle of legacy migration.

Step 5: Design Legacy Replacements

Analysts must focus on how to reconstruct logic in a later generation of software architecture. Therefore, it is important to understand the differences in generation language design. This chapter provided two types of legacy software systems: third- and fourth-generation languages. Third-generation languages were depicted as being more procedural and more difficult to convert.

Analysts must design the target applications so they will operate in accordance with the business rules and processes that will be supported in the new systems environment. Because of this integration, most replacement legacy migrations require significant reengineering activities. These activities necessitate the inclusion of new business rules that may have evolved since the legacy system was placed in production. Furthermore, new business rules can be created simply by the requirement of being a packaged software system.

Another important component of legacy migration is screen design. When replacing legacy systems, analysts must view the migration as assimilation, that is, the old system is becoming part of the new one. As a result, all existing packaged software screens need to be reviewed so that designers can determine whether they need to be modified to adopt some of the legacy functionality. This is not to suggest that all of the legacy systems screens will be absorbed into the existing packaged software system. Rather, there will be a combination of new and absorbed functionality added to the target environment.

Step 6: Design and Integrate New Databases

From an enterprise perspective, analysts must gather all of the permutations of legacy systems that exist and seek to provide a plan on how to integrate the data into one source. For "as is" solutions, legacy data files will most likely remain separate from the packaged software system until the complete legacy is migrated. However, the process of enhancing and replacing legacy data should have the objective of creating one central database source that will serve the entire packaged software enterprise system. Indeed, a central data source reduces data redundancy and significantly increases data integrity.

The process of data integration can only be accomplished by "combining user views" which is the process of matching up the multiple data element definitions that overlap and identifying data redundancies and alternative definitions. This can

only be completed by creating a repository of data elements and by representing the data graphically using an ERD. Once each system is represented in this fashion, then the analyst must perform logic data modeling as prescribed in Chap. 9. The result will be the creation of one central database system cluster that can provide the type of integration necessary for successful packaged software implementations.

While this is the goal for all analysts, the road to successful implementation is challenging. First, the process of normalization will require that some data elements be deleted (e.g., encoded values), while others will need to be added. Second, full data integration cannot be attained until all replacement screens are complete. Third, applications must be redesigned so that the centrality of the data source is assumed to exist. Since this process may be very time consuming, it may not be feasible to attempt a full database migration at one time. Therefore, the legacy data may need to be logically partitioned to facilitate incremental database migration. Thus, there will be legacy data subsets that are created to remain independent of the central database until some later migration phase is deemed feasible. Of course this strategy requires the design of temporary "bridges" that allows the entire packaged software system to appear cohesive to users.

Another important factor in planning data migration is to determine how much is really known about the legacy data itself. The less knowledge available, the longer the period where legacy data and packaged software data need to run separately and in parallel.

Step 7: Determine New Infrastructure and Environment, Including Gateways

Prior to the migration of any system, the necessary hardware and software infrastructure must be planned and installed. A common error in legacy migration is not factoring the time and effort to provide this infrastructure. Furthermore this process, which may create a new network environment, needs to determine the placement of software in a three-tier client/server platform. This means that further decomposition may be required of all processes, especially object classes. You may recall in Chap. 8 that classes may undergo further decomposition depending on the need to distribute application across the network.

Another important factor is performance. In many instances it is difficult for network engineers to predict performance in large application system environments. It may be necessary to plan for several benchmarks in performance early in the design phase. Benchmarking is the process of setting up an environment that replicates a production network so that modifications can be made, if necessary, to the design of the system to increase performance.

Another decision that must be made at this juncture is whether a gateway infrastructure will be created to mediate legacy layers. This decision, of course, is highly dependent on the migration life cycle; the more legacy layers that will be phased in over time, the higher the chances that a gateway processor for data and applications will be necessary. The decision to go with a gateway is significant, not only from the

perspective of software design but network infrastructure as well. Constructing a gateway can be very costly. It involves writing the system from scratch or tailoring a commercial product to meet the migration requirements. It is also costly because of the amount of additional hardware necessary to optimize the performance of the gateway servers. However, the benefits of a gateway are real, as it could provide a dependable structure to slowly migrate all components in the new systems environment.

Step 8: Implement Enhancements

This step requires a schedule of when legacy enhancements will be implemented and become part of the production system. Many analysts suggest that the simplest modules go into production first so that any unexpected problems can be dealt with quickly and efficiently. Furthermore, simple modules tend to have small consequences should there be a problem in processing or performance. There are some other aspects of coordination, however. For example, enhancements that feed off of the same data or use the same subsystems should obviously be implemented at one time.

Another factor in the decision of which enhanced components go first relates to the affects it has on other subsystems. This means that the priority may indeed be influenced by what other systems need or are dependent upon from other systems. Another issue could be the nature of the legacy links. Should a link be very complex or dependent on other subsystem enhancements, its schedule could be affected. Finally, the nature of the enhancements has much to do with the decision as opposed to just the application's complexity. There may be simple enhancements that are crucial for the packaged software system and vice versa.

Step 9: Implement Links

As I alluded to in Step 8, the determination of legacy links greatly affects the scheduling of the migration cycle. Once the determination is made in Step 8, the related legacy links must be put in place. This could also mean that the gateway, if designed, must also be in operation since many links might be filtered through the gateway infrastructure. So, the implementation of legacy links relates to both hardware and software. Notwithstanding whether a gateway is in place, database links often require separate servers. In many cases because these servers interface with the Internet, there is a need to install firewalls to ensure security protection.

From a software perspective, legacy links can almost be treated like conversion programs. There needs to be substantial testing done to ensure they work properly. Once legacy links are in production, like data conversions, they tend to keep working. It is also important to ensure that legacy links are documented. Indeed, any link will eventually be changed based on the incremental migration schedule. Remember that most legacy links are accomplished by building temporary "bridges." The

concept of temporary can be dangerous, in that many of these links, over time, tend to be more permanent. That is, their temporary life can sometimes extend beyond the predicted life of a permanent component. The message here should be that legacy links, while they are a temporary solution, should be designed under the same intensity and adherence to quality as any other software development component.

Step 10: Migrate Legacy Databases

The migration of data is so complex that it should be handled as a separate and distinct step in the migration life cycle. Data affects everything in the system, and often if it is not migrated properly, it can cause immense problems. First, the analyst must decide on the phasing of data based on the schedule of application migration. Hopefully, the process of data migration should be done in parallel to Steps 8 and 9.

The most challenging aspect of data migration is the physical steps in the process. Migrating new entities and schema changes are complex. For example, changes to databases require that the tables be "dropped" meaning that they are taken offline. Data dictionaries need to be updated, and changes to stored procedures and triggers are extremely time consuming. Most problematic is the process f quality assurance. While some testing can be done in a controlled environment, most of the final testing must be done once the system is actually in production. Therefore the coordination with users to test the system early is critical. Furthermore, there must be backup procedures in case the database migration does not work properly. This means that there is an alternate fail-safe plan to reinstall the old system should major problems arise. Finally, a programming team should be ready to deal with any problems that arise that do not warrant reinstalling the old version. This might include the discovery of application "bugs" that can be fixed within a reasonable period and are not deemed critical to operations (which means there is usually a "work-around" for the problem). Analysts must understand that this process must be followed each time a new database migration takes place!

Database migration is even more complex when there is a gateway. The reason is that the gateway, from an incremental perspective, contains more and more database responsibilities each time there is a migration. Therefore, for every migration, the amount of data that can be potentially affected grows larger. In addition, the number of data that becomes integrated usually grows exponentially, so the planning and conversion process becomes a critical path to successful migration life cycles. Since the migration of legacy databases becomes so much more difficult as the project progresses, the end of the life cycle becomes even more challenging to reach. That is why many migrations have never been completed!

Step 11: Migrate Replacement Legacy Applications

Once the database migration is completed, then the remainder of the legacy applications can be migrated to the new system. These applications are usually the

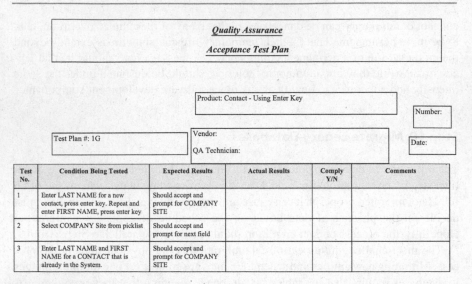

Fig. 10.25 Acceptance test plan

replacement components, which have been reengineered in the object-oriented paradigm. These programs, then, have been designed to operate against the target databases with the new functionality required for the packaged software system. Since replacement applications usually do not create links, there is typically little effect on gateway operations. What is more challenging is the quality assurance process. Users need to be aware that the code is relatively new and will contain problems regardless of the amount of preproduction testing that has been performed. In any event, programmers, database administrators, and quality assurance personnel should be on call for weeks after systems cutover.

Step 12: Incrementally Cutover to New Systems

As discussed above, testing and application turnover are two areas that frequently are overlooked. Because projects typically run over budget and schedule, the final procedures like testing and verification are usually shortened. The results of this decision can be devastating to successful legacy migrations. Because of the size and complexity of many packaged software systems, to go "cold turkey" is unrealistic and irresponsible. Therefore, an analyst should consider providing test scenarios that provide more confidence that the system is ready to be cutover. This approach is called "acceptance testing" and requires that users be involved in the determination of what tests must be performed before the system is ready to go live. Thus, acceptance test plans can be defined as the set of tests that if passed will establish that the software can be used in production. Acceptance tests need to be established early in the product life cycle and should begin during the analysis phase. It is only logical then that the development of acceptance test plans should involve analysts.

As with requirements development, the analyst must participate with the user community. Only users can make the final decision about the content and scope of the test plans. The design and development of acceptance test plans should not be confused with the testing phase of the Software Development Life Cycle.

Another perspective on acceptance testing is that it becomes a formal checklist that defines the minimal criteria for incrementally migrating systems. However, one must work with the understanding that no new product will ever be fault-free. The permutations of testing everything would make the timetable for completion unacceptable and cost prohibitive. Therefore, the acceptance test plan is a strategy to get the most important components tested completely enough for production. Figure 10.25 represents a sample acceptance test plan.

Problems and Exercises

1. What is a legacy? Explain.
2. Describe the five-generation languages. What increases with each generation?
3. What are essential components?
4. What does the object-oriented paradigm mean?
5. How does object orientation relate to Business Area Analysis?
6. What is a legacy link?
7. Explain the notion of Logic Reconstruction.
8. What is a UNIX pipe?
9. Explain how Legacy Integration operates through gateway architecture.
10. What is propagation?
11. What is the essential differences between character-based screens and GUI?
12. What is an encoded value?

References

Brodie, M., & Stonebraker, M. (1995). *Migrating legacy systems: Gateway, interfaces & the incremental approach* (Morgan Kaufmann Series in Data Management Systems). San Francisco: Morgan Kaufmann Publishers Inc.

Stair, R. M., & Reynolds, C. W. (1999). *Principles of information systems* (4th ed.). Cambridge, MA: Course Technology.

Business Process Reengineering

Business process reengineering (BPR) in Chap. 10 was specifically discussed in relation to legacy applications. This chapter provides further methods on actually replacing legacy systems as part of the redesign for a new system. That is, rather than create legacy links, replace the old application with the new system altogether. This approach can often be an attractive alternative because a packaged solution might indeed contain many of the features and functions of the legacy. The OO paradigm is again the way to accomplish this analysis, particularly using the essential components that were outlined in Chap. 10. The essential components first require the establishment of the core business requirements and then the mapping of the functionality of the organization or business unit to these components.

Many chief information officers (CIOs) today are confronted with a corporate mission to reengineer their existing applications and apply a more sophisticated and structured approach to developing what is known as the "enterprise" system. The enterprise system is composed of one common data repository for all of the organization's data. The typical enterprise configuration includes the OO paradigm and the client/server model as shown in Fig. 11.1.

The mission of BPR is to take an existing system, which is typically based on older technology and developed on the basis discussed in Chap. 9 (where the analyst is on the outside looking in), and reengineer it into one integrated system. Much has been written about the approaches or methodologies to use when applying BPR, especially by Jacobson. The focus of this book is to provide direction from a practitioner's perspective, that is, something that can realistically be applied within the typical resources and constraints that exist in most IS organizations of today.

Analyzing Legacy Systems for Replacement

The first step to applying successful BPR is to develop an approach to defining the existing system and extracting its existing data elements and applications. The data needs to be captured into the data repository and the applications need to be defined

© Springer-Verlag London Limited 2016
A.M. Langer, *Guide to Software Development*,
DOI 10.1007/978-1-4471-6799-0_11

Fig. 11.1 Client/server three-tier architecture

and compared to a new model based on essential components. Our assumption in this section is that the legacy system resides on an IBM mainframe computer. The data is stored in a VSAM format (non-database files) and the applications have been developed in COBOL. There are no central libraries or repositories of data or programs.

Data Elements

The analyst team will need to design conversion programs that will access the data files and place them in a data repository. Once all the data elements are loaded, the more rigorous process of identifying duplicate elements becomes the major effort. Duplicate elements may take on different forms. The most obvious is the same element with the same name and attributes. Another type is the same element name, but with different attributes. The third type, and the most challenging, is the duplicate elements that have different names and different attributes. This third type can be related to our discussion about combining user views. In any event, users and

analysts will need to begin the laborious process of taking each element and building a data repository.

Applications

Application documentation is more problematic but again resembles the procedures followed using flow diagrams. This means that each existing application must be flowed and included as part of a new reengineered process. Although this procedure may sound straightforward, it is not. BPR typically involves a methodology called Business Area Analysis (BAA). The purpose of BAA is to:

- Establish various business areas that make up the enterprise.
- Break down the business areas to their required data and process portions.
- Reengineer the new and old requirements of each business area.
- Develop requirements that provide an OO perspective of each business area, meaning that there is no need to map its needs to the existing physical organization structure.
- Define the links that create relationships among all of the business areas.

A business area should be developed in the same manner as depicted in Chap. 10, where we established the essential components of a bank. Each component is a business area that needs to be reengineered into its equivalent OO and client/server enterprise system. Therefore, each essential component must be functionally decomposed to its reusable parts.

Combining Structured and Object Techniques

Once the essential components or business areas have been completed and agreed to by the user community, it is time to develop the actual architecture of the new reengineered system. What modeling tools should we use? The answer is that we should be ready to use all of them when required. Figure 11.2 shows a schematic of the reengineering process within a business area.

Like OO, BPR also uses the object concept to develop cohesive and reusable processes. We use the example from Chap. 10 to demonstrate how this maps to business areas. Once the business areas are defined, the structured tools should be used to define all data and processes. BPR supports the concept that the data for a business area should be determined before the processes. You may recall that the same data represented an excellent method for creating cohesive modules. By using the same data, functional primitive DFDs and STDs can be mapped to their appropriate business area.

Logical data modeling and the ERD will need to be completed prior to creating the permanent objects and classes that belong to each business area. Normalization

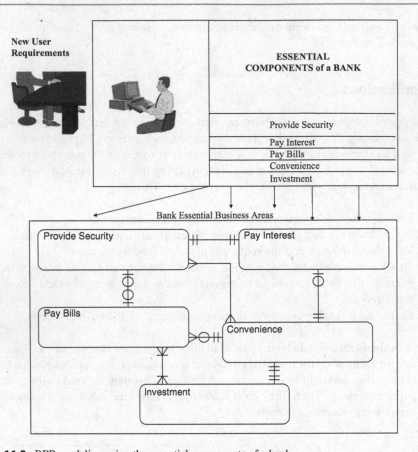

Fig. 11.2 BPR modeling using the essential components of a bank

must be applied to the required entities, which will not only have the legacy data elements but also those added as part of the reengineering analysis process.

Prior to mapping the processes and data to their logical objects, the analyst can use another tool to assist in the reconciliation that all data and processes have been found. The tool is called an Association Matrix or a CRUD diagram. CRUD stands for the four functions that can be performed on any entity: **C**reate, **R**ead, **U**pdate, or **D**elete (archive). The importance of the CRUD diagram is that it ensures:

- That an object has complete control over its data
- That a data file is accessed by at least one process
- That processes are accessing data (Fig. 11.3)

The CRUD matrix shown in Fig. 11.3 tells us a lot about the status and activities of our business area data and processes:

Processes or Business Function Data Subject or Entity	New Orders	New Products	Shipping	Sales Commission
Customers	R		R, U	
Orders	C, U		U	R
Items	R	C, U, D	R	R
Inventory	R,U	C, U	U	
Expense Category				
Salesperson	R			U

Fig. 11.3 Sample CRUD diagram

- Only the Items entity has enough component processes to control its objects data, that is, by spelling CRUD its processes have the minimum capabilities to control the cycle of any data element. Although this does not ensure that processes are not missing, it is a good indicator that the analysis has covered the life cycle of an entity.
- The Expense Category is not accessed by any process. This means that we have a file that the system is not using. This is an excellent indicator that processes are missing.
- The Customer, Expense Category and Salesperson data are created and deleted by some other processes or business area. This could be a situation where the physical location of a business function is not where it logically should be processing. The analyst should look for the missing processes to complete the spelling of CRUD before finalizing both the processes and data of any business area.

Even if BPR is not used, the CRUD diagram is an excellent tool to use to determine the processes and data needed for an object. Once the CRUD diagram is finalized, the objects and classes can be created as follows (Fig. 11.4).

It is important to recognize that many of the objects that are developed during BPR may become reusable components of other business area classes. If there are additions to an object as a result of reviewing a new business area, then the object's data and methods may need to be updated. The best approach to tracking these objects is through an integrated CASE tool, although any level of automation can be feasible.

Dealing with End Users

When applying BPR, analysts need to formulate a plan for how users and user groups will be interviewed. Most importantly, since reengineering implies change, change means discussions that must lead to decisions. Coordination of these decisions is critical, and it can get out of hand quickly. For this reason the analyst should attempt to organize BPR using multiple JAD sessions. The sessions should be

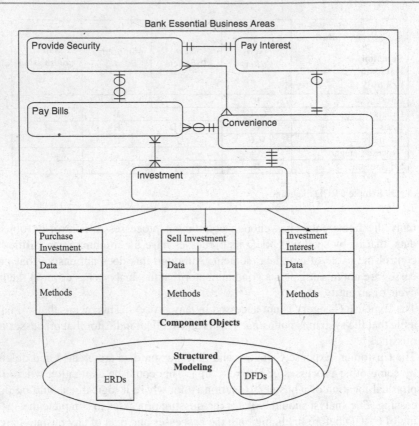

Fig. 11.4 Business area component objects and diagrams

focused first on each individual business area. Prior to actually holding the session, analysts and facilitators should educate users on the techniques and reasons for BPR. Analysts should not be afraid to show users the business area schematic and explain the concepts of essential components and how they eventually can become reusable objects. This means that there may be a need to hold a one-day training session for the users who will be involved in the JADs. This suggestion is consistent with the concept of having users prepared before they attend a meeting.

JAD sessions should be organized to have session leaders who can provide walk-throughs of the existing functions. While these walkthroughs take place, the adjust-ments and missing functionalities can be added to the business area. The issues concerning the selection of key personnel are extremely important, especially when selecting decision makers. Because of the volume of information being discussed, it is advisable to have more than one scribe available. This minimizes the risk of not capturing important business rules.

After each business area is completed, the links to the other business components must be handled. These should also take place via JADs and typically use the

Fig. 11.5 Client/server hybrid model

session leaders as attendees. Session leaders tend to have enough information at this point from the JAD sessions to determine the necessary links for each business area.

The use of prototypes for each JAD is highly recommended because it will provide the best vehicle to get agreement on the new system. This suggests that an integrated CASE product is almost a necessity for creating a successful BPR project.

Information Systems Issues

BPR is implemented on existing systems. Existing systems have IS staffs and constraints that must be addressed as part of the process. Since the current view of BPR is to create an open systems client/server enterprise system, the physical requirements of the network are critical during analysis. Remember, RAD means the combining of analysis, design and development into multiple iterative steps. In order to take the objects and classes developed from the JAD sessions, the analyst must start breaking up the data and methods of the classes into its related client and server functions. You may recall that if the client and server processing portions of an object must reside on separate hardware components, then the object/class must be separated or further decomposed into separate physical modules (Fig. 11.5).

We have emphasized the importance of analysts being involved with the network design for client/server systems. BPR thus requires that the network design be completed as soon as possible and ideally before analysis starts. This will be difficult since many of the network decisions may be altered depending on how the objects become distributed across the network. In addition, the backend database stored procedures (business rules, triggers, etc.), and middleware software components must be defined while the analysis specification is being finalized.

IT personnel must also be heavily involved in the JAD sessions to clarify questions about the existing system processes. This will involve discussions about the amount of data processed, as well as the difficulty or ease of getting additional information from the suggestions brought up during the JADs. IT can also disclose

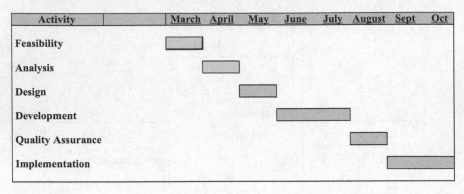

Activity		March	April	May	June	July	August	Sept	Oct
Feasibility		▓							
Analysis			▓						
Design				▓					
Development					▓▓				
Quality Assurance							▓		
Implementation								▓▓	

Fig. 11.6 The classic waterfall SDLC, showing each phase dependent on the completion of the previous one

the details of the equipment choices and how these may affect the requirements being discussed. Such input may enable quicker decisions based on predetermined IS constraints.

Finally, IT will be required to establish the information about the existing data and processes. They will most likely be responsible for the conversion of the data as well as for clarifying the meaning of many of the data elements in question. You may assume that many of the legacy data element definitions will be unknown, and as a result analysts and programmers will be spending time together figuring out what such elements do in the system. Existing process review means looking at the current application programs and how they function in the system. Most of this work will be required from IT programmers and legacy designers (if they are still around!). Since our assumption was that the existing system was developed under COBOL, there will be a more difficult mapping of how a 3GL (third-generation language[1]) is designed as opposed to today's 4GL (fourth-generation language[2]) products.

System Development Life Cycle (SDLC)

BPR changes the steps in the typical IS SDLC. The traditional SDLC is based on the waterfall approach as was shown in Chap. 1 (Fig. 11.6).

The problem with the waterfall approach is that it is unrealistic (as discussed in Chap. 1) and that it does not conform to the requirements of the OO life cycle.

[1] A generation language refers to the level of the programming language. Third-generation languages were considered high-level development systems that included C, Pascal, and COBOL.

[2] Fourth-generation languages typically include programming languages that work directly with database systems and contain simpler program instructions than its predecessor languages.

Fig. 11.7 Object-oriented
software life cycle

Therefore, IS must modify its SDLC to conform to the OO and client/server needs of BPR. The OO client/server life cycle resembles a spiral as shown in Fig. 11.7.

The spiral life cycle reflects a much larger allocation of time spent on design than in the traditional life cycle, because much of the development time is spent designing the objects for product reuse. Although this may appear unduly time consuming, there is a heavy payback in BPR if it is done correctly. Remember that the spiral life cycle is applied to the development of each object since it is a cohesive component within itself. The more reusable the object, the more spiral the effort becomes with a particular emphasis on the analysis/design phase.

Pilot Applications

Many analysts opt to have a pilot application as part of the BPR effort. The purpose of the pilot is to get users excited about the benefits of creating the new system. Because an actual application is developed, IS must be involved to ensure the pilot is successful. How can success be evaluated? The first real decision in a pilot is to select an existing application that is not working favorably and one that can demonstrate enough advantages of the OO GUI and client/server environment to pique the interest of users. Below is a suggested strategy:

* Focus on an application that can demonstrate the flexibility of the GUI front end.
* Select an application that accesses existing corporate data to show the users how easily the data can be reached. Analysts should avoid an application that gets involved with massive updates or large data queries, as this is inviting an unexpected delay in processing. Such exercises tend to involve much study and experience with the corporate network of information, and this expertise may not be available.
* Select an application that has a relatively short development time when using a GUI product. Do not try an application that might be more involved when using a client/server model.

The pilot application not only has the potential to generate more interest, but it also allows users to be more creative and understanding of the requirements of BPR.

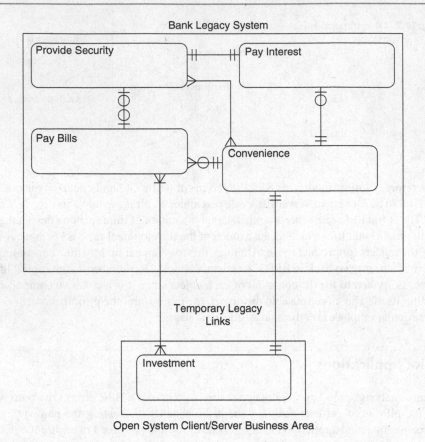

Fig. 11.8 Legacy links of a business area

Downsizing System Components

After the business areas and interfaces among them have been completed, the analyst and development must decide on a strategy for implementation. To attempt to convert an entire enterprise-level system in one project is very dangerous and very unlikely to succeed. The user community also needs to be involved with this decision since many business units can convert only at certain times of the year due to various seasonal business requirements. Therefore, the analyst must plan to migrate applications in pieces. It is only logical to do this migration by business area and to develop temporary legacy links back to the main system. Most organizations are doing just this by purchasing open systems hardware and moving complete self-contained business areas independently onto the new platforms (Fig. 11.8).

As each business area is converted to the open systems architecture, the temporary legacy links will be deleted and incorporated in the new system.

Transactions vs. Data Warehousing

Our sample system is categorized as a transaction-based operation, that is, the system was designed to maximize its performance based on the processing of transactions. This type of systems must perform under the stress of many users who are using the system for production purposes. The limit of these systems is that they do not provide the end user with online data comparisons and what-if analysis in a productive and robust environment. Such systems were designed in the early 1980s and were called decision support systems (DSS). Today's robust software goes even further than the awkward DSS systems, and users want the same level of flexibility with their enterprise solutions. The problem is simple: you cannot maximize your transactions performance while maximizing your DSS functionality. The result is many client/server systems have had trouble performing at the same level as the legacy systems. SQL-based queries that are issued during peak time enterprise processing can cause significant slowdown in processing. In most cases such delays are simply unacceptable. In fact, GUI applications will never out-perform VSAM transaction-based mainframe systems. This sounds like a disappointing state of affairs for users. The remedy is to separate the transaction processing from the DSS functionality and improve transaction processing to an acceptable user level. This is accomplished by creating a data warehouse environment. A data warehouse is an archive of the database off-loaded usually to a separate machine to provide DSS capabilities to those that need to query information.

The problem with data warehousing is the currency of the data, since off-loaded information is typically not performed real time. Therefore, users must agree to use "old" data. Many organizations have provided data warehousing capabilities within hours of the input or update of information. Nevertheless, data warehousing can work only if the user community can settle on aged data that they cannot change. There are products such as SAS that provide specific tools to create data warehouse databases. Often the data is not fully normalized because the user cannot change the information. This results in a more efficient and accessible database because the information is stored in a flatter format (fewer database files). Almost every database manufacturer will be providing data warehouse capabilities in their next release. The analyst must be involved in determining which applications (usually reporting and inquiry operations) are candidates for the warehouse function. Analysts and IS personnel must take care in explaining the role of the data warehouse to the users so that they can use it effectively. Data warehouses are discussed further in Chap. 12 (Fig. 11.9).

Fig. 11.9 Transaction/data
warehouse BPR solution

Problems and Exercises

1. Explain the objectives of BPR.
2. How is BPR consistent with the object and client/server models?
3. What is a business area?
4. Explain the relationship between BPR and structured tools.
5. What is a CRUD diagram?
6. How should BPR be introduced to users and IS personnel?
7. What is the SDLC ? Why is it called a waterfall approach?
8. Compare the SDLC with the OOLC.
9. What is the significance of the spiral approach and how does it support the development of reusable objects?
10. Describe the procedures to implement a pilot application. Why is this so important in BPR?
11. Describe the philosophy of reengineering an enterprise system.
12. What is the difference between a transaction database and a data warehouse?

Digital Transformation and Consumer Requirements

<div style="text-align:right">**12**</div>

Digital transformation is perhaps the most significant issue of the early twenty-first century. Digital transformation is defined as "the changes associated with the applications of digital technology in all aspects of human society" (Stolterman and Fors 2004, 689). From a business perspective, digital transformation enables organizations to implement new types of innovations and to rethink business processes that can take advantage of technology. From this perspective digital transformation involves a type of reengineering, but one that is not limited to rethinking just how systems work together, rather the entire business itself. Some see digital transformation as the elimination of paper in organizations. Others see it as revamping a business to meet the demands of a digital economy. This section provides a link between digital transformation and what I call "digital reengineering." To explain this better, think of process reengineering as the generation that brought together systems in a way that they talked to one another—that is, the integration of legacy systems with new application that used more robust software applications. Chapter 11 provided the structured approaches to accomplishing that challenge.

Digital reengineering represents the transformation of systems to meet the digital demands of the business' consumers. From this perspective, reengineering is no longer limited to the needs of the internal user, but rather the consumer's needs from the business. So systems must change as necessary with the changes in consumer behavior. The challenge with doing this, of course, is that consumer needs are harder to obtain and understand and can vary significantly among groups such as ethnicity, age, and gender, to name just a few.

As a result analysts need to interact with the consumer, somewhat a new type of user for them. The consumer, in effect, is the buyer of the organization's products and services. The challenge becomes how to get analysts engaged with this population, which could be across physical domains. Below are six approaches, which are not mutually exclusive of each other:

1. *Sales/marketing*: these individuals sell to the company's buyers. Thus, they have a good sense of what customers are looking for, what things they like about the

© Springer-Verlag London Limited 2016

A.M. Langer, *Guide to Software Development*,

DOI 10.1007/978-1-4471-6799-0_12

business, and what they dislike. The power of the sales and marketing team is their ability to drive realistic requirements that directly impact revenue opportunities. The limitation of this resource is that it still relies on an internal perspective of the consumer.

2. *Third-party market analysis/reporting*: there are outside resources available that examine and report on market trends within various industry sectors. Such organizations typically have massive databases of information and, using various searches and analyses, can provide various views and behavior patterns of the customer base. They can also provide competitive analysis of where the company sits with respect to alternative choices and why buyers may be choosing alternative solutions. The shortfall of this approach is that often the data may not be specific enough to feed requirements of what applications systems might be required to make a competitive advantage for the business.

3. *Predictive analytics*: this is a hot topic in today's competitive landscape for businesses. Predictive analytics is the process of feeding off large data sets (big data, discussed in Chap. 9) and predicting future behavior patterns. Predictive analytics approaches are usually handled internally with assistance from third-party products or consulting services. The value of predictive analytics is using data to design systems that can provide what might be future consumer needs. The limitation is one of risk—the risk that the prediction does not occur as planned.

4. *Consumer support departments*: internal teams and external (outsourced managed service) vendors that support consumers have a good pulse on their preferences because they speak with them. More specifically, they are responding to questions, handling problems, and getting feedback on what is working. These support departments typically depend on applications to help the buyer. As a result they are an excellent resource for providing up-to-date things that the system does not provide to them that consumers want as a service or offering. Often, however, consumer support organizations limit their needs to what they experience as opposed to what might be future needs as a result of competitive forces.

5. *Surveys*: analysts can design surveys (questionnaires) and send them to consumers for feedback. Using surveys can be of significant value in that the questions can target specific application needs. Survey design and administration can be handled by third-party firms, which may have an advantage in that the questions are being forwarded by an independent source that might not identify the company. On the other hand, this might be considered a negative—it all depends on what the analyst is seeking to obtain from the buyer.

6. *Focus groups*: this approach is similar to the use of a survey. Focus groups are commonly used to understand consumer behavior patterns and preferences. They are often conducted by outside firms. The difference between the focus group and a survey is (1) surveys are very quantitative based using scoring mechanisms to evaluate outcomes. Consumers sometimes may not understand the question and as a result provide distorted information, and (2) focus groups are more qualitative and allow analysts to engage with the consumer in two-way dialogue.

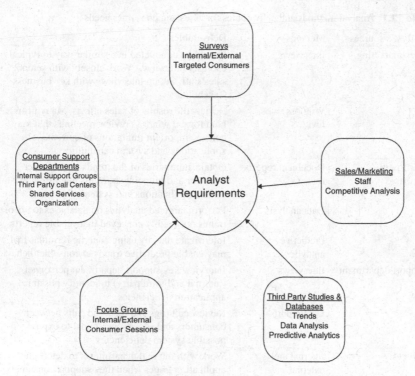

Fig. 12.1 Sources for the analysis of consumers

Figure 12.1 reflects a graphical depiction of the sources of the analysis of consumers.

Table 12.1 further articulates the methods and deliverables that analysts should consider when developing specifications.

Requirements Without Users and Without Input

Could it be possible to develop requirements for a system without user input or even consumer opinions? Could this be accomplished?

Perhaps we need to take a step back historically and think about trends that have changed the competitive landscape. Digital transformation may indeed be the most powerful agent of change in the history of business.

We have seen large companies lose their edge. IBM's fall as the leading technology firm in the 1990s is an excellent example, when Microsoft overtook them into that position. Yet Google was able to take the lead away from Microsoft in the area of consumer computing. And what about the comeback of Apple with its new array of products? The question is: why and how does this happen so quickly?

Technology continues to generate change, or as it is now referred to as "disruption." The reality is that it is getting increasingly difficult to predict what consumers

Table 12.1 Analyst methods and deliverables for assessing consumer needs

Analyst's sources	Methods	Deliverables
Sales/marketing	Interviews	Should be conducted in a similar way to typical end user interviews. Work closely with senior sales staff. Set up interviews with key business stakeholders
	Win/loss sales reviews	Review the results of sales efforts. Many firms hold formal win/loss review meetings that may convey important limitations of current applications and system capabilities
Third-party databases	Document reports reviews	Obtain summaries of the trends in consumer behavior and pinpoint shortfalls that might exist in current applications and systems
	Data analysis	Perform targeted analytics on databases to uncover trends not readily conveyed in available reports
	Predictive analytics	Interrogate data by using analytic formulas that may enable predictive trends in consumer behavior
Support department	Interviews	Interview key support department personnel (internal and third party) to identify possible application deficiencies
	Data/reports	Review call logs and recorded calls between consumers and support personnel to expose possible system deficiencies
Surveys	Internal and external questionnaires	Work with internal departments to determine application issues when they support consumers. Use similar surveys with select populations of customers to validate and fine-tune internal survey results
		Use similar surveys targeted to consumers who are not customers and compare results. Differences between existing customer base and noncustomers may expose new trends in consumer needs
Focus groups	Hold internal and external sessions	Internal focus groups can be facilitated by the analyst. Select specific survey results that had unexpected results or mixed feedback and review those results with the focus group attendees. Internal attendees should come from operations management and sales. External focus groups should be facilitated by a third-party vendor and held at independent sites. Discussions with customers should be compared with internal focus group results. Consumer focus groups should also be facilitated by a professional third- party firm

want and need—if they even know! The challenge then is: how can we forecast the changes that are brought about by technology disruptions? So the digital transformation is more about predicting consumer behavior and providing new products and services, which we hope consumers will use. This is a significant challenge for the analyst of course, given that the profession was built on the notion that good

specifications accurately depicted what users wanted. Langer (1997) originally defined this as the "concept of the logical equivalent." So we may have created an oxymoron –how do we develop systems that the user cannot specify? Furthermore, specifications that depict consumer behavior are now further complicated by the globalization of business. Which consumer behavior are we attempting to satisfy and across what cultural norms?

So the reality is that new applications will need more generic and be built with a certain amount of risk and uncertainty. That is business rules may be more questionable, risks will need to be evaluated and consistent with those practiced by the organization.

Let me state a case for my argument of designing systems for uncertainty and change.

If we look at the successful application in the 1980s with the advent of the personal computer, a standout is the electronic spreadsheet. The electronic spreadsheet was first introduced by a company called Visicorp and they named the product VisiCalc. It was designed for the Apple II and eventually the IBM PC microcomputer. The electronic spreadsheet was not built off of consumer needs, rather perceived needs. The electronic spreadsheet was designed as a generic calculator and mathematical worksheet. Visicorp took a risk by providing a product to the market and hoped that market would find it useful. Of course history shows that it was a very good risk. The electronic spreadsheet, which is now dominated by the Microsoft Excel product, has gone through multiple generations. The inventors had a vision and the market then matured its many uses. Thus Visicorp was correct, but not 100 % accurate with what consumers would want and continue to need. For example, the additional feature of a database interface, three-dimensional spreadsheets to support budgeting, and forward referencing are all examples of responses from consumers that generated new enhancements to electronic spreadsheets.

Allen and Morton (1994) established an excellent graphical depiction of the relationship between technology advancements and market needs (Fig. 12.2)

Figure 12.2 shows an interesting cycle of innovations as it relates to the creation of new products and services. The diagram reflects that innovation can be influenced by new technology capabilities or inventions that create new markets—like the electronic spreadsheet. On the other hand, the market can demand more features and functions in technology that need to respond—like the case of the upgrades made over the years to spreadsheet applications. The latter, that is, responding to the

Fig. 12.2 Technology, innovation, and market needs

market, is what most analysts are expected to handle over the past 60 years, usually working with their end user populations (those internal users that supported the actual consumer). The digital revolution; however, is placing more emphasis on "generic" applications that resemble the object paradigm. This trend will drive a new, more advanced object-driven specification. These applications will reside in a more robust object functioning library that can dynamically link these modules together to form specific application more reflective of the current consumer marketplace.

Another useful approach to dealing with consumer preferences is Porter's five forces framework. Porter's framework consists of the following five components:

1. *Competitors*: what is the number of competitors in the market and what is the organization's position within the market?
2. *New entrants*: what companies can come into the organization's space and provide competition?
3. *Substitutes*: what products or services can replace what you do?
4. *Buyers*: what alternatives do buyers have? How close and tight is the relationship between the buyer and seller?
5. *Suppliers*: what is the number of suppliers that are available which can affect the relationship with the buyer and also determine price levels?

Porter's framework is graphically depicted in Fig. 12.3.

Cadle et al. (2014) provide an approach to using Porter's model as part of the analysis and design process. Their approach is integrated with Langer's analysis consumer methods in Table 12.2.

Fig. 12.3 Porter's five forces framework

Table 12.2 Langer's analysis consumer methods

Porter's five force	Cadel et al.'s approach	Langer's sources of input
Industry competitors	How strong is your market share	Third-party market studies
New entrants	New threats	Third-party market studies
		Surveys and focus groups
Suppliers	Price sensitivity and closeness of relationship	Consumer support and end user departments
Buyers	Alternative choices and brand equity	Sales/marketing team
Substitutes	Consumer alternatives	Surveys and focus groups
		Sales and marketing team
		Third-party studies

Concepts of the S-Curve and Digital Transformation Analysis and Design

Digital transformation will also be associated with the behavior of the S-curve. The S-curve has been a long-standing economic graph that depicts the life cycle of a product or service. The S-curve is just that as shown in Fig. 12.4.

The left lower portion of the S-curve represents a growing market opportunity that is likely volatile and where demand exceeds supply. Therefore, the market opportunity is large with high prices for the product. Thus, businesses attempt to capture as much of the market at this time, which in turn requires risk-taking with associated rewards, especially in increasing market share. The shape of the S-curve suggests the life of the opportunity.

As the market approaches the middle of the center of the S, demand begins to equal supply. Prices start to drop and the market, in general, becomes less volatile and more predictable. The drop in price reflects the presence of more competitors.

Fig. 12.4 The S-curve

The S- Curve

Fig. 12.5 Extended
S-curve

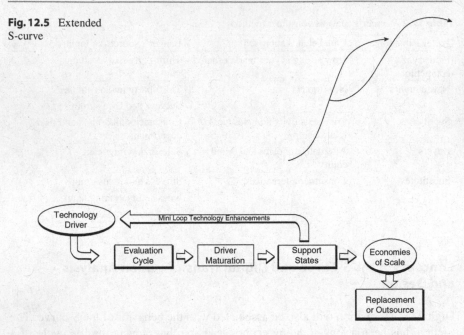

Fig. 12.6 Langer's drive/supporter life cycle

As a product or service approaches the top of the S, supply begins to exceed demand. Prices begin to fall and the market is said to have reached maturity. The uniqueness of the product or service is now approaching commodity. Typically suppliers will attempt to produce new versions to extend the life of the curve as shown in Fig. 12.5.

Establishing a new S-curve then extends the competitive life of the product or service. Once the top of the S-curve is reached, the product or service has reached the commodity level, where supply is much greater than demand. Here, the product or service has likely reached the end of its useful competitive life and should either be replaced with a new solution or considered for outsourcing to a third-party.

Langer's driver/supporter depicts the life cycle of any application or product as shown in Fig. 12.6.

Analysis and Design and the S-Curve

When designing a new application or system, the status of that product's S-curve should be carefully correlated to the source of the requirements. Table 12.3 reflects the corresponding market sources and associated risk factors relating to the dependability of requirements based on state of the consumer's market.

Table 12.3 S-curve, application requirement sources, and risk

S-curve status	Analysis input source	Risk factor
Early S-curve	Consumer	High, market volatility and uncertainty
High S-curve	Consumer	Lower, market is less uncertain as product becomes more mature
	End users	Medium, business users have experience with consumers and can provide reasonable requirements
Crest of the S-curve	End users	Low, business users have more experience as product becomes mature
	Consumer	High, might consider new features and functions to keep product more competitive. Attempt to establish new S-curve
End of S-curve	End user	None, seek to replace product or consider third-party product to replace what is now a legacy application. Also think of outsourcing application

Communities of Practice

Another technique that can be used to obtain more accurate information in the digital economy is called communities of practice (COP). COP has been traditionally used as a method of bringing together people in organizations with similar talents, responsibilities, and/or interests. Such communities can be effectively used to obtain valuable information about the way things work and what is required to run business operations. Much of this information is typically implicit knowledge that exists undocumented in the organization. Getting such information strongly correlates to the challenges of obtaining dependable information from the consumer market. I discussed the use of surveys and focus groups earlier in this section, but COP is an alternative approach to bringing together similar types of consumers grouped by their interests and needs. Communities of practice are based on the assumption that learning starts with engagement in social practice and that this practice is the fundamental construct by which individuals learn (Wenger 1998). Thus, COPs are formed to get things done by using a shared way of pursuing interests from common users. For analysts this means another way of obtaining requirements by engaging in, and contributing to, the practices of specific consumer communities. This means that working with COP is another way of developing relations with consumers to better understand their needs. Using this approach inside an organization provides a means of better learning about issues by using a sustained method of remaining interconnected with specific business user groups, which can define what the organization really knows and contributes to the business that is typically not documented. The notion of COP supports the idea that learning is an "inevitable part of participating in social life and practice" (Elkjaer 1999: 75). Thus, analysts need to become engaged in learning if they are to truly understand what is needed to develop more effective and accurate software

applications. Communities of practice also includes assisting members of the community, with the particular focus on improving their skills. This is also known as "situated learning." Thus, communities of practice is very much a social learning theory as opposed to one that is based solely on the individual. Communities of practice has been called learning-in-working where learning is an inevitable part of working together in a social setting. Much of this concept implies that learning in some form or other will occur and that it is accomplished within a framework of social participation, not solely or simply in the individual mind. In a world that is changing significantly due to technological innovations, we should recognize the need for organizations, communities, and individuals to embrace the complexities of being interconnected at an accelerated pace.

There is much that is useful in communities-of-practice theory and that justifies its use in the analysis and design process. While so much of learning technology is event driven and individually learned, it would be shortsighted to believe that it is the only way learning can occur in an organization. Furthermore, the enormity and complexity of technology requires a community focus. This would be especially useful within the confines of specific departments that are in need of understanding how to deal with technological dynamism. That is, preparation for using new technologies cannot be accomplished by waiting for an event to occur, instead, preparation can be accomplished by creating a community that can assess technologies as a part of the organization's normal activities. Specifically this means that through the infrastructure of a community, individuals can determine how they will organize themselves to operate with emerging technologies, what education they will need, and what potential strategic integration they will need to prepare for changes brought on by technology. Action in this context can be viewed as a continuous process, much in the same way that I have presented technology as an ongoing accelerating variable. However, Elkjaer (1999) argues that the continuous process cannot exist without individual interaction. As he states:

> Both individual and collective activities are grounded in the past, the present, and the future. Actions and interactions take place between and among group members and should not be viewed merely as the actions and interactions of individuals. (82)

Based on this perspective, technology can be handled by the actions (community) and consumers (individuals) as shown in Fig. 12.7.

It seems logical that COP can provide the mechanism to assist analysts with an understanding of how business users and consumers behave and interact. Indeed, the analyst can target the behavior of the community and its need to consider what new organizational structures can better support emerging technologies. I have in many ways already established and presented what should be called the "community of IT analyst practice" and its need to understand how to restructure in order to meet the needs of the digital economy. This new era does not lend itself to the traditional approaches to analysis, but rather to a more community-based process that

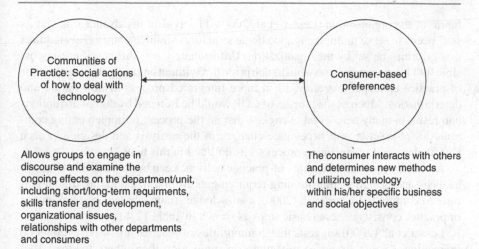

Communities of
Practice: Social actions
of how to deal with
technology

Consumer-based
preferences

Allows groups to engage in
discourse and examine the
ongoing effects on the department/unit,
including short/long-term requirments,
skills transfer and development,
organizational issues,
relationships with other departments
and consumers

The consumer interacts with others
and determines new methods
of utilizing technology
within his/her specific business
and social objectives

Fig. 12.7 Community and consumer actions

can deal with the realignment of business operations integrated with different consumer relationships.

Essentially, "communities of IT analyst practice" must allow for the continuous evolution of risk-based analysis and design based on emergent uncertain strategies. Emergent uncertain strategies acknowledge unplanned actions and evolutions in consumer behavior, which have been historically defined as patterns that develop in the absence of intentions (Mintzberg and Waters 1985). Emergent uncertain strategies can be used to gather groups that can focus on issues not based on previous plans. These strategies can be thought of as creative approaches to proactive actions. Indeed, a frustrating aspect of digital transformation is its accelerated change. Ideas and concepts borrowed from communities of practice can help businesses deal with the evolutionary aspects of consumer uncertainty.

The relationship then between communities of practice and analysis and design is significant, given that future IT applications will heavily rely on informal inputs. While there may be attempts to computerize knowledge using predictive analytics software and big data, it will not be able to provide all of the risk-associated behaviors of users and consumers. That is, a "structured" approach to creating predictive behavior reporting is typically difficult to establish and maintain. Ultimately the dynamism from digital transformations creates too many uncertainties to be handled by sophisticated automated applications on how organizations will react to digital change variables. So, COP along with these predictive analytics applications provides a more thorough umbrella of how to deal with the ongoing and unpredictable interactions established by emerging digital technologies.

Support for the above position is found in the fact that technology requires accumulative collective learning that needs to be tied to social practices; this way, project plans can be based on learning as a participatory act. One of the major advantages of communities of practice is that it can integrate key competencies into the very

fabric of the organization (Lesser et al. 2000). IT's typical disadvantage is that its staff needs to serve multiple organizational structures simultaneously. This requires that priorities be set by the organization. Unfortunately it is difficult if not impossible for IT departments to establish such priorities without engaging in communities-of-practice concepts that allow for a more integrated process of negotiation and determination. Much of the process of COP would be initiated by digital disruptions and result in many behavioral changes—that is, the process of implementing communities of practice will necessitate changes in the analysis and design approach and fundamental organization processes as outlined in this book.

As stated above, communities-of-practice activities can be very significant in the analysis and design of transitioning requirements from a transitioning digital culture. According to Lesser et al. (2000), a knowledge strategy based on communities of practice consists of seven basic steps as shown in Table 12.4.

Lesser et al. (2000) suggests that communities of practice are heavily reliant on innovation. "Some strategies rely more on innovation than others for their success..... once dependence on innovation needs have been clarified, you can work to create new knowledge where innovation matters" (8). Indeed, electronic

Table 12.4 Extended seven steps of communities-of-practice strategy in analysis and design

Step	Communities-of-practice step	Analysis extension
1.	Understanding strategic knowledge needs: what knowledge is critical to success	Understanding how technology affects strategic knowledge and what specific technological knowledge is critical to success
2.	Engaging practice domains: where people form communities of practice to engage in and identify with	Technology identifies groups based on business-related benefits. Requiring domains to work together toward measurable results
3.	Developing communities: how to help key communities reach their full potential	Technologies have life cycles that require communities to continue. Treating the life cycle as a supporter for attaining maturation and full potential
4.	Working the boundaries: how to link communities to form broader learning systems	Technology life cycles require new boundaries to be formed. This will link other communities that were previously outside of discussions and thus expand input into technology innovations
5.	Fostering a sense of belonging: how to engage people's identities and sense of belonging	The process of integrating communities: IT and other organizational units will create new evolving cultures which foster belonging as well as new social identities
6.	Running the business: how to integrate communities of practice into running the business of the organization	Digital transformation provides new organizational structures that are necessary to operate communities of practice and to support new technological innovations
7.	Applying, assessing, reflecting, renewing: how to deploy knowledge strategy through waves of organizational transformation	The active process of dealing with multiple new technologies that accelerates the deployment of knowledge strategy. Emerging technologies increase the need for organizational transformation

communities of practice are different than physical communities. Digital disruptions provide another dimension to how technology affects organizational learning. It does so by creating new ways in which communities of practice operate. In the complexity of ways that it affects us, technology has a dichotomous relationship with communities of practice. That is, there is a two-sided issue: (1) the need for communities of practice to implement IT projects and integrate them better into what consumers want, and (2) the expansion of electronic communities of practice invoked by technology, which can in turn assist expansion of the business consumer base, globally and culturally.

The latter issue establishes the fact that a consumer can now readily be a member of many electronic communities and in many different capacities. Electronic communities are different in that they can have memberships that are short-lived and transient, forming and reforming according to interest, particular tasks, or commonality of issue. Communities of practice themselves are utilizing technologies to form multiple and simultaneous relationships. Furthermore, the growth of international communities resulting from ever-expanding global economies has created further complexities and dilemmas.

Thus far I have presented communities of practice as an infrastructure that can foster improved ways to create requirements based on consumer behavior and trends. Most of what I have presented impacts the ways analysis and design needs to be approached in today's changing world. Communities of practice through the advent technology innovations have expanded to include electronic communities. While technology can provide organizations with vast electronic libraries that end up as storehouses of information, they are only valuable if it they are allowed to be shared within the community. Although IT has led many companies to imagine a new world of leveraged knowledge, communities have discovered that just storing information does not provide for effective and efficient use of knowledge. As a result, many companies have created these "electronic" communities so that knowledge can be leveraged, especially across cultures and geographic boundaries. These electronic communities are predictably more dynamic as a result of what technology provides to them. Below are examples of what these communities provide to organizations:

- Transcending boundaries and exchanging knowledge with internal and external communities. In this circumstance, communities are not only extending across business units but into communities among various clients—as we see developing in advanced e-business strategies. Using Internet and Intranets, communities can foster dynamic integration of the client, an important participant in competitive advantage. However, the expansion of an external community, due to emergent electronics, creates yet another need for the implementation of a more dynamic analysis approach to ascertaining requirements.
- Connecting social and workplace communities through sophisticated networks. This issue links well to the entire expansion of issues surrounding organizational learning, in particular learning organization formation. It enfolds both the process and the social dialectic issues so important to creating well-balanced

communities of practice that deal with organizational-level and individual development.

- Integrating teleworkers and non-teleworkers, including the study of gender and cultural differences. The growth of distance workers will most likely increase with the maturation of technological connectivity. Video conferencing and improved media interaction through expanded broadband will support further developments in virtual workplaces. Gender and culture will continue to become important issues in the expansion of existing models that are currently limited to specific types of workplace issues.
- Assisting in computer-mediated communities. Such mediation allows for the management of interaction among communities, of who mediates their communications criteria, and of who is ultimately responsible for the mediation of issues. Mature communities of practice will pursue self-mediation.
- Creating "flame" communities. A "flame" is defined as a lengthy, often personally insulting, debate in an electronic community, which provides both positive and negative consequences. Difference can be linked to strengthening the identification of common values within a community, but requires organizational maturation that relies more on computerized communication to improve interpersonal and social factors to avoid miscommunications (Franco et al. 2000).
- Storing collective requirements in large-scale libraries and databases. As Einstein stated: "Knowledge is experience. Everything else is just information." Repositories of information are not knowledge, and they often inhibit organizations from sharing important knowledge building-blocks that affect technical, social, managerial, and personal developments that are critical for learning organizations (McDermott 2000).

Ultimately the above communities of practice are forming new social networks, which have established the cornerstone of "global connectivity, virtual communities, and computer-supported cooperative work" (Wellman et al. 2000: 179). These social networks are then creating new sources of trends, changing the very nature of the way organizations deal with and use technology to change how knowledge develops and is used via communities of practice. It is not, therefore, that communities of practice are new infrastructures or social forces, but rather the difference is in the way they communicate. Digital transformation forces new networks of communication to occur and the cultural adaptation component allows these communities of practice to focus on how they will use new emerging technologies to change their business and social lives.

There is an increasing recognition that the competitive advantage of organizations depends on their "ability to create, transfer, utilize, and protect difficult-to-intimate knowledge assets" (Teece 2001, p. 125). Indeed, according to Bertels and Savage (1998), the dominant logic of the industrial era is the challenge of understanding how to break the barrier and understanding the information era. While we have developed powerful solutions to change processes and structures, most organizations have failed to address the cultural dimensions of the information era. Organizational knowledge creation is a result of organizational learning through

Fig. 12.8 Nonaka's three
steps to evaluating
organizational knowledge

| Knowledge Creation |

⇩

| Continuous Innovation |

⇩

| Competitive Advantage |

Knowledge Creation: technology provides more dynamic shifts in knowledge, thus accelerating the number of knowledge creation events that can occur

⇩

Continuous Innovation: Innovations are accelerated because of the dynamic nature of events and the time requirements to respond—therefore, continuous innovation procedures are more significant to have in order to respond on an ongoing basis.

⇩

Competitive Advantage: Technology has generated more global competition. Competitive advantages that depend of technological innovation are more common.

Fig. 12.9 Nonaka's three step model modified for technology

strategic processes. Nonaka defines organizational knowledge as "the capability of a company as a whole to create new knowledge, disseminate it throughout the organization, and embody it in products, services, and systems" (3). Nonaka used three steps to assess the value and chain of events surrounding valuation of organization knowledge in Fig. 12.8.

The question of how technology affects Nonaka's chain of actions is critical to understanding how competitive advantage can be maintained in the digital era. Without violating the model, technology has the following effects on each step as shown in Fig. 12.9.

According to Nonaka, to create new knowledge means to recreate the company and everyone in it in an ongoing process that requires personal and organizational self-renewal—that is, knowledge creation is the responsibility of everyone in the organization. The realism of this definition must be questioned. Can organizations create personnel that will adhere to such parameters, and under what conditions will senior management support such an endeavor? Once again technology has a remarkable role to play in substantiating the need for knowledge management. First, executives are still challenged to understand how they need to deal with emerging technologies as it relates to whether their organizations are capable of using it effectively and efficiently. Knowledge management addresses the theoretical construct to

a very concrete issue—it provides a way for the organization to learn how technology will be used to support innovation and competitive advantage. Second, analysts need to understand how they can best operate within the larger scope of the organization and are often searching for a true mission that contains measurable outcomes as defined by the entire organization, including senior management. Third, both executives and analysts agree that understanding the uses of technology is a continuous process that should not be utilized solely in a reactionary and event-driven way. Finally, most employees accept the fact that technology is a major component of their lives at work and at home: they accept that technology requires change and that their participation in knowledge creation is an important role for them especially in understanding how the consumers they support are transforming within their own domains. Once again, we can see that technology provides the initiator for understanding how digital transformation is important for competitive advantage in that it must meet the needs of the consumer. The combination of IT and other organizational departments, when operating within the processes outlined in digital transformation, can significantly enhance learning and competitive advantage. In order to expand on this point, I focus on the literature specifically relating to tacit knowledge and its important role in knowledge management. Scholars relate knowledge management as the ability to transfer individual tacit knowledge into explicit knowledge. Kulkki and Kosonen (2001) define tacit knowledge as combined experience-based skill type knowledge and the individual capacity to give intuitive forms to new things, that is, to anticipate and pre-conceptualize the future. Technology, by its very definition and existence, requires this anticipation and pre-conceptualization. Indeed, it is the perfect educational environment to practice the transformation of tacit to explicit knowledge. Tacit knowledge is an asset, and having individual dynamic abilities to work with such knowledge commands a "higher premium when rapid organic growth is enabled by technology" (Teece 2001, p. 140). Thus, knowledge management is likely to be greater when technological opportunity is richer.

Because evaluating emerging technologies necessitates looking into the future, it requires individuals to somehow translate valuable tacit knowledge and creatively see how these opportunities are to be judged if implemented. Examples of applicable tacit knowledge in this process are extracted from Kulkki and Kosonen (2001):

- Cultural and social history
- Problem solving modes
- Orientation to risks and uncertainties
- World views organizing principles
- Horizons of expectations

I approach each of these forms of tacit knowledge from the perspective of the components of digital transformation as shown in Table 12.5.

It is not my intension to suggest that all technologies should be or can be used to generate competitive advantage. To this extent, some technologies may indeed get rejected because it cannot assist the organization or meet consumer needs. Indeed, as Teece (2001) states: "information transfer is not knowledge transfer and

Table 12.5 Mapping tacit knowledge to digital transformation

Tacit knowledge	Digital transformation	Analyst actions
Cultural and social history		Relates to how the IT department and other departments translate emerging technologies into their existing processes and organization to support users and consumers
Problem solving modes	Internal practices that assist in determining how specific technologies can be useful and applied. Utilization of tacit knowledge to evaluate probabilities for success	Technology opportunities may require organizational and structural changes to existing applications in order to transfer tacit knowledge to explicit knowledge
Orientation to risks and uncertainties	Technology offers many risks and uncertainties. All new technologies may not be valid for the organization. Tacit knowledge is a valuable component to fully understand realities, risks, and uncertainties	Not all new applications will provide the ROI anticipated. Must build in a risk approach that establishes new expectations on success rates
World views	Technology has global effects and changes boundaries that cross business cultures and requires tacit knowledge to understand existing dispositions on how others work together	Review of how technology affects the dynamics of the way business is conducted in the target market
Organizing principles	How will new technologies actually be integrated. What are organizational challenges of how to "roll out" products, specifically relating to implementation time lines	Identify limitations of the current applications, that is, find tacit knowledge that needs to be transformed into explicit knowledge and applied to existing or new application products
	What positions are needed and who in the organization might best be qualified to fill new responsibilities	
Horizons of expectation	Consumer limitations in the tacit domain that may hinder or support evaluation process relating to determining how or if a technology can be strategically integrated into the business to support consumer needs	Determine ways in which new consumer needs can be automated and in what applications, systems, and organizational structures

information management is not knowledge management, although the former can assist the latter. Consumers and organizations can suffer from information overload" (p. 129). While this is a significant issue in many firms, the ability to have an organization that can select, interpret, and integrate information is a very valuable part of knowledge management. Furthermore much of the excitement surrounding knowledge management has been propelled by advances in IT. It is important to recognize that that consumers must be part of the analysis to ultimately determine

what new organizational knowledge is required. This is why knowledge management is so important. Knowledge must be built on its own—requiring intensive and laborious interactions among members of the organization, customers, and consumers.

Change Management

Because technology requires that organizations accelerate their actions, it is necessary for analysts to also evolve their roles to examine how business transformation relates to organizational change. Burke (2002) states that most organizational change is evolutionary; however, he defines two distinct types: planned versus unplanned and revolutionary versus evolutionary. Burke also suggests that the external environment changes are more rapid today and that most organizations "are playing catch up." I believe that many rapid changes to the external environment can be attributed to emerging technologies, in which because it creates the need, digital transformation has accelerated the divide between what an organization does and what it needs to do to remain competitive. The "catching-up" process therefore becomes more difficult because the amount of change required is only increasing because of new technologies. Burke suggests that this catch up will likely require planned and revolutionary change. Such planned and revolutionary change needs to be determined by analysts, typically by using data flow diagrams to map processes to organizational design and structure. Using technology as a need for change, it is then important that the components of analysis and design be integrated with the design of the physical organization.

History has shown that most organizational change is not successful in providing its intended outcomes because of cultural lock-in. Cultural lock-in is defined as an organization's inability to change their corporate culture even when there are clear market threats (Foster and Kaplan 2001, p. 16). Based on this definition then, technology may not be able to change the way an organization behaves, even when there are obvious competitive advantages to doing so. The concern with Foster and Kaplan's conclusion is whether individuals truly understand exactly how their organizations are being affected—or are we assuming they do? In other words, is there a process that ensures that employees understand the impact of not changing? I believe that organizational dynamism is the infrastructure that is required to support this dilemma, by establishing the processes that can support ongoing unplanned and evolutionary change.

To best show the relationship of digital transformation to organization change theory, I use Burke's six major points in assisting change in organizations:

1. *Understanding the external environment*: what are competitors and customer's expectations are certainly an issue, specifically when tracking whether expected technologies are made available in the client/vendor relationship. But more critical is the process of how emerging technologies, brought about through external channels, are evaluated and put into production. That is, having a process in

place. The analysis and design team is the infrastructure that needs to facilitate the monitoring and management of the external environment.

2. *Evaluation of the inside of the organization*: this directly relates to technology and how it can be best utilized to improve internal operations. While evaluation may also relate to a restructuring of an organization's mission, technology is often an important driver of why a mission needs to be changed, e.g., expanding a market due to digital transformation needs.

3. *Readiness of the organization*: the question here is not whether to change but how fast can the organization change to technological innovations. The analyst provides the steps necessary to design organizational structures that can evolve, integrating new consumer needs with the necessary organizational changes to support new applications.

4. *Cultural change as inevitable*: cultural change essentially dictates that organizations must dynamically assimilate new technologies and be prepared to evolve their cultures. Most important is that such evolution must be accelerated and be systemic within business units to be able to respond effectively to the rate of change created by technological innovations. Once again the analyst needs to correlate application needs with roles and responsibilities to support them.

5. *Making the case for change*: it is difficult to just explain why change is inevitable as established by Foster and Kaplan. Much of the needs for change can be supported using the reflective practices implemented in Ravell. However, such acceptance is directly related to the process of time. Major events can assist in establishing the many needs for change as discussed by Burke (2002).

6. *Sustaining change*: perhaps the most important challenge of digital transformation is in its ability to create a process that is evolutionary and systemic. It focuses on driving change to every aspect of the organization and provides organizational learning constructs to address each level of operation. It addresses what Burke spells out as "prelaunch, launch, postlaunch, and sustaining" as the important sequences of organization change (p. 286). However, the rate of change will continue to increase, so design must be very agile.

Another important aspect of change management is leadership. Leadership takes many forms and has alternating definitions. Technology plays an interesting role in how leadership can be presented to organizations, especially in terms of management style of leadership, or what Eisenhardt and Bourgeois (1988) coined "power centralization." Their study examined high-velocity environments in the microcomputer industry during the late 1980s. By high velocity, they meant "those environments in which there is a rapid and discontinuous change in demand, competitors, technology, or regulation, so that information is often inaccurate, unavailable, or obsolete" (p. 738). During the period of their study, the microcomputer industry was undergoing substantial technological change, including the introduction of many new competitors. As it turns out, the concept of high velocity is becoming more the norm today of the way organizations need to operate in constant velocities. The term "power centralization" was defined as the amount of control in decision-making by the chief executive (CEO). Their study found that the more the CEO

engaged in power-centralized leadership, the more politics existed, which in turn had a negative impact on strategic performance of the firms examined. This suggests that the less democratic the leadership in high-velocity environments, the less productive the organization. Indeed, the study found that where individuals engaged in team learning, politics was reduced and the performance of the firm improved.

The role of the analyst can provide a means of avoiding the high-velocity dilemma, especially since it utilized engineering techniques that allow for the development of more logical-based operations as well as system thinking across multiple management layers of the business. If technology is to continue to establish such high velocities, firms need to examine the Eisenhardt and Bourgeois study for its relevance to everyday operations and seek to use logical analysis and design techniques as a key basis for establishing new organizational structures.

The Role of the Analyst in Change Management for IT Organizations

While change management theories address a broad population in organizations, there is a need to create a more IT-specific approach using the analyst position to address the unique needs of any organization in digital transformation. Lientz and Rea (2004) established five specific goals for IT change managers:

1. Gain support for change from internal users and non-IT managers.
2. Implement logical flow diagrams that provide alternative organizational structures.
3. Implement new process flows where employees share more information and work more in teams.
4. Raise the level of awareness of the process and work so that there is less of a tendency for reversion.
5. Implement an ongoing measurement and review process to detect any problems and respond to new requirements.

The basis of Lientz and Rea's position is that it is particularly important that when a new culture is instilled in IT departments, it does *not* require massive management intervention. IT people need to be self-motivated to keep up with the myriad of accelerated changes in the world of technology. These changes occur inside IT in two critical areas. The first relates to the technology itself. For example, how analysts keep up with new versions of hardware and software. Many times these changes come in the form of hardware (often called "system") and software upgrades from vendors who require them to maintain support contracts. The ongoing self-management of how such upgrades and changes will ultimately affect the rest of the organization is a major challenge and one that is difficult to manage top-down. Second is the impact of new or emerging technologies on business strategy. The challenge is to develop IT personnel that can transition their technical knowledge into business knowledge and, as discussed earlier, to take this tacit knowledge and convert it into explicit strategic knowledge. A further understanding of the components of these accelerated changes is listed as follows:

- *System and software version control*: as stated earlier, the analyst must continue to track and upgrade new releases and understand the impact of these enhancements. Some product-related enhancements have no bearing on strategic use; they essentially fix problems in the system or software. On the other hand, some new releases offer new features and functions that need to be articulated to both IT, business managers, and consumers.
- *Existing legacy systems*: many of these systems cannot support the current needs of the business and consumers. This often forces IT staff to figure out how to create what are called "workarounds" to these systems. This can be problematic given that workarounds might require system changes and/or modifications to existing software. The risk of these changes both short- and long-term need to be discussed between the user and consumer communities of practice.
- *Software packages (off-the-shelf software)*: over the past decade, the use of pre-programmed third-party software packages is becoming more preferred by users. However, many of these packages can be inflexible and do not support the exact processes required by business users. IT personnel need to manage user's false expectations about what software packages can and cannot do.
- *System or software changes*: replacement of systems and/or software applications is rarely 100 % complete. Most often, remnants of old systems will remain. Analysts can at times be insensitive to the lack of a complete replacement.
- *Project completion*: analysts often misevaluate when their involvement is finished. Projects are rarely finished when the software is installed and training completed. IT staff tend to move on to other projects and tasks and lose focus on the likelihood that there will be problems discovered or last-minute requests made by business users. Given that more applications are living and breathing products, completion is never really reached, so the involvement of the analyst will continue as long as the product is in service.
- *Technical knowledge*: analysts need to keep their technical skills up to date. If this is not done, emerging technologies may not be evaluated properly as there may be a lack of technical ability inside the organization to map new technical developments to strategic advantage.
- *Pleasing users and consumers*: while pleasing business users appears to be a good thing, it can also present serious problems on IT projects. What users want and what they need may not be the same thing. Analysts need to judge when they might need assistance from business and IT management because users may be unfairly requesting things that are not feasible within the constraints of a project. Thus, analysts must have the ability to articulate what the system can do and what might be advisable. These issues tend to occur when certain business users want new systems to behave like old ones.

The above issues essentially define key risks to the success of implementation. Much of this book thus far has focused on the process of providing software solutions from an infrastructure perspective. However, the process of digital transformation posses new risks to successfully creating effective systems for consumers. These risks from the above issues along with those discussed by Lientz and Rea are summarized as follows:

- *Business-user involvement*: continuous involvement from business users is necessary. Unfortunately during the life of a project there are so many human interfaces between the analyst and business users that it is unrealistic to control these communications through tight management procedures.
- *Requirements definition and scope*: this relates to the process where analysts work with business users and consumers to determine exactly what software and systems need to accomplish, but with an understanding that it could change anytime. Determining requirements is a process, not a predetermined list that business users will necessarily have available. The discourse and language that occurs during conversations are critical pieces of whether such communities are capable of developing requirements that are unambiguous in terms of expected outcomes.
- *Business rules*: these rules have great effect on how the organization handles data and transactions. The difference between requirements and business rules is subtle, yet different. Specifically business rules, unlike requirements, are not necessarily related to processes or events of the business. As such, the determination of business rules cannot be acquired by reviewing procedures, for example, all account numbers must be numeric.
- *Documentation and training materials*: as discussed earlier, analyst staff needs to interact with business users and establish joint processes that foster the development of documentation and training that best fits user needs and business processes.
- *Data conversion*: new systems and applications require that data from legacy systems be converted into the new formats. This process is called "data mapping" where IT staff and key business users review each data field to ensure that the proper data is represented correctly in the new system. Analysts should not be doing this process without user and consumer involvement.
- *Process measurement*: organizations typically perform a post-completion review after the system or software application is installed. Unfortunately, process measurement should occur during and after project completion.

The Analyst in the Digital Transformation Era

When we discuss the digital world and its multitude of effects on how business is conducted and how the social world interacts, one must ask how this impacts the profession of analysis and design. This section attempts to address the perceived evolution of the role.

1. The analyst must become more innovative. While the business has the problem of keeping up with changes in their markets, the analyst needs to provide more solutions. Many of these solutions will not be absolute and likely will have short shelf lives. Risk is fundamental. As a result, analysts must truly become "business" analysts by exploring new ideas from the outside and continually considering how to implement the needs of the company's consumers. As a result the business analyst will emerge as an idea broker (Robertson & Robertson 2012) by con-

stantly pursuing external ideas and transforming them into automated and competitive solutions. These ideas will have a failure rate, which means that companies will need to produce more applications than they will inevitable implement. This will certainly require organizations to spend more on software development.

2. Quality requirements will be even more complex. In order to keep in equilibrium with the S-curve, the balance between quality and production will be a constant negotiation. Because applications will have shorter life cycles and the pressure to provide competitive solutions, products will need to sense market need and respond to them quicker. As a result, fixes and enhancements to applications will be become more inherent in the development cycle after products go live in the market. Thus, the object paradigm will become even more fundamental to better software development because it provides more readily tested reusable applications and routines.

3. Dynamic interaction among users and business teams will require the creation of multiple layers of communities of practice. Organizations involved in this dynamic process must have autonomy and purpose (Narayan 2015).

4. Application analysis, design, and development must be treated and managed as a living process, that is, it never ends until the product is obsolete (supporter end). So products must continually develop to maturity.

5. Organizations should never outsource a driver technology until it reaches supporter status.

Problems and Exercises

1. What is the relationship between digital transformation and analysis and design?
2. What are the six (6) sources of consumer analysis?
3. What is meant by requirements without users and without input?
4. Describe the relationship between technology and changes in the market. How does innovation play a pivotal role?
5. Describe porter's five forces framework.
6. Compare porter's five forces with Langer's sources of consumer analysis.
7. What is the S-curve?
8. Explain the effect of digital transformation on the S-curve.
9. What is an extended S-curve?
10. What is the relationship between Langer's driver/supporter theory and the S-curve?
11. How are risk factors related to digital transformation?

References

Allen, T. J., & Morton, M. S. (1994). *Information technology and the corporation*. New York: Oxford University Press.

Bertels, T., & Savage, C. M. (1998). Tough questions on knowledge management. In G. V. Krogh, J. Roos, & D. Kleine (Eds.), *Knowing in firms: Understanding managing and measuring knowledge* (pp. 7–25). London: Sage.

Burke, W. W. (2002). *Organization change: Theory and practice*. London: Sage Publications.

Cadle, J., Paul, D., & Turner, P. (2014). *Business analysis techniques: 99 essential tools for success* (2nd ed.). Swindom: Chartered Institute for IT.

Eisenhardt, K. M., & Bourgeois, L. J. (1988). Politics of strategic decision making in high-velocity environments: Toward a midrange theory. *Academy of Management Journal, 31*(4), 737–770.

Elkjaer, B. (1999). In search of a social learning theory. In M. Easterby-Smith, L. Araujo, & J. Burgoyne (Eds.), Organizational learning and the learning organisation. Developments in theory and practice. London: Sage.

Foster, R., & Kaplan, S. (2001). *Creative destruction: Why companies that are built to last underperform the market–And how to success fully transform them*. New York: Currency.

Franco, V., Hu, H., Lewenstein, B. V., Piirto, R., Underwood, R., & Vidal, N. K. (2000). Anatomy of a flame: Conflict and community building on the Internet. In E. L. Lesser, M. A. Fontaine, & J. A. Slusher (Eds.), *Knowledge and communities* (pp. 209–224). Woburn: Butterworth-Heinemann.

Kulkki, S., & Kosonen, M. (2001). How tacit knowledge explains organizational renewal and growth: The case at Nokia. In I. Nonaka & D. Teece (Eds.), Managing industrial knowledge: Creation, transfer and utilization (pp. 244–269). London: Sage.

Langer, A. M. (1997). *The art of analysis*. New York: Springer.

Lesser, E. L., Fontaine, M. A., & Slusher, J. A. (Eds.). (2000). Knowledge and communities. Boston: Butterworth-Heinemann.

Lientz, B. P., & Rea, K. P. (2004). *Breakthrough IT change management: How to get enduring change results*. Burlington: Elsevier Butterworth-Heinemann.

McDermott, R. (2000). Why information technology inspired but cannot deliver knowledge management. In E. L. Lesser, M. A. Fontaine, & J. A. Slusher (Eds.), *Knowledge and communities* (pp. 21–36). Woburn: Butterworth-Heinemann.

Mintzberg, H., & Waters, J. A. (1985). Of strategies, deliberate and emergent. *Strategic Management Journal, 6*, 257–272.

Moore, G. (2002). *Living on the fault line: Managing for shareholder value in any economy*. New York: HarperCollins.

Narayan, S. (2015). *Agile IT organization design for digital transformation and continuous delivery*. New York: Addison-Wesely.

Robertson, S., & Robertson, J. (2012). Mastering the requirements process: Getting requirements right (3rd ed.). Upper Saddle River: Addison-Wesley.

Stolterman, E., & Fors, A. C. (2004). Information technology and the good life. *Information Systems Research: Relevant Theory and Informed Practice, 143*, 687–692.

Teece, D. J. (2001). In I. Nonaka & D. Teece (Eds.), Strategies for managing knowledge assets: The role of firm structure and industrial context. Sage Publications, Tousand Oaks. *Knowledge and Process Management, 10*(4), 125.

Wellman, B., Salaff, J., Dimitrova, D., Garton, L., Gulia, M., & Haythornthwaite, C. (2000). Computer networks as social networks: Collaborative work, telework, and virtual community. In E. L. Lesser, M. A. Fontaine, & J. A. Slusher (Eds.), *Knowledge and communities* (pp. 179–208). Woburn: Butterworth-Heinemann.

Wenger, E. (1998). *Communities of practice: Learning, meaning, and identity*. Cambridge, MA: Cambridge University Press.

Data Analytics and Data Warehouses

<div style="text-align:right">13</div>

Introduction

This chapter focuses on how to extract information from packaged software systems. This information will be used for decision support purposes (DSS) and typically be presented to the user in an online display format or on a report. The concept behind DSS is that it deals with data "after the fact," meaning that the data is no longer in a production mode but rather in a storage mode where it can be used for different forms of analytical processing. The major benefit of operating on processed data is that it cannot be changed and therefore can be accessed without concern for data integrity. Another salient issue is that because the data is not subject to change, it can be copied multiple times, allowing for some interesting performance improvements and "flattening" of the data stored in the relational database. The referential integrity that was attained in a production database does not maximize performance for the query of data for reporting purposes. Almost all systems today need to determine how best to extract information for what is now being called "data analytics," that is, the ability to understand and analyze the information contained in application software systems. Increasingly, CIOs are being held responsible for providing this information.

In order to maximize the efficiency of accessing and analyzing data, it is necessary to separate it from the production system. This is accomplished by creating copies of the data solely for decision support analysis. There are a number of different ways to do this separation. One way is data warehousing, where data is reformatted from one or more data sources and placed in a special repository for analytical processing. Another approach is to create data marts. While similar to a data warehouse, data marts are defined as more strategic in nature and more specifically organized to support the gathering of departmental data. Data warehouses can be composed of many data marts. Still another method is called data mining, in which multiple definitions of data from different systems are collected and analyzed for similarities. Data mining provides more artificial intelligence features and can perform advanced analysis against multiple data warehouses and data marts,

© Springer-Verlag London Limited 2016
A.M. Langer, *Guide to Software Development*,
DOI 10.1007/978-1-4471-6799-0_13

especially when the data comes from multiple computer systems. All of these alternatives will be examined in this chapter, and its relationship to the analysis and design of packaged software systems. In order to provide effective data warehouses, data marts, and data mining, it is necessary to understand how to obtain the data that is needed to populate these data structures.

A major component of creating effective repositories of data for DSS or data analytics is how to extract the information through database query. In order to accomplish this effectively, it is important to understand the transaction processing system, since some transactions might need to be captured when they occur as opposed to after they have updated database files. Furthermore, the process of creating reports and screen displays needs to be included as part of the analyst's specification. Some reports are precoded, while others are generated through user-initiated query applications.

Data Warehousing Concepts

Operational databases are those that are designed to track business events in real time. In operational databases processing data usually correlates to cost, while the completion of the data's process relates to revenue. I have shown in Chap. 11 that the data in operational databases are accessed at the detailed level where individual records are created, read, updated, or deleted (CRUD). Entities in the relational model are constantly updated to ensure that the integrity of the data is preserved and that no historical information on the entity's previous status is stored.

Data warehouses, on the other hand, can capture both completed events *and* their original transactions. This allows data warehouse implementations with the ability to characterize more about how the data was produced at a much more detailed and granular level than usually available in operational databases. However, it is also important to remember that data warehouses are static snapshots on historical events. As a result, they are often not in sync with an operational database, which always reflects the current aggregate picture of the data. This has both advantages and disadvantages. From an advantage point of view, a data warehouse can contain multiple copies of the same data. Each set could represent the same data at a different moment in time, or could represent different views of the same data, or any combination of all of these. Figure 13.1 depicts the relationship between a data warehouse and the operational databases in a packaged software system.

The issue of data synchronization between the operational databases and the data warehouses is significant. The ultimate consideration when designing a data warehouse system relates to the age of the data in the warehouse and how often this data needs to be refreshed. For example, if an accounting department needs to produce a report by the 15th of every month on the previous month's activity, then the data refresh would need to occur sometime after the end of the previous month and before the 15th of the new month. On the other hand, if a daily report were needed on the previous day's activities, then an evening refresh would be required. Data refreshment requires that the data from the operational database be copied to the

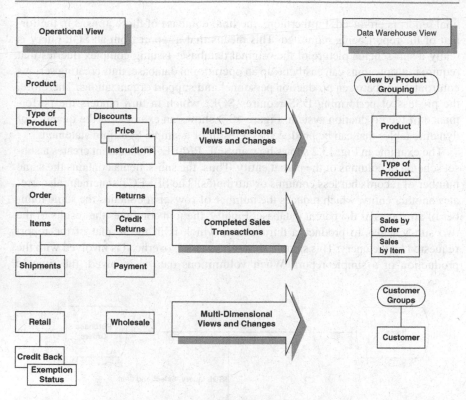

Fig. 13.1 Operational and data warehouse databases

warehouse. Unfortunately, this may not be the end of the data refresh procedure, since the format of the data in the warehouse may be very different than that of the operational system. Thus, there is typically a need for the data to be reformatted so it can be fed into the warehouse structure directly. Because a data warehouse might be an aggregation of the operational data, it can be necessary to perform mathematical computations on the ported data to produce derived data information. You might recall that derived data is a violation of normalization and not allowed in the operational database. Therefore, data warehouses are de-normalized models of the operational systems and will typically contain data elements that were removed through third-normal form implementation.

Performance Benefits of Data Warehouses

The advantages of developing a warehouse are many. First, it allows users to analyze data without interfering with the operational systems. This is a significant benefit because of the inherent problems associated with SQL. When queries are produced against an operational database to produce reports, they often require what is known as database joins. These joins create intermediate databases until the

final report is produced. Furthermore, the final database of these joins is in the format of the report being requested. This means that a report from an SQL query is really a sub-schema picture of the original database. Issuing complex queries that require multiple joins can easily tie up an operational database, thus creating serious confrontations between production personnel and support organizations. Therefore, the process of performing DSS requires SQL, which in turn hinders the performance of the production system. Figure 13.2 shows an example of the quantity of dynamic tables that can be produced as a result of a simple SQL join statement.

The example in Fig. 13.2 shows how an SQL PROJECT statement creates a subset schema of columns of the parent entity. Thus, the sub-schema contains the same number of records but less columns or attributes. The SELECT statement also creates another entity, which reduces the number of rows, but contains the same number of attributes as the parent database. Finally, the join combines the results of the two sub-schemas to produce a third entity, which is in the format of the report requested by the query. This sample shows how much overhead is involved with the production of a simple report. When voluminous data is involved, the time to

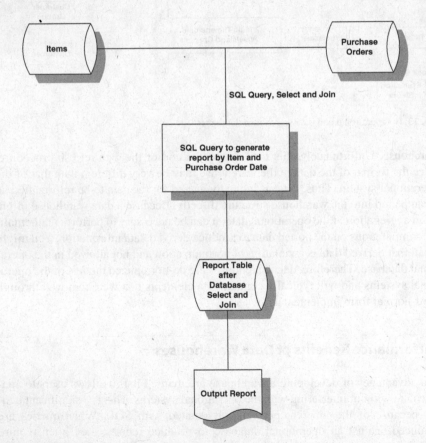

Fig. 13.2 Dynamic SQL table joins

complete the query is even more significant. Indeed, some queries have been known to run over 24 h! Therefore, data warehouse solutions should be the preferred method for analyzing data rather than using standard SQL directly against production databases.

Concept of Multiple Dimensions

Data warehousing has often been referred to as a three-dimensional way of representing data. The three dimensions are seen as a cube of data. Each cell is viewed as a box within an array. This cube brings and represents one data warehouse aggregation (combination) and provides a number of ways to view the data. Figure 13.3 shows a data warehouse aggregation of three viewable dimensions of information. The relational table is two-dimensional; it contains rows and columns, which are synonymous with records and attributes. The corresponding multidimensional cube reflects a three-attribute-dimensional view of the data. The two-dimensional part is Orders and Items, with the third dimension being Markets. Figure 13.4 reflects another third dimension, the addition of the price attribute to the array. From a reporting perspective, a user could query for Orders and Items, which would only use two of the three dimensions, or ask for Orders by Item within Market. To use all

Item	Market	Period	Quatity
Books	New York	Q1	1200
Books	New York	Q4	300
Books	St. Louis	Q2	568
Books	St. Louis	Q3	985
Books	Los Angeles	Q2	3500
DVDs	Los Angeles	Q1	5440
DVDs	Austin	Q4	1500

Fig. 13.3 Relational table and multidimensional cubes with three aggregations

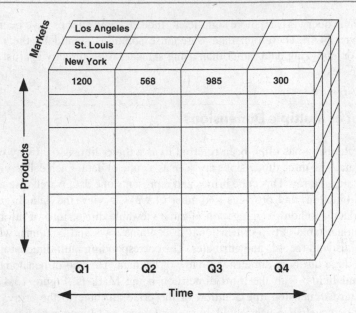

Fig. 13.4 Relational table and multidimensional cubes with four aggregations

the dimensions available, the user could search on Orders, by Item within Market by Price.

These examples picture the data warehouse from a logical perspective; that is, the cube does not exist physically, just conceptually. From a physical perspective, data warehouses use a standard data structure called the star schema. The star schema contains the main table in the center of the star, and each node represents another dimension of the data as shown in Fig. 13.5.

The star schema in Fig. 13.5 allows for queries to be performed based on an order. In many ways it resembles an entity relational diagram (ERD) in an operational database. However, most star schemas start with a multidimensioned center (concatenated primary key), so that query time is enormously reduced because there are less joins. Figures 13.6, 13.7 and 13.8 show how the number of tables is dramatically reduced as the number of primary key concatenations in the center table increases. It is important to recognize that more key concatenations in the center table greatly reduce the types of searchers that can be performed on the data, that is, the flatter the schema the less dimensions available to view the data. For example, in Fig. 13.8, there are no nodes in the star schema because there are no dimensions. Therefore, a user can only query the data warehouse to view Items within Orders, by Market and Price. It is also important to recognize that Fig. 13.8 contains no validation or look-up tables, which are normally used to validate the data of certain data elements. Data validation is not required in a warehouse architecture because the data is read-only, that is, records cannot be inserted, updated, or deleted. This is significant because this structure greatly improves data access performance. The removal of validation tables eliminates index pointers and the need for multiple

Fig. 13.5 Star schema

Fig. 13.6 Prices, order items and market as separate warehouses

Fig. 13.7 Order items and market warehouses combined

Fig. 13.8 Prices, order items and market as one warehouse

joins of tables, which simply reduces overhead and increases the performance of report queries. Figures 13.6, 13.7 and 13.8 also depict the number of dynamic searches that are needed to produce one report. It is also feasible to design packaged software data warehouses that contain all four types of star schemas. This could occur if there were four departments who had three different fixed views of how they wanted the data to be represented to them.

Because there can be multiple copies of data in a data warehouse environment, there is an advantage to create more schemas that represent the data as it is needed for a specific report or analysis, as opposed to designing an elaborate star schema that allows for multiple views of the data. The reason for this position is simple: why design a data warehouse that resembles an operation database? Another way of looking at this model is to conceptualize that every data warehouse is nothing more than a view of data for a specific user view. The more alternative searches you offer the user, the less attractive the model is from a performance perspective. However, multiple warehouses require multiple conversions from the operational systems. So, the analyst must balance the design taking into consideration both performance and overhead issues.

Data Warehouse Architecture

The first step in creating a packaged software decision support system is designing the data warehouse structure. This structure, or architecture, provides a framework for identifying how data will be utilized within the packaged software system. A basic data warehouse architecture is shown in Fig. 13.9.

The fundamental characteristics of the basic data warehouse architecture are:

- Data is extracted from operational databases, flat files, and other data sources.
- The data from all of the source systems is first integrated and transformed into another format before being loaded into the actual data warehouse.
- The data warehouse can only be used for read-only activities for DSS.
- Users obtain access to the data warehouse through a front-end application tool, usually supplied by the warehouse vendor.

Extracting Data from the Source

The data warehouse process starts with identifying the source of the data needed for the DSS. These will typically come from two places: (1) the operational databases that exist in the new packaged software system and (2) the data files that exist in legacy systems. The most difficult part of the process is to identify the meaning of the data elements in each system so they can be transformed properly into the data warehouse. This can only be accomplished by first creating a central repository of the data—typically by using a computer-aided software engineering (CASE) tool. Porting data into a central repository is easier when working with relational

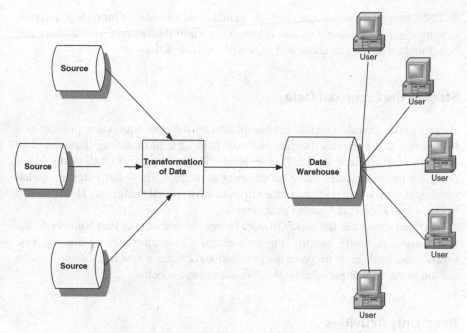

Fig. 13.9 Basic data warehouse architecture

databases because they are better documented and can be reverse engineered into a CASE tool. However, legacy data is more challenging because of their lack of documentation and less conventional data formats. Notwithstanding the format of the source data, the process to define the operational data is time-consuming but extremely valuable for the project to be successful. Many data warehouse products like Sagent provide their own metadata dictionaries that can be used instead of a CASE tool. These metadata libraries store the relationships that exist among the different yet related databases in the production systems. Analysts also need to extract data from third-party products that are part of the operational system, for example, a weekly stock price file that is integrated in to the production system. In any event, most data warehouse systems can extract data from multiple databases from multiple systems.

Many operational systems can be categorized as "transaction processing" based. This means that they are heavily geared toward capturing transactions that occur throughout the day. Typically, transaction processing systems are those that take orders, ship them, and then record financial information. Transaction processing systems have the following characteristics:

- High transaction rate.
- Constantly changing.
- Data redundancy is avoided in order to ensure integrity.
- Optimized indexes to ensure SQL query efficiency.
- Two-phase commit architecture to ensure recoverability.

DSSs using data warehouses provide tremendous advantages for transaction processing systems because they can reformat data into dimensions so that users can better understand the meaning and results of the transactions.

Staging the Extracted Data

As previously stated, a significant component of the data warehouse product is a load server that compiles the data and establishes the links among duplicate data elements. Furthermore, the load server allows for the definition of elements, especially for those attributes that have complex meanings. These attributes are called intelligent keys where portions of the attribute have special meanings. This is shown in Fig. 13.10 for a Part Number data element.

The load server has the ability to store information about the Part Number so the warehouse can easily identify the data element's components during a query. Overall, the load server prepares the raw data and creates a new repository of information in the format required by the data warehouse schema.

Read-Only Activities

As previously stated, the data warehouse is a read-only copy of operational data. The philosophy is that operational data and DSS data are inherently different. Specifically, DSS provides easy-to-understand formats of data so that analytical information can be created to support better tactical and strategic business decisions within the company. These analytical processes require that historical data be kept in different views, unlike the single normalized view required in operational databases. Indeed, one database format alone cannot efficiently provide for both types of functional need. Thus, at the core of all warehouse products is a read-only database that represents the primary component of information analysis.

Fig. 13.10 Encoded data elements

Front-End Tools

In most data warehouse systems, the data access infrastructure makes up the next most important component of the DSS architecture. This data access is composed of front-end query tools and application programs that provide useful and accessible decision support information from the data warehouse. Thus, analysts need to design the warehouse schemas, query logic, and applications to create a useful data warehouse environment that operates under the auspices of the production systems. The important component of application and query support are the third-party applications that are provided with the purchase of the data warehouse. Most warehouse products, like SAS, Sagent, and Oracle, all come with sophisticated developer tool kits that allow for the generation of advanced query and application development. These add-on application products do not, however, provide the proper analysis and design process to determine what they need to do.

Types of Data Warehouse Architecture

Thus far we have only looked as what can be called a "generic" data warehouse architecture. However, there are more sophisticated design considerations when formulating a packaged software enterprise warehouse system. Figure 13.10 depicts a slightly more complex data warehouse that loads data into what is known as business areas. A business area represents a defined segment of the organization and is based on perceived business similarities. These similarities could be based on where income is derived, type of clients, etc. Therefore, each business has its own view and use for a warehouse. All of these multiple warehouses are derived from one enterprise warehouse that has been ported from the integration of multiple data sources.

In Fig. 13.11, data is extracted from various source systems and integrated and transformed before being loaded into an enterprise data warehouse. This data is then restructured, redesigned, and moved into separate business area warehouses, which are then used for DSS. The major benefits of using a business area architecture is to:

- Ensure that all business areas are deriving data from a central warehouse system.
- Create sub-warehouses that can better facilitate the needs of smaller departments.
- Provide access to different user communities. Internal users, consumers, and customers all have different business area needs and access authorization criteria.
- Ensure that the timing of the data is consistent across all warehouses. In this way comparisons of data across the enterprise are consistent.

Another hybrid version of the business area model is to create separate area warehouses directly from the load server as shown in Fig. 13.12. While this

Fig. 13.11 Business area data warehouses

Fig. 13.12 Direct business area data warehouse

architecture does not contain a central enterprise data warehouse, it has all of the constructs that represent a true data warehouse. Obviously, the advantage is the time and space saving of creating an intermediate enterprise data warehouse. This model is advantageous when there is little need for a centralized warehouse and when there are multiple updates of the warehouse from multiple source files.

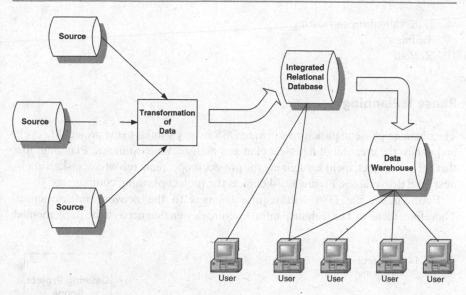

Fig. 13.13 Integrated relational data warehouse

Still another intricate architecture is shown in Fig. 13.13. This model creates an integrated relational database in third-normal form. The data that comes from source operational systems remains read-only; however, new data can be added to the integrated database directly from users. The purpose of these updates is to provide additional data that facilitates expanded decision support activities. Sometimes this process also helps to "clean up" bad data. Once the new data has been entered, the data is transformed into a data warehouse.

The Packaged Software Decision Support Life Cycle

The system development life cycle (SDLC) for packaged software DSS focuses on data, as opposed to processing and functionality. As a result of the elimination of many process-oriented steps, the DSS life cycle is much faster and less complex than its traditional counterpart. The main activity for the analysts is to take data from various sources and platforms and provide multiple strategic views of the data in another infrastructure.

The phases of the packaged software DSS are:

1. Planning
2. Gathering data requirements and modeling
3. Physical database design and development
4. Data mapping and transformation
5. Data extraction and load
6. Automating the data management process
7. Application development and reporting

8. Data validation and testing
9. Training
10. Rollout

Phase 1: Planning

The planning phase in packaged software DSS is very similar to the project life cycle and entails the creation of a project plan and realistic time estimates. Planning, like that for any project, includes defining the project scope, plan, resources, tasks, timeliness, and deliverables. Figure 13.14 depicts the project planning components.

Furthermore, the DSS will require changes to the network infrastructure. Therefore, there will be technical infrastructure design that needs to be implemented

Fig. 13.14 DSS project
planning components

while formulating the proper DSS environment. The technical components include capacity planning, archival strategies, data refresh/update strategies, and operations and job scheduling.

Phase 2: Gathering Data Requirements and Modeling

During this phase the analyst must understand the business needs and data requirements of the users of the system. Because packaged software systems are comprised of internal users, customers, and consumers, the data modeling requirements for data warehouses will vary depending on the different user views. Essentially, data requirements will involve the process of identifying what elements are needed for DSS by each group of users. The assumption should be that normalized databases exist, legacy links have been made, and intermediate transaction processing systems are in place. If a central repository of all data elements is in a CASE product, then identifying the components of the warehouse will be much easier and productive. Unlike regular data gathering, analysts should be looking at what users need to see in the form of screen displays and printed reports. Thus, it is the output that identifies what is needed for the data warehouse. Therefore, the analyst does not need to use process models like DFDs to model the data warehouse, rather the specification will consist of query screens for data access, sample reports, and screen display views. The reports and screen displays need to be in prototype form so that users can validate that the information and format are correct. Another interesting aspect of data warehouse design is to determine what users might want to see in addition to what they have already identified. Basically most users will want to see the reports and screen displays that they are used to having from their existing system. However, data warehousing allows so much more that the analysts need to consider what users might want to see given the robust power of the data warehouse query software. While this activity might seem counter to my previous position that analysts should never create requirements, I do believe that the analyst must at least inform, usually through demonstrations, the power of the data warehouse to each user constituency. Obviously, this process may not be practical for consumers, except where the marketing department is involved with focus groups. Analysts must remember to inform users that data warehouses do not contain current data. While designing real-time data warehouses is possible, it is unlikely and difficult to implement.

What is most important, however, is not the reports and displays but the strategy of designing the data warehouse (or data mart) architecture. Reports can usually be modified without great pain, but schema design is more complicated. This process requires that the analyst determines which type of warehouse designs to use. Remember that there can be multiple data warehouses produced from multiple sources, so the options for design are many to many as shown in Fig. 13.15.

Notwithstanding the relationships between data sources and data warehouses, it is important to focus on the schema design, that is, what is the design of the star schema. There are essentially three approaches. The first approach suggests that the data warehouse contains a star schema that resembles the report or screen display.

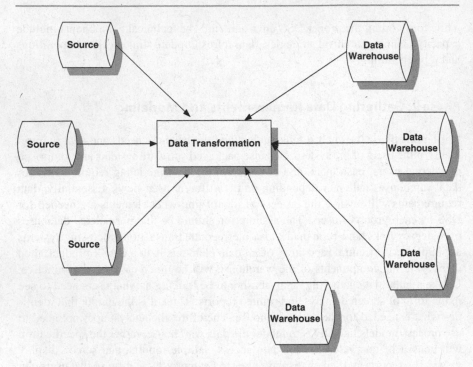

Fig. 13.15 Data source and data warehouse relationships

This design was discussed earlier in this chapter. The advantage of this approach is that data is already placed in the format required so there is little need for data manipulation. As a result, the production of the reports and displays is very efficient. Furthermore, there is little that the user needs to do other than just selecting the option to produce the report. The bad news is that the warehouse is very limited because all it can do is produce the report. The economies of scale for creating the report in a data warehouse form may seem like overkill, unless the process of obtaining the data in one central repository has significant time saving for the user. Figure 13.16 shows a data warehouse report schema.

The second approach is to create sophisticated star schemas that support a grouping of needs. Each schema would contain a central table that provides a data repository required by a group of users. Each node would provide the supplemental data that might be needed depending on the user group and the report subject. The benefit of this model is somewhat obvious in that it allows warehouses to serve multiple needs and provides for more DSS analysis of the data. The downsides are also obvious; users need more knowledge on how to query the data and therefore need training and an understanding of what data is available for analysis. In addition, the performance of the reports and displays will vary depending on the level of sophistication of the queries that are afforded to the end users. Figure 13.17 depicts a star schema for group user query.

The third approach comes back to the earlier example of the enterprise-level data warehouse. Rather than have multiple warehouses serving many users, one central

Order
Items
Market Price
Salesperson
Ship Date

Order Analysis Report					
Order #	Item ID	Market	Price	Salesperson	Date Shipped
14387	A5567	West	120.00	Joe Smith	3/15/2001

Fig. 13.16 Data warehouse report schema

Fig. 13.17 User group star schema

complex star schema can be designed to afford the needs of an entire organization, group, or department. These types of data warehouses will contain the most nodes on the schema and look very much like a third-normal form database. The advantage is that data is copied once per cycle to one data warehouse thus ensuring that all the data represents the same time period. The downside is that the warehouse becomes voluminous and requires significant data query manipulation in order to extract the needed information.

Another challenge in the movement of data from operation sources to data warehouses is derived elements. I previously discussed the handling of derived data as being a violation of third-normal form and a database redundancy. As a result, all

derived data elements were removed from the production database. However, because data warehouses are read-only, there is no need to eliminate derived data. In fact, warehouses that contain derivations will be much more efficient for query and report production. The question to answer is how to populate derived data back into the database. If a CASE tool was used to produce the normalized operational database, then there is a good chance that derived elements might exist in the data dictionary. You might recall in my earlier chapter that many derived elements are first placed in the data dictionary and defined in a process specification. Thus, the identity of these derived data elements and their calculations can be extracted from the data dictionary. Unfortunately, such is not the case when dealing with legacy databases and flat-file systems. In these situations, the analyst must reconcile each report and screen display against the existing data dictionary to determine where derived elements exist. Furthermore, just identifying them is not enough—analysts must work with users to understand how they are derived. Once all derived elements have been discovered and defined, they need to be added to the metadata dictionary usually provided with a data warehouse product. The use of metadata (data that defines data) will be discussed later in this chapter; however, its use is important when integrating derived data elements in the data warehouse. The metadata repository will allow analysts to store the calculation formula. When the data warehouse is produced (or refreshed), a triggering operation will examine the data and calculate the derived values as set forth in the metadata repository. The process of calculating derived data elements is shown in Fig. 13.18.

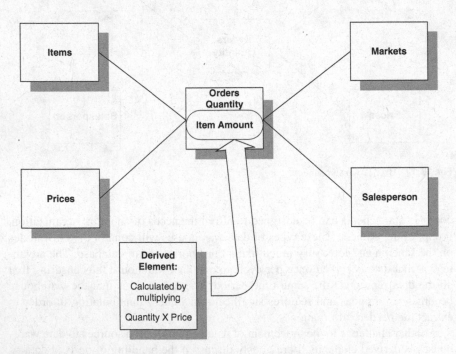

Fig. 13.18 Adding derived data elements to the data warehouse

Fig. 13.19 Porting-derived data elements directly into a data warehouse

There may also be derived data elements that cannot be directly calculated from the supplied data sources. This means that the derived elements must be calculated outside the data warehouse domain and then imported directly into the data warehouse. This is shown in Fig. 13.19.

In summary, the data gathering and modeling phase must address the following key questions:

- What will be the number and design of the data warehouses?
- How will data be reflected in the data warehouse model, particularly the derived data, which does not exist in the production database?
- Is there a CASE tool that will allow for the transformation of derived data elements from a data dictionary to the data warehouse?
- How often does data need to be refreshed?

Figure 13.20 reflects the major steps that analysts must complete in this phase.

Phase 3: Physical Database Design and Development

The physical database design entails a number of steps that enable the database to operate efficiently. There are three main components involved in the physical design process: fact tables, dimension tables, and look-up tables.

Fact tables, which are sometimes known as major tables, contain the quantitative or factual data about a business. It is, in effect, the information for which users are doing the query (Poe 1996). Fact table information is often numerical measurements of data that contain many attributes and sometimes millions of occurrences. For example, a marketing database can contain data on various sales for the company. Dimension tables or minor tables, on the other hand, are smaller than fact tables and hold descriptive data that reflect various dimensions of the facts—like

Fig. 13.20 DSS gathering data requirements and data modeling components

User Interviews

Document Results with Logic Models

Define Logical Data Model

Review Logical Designs with Users

Create Dimension Logical Data Warehouse Model

month, year, region, etc. In the previous example, dimensions of sales could be product, markets, etc. Figure 13.21 reflects the marketing data warehouse with dimension tables.

Thus, the combination of fact tables and dimension tables provides for the basis of the initial star schema. This star schema can then allow users to scan the data, and with the appropriate database constraints provide interesting analysis of the information. Look-up tables are another type of dimension table. They provide fill-in information used to describe possible values that certain fact data need. They represent entities that are similar to third-normal form validation tables. An example of a look-up table is the available colors of a particular model car. Figure 13.22 shows a combined star schema physical database that combines facts, dimensions, and look-up tables.

Fig. 13.21 Fact and dimensional data warehouse tables

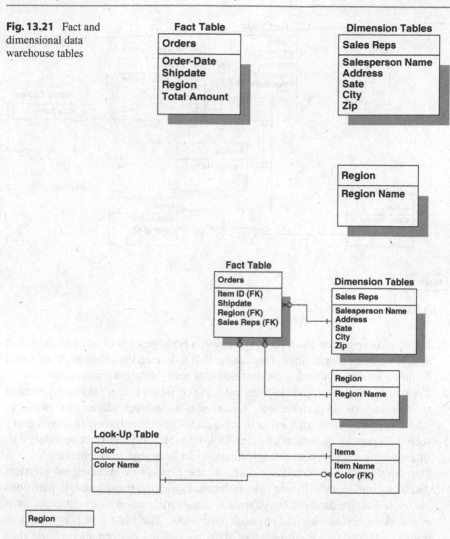

Fig. 13.22 Fact, dimensions, and look-up date warehouse tables

In many ways, much of the physical database design concepts discussed in this section could be considered part of the logic data modeling phase (Phase 2). While much of this design could be done during Phase 2, there are some related decisions that require more knowledge about the physical environment, that is, the actual data warehouse environment. Furthermore, the process of de-normalization is often accomplished during physical as opposed to logical database design. Beyond just database design, the analyst also needs to:

1. *Identify the Actual Primary and Secondary Key Structures*. Sometimes this could involve de-normalized data elements.

Fig. 13.23 Index tables

2. *Develop Aggregation Strategies.* Aggregation is the process of accumulating fact data from other transactions. This means that a derived data element transaction could be generated that depicts the results of many detailed transactions.
3. *Create Indexing Strategies.* Indexes are separate tables that are internally created to improve look-up performance. An index is an indirect address that points to where specific information exists in the database, without having to search every record. Figure 13.23 depicts an index look-up table. Any field can be indexed so that query speed to access that information can be dramatically increased.
4. *Develop Partition Tables.* Partitioning is the process of breaking up physical databases into many different storage areas. Logically, these multiple partitions are treated as one database but physically are distributed on many different areas of a disk or across multiple physical hard disks. The benefit of partitioning is purely performance. Partitioning of data maximizes performance of the data warehouse when particular parts of the data are needed by specific users. So, in theory, two users can be using the same logical data warehouse, yet be accessing two separate physical partitions of the same database.
5. *Perform Capacity Planning.* Analysts must determine the amount of storage space and processor speed that they will need in order to provide an efficient data warehouse environment. Analysts should not do this configuration alone; network architects must be involved to assist in the determination as to what processor types might best handle the load and perceived growth of the data warehouse. The key input needed from the analyst is the number of records that will be estimated in each data warehouse. There are two components that are needed to determine space requirements. The first, which was covered in an earlier chapter, calculates the size of each data warehouse record by multiplying the

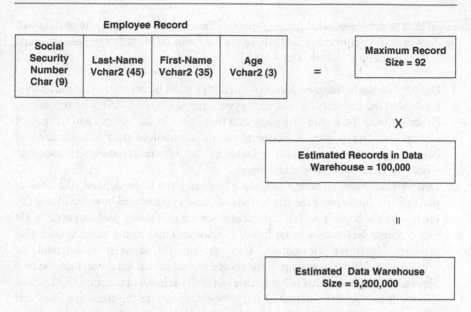

Fig. 13.24 Sample data warehouse size calculation

total number of maximum characters in each attribute within a record. By maximum I mean the largest size for all VARCHAR2 (variable length) data elements. The result of this calculation will establish each record size. The analysts need to then calculate the database size by multiplying this total record size by the estimated number of records in the data warehouse (see Fig. 13.24).

This last step might not be that easy, but sometimes estimating maximum data warehouse sizes (i.e., the largest it could be) is the safest calculation. Furthermore, analysts must take into consideration the needs for temporary storage that are required during SQL JOINS, PROJECTS, and SELECTS of data from tables. Remember that SQL-based queries generate dynamic database tables for reporting. Thus, analysts need to consider doubling or even tripling the storage requirements of the host data warehouse. This is why partitioning can be so effective; it allows network architects to scale storage by attaching more physical hard disks. The issue of how many processors to have, the memory size, and disk access speeds needs to be determined by the proper network professionals but heavily based on the input supplied by the analyst.

Phase 4: Data Mapping and Transformation

The data mapping and transformation phase is one where the analyst must locate the source of the data in the operational systems, do analysis to understand the types of data migrations and transformations that need to occur, and map the source data to

target data warehouses. This phase ultimately determines what the source data will be, how it will be converted, and where the data will be ported. The specific steps within this phase are as follows:

1. *Defining the Data Sources*: Much of this activity can be accelerated if the analyst has loaded the data elements of each system into a central CASE tool repository. Other factor is the extent of legacy data that exists in the system and the nature of how the data is stored. Furthermore, the amount of data redundancy and derived data elements all play a factor in the time requirements to ascertain where the data is and how it is defined.

2. *Determining File Layouts*: Once data sources have been defined, the analyst must clearly understand the file layouts of these systems and how the files inter-relate with each other within a particular source repository. For example, a file that contains fact data may be linked to another table in the same system that provides validation information. Thus, the analyst needs to understand the schema of each source system. If the source is a relational database, then the best approach is to generate (if not available) an entity relational diagram (ERD). The ERD will expose the referential integrity that exists at the database level and expose those relationships that have been implemented at the application level. It might also expose data redundancies. If the system is a flat-file legacy applica-tion, then the analyst should print out the file description tables (particularly if the system is written in COBOL). The file description tables will identify all of the data elements in each file. By creating a simple template or utility program, analysts can determine where duplicate elements exist among these flat files. This will allow the analyst to understand how the files link to one another, where there are redundancies, and how to schematically look at the system from a dimensional and relational perspective.

3. *Mapping Source Data to Target Data*: Once the source systems and schematic have been identified, the analyst needs to map or identify the source data to the data warehouse star schemas. This can be accomplished by creating a matrix that shows source elements and their attributes as well as their corresponding data warehouse data elements. Figure 13.25 shows a sample matching source-to-target matrix developed using a spreadsheet program.

4. *Developing Transformation Specifications*: The matrix show in Fig. 13.25 is only one component of what is called the transformation specification. Another name for a transformation specifications is conversion document. A conversion docu-ment provides the requirements for a programmer to develop a utility program that prepares, moves, and transforms source data to a data-staging file. The data-staging file is an intermediate data store that is created for actual transport to the data warehouse.

5. *Reviewing the Update Cycle*: This process establishes the refresh cycle required for each data warehouse. Refresh cycles define when a cycle begins, when it ends, and how long it runs. It is also important for the analyst to have some idea about how long a refresh cycle might take. This can be determined best by run-ning tests on sample source files and then forecasting the total update time based

Source Data Element	Attribute	Source Table	Data Warehouse Data Element	Attribute	Target Table
Company	Char(3)	Items	Company-Name	Vchar2(15)	Company
Designator	Char(15)	Items	Vendor-Style	Char(18)	PO-Item
Group-ID	Char(10)	Items	Dept-No	Char(2)	Purchase-Order
Frt-Term	Char(3)	PO	Freight-Terms	Char(1)	PO-Header
Final-Dest	Vchar2(30)	PO			
Purchase-Term	Char(4)	Contract	Import-Whse-No	Char(4)	PO-Header
Discharge-Point	Char(30)	Contract			
Arrive-By-Date	Date	Contract	FOB-Terms	Char(1)	PO-Detail
			Cancel-Date	Date	PO-Detail
Sup-Approval	Char(30)	Import	Whse-Message	Char(60)	Header-Mess
Coord-Item	Vchar(80)	Merchandise	Item-Message	Char(80)	PO-Detail

Fig. 13.25 Source-to-target data element mapping matrix

on the results of the test. The determination of conversion time could be critical since the update cycle needs to complete prior to the user wanting to see the data results. Therefore, if an update cycle runs every 24 h, then the update cycle needs to complete by the beginning of the next morning. While this might sound like plenty of time, many large-scale update cycles can take substantial time to complete. The time to complete also heavily depends on the amount of data manipulation that occurs during the conversion of data from source to target.

6. *Developing Strategies for Archival*: This step entails the decision of what portions of warehouse data can be archived or deleted from the DSS. Typically this becomes more of an issue when looking at transaction-based information. The decision is to determine when dated transactions, which are used to formulate results of the data, are no longer providing enough value to keep them actively stored in the live data warehouse. The reason for purging certain transaction is because of the performance degradation that is caused during warehouse queries. Sooner or later, historical transaction data needs to be removed from the active warehouse. Analysts have two options. Option one is to generate a summary transaction record that might represent a group of detailed transactions. This means that the summary transaction would provide a view of the meanings of the detailed transactions. Figure 13.25 provides an example of representing detailed transaction in a summary record. If this option is selected, then the detailed transactions can be deleted or archived. The creation of summary records may also require that specific program changes be made to query applications so that a summary record can be appropriately identified from a detailed transaction. The second option is to just create a separate file of purged transactions that can be accessed using a different set of query applications. This purged file would typically be resident on a separate processor so that it would not conflict with normal data warehouse activities. Regardless of which option is used, the analyst

needs to create specifications that identify the conditions for purging data and where the data is to be stored. Both options also require the development of specific query applications that can access purged data when needed.

7. *Reviewing Security Requirements*: Once the data warehouse is in place, the analyst must integrate security requirements into the specification. Unlike many security issues, because data warehouses are read-only, there are no concerns about the creation of illegal or dangerous records. However, data warehouse information is still proprietary and could provide valuable information for those with malicious or illegal intensions. Thus, securing data warehouses from unauthorized use is a key component of data warehouse design. This is especially important because most access to data warehouses in packaged software systems will occur via the Web, either from an intranet or an Internet. So who has access to what features in a Web-based data warehouse query becomes very important in the design of the warehouse system. Much of the design issues covered in Chap. 11 are relevant in data warehouse development as well. Therefore, analysts should review the security requirements of the data warehouse using the same approach as in any other system.

8. *Capacity Plan Review*: Once the data mapping and conversion methodologies have been completed, the analyst will have a much better perspective on the specific capacity requirements. This step simply suggests that the capacity planning and space determination are an iterative process in which the analyst and network architects will fine-tune the capacity needs as each phase in the life cycle is completed.

Phase 5: Populating the Data Warehouse

This phase involves the actual extract, conversion, and population of the target data warehouses. This is typically accomplished with a combination of conversion and update software supplied with the data warehouse vendor's product and with the development of specific conversion programs designed by the analyst. The steps involved with completing the population of data warehouse data is as follows:

1. *Loading and Staging the Data*: This step may involve an intermediate program that begins the process of building a repository of data where the data warehouse software will extract the information from. While many data warehouse products will allow for the loading of data directly from an operational database or file system, this is often not recommended. Accessing operational data is usually not a best practice for data architects.

2. *Converting and Integrating Data*: This step entails the execution of the actual conversion programs and the integration of multiple data sources. The process involves the confirmation that multiple data source migrations have been completed, and the execution of one or more conversion programs (that migrate the data as per the specification) have occurred. This step should result in the forma-

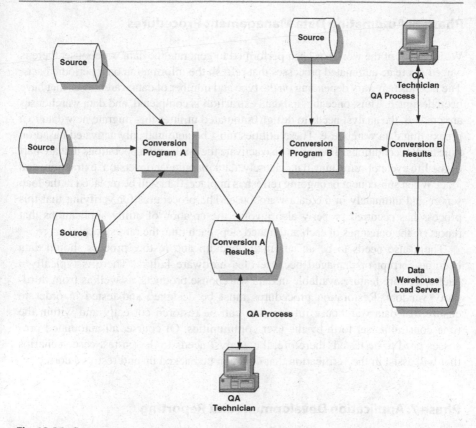

Fig. 13.26 Source conversion to data warehouse load server

tion of a warehouse load server that is ready for testing before being moved to the live data warehouse. Figure 13.26 shows the process.

3. *Testing and Loading*: The test and load phase is the final step to creating the data warehouse. The test part of this step is to provide various reconciliation results that provide assurance that data has been converted to specification. For the most part, the testing should be consistent with audit-trail philosophies including the verification that the number of records read, written, and transferred is correct. If records are rejected for whatever reason, these should also be reported. The load portion of this step involves the actual porting of the data into the warehouse for use by users. There should also be an audit-trail report specifying that the process of final load has been successful.

4. *Capacity Reviewing*: Once again, the analyst should review the capacity needs of the system after the final data warehouses have been created, since the storage at the time of completion will represent the actual storage prior to query operations on the data.

Phase 6: Automating Data Management Procedures

While much of the work has been performed to generate the data warehouse, there is a need to create automated processes that refresh the information on a periodic basis. The periods may vary depending on the type and number of data warehouses that have been designed. Thus, once the first data extraction is completed, and data warehouses are created, the analyst needs to design automated utilities that migrate new data to a preexisting data warehouse. These utilities must be automatically activated based on time and/or conditions. They must also activate the application operations that are part of the life cycle of refreshing data, namely, data mapping, conversion, extraction, and load. When subsequent or ongoing refresh is in place, data will be replaced in the load server and ultimately in the data warehouse. The procedures for verifying that this process has occurred properly also involve the creation of utility applications that report on the outcomes of each automated step, each time the refresh occurs.

There also needs to be an automatic backup and restore process should data become corrupt or damaged because of a hardware failure. There is typically a backup/restore feature available in data warehouse products, as well as from third-party vendors. Restoration procedures must be designed and tested in order to ensure that data warehouse information can be restored correctly and within the time constraints set forth by the user communities. Of course, all automated processes need to be tested; therefore, the analyst needs to design test case scenarios that will assist in the verification that data can be backed up and restored correctly.

Phase 7: Application Development and Reporting

This phase focuses on the delivery of output from the data warehouse. DSS application development is usually accomplished by using special data access tools to design and pre-build reports. Indeed, the tools selected to generate reports are critical to the success of any data warehouse. Analysts need to determine the environment to support data access and information analysis rather than just selecting a front-end software package. There are several steps that are required to understand the complexities of providing a reporting environment for users in a packaged software environment. The first issue to address is the ways in which users can receive information from the data warehouse. There are four types of reporting as follows:

1. *Parameter-Based Ad Hoc*: This allows users to enter particular information that will act as a parameter into the report application. Parameters often consist of date information or domain constraints like department or group. Users, while changing parameters, are not creating new reports but rather modifying existing reports within a predefined range of choices.
2. *Display Access*: This involves the display of reports on the Web or some other central place on the system. The important concept here is that reports are generated as needed but assumed to be effective in a view-only mode.
3. *Complete Ad Hoc*: The user interacts directly with the data warehouse using the query tools that support the warehouse product. Thus, users will need to be trained

on how to issue queries and how to manipulate the data in the warehouse. While this option provides the most versatility, it is also the most difficult report to use successfully. The problem is whether users can really master the query tool, be knowledgeable on how the data is stored, and can appropriately test their results. Indeed, the largest risk for users is generating reports that are not accurate.

4. *Hard Copy*: These are predefined and developed by the analyst. They typically have a fixed format and are printed and forwarded to the appropriate requester.

There are also a number of ways that users need to navigate through a packaged software DSS. This is based on user needs, similar to my earlier definition of user categories. The three primary methods are:

1. *Executive*: Allows executives to get predefined reports quickly and on a regular basis.
2. *Structured Decision Support*: Contains predefined and ad hoc reports and outputs. Thus, structured decision support provides another level of analysis offered to the user community. This hybrid approach is usually required by middle-tier users like line managers and supervisors, where there is a clear need to generate what-if analysis in a dynamic day-to-day environment.
3. *Unstructured Decision Support*: These users have access to all types of reports but prefer to design ad hoc reports from scratch and use them when they are needed for a particular analysis. These users are more activity based on the information they need.

The level and categories of users vary in how they use reports. What reports are needed by users also depends heavily on whether they are internal users, customers, or consumers. Typically, internal users are those that can be trained to use unstructured techniques to access data warehouse information. Figure 13.27 represents another view of how certain types of users utilize report options.

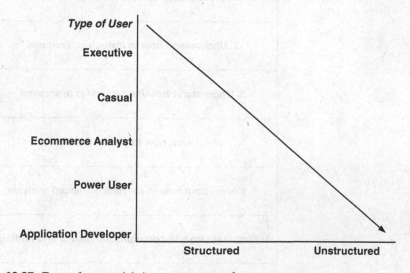

Fig. 13.27 Types of users and their report access preferences

Report Access and Analysis

A data warehouse is not an automated method of getting the information you want without working to find it. Users should not be disillusioned about what a data warehouse product will afford them to do. Misunderstanding the commitment that data warehouses require, both from designers and users, is a critical factor for success (Poe 1996). Figure 13.28 depicts the sequential steps that users should follow when using DSS and when analyzing their data.

The viewing of the reports is another important component of analysis of DSS. Users may want to specify what format they want to view the data. Thus, analysts need to provide options for users where they can select from a fixed menu of display options. While tabular and cross tabular reports are most common, graphical output is also a common way of analyzing what reports are telling users about their data. Figure 13.29 shows various types of data warehouse report presentations.

Listed below are the most common report functions that DSS should provide to users:

- Changing the axis: This allows users to swap rows and columns.
- Changing sort order.
- Adding and deleting subtotals and other information breaks.
- Creating color reports with highlighting of certain variables.
- Format options for fonts, styles, sizes, and colors.

Fig. 13.28 Report access and analysis sequence

Report Access and Analysis Sequence
1. Understand and Visualize the Data Warehouse
2. Understand how to formulate a request
3. Understand how the request is processed
4. Learn how to present results
5. Understand how to perform advanced analysis
6. Formulate how to communicate results and findings

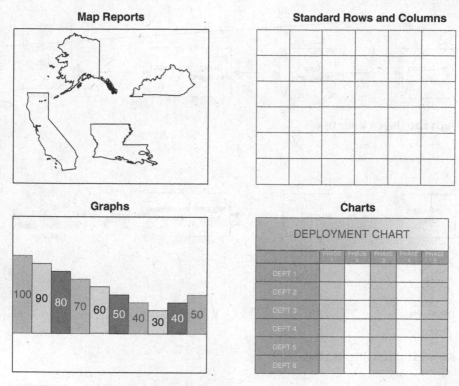

Fig. 13.29 Data warehouse report presentations

- Graphical display of information should support line graphs, dimensional and stacked bars, pie, scatter, bubble, tape, and area.
- Ability to change graph axis labels, colors, and titles.

Types of Query Tools

There are a number of types of queries that allow for the production and viewing of the information that has been defined herein. There are four types of query tools:

1. *Report Writers*: These are third-party products that access the data warehouse directly and produce reports based on SQL-type queries. Examples of third-party report writers are Crystal Reports and Cognos (see Fig. 13.30).
2. *Multidimensional Database Management Systems (MDBMS)*: These tools create a subset database that can be populated by both operational systems and data warehouses. These databases are usually multidimensional and are often defined as online analytical processing (OLAP) systems. They allow for specialized reporting of data in an aggregate form that can support advanced data mining activities (see Fig. 13.31).
3. *Advanced DSS Tools*: Advanced tools are very similar to report writers except they support more advanced query capabilities and dimensional analysis. They specifically support access to multiple data warehouses from one query.

Fig. 13.30 Report writer DSS

Fig. 13.31 MDBMS DSS architecture

Fig. 13.32 EIS DSS architecture

4. *Executive Information Systems* (*EIS*): EIS represents a higher level of DSS. These systems contain advanced metadata facilities that can create sophisticated and predefined analysis of data. EIS also supports artificial intelligence activities, which are fundamental infrastructures to the support of trend analysis and decision-making alternatives (see Fig. 13.32).

Phase 8: Data Validation and Testing

While I have mentioned that testing must occur throughout the data warehouse implementation, there is a need to have a central test plan strategy. Although each phase has a quality assurance process, the entire data warehouse life cycle requires integrated test scripts. These scripts establish what the expected results should be from each previous life cycle step. Sometimes this is best accomplished by having reports that provide reconciliation of what the warehouse contains. However, analysts should also suggest that users review the output reports. Users should be encouraged to hand check certain reports until they are satisfied that the system is calculating and collecting information based on their requirements. All too often we see users who just accept what the output of a report tells them!

Furthermore, analysts should plan for change—for change is inevitable with DSS packaged software systems. Change is not only modifications to the reporting, it's the addition or changing of what data needs to be supplied to the data warehouse and what it forms. In addition, new systems are added and need to be integrated into the overall data warehouse schema. With this in mind, analysts need to design and maintain sophisticated testing systems that can be reused each time a change is made to the warehouse infrastructure or transformation process.

Phase 9: Training

While this might not be the actual responsibility of the analyst, it is important to plan for the training of users with the objective of teaching them how to work with the data warehouse. Notwithstanding that predesigned reports do not require much data warehouse knowledge from the users, most systems will always have "super users" who want to do advanced analysis on the DSS. The training phase of the DSS life cycle includes the following considerations:

- Understanding the scope of information in the data warehouse.
- Training on the front-end tools and how to write queries.
- Understanding of how to use existing reports and how to modify them.
- Train the trainer concepts so users can eventually own the responsibility of training new employees or other users.

Phase 10: Rollout

This phase essentially involves the process of going live. It requires the actual deployment of the data warehouse into the production network environment, creating user-support infrastructures including adding new users, creating the physical procedures for users to request new reports and options, providing the procedures for backup and restore, and creating a team to troubleshoot problems that inevitably occur early in the DSS rollout.

Fig. 13.33 Metadata architecture

Understanding Metadata

Metadata is data about data. Metadata is the fundamental component that allows data warehouse systems to provide the complex information that users require. There are two primary forms of metadata: operational and DSS. Operational metadata contains the information about where the data is in the production systems and/or in the staged database system prior to conversion. The DSS metadata establishes a catalog of the data in the data warehouse and maps this data to the query applications. Figure 13.33 depicts the metadata architecture.

Therefore, the metadata infrastructure provides the front-end users with the ability to manipulate the data without working directly with the data, that is, the user works directly with the metadata, which in turn operates on the data warehouse attributes. Thus, the metadata provides a higher level of abstraction about the data. This abstraction allows for the ease of use of operating with the database.

Considerations for Using Big Data

This chapter has thus far focused heavily on data warehousing and reporting based on user requirements. While this concept of designing warehouses is consistent with the core principles of traditional analysis and design, it has significant limitations with addressing the needs of building "big data" repositories for use in predictive analytics applications. Big Data is defined as "high-volume, high-velocity and/or high-variety information assets that demand cost-effective, innovative forms of information processing that enable enhanced insight, decision making, and process automation" (Laney 2012). Big data, correctly or incorrectly, is often associated with the field of predictive analytics. Predictive analytics are methods that involve

the extraction of valuable connections of data that can assist in better business decisions. The growth of cloud computing, reduced costs of storage, and advanced algorithms have established a growing demand for gathering all kinds of data that exists inside and outside the organization.

However, the dilemma of using big data is finding all the data, especially since many of the elements have different definitions and exist in many different formats. Most important is that the user community may not be aware of such data and may not have access to it from their operations. Thus, the analyst's challenge is to go beyond what users can define and find logical relations of data that exist outside the organization and often in the consumer domain. As a result these data elements are not readily available and require a different architecture to build huge data sets that can make associations with all data that can be obtained from multiple sources. As a result, big data design requires applications that can deal with unstructured data sets. Unstructured data sets, simply by definition, are difficult to process using the database techniques presented in this chapter thus far. Indeed, for big data design to work, organizations must become more "data driven" (Brynjolfsson and McAfee 2012).

Ultimately, analysts in data-driven organizations must find and define sources of data on an ongoing basis. This data can come from multiple sources and must be integrated in large data sets that use analytics to form probabilities of the associations among these semi-defined fields. Thus, analytics and big data have inherent relationships as shown below by Sanders (2014):

$$Analytics + Big\ Data = Intelligence$$

In effect, various formats and types of data must be collected from both internal and external sources and integrated in a common repository of object data definitions and their associated relationships. Figure 13.34 reflects the types of data that can be accessed to establish comprehensive DIB data sets.

There are multiple third-party products that are used to decipher unstructured and semi-structured data. These products typically use combinations of data mapping and analytics to form associations and matches for big data processing. The analyst can utilize the matched data to add associations to the data dictionary where possible. However, the creation of many big data elements will continue to be a dynamic process, that is, the associations must be determined at application time as opposed to a stored data solution as shown in Fig. 13.35.

But analytics goes further than just the examination of the data. Consumer and user behavior represent yet another exciting area for the analyst. User and consumer

Structured Internal Data Sources		Unstructured External Data Sources	
Transactions	88%	Social Media	43%
Log Data	73%	Audio	38%
Emails	57%	Photos & Videos	34%

Fig. 13.34 Sources for big data (Source: IBM and Oxford survey, October, 2012)

Fig. 13.35 Data sources for analytics processing

behavior can provide the analyst with historical data which may not be known among the business users and provide an ability to predict behavior in the future. For example, if we look at user actions on a company application, we can capture common ways they:

1. View Web pages
2. Spend time on specific screens or processes
3. Use the information available to them, that is, what they download
4. Behave on the site that might indicate their understanding of the information being provided to them, how users react to color schemes for instance

Furthermore, analysis of Websites can identify sources of user traffic, which can lead to a better understanding on how consumer markets are reacting to a company's products and services. Much of these analytical opportunities may require that analysts participate in ethnographic consumer activities.

But analytics goes further than just the examination of the data. Consumer and user behavior represent yet another exciting area for the analyst. User and consumer behavior can provide the analyst not only with historical actions which may not be known or documented by the business but also provides a basis for probability of future behavior. For example, if we look at user actions on a company-level application, we can capture common ways consumers:

1. View Web pages
2. Spend time on specific screens or processes

3. Use the information available to them and what they download from the site
4. Traffic sources
5. Consumer behaviors on the site that indicate their understanding of the information being provided to them and how users react to colors, options, etc.

Much of these areas may require ethnographic types of investigation. Investigation typically can occur in two approaches: observation and participation. Observation involves the watching of users and how they behave without involvement. The objective of observation is to determine levels of behavior and navigation such as user confusion, satisfaction, options selected, etc. Participation, on the other hand, allows for engagement with the consumer in such a way as to possibly influence the results of the group's behavior.

There is also a plethora of third-party analytics products that can provide data analysis and reporting to assist in the management of assessment.

Data Visualization and Design

Data visualization is the presentation of data in a pictorial or graphical format. The purpose of data visualization is to communicate information clearly to users via graphic design and visual art. In many applications, data visualization is the output of analytics activities as it relates to the way in which the results are projected and presented to the business. The concept of visualization relates to the old statement: "You remember 100 % of what you see and only 50 % of what you read?" Ultimately data visualization can be seen as both an art and a science. Much of the science is in the statistical part of cognitive and analytic sciences. The art component relates to the perceptual psychology and creativity of how one provides complex data in a simple and effective way. This data must deliver a message to the viewer so they can make better management decisions.

According to Tufte's and Graves-Morris (1983) book, *The Visual Display of Quantitative Data*, there are nine key objectives for graphic displays:

1. How to show the data
2. Get the user to focus on the substance of the data rather than the details
3. Be careful not to distort the data's meaning
4. Present numbers in a small amount of space
5. Provide large data sets in an understandable way
6. Provide a way for the eye to capture data in a strategic way
7. Show the data on multiple levels of detail
8. Present the data for a purpose including appropriate description, exploration, and tabulation
9. Integrate the statistical, verbal, and visual aspects of the data

Mobile Applications

Predictive analytics also has a unique relevance when designing popular applications or porting applications for use on mobile devices. Mobile devices are a high priority for many organizations to compete in a global digital economy. Successful mobile applications must focus particularly on the use of images, compatibilities among devices, and the way input fields are entered and validated. While a part of mobile application development is consistent with traditional analysis and design techniques, which have been discussed in this book, there are differences that relate to risk assessment. Specifically this means that when consumers use mobile applications, analysts must forecast what interfaces will be esthetically pleasing and understandable for what might be the everyday common consumer. Because these applications are more focused on data input requirements, it is important to consider the data visualization issues discussed earlier. However, below is a list of additional data visualization requirement questions that should be asked for mobile applications (Nielsen Norman Group 2015).

1. Is the field absolutely necessary?
2. Is the field marked as required (*) or optional?
3. Is the label above the field (as opposed to inside or below)?
4. Have you removed placeholder from inside the field?
5. Is the field big enough so that most field values are visible?
6. Is the field visible in both orientations when the keyboard is displayed?
7. Do you have any good default for this field (e.g., history available, frequently used values)?
8. Can you use the phone features (camera, GPS, voice, contacts) to populate a field?
9. Can you compute the value from other sources in the data (e.g., State based on zip code)?
10. Do you support copy and paste in the field?
11. What is the right keyboard for this field?
12. Can you make suggestions/auto-complete based on the first letters typed?
13. Do you allow typos or abbreviations?
14. Do you allow users to enter values in whatever format they prefer (phone, credit card number) or do you automate format?

Problems and Exercises

1. What is a data warehouse?
2. What are the advantages and disadvantages of using data warehouses?
3. Describe the concept of data aggregation.
4. What is a star schema?
5. Explain the different types of data warehouses and how they should be used.

6. Describe the relationship between the concept of decision support systems and data warehouses.
7. How does data mapping relate to data warehousing?
8. What are fact tables and dimension tables?
9. What is a source-to-target element mapping matrix?
10. Describe the process of populating a data warehouse.
11. What are the different types of reporting and analytics available via warehouses?
12. What is metadata?

References

Brynjolfsson, E., & McAfee, A. (2012). Big data: The management revolution. *Harvard Business Review, 90*(10), 60–68.

IBM & Said School of Business, Oxford University. (2012). *Analytics: The real-world use of big data in financial services*. Retrieved September 30, 2015, http://www-935.ibm.com/services/multimedia/Analytics_The_real_world_use_of_big_data_in_Financial_services_Mai_2013.pdf

Laney, D. (2012). The importance of big data: A definition. *Gartner*. Retrieved 21, June 2012.

Nielsen Norman Group. (2015). *User experience for mobile applications and websites*. Retrieved September 30, 2015, from http://www.nngroup.com/reports/mobile-website-and-application-usability/

Poe, V. (1996). *Building a data warehouse for decision support*. Upper Saddle River: Prentice-Hall.

Sanders, N. R. (2014). *Big data driven supply chain management: A framework for implementing analytics and turning information into intelligence*. Upper-Saddle River: Pearson Education, Inc.

Tufte, E. R., & Graves-Morris, P. R. (1983). *The visual display of quantitative information* (Vol. 2, No. 9). Cheshire: Graphics Press.

Documentation and Acceptance Testing

Many IT organizations are faced with the ongoing issue of good product documentation. Documentation has been classically defined as having two components: user documentation and technical documentation. User documentation consists of the necessary instructions required for users to operate and maintain the system. Technical documentation, on the other hand, contains detailed information about the inner components of the product itself. Technical documentation should be designed to provide developers with the ability to support and maintain the system from a programming and engineering perspective.

Once analysis and design are completed, user documentation can be developed as a parallel function with the rest of the product life cycle components. This means that the screens and reports can be used from the design phase to build the documentation on the inputs, queries, and output reports of the system. If the software is a GUI product, then the user documentation must also adhere to the standard help facility, which is included in these types of products. Although analysts may be involved with providing information to the documentation team, it is not their responsibility to produce user documentation.

A major part of the technical documentation should be the product of the analyst's work. All of the tools used by the analyst to formulate the logical equivalent must remain as the schematic or blueprint of the product. It is not advisable to try to provide other documentation. First, there rarely is enough time, and second, it should not be necessary. Remember, the concept of using modeling tools was compared to the creation and maintenance of an architect's blueprint in which the schematic had to be self-documenting. There are, however, other components of technical documentation. This technical documentation relates to the physical software development itself. Programming source code, product libraries, and version control are examples of technical product documentation that should be the responsibility of the programming team.

Acceptance Test Plans

Acceptance test plans can be defined as the set of tests that if passed will establish that the software can be used in production. Acceptance tests need to be established early in the product life cycle and should begin during the analysis phase. It is only logical then that the development of acceptance test plans should involve analysts. As with requirements development, the analyst must participate with the user community. Only users can make the final decision about the content and scope of the test plans. The design and development of acceptance test plans should not be confused with the testing phase of the software development life cycle. Testing should be defined as the carrying out or execution of the acceptance test plans themselves.

The analysis and design of acceptance test plans are often overlooked in many IT organizations. This is because it is viewed inappropriately as a testing method rather than as a way of developing better systems. The question then is why and how do acceptance test plans improve software quality?

Quality During Analysis

If acceptance test planning is conducted as a step in analysis, then the issue of how to best test the requirements becomes part of making decisions about overall system requirements. Specifically, if a user wants something that can be difficult to test and maintain, it may force them to rethink the requirement and alter its focus. What better time to do this than when the requirement itself is being discussed? Remember, a strong part of quality software is how easy that software is to maintain.

Cannot Test 100% of Everything

One must work with the understanding that no new product will ever be fault-free. The permutations of testing everything would make the timetable for completion unacceptable and the costs prohibitive. The acceptance test plan is a strategy to get the most important components tested completely enough for production. The testing of software can be compared to the auditing of a company. Accounting firms that conduct an audit for a public company must sign a statement that the books and records of their client are materially correct, meaning that there are no significant discrepancies in the stated numbers. Accounting firms know that they cannot test everything in their client's books and records to be 100% confident that the numbers are correct. Therefore, auditors apply strategic methods like statistical sampling in order to be "comfortable" that the risk of a significant difference is improbable. Software verification is no different. Analysts and users must together decide on the minimum tests necessary to provide comfort to going live with the system. It is unfair to leave this responsibility solely with the user. Having the analyst or programmer do this alone is equally unfair. The wise strategy is to have acceptance test

plans developed by the analyst along with input from the user and verification by programming as follows:

1. As each part of a system is functionally decomposed using the various modeling tools, the analyst should develop generic test plans that are based on typical standard logic tests (e.g., Account_Number must be numeric). The analyst and users should then meet to refine the test plans by focusing on how many permutations are required for each logical test. Users should also be encouraged to establish new tests that are missing from the plan. It is highly recommended that the analyst not wait for the entire analysis to be completed before working with acceptance test plan generation. Tailoring an acceptance test plan specifically to the needs of a group of users is a good technique. This means that as the analyst completes the interviews with each user or user group, the acceptance test plans should be completed for the specifications developed for them. This philosophy is also good because it avoids the process of meeting again and rehashing old information.
2. The analyst develops inter part tests necessary to ensure that each component properly links with the other.
3. Once the acceptance test plans are approved by users, development must design tests that focus on product-specific validation. These include operating system and program tests to ensure that the operating environment is working correctly. Users and analysts need not be involved with this step as it represents the testing from an engineering perspective. Quality assurance personnel that are part of the development team should be involved in these test designs as these professionals are specifically trained to provide intricate testing that involves the mathematical aspects of finding errors. Once again, quality assurance and testers should not be confused or combined with the role the analyst and users play in the design of acceptance test plans.

More Efficient Development

Providing development personnel with the acceptance test plans is a somewhat controversial idea. Many IS professionals would object to doing so, arguing that the testing of software quality should not be carried out by programmers. However, programmers who are given the test plans are not being asked to do the testing but rather to understand what the user perceives as the most important operational qualities of the system. If the programmer is aware of the specific focus of the tests, then he/she should direct the development to ensure that such errors do not occur. In essence, we are trying to focus the programmer on the most important aspects of the system. To ask programmers to treat each component of a program in an equal manner is unfair, especially since they have no perspective on how to make the decision. If the programmer is especially focused on the tests, there should be fewer errors detected during the test review, thus supporting a more efficient development effort.

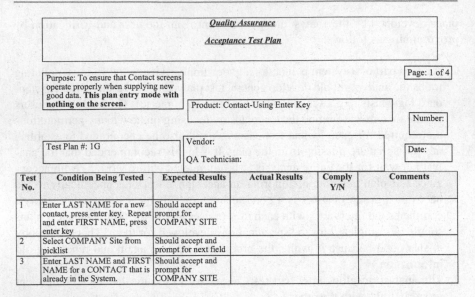

Fig. 14.1 Sample acceptance test plan

Focusing on the tests does not suggest, however, that the programmer is free to ignore the other quality areas of the program.

Now that we have established the reasons and processes of developing acceptance test plans, the analyst must provide a format for its use. The format must be user friendly so that users can participate. The format must include a record of each iteration of the test, allowing for better documentation and audit trail. The test plans should be in a machine readable format so that changes can be made. Figure 14.1 shows a sample acceptance test plan.

This particular test plan assumes that no data is on the screen and that the operator will only use the enter key (as opposed to a mouse). Each condition to be tested and its expected result must be listed. The tester will then execute each test number and fill in the results along with any comments. The test plan is then reviewed for completeness. If the test plan fails, the test will be performed again after the software is fixed. Each test iteration is part of the documentation of the testing process. Users and analysts should periodically review the test plans when the system goes live. This procedure will allow the test plans to be "fine-tuned" should any critical errors occur when the system goes into production.

Designing acceptance test plans is not a trivial task, for either the user or the analyst; however, good test plans can make the difference in the ultimate quality of the software. When GUI products are tested, the number of test iterations increases substantially. For example, the test plan shown in Fig. 14.1 is focused only on data entry (as opposed to changing existing data) and when the operator uses the enter key. Because this is GUI, operators can enter data by using the enter key, a mouse, or the tab key. Therefore, the analyst will need to repeat the same test plan two more times, one when the operator uses a mouse and the other when a tab key is used.

Task: User Interviewing

Sub-Task	Expected Hours	User Skill Set Weight .75 – Knowledgeable 1.75 – Amateur 1.00 – Novice	Weighted Hours
Selection of Users			
Determine JAD Sessions			
Pre-Meetings			
Individual Meetings			
JAD Sessions			

Fig. 14.2 User interview budget worksheet

Budget Process

We have continued to expand the role of the analyst in the life cycle of systems development. Analysts must develop the ability to view an upcoming project and submit an accurate budget for their time and effort. The best approach here is to list the generic tasks that are typically performed by an analyst and then attempt to provide an estimate of the requirements not only for each task but also for each system component within the task. Below is a step-by-step process that can be followed.

Establish the Task List

The analyst should begin the budget by listing the three standard tasks:

- Interviewing
- Modeling
- Acceptance Test Planning

Each of these tasks will then need to be expanded depending on the scope of the project.

Interviewing

The analyst will need to assess the number of users on the project and whether there will be a need for JAD sessions. Once this schedule is put together, the analyst should arrange for pre-meetings to assess the user skill sets, as this will affect the strategy and time frame of the user-interface process. Analysts should employ a weighted criterion when budgeting time. Although there is no exact science to doing this, Fig. 14.2 shows a suggested template to follow.

The table shown in Fig. 14.2 does not include the specific budget for each session, as this would require the analyst to have pre-meetings to assess the number of

Task: Modeling

Modeling Type	Estimated Hours based on Number of Diagrams or Data Elements	Automation Factor .75 – Integrated CASE 1.00 – Non-Integrated 3.00 – Manual	Factored Hours
Data Flow Diagram			
State Transition			
Data Repository			
Entity Relational Diagrams			
Process Specifications			
Object Orientation			

Fig. 14.3 Modeling budget worksheet

functions in each component and then budget the time necessary. The user interviewing tasks should take into consideration an estimate for the number of iterations. More detailed sessions can require three to four iterations before final approval is accomplished. The number of hours (or whatever time period is chosen) should be based on a novice user. Note that if the user(s) is knowledgeable, there may actually be a reduction in the budgeted time, whereas amateurs (those that know a little) may substantially increase the time frame. The latter situation is due to the likelihood that amateur users will tend to get off track and in general have more questions. The ultimate budget for JAD sessions must be based on a composite of the levels of involved users for each JAD session.

Modeling

Once the interviewing budget has been determined and there is an established understanding of the scope, objectives, constraints, and assumptions of the project, the analyst can begin to determine the time period for modeling the system requirements. Some guidelines are given in Fig. 14.3.

Analysts will need to get a sense during the preinterviews of the likely number of processes (or data elements with respect to the repository) and how many diagrams might be included. Once this is established, then the budget can be developed. Note that the weight factors are based on the level of integrated automation. Integrated automation refers to the extent of computerization (e.g., a CASE tool) that will be used to develop the models. Nonintegrated, which is the non-weighted factor, represents computerized diagramming without intelligent interfaces (which would exist with a CASE product).

Task: Acceptance Test Plan

Sub-Task	10% of User Interview Weighted Budget Hours	Estimated Hours based on Number of Diagrams or Data Elements (from Modeling budget)	Type of User Interface Factor 2.00 – GUI 1.00 – Character	Estimated Acceptance Test Plan Hours
Individual Meetings				
JAD Sessions				

Fig. 14.4 Acceptance test plan budget worksheet

Acceptance Test Plans

Acceptance test plan budgeting must take into consideration two key factors: the user interviews and the type of product. The user interview portion should be based on the original budget for user interviews applying a factor based on the modeling budget as follows (Fig. 14.4).

Essentially the matrix shown in Fig. 14.4 reflects that budget hours for acceptance test plans are approximately 10% of the original interview budget hours factored by the estimate of the number of diagrams and the level of automation. The 10% represents the portion of the interview time that is perceived to be spent discussing testing issues with the user. The final factor is the GUI. Because of the event-driven nature of GUI screens, the number of tests to be performed is dramatically increased. Many IS professionals would feel that a 2.00 factor is too low, since many favor 3.00.

Problems and Exercises

1. What is the purpose of business specifications?
2. How do Functional Overview sections relate to the entire business specification?
3. What is the use of a functional flow diagram ? Which modeling tool is used?
4. What are the five most common components of the business specification?
5. How does the business specification relate to the programming specification?
6. How does the programming specification interface with DFDs and STDs?
7. How does modeling provide the input for much of the system's documentation?
8. What is an acceptance test plan?
9. Comment on the statement: "Cannot test 100% of everything."
10. How do acceptance test plans facilitate the productivity and quality of programming?
11. Why is it important for the analyst to provide a budget for his/her tasks?

Part III

How to Implement

Project Management

<div align="right">

15

</div>

Introduction

This chapter provides guidance on system development life cycle methodologies and best practices for project management of packaged and in-house developed systems. Project organizations including roles and responsibilities are covered. There are many aspects of packaged software management that are generic; however, there are certainly unique aspects when managing packaged software systems. Thus, this chapter provides an understanding of where these unique challenges occur in the life cycle of packaged software projects. It also focuses on the ongoing support issues that must be addressed to attain best practices.

A project manager who comes from a traditional software development background and understands the phases of software development will perhaps do fine in overseeing the progress of packaged software projects. Indeed, traditional project managers will focus on budget, the schedule, the resources, and the project plan. Unfortunately, packaged software systems, because of their widespread involvement with many parts of the business, need to go beyond just watching and managing the software development process. That is, the project management of packaged systems requires much more integration with the internal and external user communities. It must combine traditional development with business creation, and because of the preexisting nature of the package, it also delves into the internal organization structure and requires their participation in every phase of the development and implementation cycle. Listed below are some of the unique components of packaged development projects:

1. *Project Managers as Complex Managers*: Packaged software projects require multiple interfaces that are outside the traditional user community. They can include interfacing with writers, editors, marketing personnel, customers, and consumers, all who might be stakeholders in the success of the system.
2. *Shorter and Dynamic Development Schedules*: Due to the dynamic nature of packaged systems, the development is less linear. Because there is less

© Springer-Verlag London Limited 2016
A.M. Langer, *Guide to Software Development*,
DOI 10.1007/978-1-4471-6799-0_15

experience and more stakeholders, there is a tendency to underestimate the time and cost to complete.

3. *New Untested Technologies*: There is so much new technology offered particularly for Web developers that there is a practice of using new versions of development software that has not matured. The method of obtaining new software is easily distributed over the Web, so it is relatively easy to try new versions as soon as they become available.

4. *Degree of Scope Changes*: Packaged systems because of their involvement with many aspects of the business tend to be much more prone to scope creep. Project managers need to work closely with internal users, customers, and consumers to advise them of the impact of changes on the schedule and the cost of the project. Unfortunately, scope changes that are influenced by changes in market trends may not be avoidable. Thus, part of a good strategy is to manage scope changes rather than attempt to stop them—which might not be realistic.

5. *Costing Packaged Systems are Difficult*: The software industry has always had difficulties in knowing how to cost a project as discussed in Chap. 6. Packaged systems are even more difficult because of the number of variables, unknowns, and use of new technologies and procedures.

6. *Lack of Standards*: The software industry continues to be a profession that does not have a governing body. Thus it is impossible to have real enforced standards as other professions enjoy. While there are suggestions and best practices, many of them are unproven and not kept current with new developments. Because of the lack of successful packaged software projects, there are few success stories to create new and better best practices.

7. *Less Specialized Roles and Responsibilities*: The software development team tends to have staff members that have varying responsibilities. Unlike traditional software projects, separation of roles and responsibilities is more difficult when operating in a Web environment. Defining the exact role of an analyst can be very tricky; for example, are they analyst programmers, database developers, or content designers? The reality is that all of these roles can be part of a developer's responsibility.

8. *Who Bears the Cost?* There is general uncertainty as to who should bear the cost of the packaged system. This refers to the internal organization of stakeholders who need to agree on the funding. This becomes even more complex when there are delays and cost overruns, because the constituents cannot easily agree on who is at fault and therefore who should bear the burden of the additional costs.

9. *Project Management Responsibilities Are Very Broad*: Packaged project management responsibilities need to go beyond those of the traditional IT project manager. Packaged project managers are required to provide management services outside the traditional software staff. They need to interact more with internal and external users as well as with nontraditional members of the development team such as content managers. Therefore, there are many more obstacles that can cause project managers to fail at their jobs.

Package Software Projects	Traditional Projects
Project managers are not always trained client managers	Different
Development project schedules tend to be short	Similar
New and untested third-party software are often implemented	Usually never
Changes in scope occur during implementation	Similar
Pricing model does not really exist	Different
Standards for package production do not exist	Similar
Team roles are less specialized	Different
Users have difficulty bearing the costs of development, especially during planning	Different
Project manager responsibilities are broad	Different

Fig. 15.1 Packaged software and traditional projects compared

10. *The Package Never Ends*: The nature of how packaged systems are built and deployed suggests that they are living systems. This means that they have a long life cycle made up of ongoing maintenance and enhancements. So the traditional begin and end project does not apply to a packaged software project that inherently must be implemented in ongoing phases.

Figure 15.1 summarizes these differences between traditional and packaged software projects.

The questions that need to be answered are not limited to what the process and responsibilities should be, but also who should do them? It is my position that a business analyst takes the responsibility of managing the process from inception to completion. The duties and responsibilities of a business analyst are excellent prerequisites for understanding the intricacies of project management. Their roles as analysts require them to have relationships with the organization and an understanding of the politics and culture that drives the business. I am not suggesting that every analyst should become a project manager, but rather that one of the analysts should also be the project manager. In order to determine the right fit, it is important to define the skill sets that are required for successful project management. These are summarized below:

- Software experience
- Understanding of budgeting, scheduling, and resource allocation
- Excellent written and verbal communication skills
- Ability to hold and lead meeting discussions
- Detail oriented yet globally motivated (can see the difference between the forest and the trees)

- Pragmatic
- A sense of humor that comes across as a natural personal trait as opposed to an acted one
- Ability to be calm and levelheaded during crisis
- Experience with Web technologies, multimedia, and software engineering

Unfortunately, it is difficult to find the project manager that has all of these traits. In many cases it is wise to promote from within and develop the expertise internally. This is especially effective because an internal individual is a known quantity and most likely already fits into the culture of the organization. Most important is that the individual is accepted in the culture. On the downside, it takes time to develop internal talent, and sometimes this trained talent leaves the company once they have received their training. There is benefit to bringing in someone from the outside because they can have a fresh view of the project and offer more objective input on what needs to be done to get the project finished on time.

Defining the Project

The first step for the project manager is to develop a mission statement for the project. A mission statement helps managers and users to focus on three core tasks:

1. Identify the projects objectives.
2. Identify the users.
3. Determine the scope of the project.

Identify Objectives

Project objectives are defined as the results that must be attained during the project. According to Lewis (1995), project objectives must be specific, measurable, attainable, realistic, and time limited. The most difficult of these objectives tends to be "measurable" and "attainable." Ultimately, objectives state the desired outcomes and focus on how the organization will know when it is reached? Objectives are typically devised by the project's stakeholders. These individuals are usually executives and managers that have the most to gain from the successful implementation of the packaged software system. Unfortunately, while this sounds good, it is difficult to implement. In reality, it is difficult for executives to articulate on what they are looking for. Indeed, the packaged software paradigm has simply forced many executives to create products because they think it is a competitive advantage for their companies to have one. This, in essence, means that executives might be driven by the fear that they must do something or something is better than nothing.

Packaged software objectives evolve and cause many iterative events to occur, especially in the early phases of the project. Good and effective objectives tend to be short sentences that are written down. Using this format, objectives can be used

by project managers to effectively avoid scope creep. The objectives should be distributed to all stakeholders and project members so that everyone understands them.

Identify Users

Chapter 2 covered the significance of users and their importance to the success of any project. In the chapter I defined three types of users: internal, customers, and consumers. It is important for project managers to understand the value of the input from each of these users. Indeed, the content of the website will ultimately be determined by the users who access the site. However, managers and developers often disagree on how much input is needed from users. This is further complicated when managing packaged software projects because of the diversity of the users and the complexity of decisions that must be made. Furthermore, there is always limited time, so packaged software project managers need to be as productive as possible with how user input is obtained, the types of interviewing that is done, and the method of measuring the value of the user's input.

Since the only way to measure a site's success is to determine whether the objectives have been met, the philosophy of who gets interviewed and how much value their input has should be mapped to the original objectives set forth by management. Thus, besides the internal users, the real obstacle for project managers is to identify which users know best what they want from the packaged software system. Besides one-on-one interviews and JADs, the project manager can also obtain information from two other sources: market research and focus groups.

There are many firms that provide market research services. Such firms have databases of researched information relating to user preferences and behaviors. They also collect information about packaged solutions and what users expect from them. Every packaged software system should have a budget using a market research firm so that they can obtain an objective and independent opinion about user preferences, particularly within a certain market segment. Conducting a focus group is a cheaper yet effective way to get objective input from users. It is particularly useful when attempting to assess consumer preferences. Focus groups involve the selection of sample consumers that the project manager feels represents the typical user. The sessions are filmed behind a mirror, and users respond to questions about their preferences when using a packaged software system. The focus group typically needs a moderator who controls the meeting agenda and ensures that all of the research questions are answered by the participants. During all sessions it is important that the project manager ensure that the objectives of the packaged software system be clearly defined to the audience. The objectives should be in writing and reviewed before the start and end of each session. In addition, the objectives should be written on a whiteboard or flip chart so participants can be reminded of the scope of the project should certain users start discussions on tangent subjects.

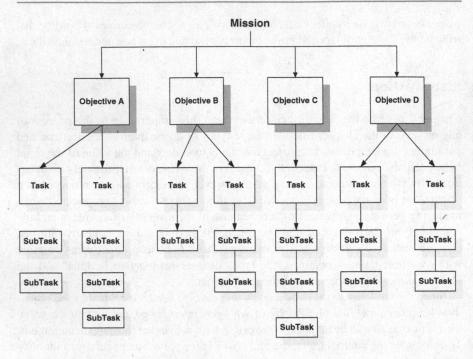

Fig. 15.2 Sample work breakdown structure

Determining the Scope of the Project

The scope of the project relates to the time and budget of when it needs to be completed. Because there is always a limited amount of time and money to create product, the scope of the project must be negotiated against what can be done with what users want done. Thus, scope is the domain of functions and features that will be included in the packaged software system based on a specific time commitment and cost outlay. The best approach to formulating a scope statement is to first create a work breakdown structure that contains the mission statement, lists the objectives, and formulates the tasks and subtasks to complete each objective. Thus, a work breakdown structure is really a form of functional decomposition of the tasks necessary to meet the objectives. Once stakeholders and the project manager agree on the objectives and what tasks will be done to attain them, then the scope of the project is complete. Figure 15.2 depicts a sample work breakdown structure.

Once tasks and subtasks have been determined, the packaged software project manager needs to determine the time and cost of completing each component. Thus, the work breakdown structure will eventually contain the costs for each task within each objective for the entire project as proposed. Management and the project manager can then begin the process of negotiating what can be completed on time and on budget by removing subtasks or tasks as appropriate.

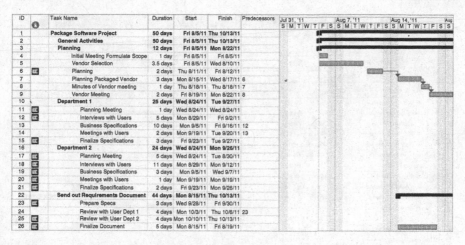

Fig. 15.3 Packaged software project plan

Another valuable approach to building packaged software projects is phasing deliverables. Because packaged software projects tend never to be finished, it might be advisable to deliver some portion of the system first and then add-on functionality in subsequent releases of the system. Obviously this might not always be feasible; there are packaged software systems that cannot be phased, that is, they are all or nothing at all. However, I believe that all projects can have some level of phased development and that such development in the long run benefits the entire scope of the project. Indeed, first releases of a packaged solution typically need revision anyway, and the second phase or version might be a better time to add certain features and functions.

I stated that the final work breakdown schedule represents the scope of the project. Typically, the packaged software project manager will finalize the scope statement by preparing a document that includes the work breakdown structure and articulates how this structure will be formulated into deliverables for the project. In many ways the scope document acts as a management report and reiterates the mission and objectives of the project along with the project plan. Figure 15.3 shows a typical project plan developed in Microsoft Project.

Managing Scope

A project plan can sometimes be referred to as a work breakdown schedule or WBS. As shown in Fig. 15.3, it depicts every step in the project and can enforce dependencies within tasks and subtasks. This is important, because changes to the plan may affect other tasks. A WBS product like Microsoft Project provides an automated way of tracking changes and determining its effect on the entire project. A popular method of tracking changes is called "critical path analysis." Critical path analysis involves the monitoring of tasks that can have an effect on the entire scope

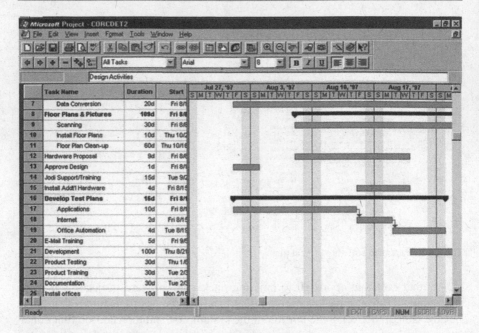

Fig. 15.4 Critical and noncritical tasks using Microsoft Project

of the project, meaning it can change the time frame and cost of delivery. A critical path is defined as a task that if delayed will cause a delay in the entire project. A task that can delay the project is then called a critical task. The importance of managing critical tasks is crucial for successful management of packaged software projects. Project managers are often faced with the reality that some task has slipped behind schedule when faced with this dilemma. The project manager needs to decide whether dedicating more resources to the task might get it back on schedule. However, the first thing that the project manager needs to assess is whether the task can affect the critical path. If the answer is yes, then the project manager must attempt to use other resources to avoid a scope delay. If the task is not critical, then the delay may be acceptable without needing to change the project plan. Figure 15.4 shows a critical task and a noncritical task.

The Budget

Budgeting is one of the most important responsibilities of a project manager. The budget effectively prices the tasks that must be delivered and rolls them up to the project cost level. It is important to recognize that all budgets are estimates. Therefore they are never 100 % accurate—if they were they would not be budgets. The concept behind budgeting is that some tasks will be over-budget and others will be underbudget resulting in an offset that essentially balances out to the

Project Budget Sample 12/12/2010

Description		Low	High	Comments				
Hardware								
Servers	$	150,000	200,000					
Workstations		400,000	600,000					
Modems		25,000	30,000					
Scanners		5,000	20,000					
Total Hardware		580,000	850,000					
Software								
Base Product		250,000	350,000	Cost of vendor base product software				
Database		100,000	250,000	Database vendor software license				
Office Automation		40,000	100,000	Forms elimination and e-mail intranet				
CAD/CAM-Scanning		40,000	100,000	Scanning software				
Media Production		90,000	150,000					
Software Modifications		75,000	125,000	Modification costs to vendors product meet needs				
Total Software		595,000	1,075,000					
Services								
Network and Software Design		5,000	8,500	Analysis & design of system				
Consultants		240,000	285,000	Specialists that may be needed				
Scanning Documents		125,000	135,000	Service to put all plans in system				
Conversion of Data		120,000	130,000					
Installation		45,000	87,000	low: 300 × 150 high 300 × 250 plus servers				
Training		25,000	85,000	Train the trainer all train everyone				
Total Services		560,000	730,500					
Total	$	1,735,000	2,655,500					

Fig. 15.5 Sample e-business project budget expense categories

assumptions outlined in the original plan. Budgets are typically built on expense categories. Figure 15.5 shows the common budget categories that projects should be tracking.

As stated earlier, a project budget is a set of assumptions. Typical budget assumptions are:

- All content will be provided in machine-readable form.
- The content manager will approve content design within 24 h.
- The Web design team will present two alternate design schemas.
- Graphics for the website are finalized and ready for integration.

It is not a bad idea for the project manager to create a budget document that includes a list of the assumptions because it allows the manager to track whether incorrect assumptions caused delays in the scope of the project. Unfortunately, there are also hidden costs that tend not to be included in project budgets. The following is a list of common hidden costs that are missed by the project manager:

- Meetings
- Phone calls
- Research
- Development of documents and status reports
- Project administration
- Review sessions
- Presentations to management

As previously discussed, some project managers add a 10–15 % cushion to their budgets to absorb common hidden costs. While I do not support cushions, it is acceptable if actually listed as a budget item, as opposed to a cushion on each budget line item.

The Project Team

The project team is unique from other traditional project organizations. Most of the significant differences are attributable to the addition of the packaged software responsibilities. Today, the roles and responsibilities for developing and supporting packaged software team are far more complex and specialized. The project team has evolved because business managers understand the importance of technology in transforming the way business is done. On the other hand, there are certainly traditional roles and responsibilities that have not changed and are generalizable across any software development project.

While the structure of project teams can vary depending on the type of project, the size of the system, and the time to complete, typical organizations contain the following roles and responsibilities:

- *Project Manager*: The project manager is responsible for the scope of work, developing the project plan, scheduling, allocating resources, budgeting, managing the team, interfacing with users, and reporting to management on progress. The project manager also deals with politics and other business issues, which include but are not limited to contract negotiations, licensing of third-party products, and staff hiring. In some instances the project manager is responsible for handling customer and consumer needs as it relates to the design and development of the packaged software system. Perhaps the most important responsibility of the packaged software project manager is to know at all times what has been done and what needs to be done.

- *Account Manager*: The account manager is usually a senior manager who is responsible for a number of projects. Account managers also serve clients in a number of ways, from selling new product to providing client support. In many ways, the account manager is the representative of the client's needs to the internal development team. Account managers can be called upon to obtain information from customers about their needs and their feedback on how the system supports their needs.
- *Technical Manager*: This individual is the senior technologist of the project. He/she is usually from the development team and is the most experienced developer. The technical manger is responsible for ensuring that the correct technology is being used and deployed properly. This individual manages the programmers, database developers, and other system integrators. The technical manger provides feedback on the development status of each task and reports to the project manager.
- *Programmer*: A programmer may be needed to do certain custom modifications if not outsourced. He/she is responsible for coding applications for the project. These applications are coded to spec and can include a myriad of technologies including but not limited to server scripts, database applications, applets, and ActiveX controls. Development languages used on packaged software projects vary, but the Web uses such languages as Java, JavaScript, Visual Basic, VBScript, SQL, and C/C++. The technical manager usually manages this individual; however, large projects may employ multiple levels of programmers. In certain situations, junior programmers report to senior developers who act as mentors to them.
- *Business Analyst*: This individual is responsible for gathering all of the user requirements and designing the logic models and architecture of the system, which include process models, data models, transactions system design, and process specifications. Ultimately the business analyst is responsible for site architecture, navigation, search and data retrieval, and interaction design. This role is sometimes called an information architect.
- *Designer*: Designers create the look and feel of the screens. They use various tools to design template content and overall screen structure. Screen designers report to the project manager who sets the overall project philosophy.
- *Database Administrator (DBA)*: The DBA is responsible for all physical database design and development. This individual must also fine-tune the database to ensure efficient operation. Other responsibilities include data partitioning, data warehouse setup, data replication, and report generation.
- *Network Engineers*: These individuals are responsible for designing network configurations that support the packaged software system. Sometimes a network engineer is also a security specialist who is responsible for registering domain names, setting up email servers, and chat rooms.
- *Security Expert*: While this might be the network specialist, larger packaged software projects employ a dedicated security expert who works with encryption formulas, integrates with content systems, and focuses on securing online

Type of Project Activity	Staff Organization
Marketing and Media	Account executive, project manager, creative manager, designer, copywriter, production artist, quality assurance specialist
Project transactions	Project manager, technical manager, analyst, creative manager, database administrator, tester
Input/Output data	Project manager, technical manager, creative manager, database administrator, analyst, Web production specialist, quality assurance specialist
Intranet	Project manager, Technical manager, creative manager, network engineer, Web production specialist, quality assurance specialist

Fig. 15.6 Project team roles and responsibilities matrix

Skill Set	Description
Project Management	Ability to communicate with staff, executives, and users. Keep project on schedule.
Architecture	Ability to design the user interface and interact with technical development personnel
Graphic Design	Ability to transform requirements into visual solutions
Graphic Production	Ability to develop efficient graphics for Web browser use
Content Development	Ability to design and develop text and interactive content
Programming	Ability to use HTML, Javascript, etc.

Fig. 15.7 Necessary project skill sets

transactions. This individual can also advise the project manager on strategies to implement certain component applications.

- *Quality Assurance Specialist*: This individual is responsible for creating test scripts to ensure that the packaged software system operates within spec. The purpose of the test plans, sometimes called acceptance test plans, is to provide the minimal set of tests that must be passed for the site to go into production. The reporting structure for quality assurance personnel varies. Some believe that it is part of the development team and therefore should report to the technical manager, while others believe that it needs to report directly to the project manager. There are still others that believe that the quality assurance staff should report to

the chief information officer (CIO). The reporting structure is dependent on how highly the department values the independence of the testing function.

* *Tester*: A tester is simply a person who carries out the test plans developed by the quality assurance staff. These people typically report to quality assurance staff; however, sometimes testers are users who are working with the account manager to assist in the testing of the product. These testers are in a sense a beta test user (beta test means that the software is tested in a live environment).

While this is an exhaustive list of potential positions to have on a project, it is unlikely that every one of these positions will exist in any given packaged software project. In reality, it is more important that the functionality of each of these positions is carried out, regardless of who takes on the responsibility. In order to provide better insight to the roles and responsibilities of each position, Fig. 15.6 reflects a matrix that compares roles with responsibilities.

Figure 15.7 identifies the necessary skills of each of the critical members of the project team.

Project Team Dynamics

It is not unusual for packaged software development projects to operate from multiple sites with multiple interfaces. This may require much more organization and communication among the members of the team.

Set Rules and Guidelines for Communication

When project members are separated by locations or even by work schedules, it is very important that everyone know what their roles are and what everybody else's responsibilities are to each other. Project managers should establish guidelines on communication and require each member to provide short statuses on where they are in the project. While this might seem like a bother to team members, I have found that it provides immense value to the project manager because it forces each person to discipline themselves and report on where they are in their respective worlds. Furthermore, it forces project staff to articulate in writing what they have accomplished, what is outstanding, and what they plan to get done. Figure 15.8 shows a sample status report that tracks previous objectives with current objectives. It should not take more than 15 min to complete.

Extranet Review Sites

Project managers should create extranets that allow project staff to view the work of the project team. This also allows work to be approved virtually over the Web. Furthermore, status reports and general announcements can be viewed by

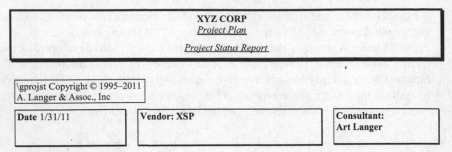

XYZ CORP
Project Plan

Project Status Report

\gprojst Copyright © 1995–2011
A. Langer & Assoc., Inc

| Date 1/31/11 | Vendor: XSP | Consultant:
Art Langer |

Previous Objectives: Objective	Previous Target Date	Status
Send out Software Proposals	1/23/11	Done
Send out Hardware Bids and check labor rates	1/25/11	2/6/11
Get XSP to modify detail design contract to include specifics on deliverables.	1/23/11	Done, waiting approval
Speak with product consultant and contract with him for data and layouts	1/25/11	2/3/11
Finalize Network Design Requirements Document	1/23/11	2/3/11

New Project Objectives: Objective	Target Date
Get specification on hardware certification machines from XSP	2/5/11
Get room to do JAD interviews and reviews	2/10/11
Ensure that accounting features are integrated in specs	2/10/11
Art to interview Joe	2/3/11
Check ability of MAS to create output files for display on Web	2/6/11
Identify and meet with brokers as part of interviews	2/3/11
Get prices for Scanning of floor plans for Web browsing	2/10/11

| Attendees | A. Langer & Assoc. Art Langer | XSP |

Fig. 15.8 Sample project status report

authorized members of the project team, as well as by stakeholders and users. Often extranet documents can be coupled with regular conference call sessions where project members can openly discuss reports and website samples and determine new milestones as appropriate. Unfortunately, managing an extranet review site requires overhead and someone who can do the work. This simply means that someone on the project's staff or some assigned administrative person needs to take on the responsibility. There is also the challenge of dealing with staff that do not comply with procedures or need to be reminded about delivering their status reports on a regular basis. While this is unfortunate, it is a reality. However, it also tells the project manager who needs to be watched closer than other team members.

Working with User Resources

Users are an interesting yet challenging resource. While they are clearly needed to perform reviews and quality assurance, they are not officially assigned to the project and are therefore not under the control of the project manager. Unfortunately this can cause problems if a user is not responsive to the needs of the project team. This can be very damaging because the staff will be dependent on receiving timely feedback from these resources. Lack of responsiveness from a user can also alienate them from the project team. Indeed, there is nothing more damaging than a user that shows disinterest in the project that is being designed to serve them. Therefore, the packaged software project manager needs to be careful on what commitments are made when a user resource is made available to them. Obviously, the project manager would want the individual to report directly to him/her and be a full-time resource. This could also be wishful thinking. It certainly can be dangerous to turn down the help. While this may appear to be a catch-22, it can be managed. First, the packaged software project manager should establish the need for user assistance early in the project and include it in the requirements documentation (it should be part of the assumptions section). Second, the project manager may need to limit the amount of work assigned to the user if they indeed are just part-time resources.

Outsourcing

As discussed in earlier chapters, not all packaged projects can be completed using internal staff. In fact, most are not. Using outsourced resources makes sense for many projects, especially those that might need very unique and qualified personnel that is not on staff or not deemed worthy of full-time employment. There may also be a lack of talent, which is the usual reason why consultants are hired in the first place. Sometimes, outsourced relationships are managed as strategic partnerships, which mean that an outside business provides specific services for the firm on a regular basis. Project strategic partnerships can be made in many different areas or phases of the project. Outsource firms can provide video or audio engineers as needed or network support personnel to assist in installing the packaged solution. On the other hand, the entire project should not be outsourced because there may be a false sense of comfort that the firm's personnel need not be involved in the responsibility. I believe in the long run this is a mistake. Remember that outsourced firms have their own destiny and growth to manage.

Planning and Process Development

In order to operationalize the project plan and to meet the budget, it is necessary to develop a phased implementation guide that helps members of the team understand where they are in the process. Unfortunately the project task plan is much too detailed to use, so it is a good idea for the project manager to develop a higher-level

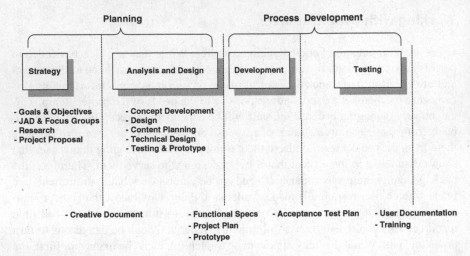

Fig. 15.9 Packaged software development phases

document that can be used during the development project. Such a plan typically contains four phases: (1) strategy, (2) design, (3) development, and (4) testing. Figure 15.9 reflects the major software phases and includes the activities and output of each phase:

1. *Strategy*: This phase requires that the stakeholders, account executive, users, and the project manager all meet to agree on the objectives, requirements, key milestones, and needs of the target audience. The activities in this phase comprise of the goals and objectives, feedback from users, research from outside sources, and the project proposal document. The culmination of these steps should be summarized in a document to be used by the project team. This document is sometimes referred to as a creative brief. The creative brief is really a summary of the original proposal in template form and created so that project team members can quickly refer to it and obtain the information they need. Figure 15.10 depicts a creative brief template.

 Creative briefs allow the project manager to conduct effective brainstorming sessions with staff. The document acts as an agenda and also a checkpoint to ensure that discussions are not going beyond the objectives of the project and that the products are designed in accordance with the target audience's needs.

2. *Design*: Design represents the second major phase. It is comprised of all the tasks that participate in the design of the user interface, the analysis and design of technical specifications, and the overall architecture of the packaged software system. The results of the design phase are the functional specifications, detailed project plan timeline and budget, and website and report prototypes. The design phase typically requires stakeholders and other users to review and sign off on the specification document before the project can proceed. Of course, the

Creative Brief Template

XYZ, INC

Dates:	Dept:	User:

Project Scope

Objectives:

Target Audiences:

Image: (Explain the image that the system must convey to users)

Current Brand: (Explain the current brand and image of the business to its users)

User Experience: (Explain the most important thing that users should experience from using the system)

Fig. 15.10 Sample creative brief

approval process of the design document can be done in phases, that is, portions of the document can be approved so that the implementation can go forward on some limited basis. During the process of designing the packaged system, it is important that the project team have access to the content of all screens and programs. This is especially important for large projects where there can be more than one design group creating content. As stated in the previous chapter, content development is an iterative process; therefore, the team members need to con-

	Quality Assurance *Acceptance Test Plan*

Purpose: To ensure that Contact screens operate properly when supplying new good data. **This plan entry mode with nothing on the screen.**	Product: Contact - Using Enter Key	Page: 1 of 4
Test Plan #: 1G	Vendor: QA Technician:	Number: Date:

Test No.	Condition Being Tested	Expected Results	Actual Results	Comply Y/N	Comments
1	Enter LAST NAME for a new contact, press enter key. Repeat and enter FIRST NAME, press enter key	Should accept and prompt for COMPANY SITE			
2	Select COMPANY Site from picklist	Should accept and prompt for next field			
3	Enter LAST NAME and FIRST NAME for a CONTACT that is already in the System.	Should accept and prompt for COMPANY SITE			

Fig. 15.11 QA test plan

stantly have access to the current site architecture and schematic designs. That is why it is so important to have the technical specifications in a CASE tool and content system so that all members can have instant access to the current state of the project.

3. *Development*: This phase includes all of the activities that are involved with actually building the site. The challenge for project managers is to control changes made to the original specifications. This typically occurs after the first prototype reviews where users begin to change or enhance their original requirements. While it is not impossible to change specifications, it is certainly dangerous and can be a major cause of scope creep.

4. *Testing*: During this phase developers and users are testing the site and reporting errors. Errors are tricky issues; they must be classified in particular areas and levels of severity. For example, some errors cause an application to abort, which would be considered a critical error. Others might be aesthetic in nature and can be scheduled for fixing but are not severe enough to holdup going live. Still other errors are not really errors, but rather deficiencies in design. This means that the program is performing to the specification but not in the way the user really expects. All of these issues need to be part of an overall test plan, which identifies what types of errors are critical and how they affect the development process. Figure 15.11 shows a typical test plan.

Technical Planning

Technical planning is the process where the project team develops a working strategy for how they will use the features of the packaged system. These features include all of the components of development including database, programming, transaction systems, multimedia, and scripting. Technical planning is simple in concept; how do all of the technology pieces come together, how do they interface, and what is the schedule of implementation? Because of the object-oriented methods that are employed by packaged software systems, it is easy to have components developed in separate teams of programmers. However, there comes a time when all components must come together and interface with each other. When the components interface correctly, the system works. Project managers never quite know if interfaces will work until they are actually tested. The concept of "working" means many things in software development. The obvious definition is that the program performs its tasks correctly and to specification. There is another part of what "working" means. This relates to performance of the application. While an application might calculate the correct output, it may not do so efficiently. Application performance problems tend to first show up during component interface testing. Fortunately this is at a time where applications can be fine-tuned before they go into production. Unfortunately, many interface-oriented performance problems first appear in the production system because the testing environment was not a true representation of the live system. Therefore, it is important for project managers to ensure that the test system correctly matches the live environment. Indeed, many performance problems occur because of the unexpected stress load on the system. Notwithstanding when an application performance problem is discovered, the main challenge is to fix the problem. Sometimes performance interface problems can be a serious problem especially if the solution requires a redesign of the application architecture or substantial changes to the network infrastructure. Any serious problems of this caliber could cause serious setbacks to the project schedule and its cost. In many ways the planning and decision-making regarding how applications are designed, which program languages should be used, and what network platforms to choose are crucial steps for the project team to make. The project manager must attempt to surround himself/herself with the best knowledge available. This knowledge base of people might not exist in the organization. Therefore, the project manager might need to seek guidance from third-party consultants who can act as specialists during these critical decision times.

Defining Technical Development Requirements

A large part of whether systems are implemented properly has to do with how well the detailed technical requirements are prepared. The technical project team needs to define the technical requirements to implement the logical specifications. Remember that logical specifications do not necessarily specify what hardware or software to use. Thus, the technical team must evaluate the logical specification and

make recommendations on how the actual technical specifications are to be built. The project manager can be more effective if they ask some key questions:

- *Are we thinking of using technologies that we have not used before?* Using unknown technologies can be very dangerous. An unknown technology is not only a new product; it is a product that the development team has never used. Because of the extent of new developments in technology, dealing with unknown hardware and software needs to be addressed and risks assessed by the project manager.
- *What benefits will be derived from new technologies?* Implementing new technologies for the sake of new technologies is not a good reason to implement unknowns. This concept gets back to the old cliché: "if it's not broken don't fix it!"
- *What type of coding is being done?* This relates to whether program code is being developed from scratch or via modified software packages. Each has its advantages and disadvantages. Writing code from scratch takes longer, but provides the architecture that best fits the design. Packaged software is faster to develop, but may not fit well with the overall needs of the company. The rule of thumb is never to modify packages by more than 20 % of their total code. When this percent is exceeded, the benefit realized from the package is so minimum that developers might as well start from scratch.
- *Will there be access to production-like testing environments?* This was covered earlier. Project managers must ensure that the proper testing facilities are available to mirror the production environment.

Maintenance

Packaged software projects should never be implemented without considering how to preserve maintainability. Maintainability is a universal concept that relates to what defines a quality product. Products that work is one thing, those that work and are maintainable is another. In packaged software systems, product that cannot be maintained easily is problematic. I have previously discussed the power of content management systems and CASE software as vehicles to support maintenance of packaged software systems. There are other best practices that need to be performed during the planning stage. First, the manner in which code will be developed and the standards to be upheld needs to be agreed upon and put in writing. Technical managers should also define how they intend to enforce these standards. Documentation of code should also be addressed in the documents. Furthermore, there needs to be agreement on the database design as well. This involves getting the database administrators to agree on limits to de-normalization, naming standards, and the methods of coding stored procedures and database triggers.

Another important component of maintenance quality is planning for growth. The issue of growth relates more to network infrastructure than software development. First, the project manager needs to address issues of hardware scalability.

This relates to the capacity of the network before the hardware architecture needs to be changed to accommodate new applications. Second, database servers must be configured with real-time backup architecture (no single point of failure concepts) and data warehouses need to be designed to perform at peak times.

Project Management and Communication

Successful project managers communicate well, not only with their staffs, but with vendors, management, and users. Indeed, sometimes communications skills are more important than technical ones. Obviously a complete project manager has both. However, the advent of packaged software systems has placed even more emphasis on the importance of communication within the project team. There are many reasons why poor communications occur during project life cycles. According to Burdman (1999), there are 11 leading causes for communication problems on a project team.

1. *People Come from Different Disciplines*: Communication is difficult enough among those that work together everyday. The influx of many different disciplines on a packaged software project creates more challenges because staffs are not as familiar with each other. Remember that relationships are very important for team interaction. Many teams need to spend time just getting acclimated to each other's business styles.
2. *Lack of Mutual Understanding of the Technology*: Project members do not have consistent understandings of the technology. For example, some staff might use the word "table" to define a logical database entity, while others call it a file. The best solution to this problem is to distribute a list of common technology definitions to all project participants.
3. *Personalities*: This occurs in all projects. Some people have conflicting personalities and do not naturally get along.
4. *Hidden Agenda*: There are often political agendas that team members have. They are sometimes difficult to assess, but they definitely cause problems with communication among project staff. These individuals are set in their ways and have questionable dedication to the success of the project, that is, they have a more important political agenda.
5. *Ineffective Meetings*: Meetings for the sake of meetings are no reason to meet. Sometimes too many meetings can be counterproductive to getting things done. It can sometimes be a false solution to other problems that exist in the project team. Some meetings are necessary but run too long, and participants begin to lose focus on the agenda. Project managers need to be cognizant of the time allotments they make to meetings and to respect those time frames.
6. *Proximity*: The demographics of where project team members reside are obviously a factor in hindering communications among the team members. While this is a disadvantage, teleconferencing and videoconferencing are all possible anecdotes for managing communication projects at a distance. Communication

can be further hindered because of long distances between staff especially when there are time zone changes. In these situations, even conferencing is not feasible. Usually the best way of communicating is through email and extranets.

7. *Assumptions*: Team members can often make assumptions about things that can cause communication breakdowns. Usually assumptions create problems because things that are believed to be true are not written down.

8. *Poor Infrastructure and Support*: The severity of this problem is often overlooked. It includes the frustrations of having computer troubles, email incompatibilities, and other hardware failures that contribute to communications problems. The best approach to avoiding these frustrations is for the project manager to be very aggressive on having them fixed timely and properly.

9. *Being an Expert*: Every project has one or two "know-it-allers" who attempt to dominate meetings and want to orchestrate their point of view on the rest of the staff. These individuals spend so much time telling others what to do that they forget what they have to do to make the project successful. Project managers should be very aggressive with these types of participants by making it clear what everyone's role is, including the project manager's responsibilities!

10. *Fear*: Fear is a very large barrier with certain staff. These staff members become overwhelmed with the size, complexity, and length of packaged software project and it can cause them to lose their perspective and creativity. Project managers need to interject and provide assistance to those members who struggle with a packaged software system.

11. *Lack of Good Communications Structure*: Good communications systems fit in with the culture of the organization and are realistic in what they might accomplish. Many communications problems exist simply because the infrastructure does not relate to the needs of the staff.

Summary

This chapter attempted to provide a project manager with a perspective on the salient issues that can help them be successful. This chapter was not intended to provide a complete step-by-step approach to managing complex projects. I included this chapter because I believe that many analysts can also serve as excellent project managers. Indeed, much of the important issues discussed in this chapter relate to many of the skills that analysts must have to perform their responsibilities as software engineers. These include:

- *Communications Skills*: Analysts have significant experience in working with users to obtain input so they can develop system requirements properly.
- *Meeting Management*: JAD sessions are more complex meetings than typical project meetings. Analysts that have also been JAD facilitators are very well trained on how to control meetings.
- *Politically Astute*: Analysts are experienced with working with people who have hidden agendas and are driven by politics.

- *Technically Proficient*: Analysts are educated in logic modeling and are familiar with much of the technical issues that come up during the project life cycle.
- *Project Planning*: Analysts are used to developing project plans and managing to deliverables; each analysis and design task can be seen as a mini-project.
- *Documentation*: Analysts are supporters of good documentation and understand the value of having maintainable processes.
- *Executive Presence*: Analysts work with executive users and understand how to interact with them.
- *Quality Assurance*: Analysts are familiar with quality assurance test plans and testing methodologies. They are often involved with test plan development.

Problems and Exercises

1. Describe five unique aspects of packaged software projects.
2. Compare packaged products with traditional ones.
3. What is a mission statement for a project mean? How should a project manager define the project mission?
4. Explain how the scope of a project is determined and how it is controlled.
5. What are the key categories of a project budget?
6. What are the roles and responsibilities of the project team? Who determines the members?
7. Explain the components of a project status report? How often should the report be issued and to whom?
8. What is a creative brief? What are the key components?
9. What are the important aspects of project management communication?

References

Burdman, J. (1999). *Collaborative web development*. New York: Addison-Wesley.
Lewis, M. (1995). *Project management: 25 popular project management methodologies*. New York: Amazon Digital Services LLC.

Virtual Teams and Outsourcing

16

Much has been written and published about managing virtual teams, which are mostly defined as those that are geographically dispersed. Technology has been the main driver of the expansion of using virtual teams. In fact, technology organizations, due mostly to the advent of competitive outsourcing abroad, have pushed IT teams to learn how to manage across geographical locations. These locations are typically countries such as India, China, Brazil, Ireland, among many others. These countries are not only far away but also present cultural as well as language barriers. These barriers often impede communications on project status and affect a project's ability to be delivered timely and within forecasted budgets. With these major challenges then, what is it that makes virtual teams so attractive? The answer is simple: cost savings and talent supply. If we look closely into how virtual teams in IT have become so relevant and popular, the case of India stands out as the epitome of this phenomenon. The migration of IT talent to the South Asian country begun with the nation's growth in providing cheap and educated talent. The "cheaper" part of the equation caused many IT development departments to start transitioning to use more Indian-based firms, hence resulting in less students entering into IT curriculums at universities for fear of not being able to find work post-graduation. This then initiated a cycle of job losses and further talent growth needs abroad. So, the reality is that technology organizations themselves are faced with the complex challenges of learning how to manage virtually, because the talent is far away.

From an IT perspective, outsourcing and virtual teams have a strong relationship in that outsourcing success is predicated heavily on the effectiveness of the team's ability to communicate and operate in a virtual environment and ultimately manage projects. However, the converse is not true, that is, the existence of virtual teams does not necessarily imply outsourcing. Virtual teams can simply be those workers who are working from a distance as opposed to someone who comes to work at the office. This section addresses both virtual teams from an "internal" perspective as well as from an outsource one. Additionally, it provides project managers with an understanding of when and how to consider outsource partners as part of the analysis and development process. The project topics include: management

© Springer-Verlag London Limited 2016
A.M. Langer, *Guide to Software Development*,
DOI 10.1007/978-1-4471-6799-0_16

considerations, dealing with multiple locations, contract administration, and in-house alternatives. Most important, this section will extend how outstanding project management is a critical component for success in using virtual organizations.

When reviewing the success factors of managing projects virtually, we see that most failures relate to poor communication. From an organizational learning perspective, we would define this as differences in meaning-making—stemming mostly from cultural differences of the meaning of words and behavioral norms. There is also no question that time differences play a role in certain malfunctions of teams, but the core issues remain to be communication related.

My previous research has shown that cultural transformation is slow to occur (Langer 2011) and often happens in small intervals. In many virtual team settings, team members never physically meet and may never do more than talk via email. As an example, I had a client that was outsourcing production in China. One day they received an email stating "we cannot do business with you." Of course the management team was confused and worried, seeking to understand why the business arrangement was ending without any formal discussions of the problem. A translator in China was hired to further understand the dilemma. As it turned out, the statement was meant to suggest that the company needed to provide more business—more work that is. The way the Chinese communicated that need was very different than the Western interpretation! This is just a small example of what can happen without a well-thought-out project management scheme. We must think how often specifications and product requirements are changing and need virtual teams to somehow come together and agree on how to get the work done—or think they agree!

Still, another aspect of managing virtual teams is the simple expansion of employees that want to have more personal flexibility. Indeed, companies are having employees work from home more often—and have found the experience to be most productive. However, this type of virtual team management is different in that it is a more hybrid model. While workers are not in the office every day, they do come in for critical meetings and sessions, which dramatically help with communication and the ability for the management to have quality checkpoints.

So the main purpose of this section is how to formulate approaches that provide formidable solutions to a growing dilemma of how teams work, especially those that are 100 % virtual. Obviously the advent of virtual teams creates another level of complexity for designing and maintaining project teams. It also furthers the value proposition of why project management, in general, is required for successful transformation into a virtual community of workers.

Prior research and case studies typically provide tools and procedures as ways to improve productivity and quality of virtual team operations. While these processes and methodologies are needed, they will not necessarily ensure the successful outcomes that are being sought by analysis and design teams. We must also remember that virtual team operations are not limited to IT staffs. Business users are often needed to be involved as they would in any project, particularly when users are needed to validate requirements and test the product. Furthermore, as discussed in Chap. 11, digital transformation also includes consumers, who in turn can also be virtual across the globe.

Status of Virtual Teams

The general consensus tells us that virtual teams render results. According to Bazarova and Walther (2009) "virtual groups whose members communicate primarily or entirely via email, computer conferencing, chat, or voice—has become a common feature of twenty-first century organizations" (p. 252). Lipnack and Stamps (2000) state that virtual teams will become the accepted way to work and will likely reshape the work world. While there is certainty in the predictions, there has also been evidence of negative attribution or judgment about problems that arise in virtual team performance. Thus, it is important to understand the complexities of adjusting to how virtual teams need to be managed and the how expectations need to be formed.

Project Management Challenges

Attribution theory "describes how people typically generate explanations for outcomes and actions—their own and others" (Bazarova and Walther 2009, p. 253). This theory explains certain behavior patterns that have occurred during dysfunctional problems occurring in managing virtual project teams. The significant difference in virtual project teams is that members often do not have accurate information about the other members because of the limitations of interaction. Therefore, project members can easily develop perceptions as to why members take specific actions that are inaccurate or distorted by their own cultural norms or those of their other members. Research also shows us that virtual project team members typically attribute failure to the external factors and successes to internal factors. The successes then tend to reinforce that virtual teams are problematic because of their very nature. This then establishes the dilemma of the use of virtual project organizations—its use will continue to increase and dominate workplace structures and yet will present challenges to organizations that do not want to change. The lack of support to change will be substantiated during failures in expected outcomes. Some of the failures, however, can and should be attributable to distance. As Olson and Olson (2000) state: "distance will persist as an important element of human experience" (p.2). So despite the advent of technology, it is important not to ignore the social needs that project teams need to have to be effective.

Dealing with Multiple Locations

Perhaps the greatest difficulty in implementing virtual project teams is the reality that it spans across multiple locations. More often these locations can be in different time zones and across multiple cultures. In order to properly understand the complexity of interactions, it makes sense to revisit the organizational learning tools discussed in prior chapters. Perhaps another way of viewing virtual project teams is to compare them to multiple layers in a spreadsheet. This means that virtual teams

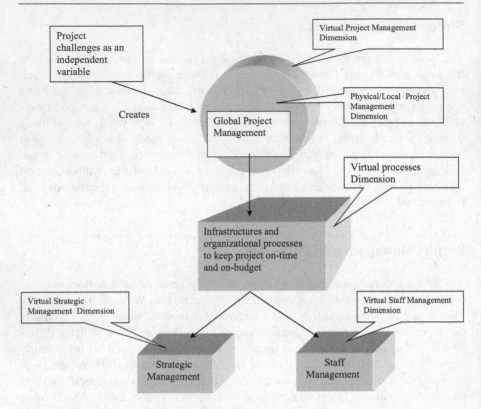

Fig. 16.1 Virtual project management dimensions

affect projects in a third dimension. Figure 16.1 reflects how this dimension should be observed.

In other words the existence of virtual project teams should be viewed as a subset of the study of project management. When one talks about workplace activities, we need to address the issues at the component level. In this example the components are the "physical organization" and the "virtual organization." The two together make up the superset or the entire organization! Therefore, we can no longer limit the conversation in one dimension; rather the sum of the two components comprises the complete topic of project management.

In Chap. 11, I provided an introduction to the complexities surrounding communities of practice (COP). In this section I will expand that discussion to include virtual organizational structures.

Virtual project teams perhaps will facilitate the complete integration of IT and non-IT workers. The ability to connect from various locations using technology in itself provides an ability to expand the building of COP. But as stated in Chap. 11, it also presents new challenges, most of which relate to the transient nature of

Table 16.1 Operating differences between traditional and virtual project teams

Traditional project teams	Virtual project team members
Teams tend to have fixed participation and members	Membership shifts based on topics and needs
Members tend to be from the same organization	Team members can include people from outside the organization (clients and collaborators)
Team members are 100 % dedicated	Members are assigned to multiple teams
Team members are co-located geographically and by organization	Team members are distributed geographically and by organization
Teams tend to have a fixed term of membership, that is, start and stop dates	Teams are reconfigured dynamically and may never terminate
Teams tend to have one overall manager	Teams have multiple reporting relationships with different parts of the organization at different times
Teamwork is physical and practiced in face-to-face interactions	Teamwork is basically social
Engagement is often during group events and can often be hierarchical in nature	Individual engagement is inseparable from empowerment

members that can participate based more on a subject or transactional basis as opposed to a permanent membership in a group. Table 16.1 reflects some of the key differences between physical project teams and virtual project forms.

Much has been stated about whether everyone is suited to perform effectively in a virtual community. Members need to be self-motivated and able to work independently, and people need to communicate clearly and in a positive way. Such a requirement seems a bit ridiculous given that workers in general may not have such skills. The reality is that virtual team success must be predicated more on the ability of workers to understand and learn how to be more adaptive or face the reality that their value will become marginal in their organizations.

To better understand this issue, I have extended the communities-of-practice matrix (Table 16.2) presented in Chap. 11 to include virtual project team considerations.

Item 7 in Table 16.2 links the study of knowledge management with communities of practice. The study of managing knowledge in virtual communities within an organization has become associated directly with a firm's ability to sustain competitive advantage. Indeed, Peddibhotla and Subramni (2008) state that "virtual communities are recognized as important contributors to both the development of social networks among individuals but also individual performance and firm performance" (p. 229). However, technology-enabled facilities and support, while providing the repository for better documentation, also create challenges particularly in maintaining such knowledge. The process of how information might become explicit has also been dramatically changed with the advent of virtual project team communications. For example, much of technology-related documentation evolves more from bottom-up sources as opposed to what has been traditionally a top-down-oriented process. In effect, virtual communities share knowledge more on a peer-to-peer basis or through mutual consensus of the members. As a result, virtual project communities have

Table 16.2 Communities of practice matrix for virtual teams

Step	Communities-of-practice step	Traditional project management extension	Virtual project management extension
1.	Understanding strategic knowledge needs: what knowledge is critical to project success	Understanding how project phases affect outcomes and is critical to success	Understanding how to integrate multiple project phases that need to be integrated into one overall project plan
2.	Engaging practice domains: where people form communities of practice to engage in and identify with	The project manager identifies groups based on business-related benefits. Requiring domains to work together toward measurable results	Virtual domains are more dynamic and can be formed for specific purposes and then reconfigured based on project needs
3.	Developing communities: how to help key communities reach their full potential	Technologies have life cycles that require communities to continue. Treating the life cycle as a supporter for attaining maturation and full potential	Communities can be reallocated to participate in multiple objectives. Domains of discussion have no limits to reach organizational needs
4.	Working the boundaries: how to link communities to form broader learning systems	Project life cycles require new boundaries to be formed. This will link other communities that were previously outside of discussions and expand domain of project input	Virtual abilities allow for consumer interfaces, vendors, and other interested parties to join project community
5.	Fostering a sense of belonging: how to engage people's identities and sense of belonging	The process of integrating communities: IT and other organizational units will create new evolving cultures which foster belonging to the project goals	Communities establish belonging in a virtual way. Identities are established more on content of discussion than on physical attributes of members
6.	Running the business: how to integrate communities of practice into running the business of the organization	The project provides new organizational structures that are necessary to operate communities of practice and to manage the plan	The project functions more as a virtual community or team, being more agile to demands of the business and interactions may not always include all members
7.	Applying, assessing, reflecting, renewing: how to deploy knowledge strategy through waves of organizational transformation	The active process of dealing with multiple components of the project accelerates the need for organizational transformation	Virtual teams require clear communication and documentation which results in establishing explicit knowledge during the project

historically failed to meet expectations, particularly of management objectives. To better understand the complexities of knowledge management and virtual project teams, Sabherwal and Becerra-Fernandez (2005) expanded on Nonaka's (1994) work on knowledge management that outlined four modes of knowledge creation: *externalization, internalization, combination, and socialization.*

Externalization

Externalization is the process of converting or translating tacit knowledge into explicit forms. The problem with this concept is whether project members really understand what they know and how it might affect the project. Virtual project communities have further challenges in that the repository of tacit information can be found in a myriad of storage facilities, namely, audit trails of email communications. While Sabherwal and Becerra-Fernandez suggest that technology may indeed assist in providing the infrastructure to access such information, the reality is the challenge is not one of process, rather of thinking and doing. That is, it is more a process of unlearning existing processes of thinking and doing into new modes of using knowledge that is abundantly available.

Internalization

Internalization is a reversal of externalization in that it is the process of transferring explicit knowledge into tacit—or individualized project learning. The individual thus makes the explicit process into his/her own stabilized thinking system so that it becomes intuitive in project operations. The value of virtual project team interactions is that it can provide more authentic evidence of why explicit knowledge is valuable to the individual. Virtual project management techniques simply can provide more people that find such knowledge useful, and such individuals, coming from a more peer relationship, can associate with others why their procedures can be internalized and become part of the everyday operations.

Combination

Perhaps combination provides the most evolving of virtual project team advantages. The association, particularly in a global environment, allows virtual team members to integrate new explicit forms into their own, not by replacing their beliefs, but rather establishing new hybrid knowledge systems. This is particularly an advantage across multiple cultures and business systems that differ among countries who hold different and possibly complimentary knowledge about how things can get done. Nonaka's concept of combination requires participants in the community to be at higher levels of management—suggesting that this form can only be successful among certain levels or positions of project members.

Socialization

As Nonaka defined, individuals learn by observation, imitation, and practice. The very expansion of conversations via technology can provide a social network where individuals can learn simply through discourse. The challenge in virtual social

networks is the ability for participants to ascertain the authenticity of the information being provided by those in the community.

The four modes of knowledge management formulated by Nonaka needs to be expanded to embrace the complexities of virtual project team communities of practice. Most of the adjustments are predicated to the team's ability to deal with the critical factors that are key in virtual team project management success. Below is a mapping of virtual project management to Nonaka's four modes.

Externalization Virtual Project Management

The externalization mode must be dynamic, ongoing, with little ability to forecast the longevity of any tacit to explicit formulation. In other words, tacit to explicit project knowledge may occur daily, but may only operate effectively for a shorter period due to additional changes brought on digital transformation and changes in consumer behavior as outlined in Chap. 11. This means that members in a community must continually challenge themselves to revisit previous tacit processes and acknowledge the need to reformulate their tacit systems. Thus, transformation from tacit knowledge to explicit knowledge can be a daily challenge for community of practice virtual project organizations.

Internalization Virtual Project Management

This process of internalizing explicit forms must be carefully reflected on. Given the differences in cultures and acceleration of business change, individualized learning creating new tacit abilities may not operate the same in different project settings. It may be necessary to adopt multiple processes depending on the environment where tacit operations are being performed. As stated previously, what might work in China may not work in Brazil, for example. Tacit behavior is very culture-oriented, so multiple and simultaneous versions must be respected and practiced. Further expansion of internalization is a virtual team's understanding of how such tacit behaviors change over time due to the acceleration of new business challenges.

Combination Virtual Project Management

I believe this mode is the most important component of virtual team formation. Any *combination* or hybrid model requires a mature project team. This means that individuals in virtual teams must be capable of dealing with the complexities of changing dispositions. This suggests that members of COP need to be observed and a determination of readiness needs to exist for such new structures to develop in a virtual world. Thus, COP project members need training and this need might provide why to date so many virtual teams have had disappointing results. What does this really mean? The suggestion is that readiness for virtual team participation

requires a certain level of relativistic thinking in order to be successful. The complexity of COP issues that will occur in a virtual process requires that members see themselves outside of their own world and have the ability to understand the importance of what "others" need. This position suggests that individuals need to be tested to the extent that they are ready for such challenges. Training techniques remain as a valid method to develop workers that can cope with dynamic change requirements required in virtual team organizations.

Socialization Dynamism

Socialization challenges the virtual team members' ability to understand the meaning of words and requires critical reflection of its constituents. This requires that virtual teams need to be agile especially to the emotions displayed by others in the community. This may require individuals to understand another member's culture and meaning-making. Thus, virtual team members need to have the ability to assess others' situation with local needs. Assessment in a virtual collaboration becomes a necessity especially given the existence of the unpredictability of technology-based virtual projects.

Ultimately knowledge management in a virtual project management context has significant factors that must be addressed to improve its success. These factors include management commitment, resource availability, modification of work practices, marketing of the initiative, training, and facilitation of cultural differences (Peddibhotla and Subramani 2008).

Below are some action steps that organizations need to take to address these factors:

1. The executive team needs to advocate the commitment and support for virtual project teams. The CIO and his/her counterparts need to provide teams with the "sponsorship" that the organization will need to endure setbacks until the virtual operation becomes fully integrated into the entire project. This commitment can be accomplished via multiple actions including but not limited to a kickoff meeting with staff, status reports to virtual teams on successes and setbacks, emails and memos on new virtual formations, and a general update on the effort perhaps on a quarterly basis. This approach allows the organization to understand the evolution of the effort and know that virtual teams are an important direction for the project.
2. Training and practice sessions with collocated groups that allow virtual project teams to voice their concerns and receive direction on how best to proceed. Practice sessions should focus on team member responsibilities and advocating their ownership of responsibility. These sessions should cover lessons learned from actual experiences so that other groups can learn from others. Training should set the goals and establish the criteria for how virtual teams interact in the firm. This should include the application software and repositories in place and the procedures for keeping information and knowledge current.

3. External reminders should be practiced so that virtual project teams do not become lax and develop bad habits since no one is monitoring or measuring success. Providing documented processes or procedures and measurements is a good practice for monitoring compliance.

Dealing with Multiple Locations and Outsourcing

As stated earlier in this chapter, virtual organizations are often a given in outsourcing environments especially those that are offshore. Offshore outsourcing also means that the virtual communications will occur from multiple locations. The first part of dealing with multiple locations is typically time differences. In a global world, dealing at different time zones is not an unusual situation. But viewing the complexities of project management across virtual members gets complicated when meetings occur at obscure times for certain members of the community. It also presents problems when attempting to deal with unanticipated problems that occur where pulling together the team may not be feasible because of time differences. The second major issue is culture. Cultural norms governing behavior of team members can be significant. This especially causes problems during off-hour virtual sessions. For example, European work culture does not often support having meetings outside of work hours. In some countries work hours may be governed by the government or very powerful unions.

What makes outsourcing a further complication is that the virtual teams may be across different companies. That is, part of the community is comprised of a vendor who has assigned staff resources to the effort. These outsourced project team members belong to the community of the project, yet also work for another organization. The relationship between an outside consultant and the internal team is not straightforward and varies among projects. For example, some outsourced technical resources may be permanently assigned to the project, so while they actually work for another firm, they behave and take daily direction as if they were an employee of the business. Yet, in other relationships, outsourced resources work closely under the auspices of the outsourced "project manager" who acts as a buffer between the firm and the vendor. Such COP formations then will vary. Still other outsourced relationships have very virtual members—so virtual that the firm does not know who they are per se—unless there is a problem, then outsourced staff get involved. This latter example is usually relevant when organizations outsource complete systems—so that the expectation is based more on the results than on interaction. Notwithstanding the arrangement or level of integration, a COP must exist and its behavior in all three of these examples varies in participation, but all are driven in a virtual relationship more by dynamic business events than by preplanned activities.

Typical outsourced development projects may include multiple distributed teams, some using internal staff mixed with third party vendors. In summary then, outsource projects have a number of challenges that relate to virtual teams including:

- Getting timely and consistent input requirements from multiple sources and countries. Conflicts may arise from cultural norms, working hours, and management styles.
- Contract definitions and legal ramifications across borders (see Chap. 18).
- Conflict in different consumer bases including buying preferences and brand loyalties.
- Time zone resolutions in communications, meetings, and releases of products.
- Differences in written and verbal communications and a more strict need for clearly defined procedures.
- Outsourced teams may lack business and organizational experience.

If we look closely at COP approaches to dealing with outsourced operations, the extension of project management in a virtual team community shows the pressure on transactions and what may be defined as temporary team formation based on demographic similarity needs. Table 16.3 shows the expansion of virtual project management on the learning in a social setting of COP.

Thus, the advent of modern-day IT outsourcing has created a complexity of how project communities of practice function. IT outsourcing has simultaneously brought attention to the importance of COP and knowledge management in general.

Table 16.3 Virtual project management COP

COP physical social settings	COP virtual project management
Shared pursuit of interest accomplished through group meetings	Interest in discussion based more on dynamic transactions and remote needs to satisfy specific personal needs
Creation of the "community" is typically established within the same or similar departments	The notion of permanency is de-emphasized. Specific objective at based on the need of the group will establish the community
Demographic similarity is a strong contributor to selection of community members	Demographic similarity has little to do with community selection. Selection is based more on subject matter expertise
Situated learning is often accomplished by assisting members to help develop others. Learning occurs within a framework of social participation	Situated learning to help others has less focus. It may not be seen as the purpose or responsibility of virtual team members. Social participation has more concrete perspective
Community needs to assess project activities in more physical environments requiring a formal infrastructure	Community is less identifiable from a physical perspective. Project activities are accomplished by members who have special interests at the subject level as opposed to the group level
COP works well with formal work groups where participants are clearly identified	Work groups in virtual settings are more transaction -based
COP can be used for realignment of work departments based on similar needs	COP in a virtual environment creates temporary realignments based on similar needs during the process
COP supports continual learning and dealing with unplanned action	COPs are continually reconfigured and do not have permanency of group size or interest

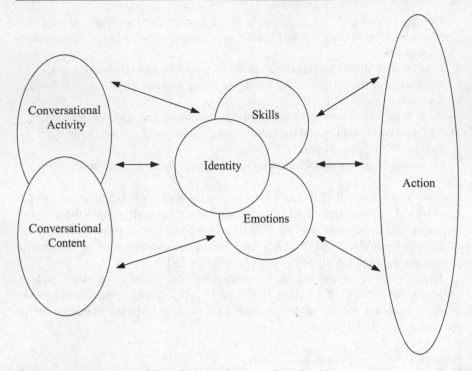

Fig. 16.2 Grant's schema of the relationship between talk and action

Social Discourse in Virtual Project Management

The importance of social discourse and the use of language is a distinct component that affects the success of virtual projects that use communities of practice. Grant et al. (1996) developed an interesting schema that links talk and action. It contains three components: identity, skills and emotion. Figure 16.2 shows this relationship again.

The expansion of virtual team communications further emphasizes the importance of discourse and the need to rethink how Grant's three components relate to each other in a virtual project context.

Identity

Human identities can be very transactional—in such ways that an individual may be a member of multiple COP environments and have different identities in each one. This presents an emphasis on the multitasking aspect of the virtual project management teams. Ultimately social discourse will dynamically change based on the COP that an individual belongs to, and that individual needs to be able to "inventory" these multiple roles and responsibilities. Such roles and responsibilities themselves

will transform due to the complexity of events that occur in IT projects. So what this means is that project members will have multiple identities and must be able to manage those identities across different COPs and via different contexts within those COPs. This requires project teams to use discourse to transform their interests and opinions into action.

Skills

Persuasion is often thought of as a skill to transform talk into action. Having the ability to persuade others across virtual project teams is critical. Often skills are misrepresented as technical abilities that give people a right of passage. Among multiple cultures, individuals in teams must be able to recognize norms and understand how to communicate with others to get tangible results on their projects. What is most difficult is doing such determinations with an individual that one has never physically met. Furthermore, virtual meetings may not provide the necessary background required to properly understand a person's skill sets, both "hard" and "soft." The "soft" skills analysis is more important as the individual's technical credentials become assumed. We see this assumption when individuals transition into management positions. Ascertaining technical knowledge at the staff level is easier—almost like an inventory analysis of technical requirements. However, determining individual soft skill ability and understanding whether a person possesses such skills is much more challenging. Virtual project teams will need to create more complex and broadened inventories of their team's skill sets, as well as establishing better criteria on how to measure soft skills. Soft skills will require individuals to have better "multicultural" abilities so that members can be better equipped to deal with multinational and cross-cultural issues.

Emotion

Along with persuasion, emotion involves an individual's ability to motivate others and to create positive energy. Many of those who successfully use emotion are likely to have done so in a more physical context than from a virtual perspective. Transferring positive emotion in a virtual world can be analogous to what organizations experienced in the e-commerce world, where organizations needed to re-brand themselves across the web in such a way that their image was reflected virtually to their customers. This meant that marketing had to be accomplished without having the physical capacities to be in front of the buyer during purchase decisions. Virtual COPs are similar—representation must be what the individual walks away with, without seeing the results physically—certainly a new dimension for managing teams. This means that the development requirements for virtual members must include advanced abstract thinking so that the individual can better forecast virtual team reactions to what *will* be said, as opposed to reacting while the conversation is being conducted or thinking about what to do after virtual meetings.

Fig. 16.3 Marshak's types of talk

Marshak's (1998) work on types of talk that leads to action is useful here. It includes three components: tool-talk, frame-talk, and mythopoetic-talk:

Tool-talk includes "instrumental communities required to discuss, conclude, act, and evaluate outcomes" (22). What is most important in its application is that tool-talk be used to deal with specific issues for an identified purpose.

Frame-talk focuses on interpretation to evaluate the meanings of talk. Using frame-talk results in enabling implicit and explicit assessments, which include symbolic, conscious, pre-conscious, and contextually subjective dimensions (Marshak 1998).

Mythopoetic-talk communicates idiogenic ideas and images (for instance, myths and cosmologies) that can be used to communicate the nature of how to apply tool-talk and frame-talk within the particular culture or society. This type of talk allows for concepts of intuition and ideas for concrete application.

Virtual project teams require modification to the sequence of talk, that is, the use of talk is altered. Let us first look at Fig. 16.3 representing the Marshak model.

The effects of virtual teams on this model are in its sequence. That is, the virtual project team must focus on mythopoetic-talk in the center as opposed to an outer ring. This means that idiogenic issues must precede interpretation in a virtual world. Thus, tool-talk, which in the more physical world was at the center of types of tools, is now moved to the outside rectangle. In other words instrumental actions lag those of ideology and interpretation. This is restructured in Fig. 16.4.

Indeed, mythopoetic-talk is at the foundation of grounding ideas at virtual COP. It would only make sense that a COP-driven talk requires idiogenic behavior before migrating to instrumental outcomes! Remember idiogenic talk allows for concepts of intuition and ideas for concrete application especially relevant among multiple cultures and societies. So we once again see that virtual teams require changes in the sequence of how learning needs to transpire. This change in sequence places more emphasis on the need for an individual to be more developmentally mature—mature with respect to the way one thinks and handles

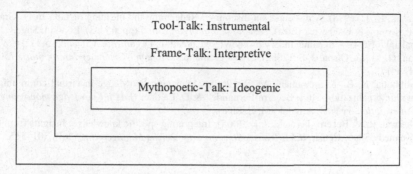

Fig. 16.4 Virtual team depiction of Marshak's types of talk

differences, and an emphasis to think more abstractly. This new "abstract individual" must be able to deal with digital transformation and acceleration of changes we see in many IT projects.

Problems and Exercises

1. What are the major factors that have accelerated the need for virtual teams?
2. Discuss the relationship between virtual teams and the need for outsourcing?
3. Explain five (5) key challenges of managing virtual teams.
4. What is meaning of project management dimensions?
5. What is the relationship between communities of practice (COP) and virtual project management?
6. Define knowledge management.
7. Why is knowledge management important in managing virtual teams?
8. Define and compare the four (4) modes of knowledge creation.
9. What is meant by "dynamism?"
10. What is tool-talk, frame-talk, and mythopoetic-talk?
11. Describe the relationship between talk and action.

References

Bazarova, N. N., & Walther, J. B. (2009). Virtual groups: (Mis) attribution of blame in distributed work. In P. Lutgen-Sandvik & B. Davenport Sypher (Eds.), *Destructive organizational communication: Processes, consequences, and constructive ways of organizing* (pp. 252–266). New York: Routledge.

Grant, D., Keenoy, T., & Oswick, C. (1996). *Discourse and organization*. London: Sage Publications.

Langer, A. M. (2011). *Information technology and organizational learning: Managing behavioral change through technology and education* (2nd ed.). New York: CRC Press.

Lipnack, J., & Stamps, J. (2000). *Virtual teams* (2nd ed.). New York: Wiley.

Marshak, R. J. (1998). A discourse on discourse: Redeeming the meaning of talk. In D. Grant, T. Keenoy, & O. Oswick (Eds.), *Discourse and organization* (pp. 65–83). London: Sage.

Nonaka, I. (1994). A dynamic theory of knowledge creation. *Organization Science, 5*(1), 14–37.

Olson, G. M., & Olson, J. S. (2000). Distance matters. *Human –Computer Interactions, 15*(1), 139–178.

Peddibhotla, N. B., & Subramani, M. R. (2008). Managing knowledge in virtual communities within organizations. In I. Becerra-Fernandez & D. Leidner (Eds.), *Knowledge management: An evolutionary view*. Armonk: M. E. Sharp.

Sabherwal, R., & Becerra-Fernandez, I. (2005). Integrating specific knowledge: Insights from the Kennedy Space Center. *IEEE Transactions on Engineering Management, 52*(3), 301–315.

Cyber Security, ISO 9000, and the Software Development Life Cycle

<div style="text-align:right">

17

</div>

Cyber Security in Analysis and Design

The overall challenge in building more resilient applications that are better equipped to protect against threats is a decision that needs to address exposure coupled with risk. The general consensus is that no system can be 100 % protected and that this requires important decisions when analysts are designing applications and systems. Indeed, security access is not just limited to getting into the system, rather on the individual application level as well. How then do analysts participate in the process of designing secure applications through good design? We know that many cyber security architectures are designed from the office of the chief information security officer or CISO, a new and emerging role in organizations. The CISO role, often independent of the CIO (chief information officer), became significant as a result of the early threats from the Internet, the 9/11 attacks, and most recently the abundant number of system compromises experienced by companies such as JP Morgan Chase, SONY, Home Depot, and Target to name just a few.

The challenge of cyber security reaches well beyond just architecture. It must address third-party vendor products that are part of the supply chain of automation used by firms, not to mention access to legacy applications that likely do not have the necessary securities built into the architecture of these older, less resilient technologies. This challenge has established the need for an enterprise cyber security solution that addresses the need of the entire organization. This approach would then target third-party vendor design and compliance. Thus, cyber security architecture requires integration with a firm's software development life cycle (SDLC), particularly within steps that include strategic design, engineering, and operations. The objective is to use a framework that works with all of these components.

© Springer-Verlag London Limited 2016
A.M. Langer, *Guide to Software Development*,
DOI 10.1007/978-1-4471-6799-0_17

Cyber Security Risk in the S-Curve

In Chap. 12, I discussed the importance of the S-curve and its relationship to the risk in accuracy when determining requirements sources. The S-curve also needs to be considered in the design of the cyber security architecture. When designing systems to protect against cyber attacks, risks must be factored into the decision-making process. A number of security experts often ask business executives the question, "How much security protection do you want, and what are you willing to spend to achieve that security?"

We see a much higher tolerance for increasing cost as a result of the recent attacks on companies. This section provides guidance on how to determine appropriate security risks based on where the product exists on the S-Curve.

Security risk is typically discussed in the form of threats. Threats can be categorized based on Schoenfield (2015), analysis below:

1. Threat agent: where is the threat coming from and who is making the attack?
2. Threat goals: what does the agent hope to gain?
3. Threat capability: what threat methodology or type is the agent possibly going to use?
4. Threat work factor: how much effort is the agent willing to put in to get into the system?
5. Threat risk tolerance: what legal chances is the agent willing to take to achieve their goals?

Table 17.1 is shown as a guideline.

Depending on the threat, its associated risks, and related work factors, the use of threat analysis will provide important input to the security design at the application design level. Such application securities in design typically include:

1. The user interface (sign in screen, access to specific parts of the application)
2. Command-line interface (interactivity) in online systems
3. Inter-application communications. How data and password information are passed and stored among applications across systems

Table 17.1 Threat analysis

Threat agent	Goals	Risk tolerance	Work factor	Methods
Cyber criminals	Financial	Low	Low to medium	Known and proven

Source: Schoenfield (2015)

Decomposition in Cyber Security Analysis

Flow diagrams and database normalization is not the only application for functional decomposition. The concept of decomposition is very relevant to the architecture of systems that guard against attacks. Simply put, integrating security at the functional decomposed levels of applications can improve protection. However, security at this level does not negate threat exposure but will reduce risk. Figure 17.1 shows a scheme of how security is implemented at all levels during the decomposition process.

Figure 17.1 demonstrates how analysts need to ensure that various security routines exist at multiple layers including the front-end interface, applications, and databases. The reason for this level of security is to provide the maximum amount of resistant to the ways threats enter a system. Indeed, once a virus enters, it can find its way through many parts of the system—that is, entry points serve as gateways into the environment. Some of these points of potential entry could require special third-party applications, but these decisions should be discussed with the cyber security team. The analyst must continue to stay focused on the logical view of the system.

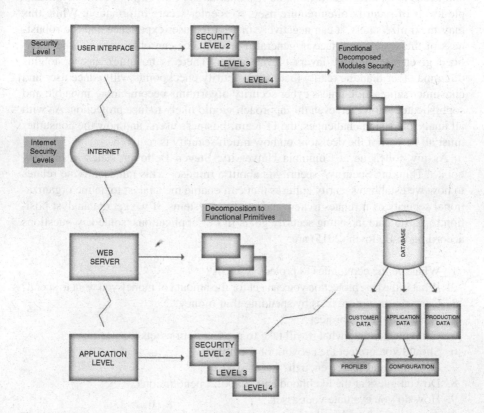

Fig. 17.1 Cyber security and decomposition

At each decomposed level, the analyst should consider the specific checklist of threat potentials as I outlined in Chap. 15. The number of security interfaces needed will depend on the amount of risk tolerance and the associated costs to implement a solution. An important consideration prior to the determination of the levels of security is always the impact it might have on the user interface and on overall performance of the system.

Risk Responsibility

Schoenfield (2015) suggests that someone in the organization is assigned the role of the "risk owner." There may be many risk owners and as a result this role could have complex effects on the way systems are designed. For example, the top risk owner in most organizations today is associated with the CISO, or cyber security information systems officer. However, many firms also employ a CRO or chief risk officer. This role's responsibilities vary.

But risk analysis at the application design level requires different governance. Application security risk needs involvement from the business and the consumer and needs to be integrated within the risk standards of the firm. Specifically, multiple levels of security often require users to reenter secure information. While this may maximize safety, it can negatively impact the user experience and the robustness of the system interface in general. Performance can obviously also be sacrificed given the multiple layers of validation. There is no quick answer to this dilemma other than the reality that more security checkpoints will reduce user and consumer satisfaction unless cyber security algorithms become more invisible and sophisticated. However, even this approach would likely reduce protection. As with all analysts' design challenges, the IT team, business users, and now the consumer must all be part of the decisions on how much security is required.

As my colleague at Columbia University, Steven Bellovin, states in his new book, "Thinking Security," security is about a mindset. This mindset to me relates to how we establish security cultures that can enable the analyst to define organizational security as it relates to new and existing systems. If we get the analyst position to participate in setting security goals in our applications, some key questions according to Bellovin (2015) are:

1. What are the economics to protect systems?
2. What is the best protection you can get for the amount of money you want to spend?
3. Can you save more lives by spending that money?
4. What should you protect?
5. Can you estimate what it will take to protect your assets?
6. Should you protect the network or the host?
7. Is your Cloud secure enough?
8. Do you guess at the likelihood and cost of a penetration?
9. How do you evaluate your assets?
10. Are you thinking like the enemy?

The key to analysis and design in cyber security is recognizing that it is dynamic; the attackers are adaptive and somewhat unpredictable. This dynamism requires constant architectural change accompanied with increased complexity of how systems become compromised. Thus, analysts must be involved at the conceptual model, which includes business definitions, business processes, and enterprise standards. However, the analysts must also be engaged with the logical design, which comprises two sub-models:

1. Logical architecture: depicts the relationships of different data domains and functionalities required to manage each type of information in the system.
2. Component model: reflects each of the sub-models and applications that provide various functions in the system. The component model may also include third-party vendor products that interface with the system. The component model coincides in many ways with the process of decomposition.

In summary, the analysis and design interface with cyber security is complex. It must utilize the high level and decomposed diagrams and pictures that reference the specific hardware and software that comprise the needs for security. Security is relative, and thus analysts must be closely aligned with the CISO, executive management, and network architects to keep current with the threats and fixes when systems get compromised.

Developing a System of Procedures

Perhaps one of the most significant challenges in analysis today is its role in the software life cycle. There has been much criticism of the lack of discipline applied to software development projects and personnel in general, and we continue to be an industry that has a poor reputation for delivering quality products on schedule. This is even more evident with the exposures to cyber security attacks as articulated above. Although many organizations have procedures, few really follow them and fewer still have any means of measuring the quality and productivity of software development. A system of procedures should first be developed prior to implementing a life cycle that can ensure its adherence to the procedure. These procedures also need to be measured on an ongoing basis. This book restricts its focus to the set of procedures that should be employed in the analysis and design functions.

The process of developing measurable procedures in an organization must start with the people who will be part of its implementation. Standard procedures should not be created by upper management, as the steps will be viewed as a control mechanism as opposed to a quality implementation. How then do we get the implementers to create the standards? When examining this question, one must look at other professions and see how they implement their standards. The first main difference between computer professionals and members of many other professions is they lack a governing standards board like the American Medical

Association (AMA) or the American Institute of Certified Public Accountants (AICPA). Unfortunately, as mentioned in previous chapters, it seems unlikely that any such governing board will exist in the near future. Looking more closely at this issue, however, we need to examine the ultimate value of a governing board. What standards boards really accomplish is to build the moral and professional responsibilities of their trade. Accountants, attorneys, and doctors look upon themselves as professionals who have such responsibilities. This is not to imply that governing boards can resolve every problem, but at least they can help. With or without the existence of a standards board, analysts within an organization must develop the belief that they belong to a profession. Once this identification occurs, analysts can create the procedures necessary to ensure the quality of their own profession. There simply are not many analysts who view themselves as part of a profession.

If analysts can create this level of self-actualization, then the group can begin the process of developing quality procedures that can be measured for future improvement. The standard procedures should be governed by the group itself and the processes integrated into the software life cycle of the organization. In fact, analysts should encourage other departments to follow the same procedures for implementing their respective quality procedures.

Although not typically required, many firms have elected to employ ISO 9000 as a more formal vehicle to implement the development of measurable procedures. ISO 9000 stands for the International Organization for Standardization, an organization formed in 1947 and based in Geneva, which currently has 91 member countries associated with it. ISO 9000 was founded to establish international quality assurance standards focused on processes rather than on products.

Why ISO 9000?

ISO 9000 offers a method of establishing agreed-upon quality levels through standard procedures in the production of goods and services. Many international companies require that their vendors be ISO 9000 compliant through the certification process. Certification requires an audit by an independent firm that specializes in ISO 9000 compliance. The certification is good for 3 years. Apart from the issue of certification, the benefits of ISO 9000 are in its basis for building a quality program through employee empowerment. It also achieves and sustains specific quality levels and provides consistency in its application. ISO 9000 has a number of subcomponents. ISO 9001, 9002, 9003 codify the software development process. In particular 9001 affects the role of the analyst by requiring standards for design specifications and defines 20 different categories of systems. Essentially ISO 9000 requires three basic things:

1. Say what you do.
2. Do what you say.
3. Prove it.

 This means that the analyst will need to completely document what should occur during the requirements process to ensure quality. After these procedures are documented, the analyst needs to start implementing based on the standards developed and agreed upon by the organization. The process must be self documenting, that is, it must contain various control points that can prove at any time that a quality step in the process was not only completed but done within the quality standard established by the organization. It is important to recognize that ISO 9000 does not establish what the standard should be but rather simply that the organization can comply with whatever standards it chooses to employ. This freedom is what makes ISO 9000 so attractive. Even if the organization does not opt to go through with the audit, it can still establish an honorable quality infrastructure that:

- Creates an environment of professional involvement, commitment, and accountability
- Allows for professional freedom to document the realities of the process itself within reasonable quality measurements
- Pushes down the responsibilities of quality to the implementer as opposed to the executive
- Identifies where the analyst fits in the scope of the software life cycle
- Locates existing procedural flaws
- Eliminates duplication of efforts
- Closes the gap between required procedures and actual practices
- Complements the other quality programs that might exist
- Requires that the individuals participating in the process be qualified within their defined job descriptions

How to Incorporate ISO 9000 into Existing Software Life Cycles

The question now is how to incorporate an ISO 9000-type process for the analyst function and incorporate it into the existing software life cycle. Listed below are the essential 9 steps to follow:

1. Create and document all the quality procedures for the analyst.
2. Follow these processes throughout the organization and see how they enter and leave the analyst function.
3. Maintain records that support the procedures.
4. Ensure that all professionals understand and endorse the quality policy.
5. Verify that there are no missing processes.
6. Changes or modifications to the procedures must be systematically reviewed and controlled.
7. Have control over all documentation within the process.
8. Ensure that analysts are trained and that records are kept about their training.
9. Ensure that constant review is carried out by the organization or through third-party audits.

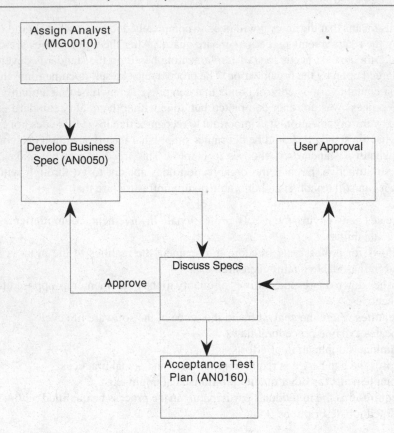

Fig. 17.2 Sample work flow diagram

In order for ISO 9000 guidelines to be implemented, it is recommended that the analyst initially provide a work flow diagram of the quality process (Figs. 17.2, 17.3, 17.4, 17.5, 17.6, and 17.7):

The diagram in Fig. 17.2 reflects some of the steps in a quality process for an analyst. Note that certain steps reflect that there is an actual form that needs to be completed in order to confirm the step's completion.

The forms shown in Figs. 17.3–17.5 represent the confirmation of the activities in the quality work flow process outlined by the analyst. At any time during the life cycle, an event can be confirmed by looking at the completed form.

In order to comply with the documentation standards, each form should contain an instruction sheet (as shown in Fig. 17.3). This sheet will ensure that users have the appropriate instructions. Confirmation documents can be implemented in different ways. Obviously if forms are processed manually, the documentation will contain the actual storage of working papers by project. Such working papers are typically filed in a documentation storage room similar to a library where the

Fig. 17.3 ISO 9000 project status report

original contents are secure and controlled. Access to the documentation is allowed but must be authorized and recorded. Sometimes forms are put together using a word-processing package such as Microsoft Word. The blank forms are stored on a central library so that master documents can be accessed by the analyst via a network. Once the forms are completed, they can be stored in a project directory. The most sophisticated method of implementing ISO 9000 is to use a Lotus Notes electronic filing system. Here, forms are filled out and passed to the appropriate individuals automatically. The confirmation documents then become an inherent part of the original work flow. In any event, these types of forms implementation affect only automation, not the concept of ISO 9000 as a whole.

Analysis Acknowledgment

User: _____

Date:		Analyst:		Date of Request	Project #

Confirmation Type	Y/N	Cost	Expected Days	Expected Delivery	Deliverable/Comments
Requirements Definition					
Conceptual Detail Design:					
Development:					
System Tested Enhancements					
User Accepted Enhancements					

\an0050 Rev. 3/21/11

Fig. 17.4 ISO 9000 analysis acknowledgment

Quality Assurance

Acceptance Test Plan

Purpose:

Test Plan #:		Product:		Number:
		Vendor:		Date:
		QA Technician:		Page: 1 of

Test No.	Condition Being Tested	Expected Results	Actual Results	Comply Y/N	Comments
1					
2					
3					

Fig. 17.5 Quality assurance test plan

Interfacing IT Personnel

We mentioned earlier that ISO 9000 requires qualified personnel. This means that the organization must provide detailed information about the skill set requirements for each job function. Most organizations typically have job descriptions that are not very detailed and tend to be vague with respect to the specific requirements of the job. In addition, job descriptions rarely provide information that can be used to measure true performance. Questions such as "How many lines of code should a programmer generate per day?" cannot be measured effectively. There is also a question about whether lines of code should be the basis of measurement at all.

Name:	Date Issued: 3/8/11
Confirmation/Service Acknowledgment	
Form Instructions	Supersedes:
	Revision: 1.00

The purpose of this form is to track the status of various services such as Requirements Definition, Conceptual Detail Design, Development, System Tested Enhancements and User Accepted Enhancements.

The appropriate project # must be attached. The type form must be checked for each type of Confirmation.

\an0050i Rev. 3/8/11

Fig. 17.6 An ISO 9000 form instruction page

A solution to this dilemma is to create a job description matrix which provides the specific details of each job responsibility along with the necessary measurement criteria for performance.

The document shown in Fig. 17.7 is a matrix of responsibilities for an analyst. Note that the analyst has a number of efficiency requirements within the managing engagements (projects) responsibility. Efficiency here means that the analyst must perform the task at a certain indicated level to be considered productive at that task. To a degree, efficiency typically establishes the time constraints to deliver the task. Measurement defines the method used to determine whether the efficiency was met. Reports are simply the vehicle in which the analyst proves that the task was completed and on what basis.

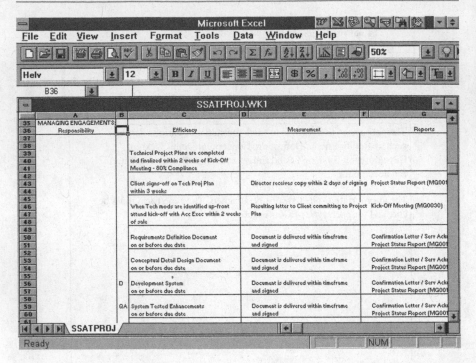

Fig. 17.7 Job description matrix

The job description matrix represents a subset of the entire job description that strictly focuses on the procedural and process aspects of the individual's position. It not only satisfies ISO 9000 but represents a healthier way of measuring individual performance in an IS environment. Most individuals should know exactly their performance at any time during the review period. Furthermore, the matrix is an easy tool to use for updating new or changed performance tasks.

Committing to ISO 9000

We have outlined the sequential steps to implement an ISO 9000 organization. Unfortunately, the outline does not ensure success, and often just following the suggested steps leads to another software life cycle that nobody really adheres to. In order to be successful, a more strategic commitment must be made. Let's outline these guidelines for the analyst functions:

- A team of analysts should meet to form the governing body that will establish the procedures to follow to reach an ISO 9000 level (this does not necessarily require that certification be accomplished.)
- The ISO 9000 team should develop a budget of the milestones to be reached and the time commitments that are required. It is advisable that the budget be forecasted like a project, probably using a Gantt chart to develop the milestones and timeframes.

- The ISO 9000 team should then communicate their objectives to the remaining analysts in the organization and coordinate a review session so that the entire organization can understand the benefits, constraints, and scope of the activity. It is also an opportunity to allow everyone to voice their opinions about how to complete the project. Therefore, the meeting should result in the final schedule for completing the ISO 9000 objective.

- The ISO 9000 team should inform the other IS groups of its objectives, although analysts should be careful not to provoke a political confrontation with other parts of the IS staff. The communication should be limited to helping other departments understand how these analyst quality standards will interface with the entire software life cycle.

- The work flows for the analyst tasks must be completed in accordance with the schedule such that everyone can agree to the confirmation steps necessary to validate each task. It is important that the ISO 9000 processes allow for a percentage of success. This means that not every process must be successful 100 % of the time, but rather can be acceptable within some fault tolerance level. For example, suppose that the analyst must have a follow-up meeting with the users within 48 h after a previous step has been completed. It may not be realistic to meet this goal every time such a meeting is necessary. After all, the analyst cannot always force users to attend meetings in a timely way. Therefore, the ISO 9000 step may view this task as successful if it occurs within the 48 h 80 % of the time, that is, within a 20 % fault tolerance.

- All task steps must have verification. This will require that standard forms be developed to confirm completion. While we have shown samples of these forms earlier, the ISO 9000 team should beware of producing an unwieldy process involving too many forms. Many software life cycles have suffered the consequences of establishing too many checkpoints. Remember, ISO 9000 is a professional's standard and should cater to the needs of well trained professionals. Therefore, the ISO 9000 team should review the initial confirmation forms and begin the process of combining them into a smaller subset. That is, the final forms should be designed to be as generic as possible by confirming multiple tasks. For example, form AN0010 (Fig. 15.2) represents a generic project status report that was used to confirm various types of information attributable to different tasks.

- There should be meetings held with the analysis group that focus on the alternatives for automating the confirmation forms as outlined earlier in this chapter. It is advisable that this topic be confirmed by the group since their full cooperation is needed for the success of the program.

- Allow time for changing the procedures and the forms. Your first effort will not be the final one; therefore, the ISO 9000 team must plan to meet and review the changes necessary to make it work. Analysts should be aware that the opportunity for change always exists as long as it conforms to the essential objectives of ISO 9000.

- The ISO 9000 project should be at least a 1-year plan, from inception of the schedule to actual fulfillment of the processes. In fact, an organization must demonstrate ISO 9000 for at least 18 months prior to being eligible for certification.

- The ISO 9000 group needs to be prepared and authorized to make changes to the job description of the analyst. This may require the submission of requests and authorizations to the executive management team or the human resources department. It is important not to overlook this step since an inability to change the organization structure could hinder the success of the ISO 9000 implementation.

As we can see from the above steps, establishing an ISO 9000 group is a significant commitment. However, its benefits can include a professional organization that controls its own quality standards. These standards can be changed on an ongoing basis to ensure compliance with the business objectives and requirements of the enterprise. Certification, while not the focus of our discussion, is clearly another level to achieve. Most companies that pursue certification do so for marketing advantage or are required to obtain it by their customers. Implementing ISO 9000 should not require that the entire company conform at once; in fact it is almost an advantage to implement it in a phased approach, department by department. The potential benefits of ISO 9000 concepts may fill the void in many of the IS organizations which lack clearly defined quality standards.

Problems and Exercises

1. Provide the key issues when designing systems to deal with cyber security attacks.
2. How does the analyst role change when being engaged with cyber security design?
3. Explain why ISO 9000 represents a system of procedures.
4. What are the three fundamental things that ISO 9000 tries to establish?
5. What are the overall benefits of ISO 9000?
6. How is ISO 9000 incorporated into the life cycle?
7. Why are work flows the most critical aspect of developing the ISO 9000 model?
8. Why are forms used in ISO 9000?
9. How are personnel affected by ISO 9000?
10. What is a job description matrix?
11. What steps are necessary for an organization to adopt ISO 9000?
12. Does ISO 9000 need to be implemented in all areas of the business? Explain.

References

Bellovin, S. M. (2015). To appear. In *Thinking security: Stopping next year's hackers*. Boston: Addison-Wesley.

Schoenfield, B. S. E. (2015). *Securing systems: Applied security architecture and threat models*. Boca Raton: CRC Press.

Vendor Contract Considerations

18

It becomes increasingly important that contract considerations be included as part of the final selection process of any vendor solution (package or customized development). Organizations tend to make the mistake of leaving the contract negotiations toward the end of the selection process as opposed to making it inherently part of the process throughout each phase. That is, the contract is more a "living" document that may change as the needs of the product become more obvious to the stakeholders. In other words, the process feeds the contract needs. Thus, the purpose of this chapter is to provide guidance on the relevant stages, considerations, and content of the contract agreement. It is important to note that the information contained in this chapter is prescriptive in nature and not intended to suggest that technology or business personnel can determine whether a contract should be signed without the assistance of legal counsel, but it does provide a checklist of things to ensure that lawyers are aware about and ensures that the organization is protected.

What everyone wants out of a contract is to be protected, both from the organization (buyer) to the vendor (seller). The question really becomes how to provide an agreement where both sides feel that it is fair. The core factors typically include:

- *Ownership and rights*: this part contains the legal aspects of who owns the product and what rights does each party have in the use of the software.
- *Legal protection and coverage*: this contains various protections such as insurance requirements, indemnifications, and liabilities of each party.
- *Financials*: simply the cost for license of software, cost for development and programming, support and maintenance, and payment schedules.
- *Deliverables and performance*: specific things that the vendor agrees to deliver to the organization.

Each of these components will be defined and analyzed as follows.

© Springer-Verlag London Limited 2016
A.M. Langer, *Guide to Software Development*,
DOI 10.1007/978-1-4471-6799-0_18

Ownership and Rights

The most salient issue of ownership is whether the software is a package owned by another company—in which case it is likely that the product is being licensed for what is known as a "limited" use—that is, the organization is paying a license fee for the right to use the product under the conditions set forth in the agreement. Licensing does not mean ownership even if the source code of the system is delivered for use. Thus it is important to carefully understand the conditions of use, particularly reviewing any limits on use at locations, transferability (e.g., if the company is sold), conditions for forfeit of license (usually nonpayment), requirements for maintenance, and limits on disclosure about the product's source code and other proprietary information. Software license agreements are usually standard formats.

The licensed software agreement also includes provisions for the following information:

- *Operating environment*: the software may be restricted to operate within a certain hardware and software environment or platform. Packaged software license agreements normally require the vendor (or licensor) to be responsible for determining the terms of compatibility.
- *Warrantees*: this relates to safeguards that guarantee certain performance, application run-times, and specific response times of the product. All warrantees are subject to restrictions on performance based on certain peak periods.
- *License fees*: these can be complex especially when there are discounts available for volume use or use over a number of physical sites or versions (e.g., Windows, UNIX, mainframe). Organizations should concentrate on whether there are clauses for increased fees over time, especially relating to maintenance fees for updates and support from the vendor.
- *Refreshment*: this covers bug fixes and patches to software that cannot wait for regularly scheduled maintenance updates. This is a critical clause in that the organization wants to know that serious bugs or needed patches can be fixed timely.
- *Documentation*: almost all licenses come with some form of operating documentation. Today many products have documentation as part of the Help portion of the product itself, but in either case, documentation must be available.
- *Source code*: a popular part of third-party licensing is access to source code if not included as part of the license. Organizations have been using attorneys that hold the source code in escrow and will deliver the code to the organization should the vendor default. Default should include failure to perform or that the vendor goes out of business. In this way an independent agent can judge whether a default has occurred and whether the organization can protect its interests by obtaining the current code. What is also important are the procedures for ensuring that the attorney receives timely updates to the source code. This is most critical if there are customizations being applied to the source on during the project.

Legal Protections and Coverage

Agreements for software also contain a myriad of legal items that protect both organizations. These items and clauses are not necessarily unique to software agreements but important to include in any contract. Some key elements are described below:

- *Intellectual property and other indemnification (IPOI)*: IPOI clauses are very common in software license agreements. Essentially, IPOI protects the organization against any third-party law suits that have a claim against the vendor's violation of intellectual property rights of another. Thus, the buyer is protected against any suit against a claim that the software being used by the organization violates the rights of another party. The only complication on IPI is that the laws are different internationally. The laws in many countries may not uphold the same definition of what constitutes violation of intellectual property. It is therefore important in any international indemnity to clearly state that the contract will be upheld based on the laws of the USA or the UK. In this way, the organization agrees to use *that law* to resolve matters even if they occur in another country.
- *Limitation of liability*: basically this clause sets boundaries on an agreed-upon economic exposure to the organization. Specifically the limitation of liability restricts the amount of damages that can be recovered from the vendor due to contractual breaches and/or negligence. Obviously, the organization should attempt to have a provision of "unlimited" liability that covers all costs, including legal and out-of-pocket expenses should the vendor be found guilty. Such clauses, if enacted, could easily bankrupt the vendor. Thus, vendors try to limit their exposure and risk by restricting contractually what can be recovered. Most vendors will suggest that the limit be set to the amount of the vendor's insurance coverage, which means that the amount must be known and possibly increased to an amount that the organization is comfortable with having should something occur. Setting a limit on the liability then becomes an organizational risk necessitating analysis from the management team and legal counsel.
- *Waivers*: a waiver clause allows the vendor to be excluded from a responsibility in the contract. It is suggested that no waivers be granted unless they are expressly agreed upon in writing by the organization and that waiver only be given for that specific instance. Effectively a waiver is an override to a condition in the agreement, like making a payment or delivering product by a certain time.
- *Assignment*: this clause would allow the vendor or the organization to transfer responsibilities to another party. License agreements should not allow the vendor to assign responsibility without the express written consent of the organization. Assignment gets a bit tricky when a vendor is acquired by another entity. The buyer would likely allow the new firm to assume responsibility.
- *Severability*: this clause is needed in the situation where a particular component of the contract is held illegal. The question becomes, how is the remainder of the contract to be handled? Agreements normally state that the remainder of the

contract will continue to be in force. The purpose then of severability is to avoid a complete contact becoming void should one item be found problematic.

- *Notice*: this statement provides information for both the vendor and the organization. It instructs both parties on how notifications are to be communicated between the parties and typically provides a physical address and department where the parties need to be notified. This ensures that both parties are aware should there be a contractual problem.
- *Force majeure*: stands for "superior force" in French and is used to excuse both parties from contractual obligation when there is an unusual event—or as they say, "act of God," like an earthquake, hurricane, etc. The clause does not excuse neglect of duties, however.
- *Confidentiality/privacy*: this clause protects the proprietary information of the entities. It typically states that any information discovered or used during the engagement remains the property of the associated entity (vendor or organization) and that it cannot be shared with any other parties without the written approval of the other party.
- *Proprietary rights/work for hire*: this clause protects the ownership rights of each party. The proprietary rights protect the vendor and the organization. That is, the vendor maintains ownership of the packaged product, but the organization may have ownership of the custom modifications made to the product. This can be a very sticky part of the contract. Certain packaged software vendors will attempt to absorb any custom modifications into their core product and market it to other organizations. In some cases this has advantages for both parties in that the customized portion, if part of the base product, must be maintained by the vendor. On the other hand, if the customizations are proprietary to the organizations or are deemed to be competitive advantages, then it is important that such customizations remain under the ownership of the organization. In these cases, the organization should specify these customizations as a "work for hire" which stipulates that the vendor is being paid to develop an application solely for the use by the organization and becomes the exclusive ownership of the paying organization.

Financials

Financials is usually found in a section of the contract called "fees and payments." This section provides information about license fees, maintenance fees, programming fees, and any other fees associated with delivery. The financial section also contains information about payroll tax liabilities, sales tax responsibilities, and invoicing procedures. Details of each of these issues are discussed below:

- *License fees and rates*: this information is usually contained in an exhibit or addendum of the contract. Thus, the body of the agreement "points" to the exhibit which contains specific information regarding license fees, maintenance rates, per diem programming costs, and any other agreed-upon costs such as a fixed price for custom modifications. The reason for having these costs identified in an

exhibit is to allow for easier modifications should they arise. These modifications could be the result of an expansion of the original contract which would normally require the re-execution of the agreement. Exhibits, therefore, usually have a separate signature page so that if a change is required, only the Exhibit page needs to be resigned. This is shown in the sample contract in Fig. 16.1.

- *Sales taxes*: this is an important section to ensure that the organization is not responsible for paying the sales tax should the vendor either not collect it or not pay the tax to the appropriate state. Sales taxes can be complicated especially since it is collected separately for each state and may depend on where the software is licensed, where the vendor resides, and ultimately where the software is actually used. All of these issues and corresponding liabilities need to be the responsibility of the vendor. Furthermore, the fact that it is part of the agreement establishes the disclosure of the responsibilities and will certainly expose the responsibility to pay sales tax to the vendor.
- *Payroll taxes*: this is another important clause for protecting the organization. Should the vendor use contract labor on the engagement, they may be considered an employee of the vendor by the IRS. IRS rulings in this area can be vague in terms of what constitutes an employee. In either case, you want to protect the organization against any liabilities should the IRS determine that a vendor's consultant must be treated as an employee of that vendor. This section should also address the vendor's employees, that is, that the vendor agrees that they must pay federal, state, and local withholding taxes. While this might seem obvious, government agencies might seek those funds from the organization should the vendor be late or in default of paying.
- *Invoicing*: this section addresses two important issues: (1) where invoices should be sent and (2) net terms of payment. The latter states the number of days before invoices will be paid to the vendor. Some organizations and/or vendors will offer a discount on the amount due if payment is made sooner. Depending on the situation with cash flow and the general philosophy of the organization, discounts can be advantageous for both the vendor and the organization. Some organizations, particularly those that are cash rich, may not want to participate in a discount plan. This should all be addressed in the invoice section.
- *Insurance*: this section requires the vendor to have certain insurance provisions above and beyond just indemnifications. This usually includes comprehensive general liability and property coverage, which protects the organization against any damages that a vendor's employee or consultant does purposefully or inadvertently (e.g., damaging a PC) while on premise. The organization might also require errors and omissions (E&O) coverage. E&O protects the organization from any professional errors made by the vendor that can cause problems—such as converting data incorrectly and creating a false representation of information. Other insurance requirements include auto insurance, and inappropriate advertising liability. The organization should require the vendor to provide a "certificate of insurance" that evidences the coverage and names the organization as an insured.

Deliverables and Performance

This section of the agreement should contain specific information about what the vendor has agreed to deliver to the organization. This should include the product itself, custom modifications, and in general particular features and functions that are deemed critical for the application to be useful to the organization. Another way of stating this is that this section should include critical things about the application that if not delivered would be detrimental to the success of the project. Some key subsections are described below:

- *Warranty*: this clause states that the vendor warrants all of its software and services to the specifications provided to the organization. The specifications should be included in the agreement and/or point to a particular set of documents that provide more detail about what the product/services provide. Typically such a document could include the vendor's user manual, advertisement materials, and requirements documents prepared by the organization or the vendor's consultants. Often the list of warranty information is contained in an addendum or exhibit of the contract. This type of warranty differs from the warranty of runtime performance but can be included in the same section of the contract.
- *Disputes and remedies*: this subsection addresses the procedures for dealing with problems that arise during the completion of the contract. It could include things that are not specifically addressed in the contract or new things that may be deemed as "implied" in the contract. It could also relate to when something is considered complete and therefore relates when a specific payment is due in the contract.
- *Security*: this section requires the vendor to abide by the organizations internal security requirements. This typically includes access to system policies, on-site behavior and accommodations, and in general protection of the data that a vendor will have access to during the implementation.

Figure 18.1 provides a sample of how the above provisions are formatted in a contract for software and services.

This SOFTWARE and CONSULTING SERVICES AGREEMENT ("Agreement") is made

this ___ day of XXXXXXX, 2011 ("Effective Date") by and between Sample

Applications Contract ("SAC"), with a place of business at Xyz Blvd, New York, NY

10026, and the consultant identified below ("Vendor").

Vendor Name: A. Langer & Assoc.

Address: 510A James Hall

City: New York State: Zip: 10027
 NY

Telephone: 914 261-6142 Fax: 212 865-1324

VENDOR HAS READ AND AGREES TO THE TERMS AND CONDITIONS ANNEXED
HERETO.

A. Langer & Assoc., Inc **Sample Application Contract**

By: _____ By: _____

Print Name: _Arthur M. Langer_____ Print Name: _____

Title: _President_____ Title: _____

Date: _____ Date: _____

Fig. 18.1 Software and consulting services agreement

TERMS AND CONDITIONS

Subject to the terms and conditions set forth in Exhibit I executed by SAC and Vendor, Vendor agrees to perform the consulting services described below. .

1. SOFTWARE and SERVICES.

1.1 Vendor shall, in a professional manner, provide to SAC the software and services described in Exhibit I for the fees or compensation set forth therein.

1.2 All rights and benefits granted hereunder to SAC and the terms of this Agreement extend to and may be used and/or exercised by SAC, their affiliates, subsidiaries and business divisions (the "SAC Organization"). The term "SAC" as used throughout this Agreement includes each entity in the SAC Organization. Notwithstanding the foregoing, any modification of this Agreement executed by the signatories is binding upon any SAC Organization, and any action or consent taken by SAC on its own behalf is binding upon any SAC Organization for the purposes of this Agreement. This Agreement is not intended to, nor may it be deemed to, create any enforceable rights, remedies or performance obligations upon any SAC Organization except with respect to Exhibit 1 & Exhibit 2.

2. PROPRIETARY RIGHTS.

2.1 Vendor acknowledges and agrees that the Services performed hereunder, and all materials, products, reports, audio and/or visual works, computer programs (source and object code), documentation, deliverables and inventions conceived, developed or prepared for SAC by Vendor in performance of the Services and all elements thereof (the "Work Product") are Confidential Information (as defined in Section 3.1 below) and the property of SAC. All right, title and interest in and to the Work Product vests in SAC and shall be deemed to be a work made for hire, made under the copyright laws of the United States in the course of performing the Services. To the extent that title to any such Work Product does not vest in SAC by operation of law, or such Work Product is not considered a work made for hire under such copyright laws, all right, title and interest therein are hereby irrevocably assigned to SAC. All Work Product belongs exclusively to SAC, with SAC having the right to obtain and to hold in its own name copyright registrations, patents and such other intellectual property protection as may be appropriate to the subject matter, and any extensions and renewals thereof. Vendor agrees to give SAC, and any person designated by SAC, reasonable assistance, at SAC's expense, required to perfect the rights defined in this Section, including, but not limited to, executing and delivering all assignment of copyright and ancillary and confirmatory documents requested by SAC in connection therewith. Alternatively, Vendor irrevocably appoints SAC as Vendor's attorney-in-fact with full powers of substitution and delegation to sign all documents that may be necessary to evidence SAC's ownership rights in the Work Product or any copyright. Vendor waives any moral rights that it may have in the Work Product and

represents that it will obtain a waiver of the moral rights of all authors of the Work Product. Vendor may use the Work Product only to perform its obligations under any Engagement Schedule. Unless otherwise directed by SAC, upon the completion of the Services or upon the earlier termination of the engagement, Vendor shall immediately turn over to SAC all Work Product as well as all materials and deliverables developed by Vendor, including, but not limited to, working papers, descriptions, reports, notes and data. All Work Product shall bear SAC's copyright and trade secret notices, as specified by SAC. No rights to the Work Product remain with Vendor.

2.2 Notwithstanding the foregoing, unless otherwise provided for in this agreement, Vendor reserves all rights in and to the tools, utilities and standards developed by Vendor prior to or independent of the Services hereunder and utilized to provide the Services ("Vendor Tools"). Work Product does not include any Vendor owned software or software licensed from any third party, including without limitation, open source software, unless such software is specifically identified in an Engagement Schedule issued hereunder. In the event and to the extent that the Work Product contains any software or other items or elements which may be proprietary to Vendor or a third party, Vendor hereby grants SAC, its agents, consultants and other third parties, an irrevocable, worldwide, royalty free, nonexclusive license to use, execute, reproduce, modify, display, perform, and distribute copies of and prepare derivative works based on the Vendor Tools and/or any Vendor or third party software, items or elements which may be contained in the Work Product, and to authorize others to do any of the foregoing.

3. CONFIDENTIALITY/PRIVACY.

3.1 Vendor acknowledges that in the course of its engagement by SAC, Vendor may receive or have access to confidential and proprietary information about, and Vendor's engagement by SAC may bring it into close contact with confidential and proprietary information of SAC or third parties with whom SAC conducts business. Such information is defined below and collectively referred to as "Confidential Information." In recognition of the foregoing, Vendor covenants and agrees that:

3.1.1 it will keep and maintain all Confidential Information in strict confidence, using such degree of care as is appropriate to avoid unauthorized use or disclosure;

3.1.2 it will use and disclose Confidential Information solely for the purposes for which such information, or access to it, was provided pursuant to the terms of this Agreement, and will not use or disclose Confidential Information for Vendor's own purposes or for the benefit of anyone other than SAC;

3.1.3 it will not, directly or indirectly, disclose Confidential Information to anyone outside SAC, except with SAC's prior written consent as permitted under the terms of this Agreement; and

3.1.4 it shall, upon the earlier of (i) completion of an engagement or termination of this Agreement or the applicable Engagement Schedule; (ii) determination that it has no need for Confidential Information; or (iii) at any time SAC requests, dispose of all records, electronic or otherwise (including all backup records and/or other copies thereof) regarding or including any Confidential Information that Vendor may then possess or control. Disposal may be achieved, at SAC's option, through prompt delivery of the records to SAC or destruction pursuant to Vendor's written policy governing such destruction and in a manner that renders the records unreadable and undecipherable by any means. Upon any occurrence of (i), (ii), or (iii) above, Vendor shall promptly certify in writing to SAC, in a form acceptable to SAC and executed by an authorized officer of Vendor, that all such Confidential Information has been destroyed or returned.

Vendor shall be permitted to disclose Confidential Information only to its employees and permitted subcontractors (individually an "Employee" and collectively, "Employees") having a need to know such information in connection with the performance of the Services, provided that any subcontracting and disclosure of Confidential Information to a subcontractor shall be subject to SAC's prior written consent pursuant to Section 8.1 hereof. Vendor shall instruct all Employees as to their obligations under this Agreement, and shall obtain from each Employee his or her written acknowledgment and agreement to be bound by the terms and conditions of this Agreement prior to such Employee being given access to the Confidential Information. SAC may provide Vendor with a confidentiality agreement to be executed by each Employee providing Services hereunder or Vendor shall otherwise obtain SAC's written consent to Vendor's form. Vendor shall be responsible for all Employees' compliance with the terms of this Agreement. If Vendor is required by law to disclose Confidential Information, Vendor shall promptly notify SAC in writing in advance of such disclosure, and provide SAC with copies of any related information so that SAC may take appropriate action to protect the Confidential Information.

3.2 Confidential Information includes all business and other proprietary information of SAC, written or oral, including without limitation the following:

3.2.1 information relating to planned or existing businesses or business initiatives; organizational restructuring plans; and actual and projected sales, profits and other financial information;

3.2.2 information relating to technology, such as computer systems and systems architecture, including, but not limited to, computer hardware, computer software, source code, object code, documentation, methods of processing and operational methods;

3.2.3 information that describes insurance, annuities and financial services products and strategies, including, but not limited to, actuarial calculations,

product designs, product administration and management; tax interpretations, tax positions and treatment of any item for tax purposes;

3.2.4 confidential information, software and material of third parties with whom SAC conducts business;

3.2.5 information about SAC employees and personnel;

3.2.6 "Personal Information," which means information provided by or at the direction of SAC, or to which access was provided in the course of Vendor's performance of this Agreement that (i) identifies an individual (by name, signature, address, telephone number or other unique identifier), or (ii) that can be used to authenticate that individual (including, without limitation, passwords or PINs, biometric data, unique identification numbers, answers to security questions, or other personal identifiers). An individual's social security number, even in isolation, is Personal Information. SAC business contact information is not by itself Personal Information.

Notwithstanding the foregoing, Confidential Information does not include information that (i) is lawfully made available to the general public from federal, state, or local government records, (ii) is or becomes generally known to the public not as a result of a disclosure by Vendor, (iii) is rightfully in the possession of Vendor prior to disclosure by SAC, or (iv) is received by Vendor in good faith and without restriction from a third party not under a confidentiality obligation to SAC and having the right to make such disclosure. The foregoing exceptions do not apply to the disclosure of Personal Information, which shall not be disclosed without SAC's prior written consent unless required by law.

3.3 Vendor agrees to comply with any and all privacy and/or security policies, rules and practices, as SAC may issue, amend, or otherwise make available from time to time pursuant to Section 11.18 of this Agreement.

3.4 Vendor shall notify SAC, promptly and without unreasonable delay, but in no event more than forty-eight (48) hours of learning that unauthorized access to, disclosure of, or breach in the security of Confidential Information may have occurred or been attempted (a "Security Incident"). Thereafter, Vendor shall, at its own cost and expense:

3.4.1 promptly furnish to SAC full details of the Security Incident;

3.4.2 assist and cooperate fully with SAC in SAC's investigation of Vendor, Employees or third parties related to the Security Incident, including but not limited to providing SAC with physical access to the facilities and operations

affected, facilitating interviews with Employees and others involved in the matter, and making available all relevant records, logs, files, and data;

3.4.3 cooperate with SAC in any litigation or other formal action against third parties deemed necessary by SAC to protect its rights; and

3.4.4 promptly use its best efforts to prevent a recurrence of any such Security Incident.

In addition to the foregoing, Vendor agrees that in the event of a Security Incident, SAC shall have the sole right to determine (i) whether notice is to be provided to any individuals, regulators, law enforcement agencies, consumer reporting agencies, or others as required by law or regulation, or in SAC's discretion; and (ii) the contents of such notice, whether any type of remediation may be offered to affected persons, and the nature and extent of any such remediation. Any such notice or remediation shall be at Vendor's sole cost and expense.

3.6 Vendor certifies that its treatment of Personal Information is in compliance with applicable laws and/or regulations with respect to privacy and data security and that it has implemented and currently maintains an effective information security program that includes administrative, technical, and physical safeguards to (a) ensure the security and confidentiality of Personal Information; (b) protect against any anticipated threats or hazards to the security or integrity of such Personal Information; and (c) protect against unauthorized access to, destruction, modification, disclosure or use of Personal Information which could result in substantial harm or inconvenience to SAC, or to any person who may be identified by such Personal Information. Vendor shall immediately notify SAC if Vendor is in material breach of this Section. At SAC's request, Vendor agrees to certify in writing to SAC, its compliance with the terms of this Section.

3.7 Notwithstanding any remedy of a material breach of this Section 3, SAC reserves the right to terminate this Agreement within 90 days upon written notice to Vendor should such material breach occur, and SAC may pursue all such remedies as may be available to it at law or in equity.

4. FEES AND PAYMENT.

4.1 **Fees and Expenses**.

4.1.1 Fees for the Services and payment schedule is specified in Exhibit 2. The fees for Services are fixed for the term of the Agreement or any addendums.

4.1.2 SAC agrees that additional needs above those identified in Exhibit 1 could require more or different Vendor consultants. Such increases or changes

in scope shall be negotiated and additional Exhibits or Engagement Schedules will be added to this Agreement as required.

4.1.3 Except as set forth otherwise in Exhibit 1, Vendor is entitled to reimbursement from SAC only for documented "out-of-pocket" expenses that are reasonably incurred and necessary for Vendor's performance of the Services. SAC must pre-approve in writing all expenses for reimbursement. In the event that any travel is required, Vendor shall comply with SAC's travel policies. Under no circumstances will SAC reimburse Vendor for first class or business class travel.

4.2 **Invoices.**

4.2.1 Vendor shall invoice SAC monthly for all fees due hereunder by submitting each invoice to the address indicated in this Agreement.

4.3 **Taxes.** In addition to the fees payable hereunder:

4.3.1 Vendor shall specifically state and bill all applicable taxes related to SAC's acquisition of Services in its invoices. Vendor shall indicate on each invoice the jurisdiction, or jurisdictions as the case may be, for which any such tax is being collected. Vendor shall remit all such taxes collected from SAC to the appropriate taxing authority. Vendor shall be responsible for interest and penalties associated with a failure by Vendor to appropriately collect, remit or timely file appropriate tax returns for any such tax to the appropriate tax authority.

4.3.2 In the event that SAC supplies Vendor with appropriate exemption certificates, the parties agree that the determination of the amount of sales tax, if any, and any other determinations of a substantive or procedural nature relating to such tax, will be the responsibility and prerogative of SAC, in its sole discretion.

4.3.3 In those states in which Vendor has no obligation to collect sales tax and only in those states in which SAC has an obligation to report and remit sales, use or similar tax, SAC shall be responsible for payment directly to such taxing authority of any sales, use or similar tax imposed in connection with the Services.

4.3.4 Vendor further agrees that in the event that Vendor has no obligation to collect and remit sales tax, Vendor shall not include any such tax on any invoices or payment requests. Further, if Vendor does erroneously include such tax that SAC is not required to remit, and SAC does remit such tax to Vendor, Vendor shall promptly reimburse SAC for such erroneously charged tax.

4.3.5 If Vendor is notified by any jurisdiction that it had an obligation to collect sales, use or similar tax from SAC, and Vendor has failed or neglected to include such tax in its invoice to SAC, Vendor shall so advise SAC in a timely manner and Vendor shall allow SAC the right to actively participate in the contest or settlement of such tax. If the resolution of this issue is held to be taxable, SAC shall promptly remit such tax to Vendor or demonstrate that the tax has already been paid by SAC to the taxing authority. Vendor is responsible for interest and penalties where it had an obligation to collect sales, use or similar tax from SAC, and Vendor failed or neglected to include such tax in its invoice to SAC.

4.3.6 Vendor shall be solely responsible for the payment of all withholding taxes for its Employees, including, but not limited to, federal and state income taxes, social security taxes, unemployment insurance taxes and any other applicable taxes.

5. WARRANTIES

5.1 **Warranty**. Vendor warrants that:

5.1.1 it has the expertise to perform the Services in a professional and workmanlike manner and it will perform the Services in accordance with the specifications and description of such Services as set forth in Exhibit I or the applicable Engagement Schedule;

5.1.2 all Work Product conforms to the specifications or descriptions thereof in Exhibit I or the Engagement Schedule;

5.1.3 it will not introduce into any Work Product and the Work Product does not contain any virus or any other contaminant, or disabling devices including, but not limited to, codes, commands or instructions that may have the effect or be used to access, alter, delete, damage or disable the Work Product, other software, SAC information or other SAC property, in a manner other than in accordance with specifications;

5.1.4 all Work Product and Vendor Tools (i) is original to Vendor (or its subcontractors, as the case may be); (ii) is in all respects copyrightable; (iii) does not violate any patent, copyright, trade secret or other property right of any other party; (iv) has been written and developed by Vendor or its subcontractors without referring to or copying lines of code, or the structure, sequence or organization of any software owned by another person or entity or in which another person or entity has a valid and existing copyright;

5.1.5 it has all consents, permissions and/or licenses necessary to perform the Services and Vendor shall comply with all applicable federal, state and

local laws, rules and regulations, and shall obtain all applicable permits and licenses required to perform the Services;

5.1.6 Vendor shall not (i) include in any Work Product prepared or provided to SAC, or (ii) use in conjunction with the performance of Services for SAC on SAC's premises, any existing software or materials licensed from any third party, including without limitation open source software, without the prior written consent of SAC. Vendor shall specifically identify any such third-party software or materials for which it seeks SAC's consent in the applicable Engagement Schedule. With respect to any such third party software and materials to be included in Work Product, Vendor warrants and represents that it has all rights necessary to provide such software and materials to, and/or use such software and materials for the benefit of, SAC;

6. INDEMNITIES; LIMITATION ON LIABILITY

6.1 **Vendor Indemnity.** Vendor agrees to indemnify, defend and hold harmless SAC, its assignees, directors, officers, employees and agents, from and against any action brought against same with respect to any claim, loss, demand, cause of action, debt, liability, penalty or fines, including legal fees and expenses, to the limit of WOS' insurance coverage and based upon:

6.1.1 a claim that any Work Product, Services, Vendor Tools or any other software or other material provided, used or delivered by Vendor hereunder infringes or violates any patents, copyrights, trade secrets, licenses, or other property rights of any third party;

6.1.2 personal injury or property damage caused by the fault or negligence of Vendor;

6.1.3 any breach of the terms and warranties provisions contained herein or willful, intentional or negligent actions or failures by Vendor or its agents hereunder;

6.1.4 a claim that any Employee or any person provided to SAC by Vendor to perform services under this Agreement is a SAC employee and not Vendor's employee or an independent contractor, including, but not limited to: (1) any taxes SAC is required to pay on behalf of any Employee; (2) the cost of any employee benefits SAC is required to provide to or pay for on behalf of any Employee; (3) any claim, lawsuit, or proceeding brought by Vendor's Employees against SAC based upon the employer-employee relationship; and (4) breach by any Employee of any of the provisions of this Agreement, including, but not limited to, the provisions regarding subcontractors looking only to Vendor for payment for services which may be rendered.

6.2 **LIMITATIONS ON LIABILITY.**

6.2.1 NEITHER PARTY SHALL BE LIABLE FOR ANY LOST PROFITS, LOST SAVINGS, OR OTHER CONSEQUENTIAL DAMAGES, EVEN IF SUCH PARTY HAS BEEN ADVISED OF THE POSSIBILITY OF OR COULD HAVE FORESEEN SUCH DAMAGES. THE AGGREGATE LIABILITY OF EACH PARTY UNDER THIS AGREEMENT SHALL NOT EXCEED THE TOTAL FEES PAID BY SAC TO VENDOR HEREUNDER.

6.2.2 THE LIMITATIONS ON LIABILITY AND REMEDIES CONTAINED IN SECTION 6.2 ABOVE SHALL NOT APPLY TO:

(a) LIABILITY ARISING UNDER SECTION 6.1 OF THIS AGREEMENT; AND/OR

(b) DAMAGES INCURRED DUE TO INTENTIONAL OR GROSSLY NEGLIGENT ACTS OR NON-PERFORMANCE BY VENDOR; AND/OR

(c) DAMAGES INCURRED DUE TO ABANDONMENT OR DELIBERATE BREACH OF VENDOR'S OBLIGATIONS HEREUNDER; AND/OR

(d) DAMAGAES INCURRED DUE TO A BREACH OF VENDOR'S CONFIDENTIALITY OR SYSTEM SECURITY OBLIGATIONS.

7. OTHER RIGHTS AND OBLIGATIONS.

7.1 **Independent Contractor.** Vendor is acting in performance of this Agreement as an independent contractor. Vendor's employees are not employees or agents of SAC, and are not entitled to any of SAC's employee benefits. SAC is not responsible for payment of workers' compensation, disability benefits or unemployment insurance, nor is SAC responsible for withholding or paying employment related taxes for Vendor or its employees. Vendor shall not subcontract the Services, or any part thereof, without the prior written consent of SAC. With respect to any Services which are subcontracted or provided by any third party: (i) Vendor hereby assumes all liability and responsibility for such subcontractors' and third parties' compliance with and breach of the terms of this Agreement and Engagement Schedules, and for all acts and omissions of such subcontractors and third parties; and (ii) Vendor shall include a provision in all of its agreements with subcontractors stating that such subcontractors shall look to Vendor for payment and shall under no circumstances look to any other party, including SAC, for payment.

7.2 **Vendor Resources.** In the event that any Employee assigned to perform Services is found to be unacceptable to SAC, SAC shall notify Vendor of such fact and Vendor shall immediately remove such individual from the engagement, and, if

requested by SAC, use diligent efforts to provide replacements acceptable to SAC within three (3) days of said notice, or such other period as may be agreed to by the parties.

7.3 **Security**. Vendor shall comply with SAC's system security policies, procedures and requirements ("Security Regulations") for computer systems and software used to access Confidential Information ("Systems"). Vendor and its Employees will not tamper with, compromise or circumvent any Security Regulations. Vendor shall ensure that only those users who are specifically authorized to gain access to SAC's Systems gain such access. Vendor shall prevent unauthorized destruction, alteration or loss of information contained in SAC's Systems. If at any time SAC or Vendor determines that any Employee has sought to circumvent or has circumvented SAC's Security Regulations or that an unauthorized person has accessed or may access SAC's Systems or a person has engaged in activities that may lead to the unauthorized access, destruction or alteration or loss of data, information or software, Vendor shall immediately terminate any such person's access and immediately notify SAC. If SAC reasonably determines that an Employee has attempted to or has circumvented SAC's Security Regulations, SAC may immediately terminate such person's access to the Systems and shall immediately advise Vendor. SAC may audit Vendor's use of the Systems. Vendor agrees that SAC may review any information, electronic mail communications, or other data stored on or contained in any computer hard drive, disk, or any other storage medium located on SAC's premises to determine whether there has been any breach of security or violation of this Agreement, regardless of whether such computer hard drives, disks, storage media or electronic mail communications are on equipment owned or leased by SAC or are brought or sent onto SAC's premises by Vendor or its Employees. In the event that SAC concludes that there has been any breach of security or violation of this Agreement by Vendor or its Employees, SAC reserves the right to disclose any computer files or electronic mail message to third parties, including (but not limited to) law enforcement officials, as SAC deems appropriate without any prior notice to any individuals who may have written, sent or received such files or message.

7.4 **Consultant Screening**. Prior to placing any Manager or Supervisor level Employee with SAC, Vendor is required to:

7.4.1 allow identified SAC personnel to interview and approve any such placement;

7.4.2 agree that it will not place on assignment at SAC any Employee who has not consented to, and/or satisfied the conditions contained in this Agreement, subject to applicable federal, state or local laws.

7.5 **SAC Policies**. Vendor agrees to comply with SAC's information systems related policies and standards (which include technology, product, and process standards) when delivering Services and Work Products to SAC.

8. TERMINATION.

8.1 This Agreement is effective as of the Effective Date and continues until terminated in accordance with the terms of this Agreement or any applicable Engagement Schedule. SAC, however, may terminate the Services to be provided pursuant to any Engagement Schedule for the reasons set forth in this Section without terminating this Agreement.

8.2 SAC may terminate this Agreement or the Services to be provided under any Engagement Schedule, as follows:

> 8.2.1 Termination for Cause. SAC may terminate this Agreement or any Engagement Schedule in the event that Vendor or any of its agents breaches any of the terms of this Agreement and said breach is not cured within ten (10) days after written notice thereof to Vendor..

> 8.2.2 Termination without Cause. SAC may terminate this Agreement or any Engagement Schedule at any time and for any reason upon 90 days' written notice to Vendor.

8.3 If SAC terminates this Agreement without cause, then SAC's sole obligation is to reimburse Vendor for Services satisfactorily performed by Vendor up to the effective date of such termination. If SAC terminates this Agreement or any Engagement Schedule for cause, then SAC has no obligation to make any further payment to Vendor or any third party for any outstanding charges or invoices for Services performed.

9. INSURANCE.

Vendor shall obtain from a company or companies acceptable to SAC, having a current A.M. Best Rating of A- VIII or better, and maintain in force during the term of this Agreement and for not less than two (2) years thereafter, the following insurance coverage in the minimum amounts indicated:

TYPE OF COVERAGE	REQUIRED AMOUNT
Comprehensive General Liability Insurance including Broad Form Contractual, Broad Form Property damage Personal Injury and Advertising Liability, Completed Operation and Products coverage	$1,000,000 combined single limit/general aggregate $2,000,000

Where applicable, the above policies shall name SAC and/or the applicable SAC Organization as additional insureds. Vendor shall, upon request, provide SAC with a Certificate or Certificates of Insurance evidencing that the above insurance requirements have been satisfied and specifying that SAC shall receive a minimum 30-day written advance notice of any cancellation of or reduction in coverage.

10. GENERAL.

10.1 **No Publicity.** Vendor shall not use the name, trademark, service mark, trade name, logo or other commercial or product designations of SAC in any way, in print or electronic format or on a web or internet site, without the prior written consent of SAC in each instance.

10.2 **No Waiver; Remedies**. A party may not waive a right or remedy except pursuant to a writing executed by such party. No failure or delay in exercising any right or remedy or requiring the satisfaction of any condition under this Agreement, and no course of dealing between the parties, operates as a waiver or estoppel of any right, remedy or condition. A waiver made in writing on one occasion is effective only in that instance and only for the purpose that it is given and is not to be construed as a waiver on any future occasion. No single or partial exercise of any right or remedy under this Agreement precludes the simultaneous or subsequent exercise of any other right or remedy. The rights and remedies of the parties set forth in this Agreement are not exclusive of, but are cumulative to, any rights or remedies now or subsequently existing at law, in equity or by statute.

10.3 **Severability.** If a court of competent jurisdiction determines that any provision of this Agreement is invalid, illegal or unenforceable under any applicable statute or rule of law, such provision is to that extent deemed omitted, and the balance of the Agreement remains in full force if the essential terms and conditions of this Agreement for each party remain valid, binding and enforceable.

10.4 **Assignment.** This Agreement is binding upon the parties' respective successors and permitted assigns. Vendor shall not assign any of its rights or delegate any performance under this Agreement, voluntarily or involuntarily, whether by merger, consolidation, dissolution, change of control, operation of law or any other manner, except with the prior written consent of SAC. Any purported assignment by Vendor of rights or delegation of performance without SAC's prior written consent is void, and SAC is entitled to terminate this Agreement effective as of the date SAC obtains knowledge of the purported assignment or delegation without prejudice to SAC's claims for damages. SAC may assign this Agreement in whole or in part and/or any of its rights, licenses, duties and/or obligations hereunder, upon written notice to Vendor and without Vendor's consent, to any SAC Organization, or in connection with a reorganization, demutualization or change of control of SAC, a business unit, division or line of business

10.5 Governing Law. The laws of the State of New York, without giving effect to its choice of law principles, govern all matters arising under or relating to this Agreement and all of the transactions it contemplates, including, without limitation, its validity, interpretation, construction, performance and enforcement. The parties further agree that the Uniform Computer Information Transactions Act (UCITA) does not apply to this Agreement.

10.6 Forum. Any party bringing a legal action or proceeding against any other party arising out of or relating to this Agreement shall bring the legal action or proceeding in the United States District Court for the District of New York City. Each party waives, to the fullest extent permitted by law, (a) any objection which it may now or later have to the laying of venue of any action or proceeding arising out of or relating to this Agreement brought in the United States District Court for the District of New York, or any court of the State of New York sitting in New York City; and (b) any claim that any action or proceeding brought in any such court has been brought in an inconvenient forum.

10.7 Waiver of Trial by Jury. EACH PARTY, TO THE EXTENT PERMITTED BY LAW, KNOWINGLY, VOLUNTARILY AND INTENTIONALLY WAIVES ITS RIGHT TO A TRIAL BY JURY IN ANY ACTION OR LEGAL PROCEEDING ARISING OUT OF OR RELATING TO THIS AGREEMENT AND THE TRANSACTIONS IT CONTEMPLATES. EACH PARTY ACKNOWLEDGES THAT IT HAS RECEIVED THE ADVICE OF COMPETENT COUNSEL.

10.8 Notices. Each party shall deliver any notices required or desired pursuant to this Agreement in writing. Notices are deemed given (i) if by hand delivery, upon receipt thereof; (ii) if mailed, five (5) days after deposit in the U.S. mails, postage prepaid, certified mail, return receipt requested, or (iii) if sent via overnight courier upon receipt. SAC shall address all notices to the Vendor at the address indicated on the first page of this Agreement. Vendor shall address all notices to SAC pursuant to the notice provision contained in the applicable Engagement Schedule.

10.9 Survival. All provisions hereof relating to proprietary rights, confidentiality and non-disclosure, indemnification and limitation of liability survive the completion of the Services or any earlier termination, expiration or rescission of this Agreement.

10.10 EEO Requirements. To the extent applicable, the equal employment opportunity and affirmative action requirements set forth in 41 C.F.R. Part 60-1.4(a) (women and minorities), 41 C.F.R. Part 60-250.5(a) (covered veterans) and 41 C.F.R. Part 60-741.5(a) (individuals with disabilities) are hereby incorporated by reference into this Agreement.

10.11 Right to Hire. SAC shall have the right to hire any Vendor Employee for no additional fee. SAC agrees to provide Vendor with 90 days notice to allow Vendor to replace hired Employee.

10.12 **Further Assurances.** After the Effective Date at SAC's request, Vendor shall execute and deliver to SAC any such additional instruments, documents, conveyances or assurances and take such other actions as are necessary or appropriate to confirm and assure the rights and obligations provided for in this Agreement and consummate the transactions contemplated hereby, or otherwise to effectuate the intent and purposes of this Agreement.

10.13 **Headings.** The section headings are used in this Agreement for reference and convenience only and do not affect this Agreement's construction or interpretation.

10.14 **Subsequent Modifications.** No amendment, alteration or modification of this Agreement is effective or binding unless it is set forth in a writing signed by duly authorized representatives of both parties.

10.15 **Counterparts.** The parties may execute this Agreement in any number of duplicate originals and in multiple counterparts, each of which constitutes an original, and all of which, collectively, constitute only one agreement. The signatures of all of the parties need not appear on the same counterpart, and delivery of an executed counterpart signature page by facsimile is as effective as executing and delivering this Agreement in the presence of the other party to this Agreement. This Agreement is effective upon delivery of one executed counterpart from each party to the other party. Any party delivering an executed counterpart of this Agreement by facsimile shall also deliver a manually executed counterpart of this Agreement as soon as reasonably practicable following transmittal by facsimile, but the failure to do so does not affect the validity, enforceability or binding effect of this Agreement.

10.16 **Entire Agreement.** This Agreement, together with the exhibits and Engagement Schedules, constitutes the entire agreement between the parties in connection with the subject matter hereof and supersedes all prior and contemporaneous agreements, understandings, negotiations and discussions, whether oral or written, of the parties, and there are no warranties, representations and/or agreements between the parties in connection with the subject matter hereof except as set forth in this Agreement. The parties also understand, acknowledge and agree that, unless otherwise specified in a written instrument signed by an officer of each party, no additional terms or changes to these terms are valid or binding on the parties, even if such additional terms or changes contain provisions to the contrary.

Contract Considerations in a Global Economy

This chapter has provided common issues and consideration when working with third parties. Because of the expansion of the global economy, many companies are working with vendors who exist everywhere in the world. This is particularly true in the new "supply chain" of how products and services are delivered ultimately to their final destination. For example, the raw materials to create a product may begin in a foreign country, be shipped to another country where a different vendor provides packaging, and so forth. So the challenge for businesses is to establish contractual relations with multiple vendors in different countries, all who may have different legal systems and regulations. From an IT perspective, this may involve issues of ownership rights, particularly with who might own the product and data. Data ownership has become an enormous issue, as separate countries all have restrictions on data use and how outside companies can access and use it for their own advantages. To say the least, it is a complex issue that has yet to mature from a global legal perspective. What we see is that digital disruptions are occurring at an exponential rate where our legal systems appear to be falling further and further behind.

Furthermore, IT supply systems typically avoid a "single-point" of failure, meaning that there needs to be multiple paths to delivering a product or service in case of physical location failures (catastrophic weather or other natural disasters, for example) or political restrictions due to government changes in the legal system or in administration. In addition, a vendor's business could fail, which would immediately cause a blockage to the supply chain. As a result, businesses need to deal with multiple levels of legal advice, both internally and externally. Multiple outside counsels are typically necessary and IT must now be intimately aware of the legal aspects of everything within the supply chain. As with most legal issues, risk of exposure and ramifications of decisions can be critical to the success or failure of any global IT project. In effect, all of the information discussed in this chapter becomes more dimensional in the global context. Worst-case scenarios must be discussed and decisions on IT projects might need executive review given the potential for exposures both from a legal and reputation point of view. Bad press can come quickly across global markets as we have seen with companies like Amazon and Google who are continually at odds with country legal restrictions on their business endeavors.

EXHIBIT 1
ENGAGEMENT SCHEDULE Schedule No. _1_
Project Scope
1. License base XYZ enterprise software for 250 users
2. Customized programming per requirements document
3. User training
4. Annual maintenance including 8 h help desk support

IN WITNESS WHEREOF, the parties have executed this Engagement Schedule by their duly authorized representatives.

A. Langer & Assoc., Inc	Sample Application Contract
By: _____	By: _____
Print Name: Arthur M. Langer	Print Name: _____
Title: President	Title: _____
Date: _____	Date: _____

EXHIBIT 2	
FEES	
XYZ License Software for 250 users	$ 250,000
Custom Programming for modifications per requirements document	$ 95,000
Additional Per Diem programming rate	$ 600 per day
Per diem user training rate	$ 250 per day
Annual Maintenance on base product 15 % of current advertised license fee	

Problems and Exercises

1. What are the four factors in a software and services contract?
2. What is a proprietary right?
3. What is error and omissions insurance? Who does it favor, the vendor or the organization?
4. What is indemnification? Under what conditions does indemnification apply?
5. What are the key aspects of nondisclosure?
6. How should management handle multinational agreements? What is the best way to protect the organization when dealing in multiple countries?

This chapter deals with the final part of software implementation: going live or moving the system into production. It is also fitting that this chapter contain conclusions about the methods and approaches discussed in this book. There are three major steps necessary to move the application into a production environment: user training, IT's role, and the preparation steps for going live.

User Training

This step can often be underestimated especially with the standardization of help text in products and the perception that software applications are robust. Robust is defined as applications that are "intuitively obvious" to use, so that formal training is not required. Such is likely not the reality with most integrated enterprise-level package software products. Furthermore, user training becomes more complicated when there are custom modifications to the application. Finally, if the product is developed in-house, then training may be a very comprehensive part of rolling out the application into production.

There are a number of steps to develop the right training materials:

1. Focus on the business aspects of the material, that is, what do your users need to know in terms of operating the system.
2. How many users need to be trained?
3. Utilize prototypes during the early stages of training before the product is actually ready. Prototypes are screen pictures that can be populated with data and provide users with an understanding of how data travels through the system. Some of the prototypes need to be done in demo form.
4. Provide exercises for the user groupings. Thus, it is important to develop a strategy on who should be trained and when and what are the groupings of the users.

© Springer-Verlag London Limited 2016
A.M. Langer, *Guide to Software Development*,
DOI 10.1007/978-1-4471-6799-0_19

Training Step	SDLC Stage
Determine the number of users to be trained, locations, etc.	Feasibility/Analysis and Design
Determine topics	Analysis
Design materials	Design
Determine who will train	Make/Buy
Update and Feedback	QA
Actual training	Prior to Go Live
Training iterations, including feedback	During various phases of production

Fig. 19.1 Training steps in the SDLC

5. Training needs to be iterative; do not expect that training will be effective the first time.
6. Ensure that training includes product setup requirements. New products tend to need tables that are initialized, e.g., user access rights and security.
7. Determine how the training will be delivered—that is, in a traditional classroom, online (Internet) and on demand using CBT (computer-based training), packaged delivery, or all of these!
8. Determine who will train. Is the training done by the vendor? Or does the vendor train trainers in the organization? Or some combination?
9. Where should the training take place? Are there multiple locations? Are there components of the product that are only used in specific businesses within the company?
10. Prepare for feedback from users and common problems that might be discovered during the training.
11. Determine whether certain training sessions should be taped and made available via video.

Clearly many of the above points need to be developed and planned during the SDLC, but most of the actual training must be done as close as possible to going live. If the training takes place too early, users will forget much of the details. Figure 19.1 provides additional guidance on the steps to take and decisions to be made during the SDLC.

The Role of IT

Where and when the IT organization participates in the Go Live process is another important question. There are some obvious areas where IT personnel are required:

• Placing the application on the servers and general network availability.
• Assisting with the review of technical aspects of the license agreement, e.g., runtime licenses.
• Ensuring that appropriate security is in place to protect applications and data.
• Performance testing both before and during Go Live.

- Appropriate backup and restore procedures are in place.
- Help desk personnel are available to handle peak calls during Go Live.

Another important issue is whether IT should be responsible for project management. My experience suggests that most often IT is in charge of the project. This can be both good and bad. The good part is what most would expect—that IT is the experienced organization to perform the project management. The bad part is that IT is not integrated enough in the business units and cannot really manage the project without the help from key stakeholders. I have found the best approach is to form a joint management team, where someone from IT is the project manager, but an associate from the business side provides the business side interface. There might also be a project manager from the vendor. It is this team that ultimately can get the project completed assuming that executive support is available from each of these units. This means that there must be an executive from each business unit that will use the system (or someone who has management over all of them, which is rare), the CIO from the IT side, and a senior executive from the vendor(s).

The IT project manager (IT PM) should provide most of the SDLC supervision; the business project manager (Bus PM) should organize training, plan for "go live," coordinate key events, and most importantly confirm that the requirements are accurate and complete. The Bus PM must also deal with disagreements and escalate as necessary to his/her senior management. Both the IT PM and Bus PM should jointly manage the vendor project manager. The IT PM should handle the technical and system issues and the Bus PM should ensure that the features and functions of the product are correct.

Perhaps the most salient role for IT is coordinating the Go Live administration. This includes ensuring that the systems are ready, parallel systems are in place, help desk people are ready in case of problems, and that the vendor is available to deal with problems that occur during the launch. Additionally, IT should plan to do system fine-tuning in the advent that there are performance problems with the application.

Conclusions

This book has been organized to define the necessary steps in today's SDLC. The premise of the book is that managers need to spend more time ensuring that the requirements are accurate. This may seem like an old story—get the requirements correct before implementing. However, there is little evidence to show that the success rate has changed over the past two decades. Furthermore, the days of developing software from scratch may have come to an end. The library of software routines, packages, and legacy code are vast, and the key to success is more about selecting the right software partners and managing the process. Indeed, there should be less focus on the actual development and more on the architecture and management. IT and business managers need to finalize the specifications and select the right vendors.

The realities of developing applications today, then, are to create what I call the Packaged Software SDLC. This modified SDLC is designed as a *unified* solution to what otherwise has been considered separate SDLCs depending on whether the software was developed in-house or by a third-party package. It was my intent to dispel any credibility to this notion. The SDLC is now too complex and needs to unify all the SDLCs into one cycle. The SDLC is no longer limited to IT; rather it must incorporate a much larger user interface. Business users need to be much more active in the determination of application needs. That is why assessment of needs is more important than feasibility. I also incorporated the build vs. buy and RFI/RFP steps as inherently part of that decision. I included the vendor search and selection as part of the SDLC, as opposed to a precursor or an afterthought of analysis and design. Simply put they are part of the process. Organizations can no longer just do requirements and look for the solution—the solution itself affects the completion of requirements. In addition, I included the Budget and ROI as part of the SDLC and at a much later stage than otherwise considered on traditional projects. Specifically, the traditional SDLC had feasibility as the first step. I understand why this was the case, but technology solutions today must be far more agile on spending commitments; it just changes too often during the life cycle. Once the business units know what technology and applications they need, it should not be about whether it is feasible, rather more about how much to spend versus the cost for not implementing. Budgets today need to be more about control, explanation, and negotiation than about "go" or "no go."

I also explained my driver and supporter theory, which continues to be an effective way of explaining why projects are needed, why they might change, and how to determine costs. All new projects must show why they are a driver, and this alone can help executive managers to better comprehend why the application can change the market, the risks inherently involved in the undertaking, and the importance of providing agile funding when market conditions are dynamic. I emphasize the supporter side as well, since most current applications by definition are legacies that should have been replaced decades ago, but because IT was not positioned to articulate why they needed to be redone, they have now become major impediments to creating new enterprise systems.

This book has also integrated project management and quality assurance. These two areas increase the success that projects will be more accountable and delivered on time. Too often project management and quality assurance are treated as separate subjects. Included in the chapter on project management was an emphasis on the importance of vendor contracts and adherence to standards like ISO 9000. I also transformed the Balanced Scorecard into a workable version for packaged software implementations. The Balanced Scorecard can be an effective reconciliation tool to understand how the application contributes to the organization. In addition, the strategy map provides the schematic of how learning, support, and users ultimately contribute to the financial performance of the firm.

However, the essence of this book still focuses on the importance of understanding the technical components of analysis and design. Regardless of who reads this book, whether a business user or a systems analyst, a director, or a CIO, the message is that one must know how to do architecture to have success. So everyone involved needs to understand flow diagrams, functional decomposition, pseudocode, logic data modeling, and the object paradigm. They also need to know about test planning and quality assurance as part of how the system is designed, developed, and implemented. Without adherence to the tools of analysis and design, the core of systems development cannot achieve consistent success.

Appendix A
Case Study: The Rainforest Book Company Problem

The following four events are services provided by the Rainforest Book Company:

Event I

A customer wishes to set up an account to purchase books. The Sales Department at the Rainforest Book Company receives the request and sends out a blank Account Request form. The form has space for the following information:

Customer Name
Customer Address
Customer Phone Number
Customer Fax Number
Credit Card Information (if applicable)
Credit Card Number
Type of Credit Card
Expiration Date
Cardholder's Name
Zip or postal code of the billing address for this card

The customer sends back a completed Account Request form. The "for office use only" section is filled out by the Sales Group. This information includes the processor's identification, the date the account is opened and a customer account number which is assigned. The customer account file is updated and the Account Request form is filed. The Account Processing Department receives notification of the new account and sends the customer a confirmation letter. This letter notifies the customer of their customer account number. This number can be used to expedite the ordering process.

Event II

A customer makes a book inquiry. The customer can request a book by giving any of the following information: (book title and book author) or ISBN number. The Sales Department first verifies that the customer has a valid account. If the book is found based upon the information that was given, the customer receives the following information about the book:

© Springer-Verlag London Limited 2016
A.M. Langer, *Guide to Software Development*,
DOI 10.1007/978-1-4471-6799-0

Title of the book
Author of the book
Paperback/Hardcover
Price
Date Published
Availability
Reviews

If the book is not available in stock, all of the above information is returned and an out-of-stock notice is sent specifying the approximate date the book will be in stock. If the book is no longer in print and has been discontinued, an out-of-print notice is sent to the customer. This out-of-print notice includes a list of Used-Book Stores in the customer's county.

Event III
A customer decides to purchase books, places the order for the books, and requests a book order form from the Sales Department. A blank book order form is forwarded to the customer. The customer account number and the date the order is being placed is entered. The following information is included in the book order:

Customer Account Number
Date Order is placed
Title of the Book
Author
Paperback or Hardcopy
ISBN, if available

In addition, the customer indicates the shipping option by entering the following information:

Standard Shipping or
Second Day Air or
Next Day Air

Placed orders are sent to the Warehouse and the customer account file is updated. The warehouse issues an order confirmation when the books are shipped. The invoice is generated and then sent to the customer. The customer then sends the invoice slip and payment or authorizes the use of a credit card on file to the Accounting Department. The Accounting Department processes the payment and updates the customer account.

Event IV
The Sales Department generates a monthly sales report and forwards it to Management.

Assignment:
1. Create DFDs for the four events.
2. Decompose the four top-level DFDs into their respective functional primitives.
3. Create the data dictionary entries for all the named data flows found in the child diagrams from (2). The entries in the resulting data dictionary should be reported in alphabetical order.
4. Write process specifications for all of the functional primitives from (2).

Case Study created by Cynthia Hernandez.

Appendix B
Case Study: Northwest General Practitioner's Office

The following represents information obtained during an interview with the Northwest General Practitioner's office:

> Potential patients contact the Northwest General Practitioner's office to make appointments to see a General Practitioner. All patient information is stored in a patient medical history folder.
>
> The patient must provide the following information:

Name
Social Security Number
Address
Home Telephone Number
Work or Mobile Telephone Number
Insurance Provider Name
Insurance Provider ID
Name of Primary Insurance Holder
Reason for Visit
Medical History
Family Medical History
List of Allergies

> The office examines the patient medical history file and tries to make an appointment for the patient to see the General Practitioner the patient has specified as his/her "preferred" doctor. If the patient's preference is not available at the time the patient requests for the appointment, then the office provides the patient with a list of practitioners who *are* available at that time.
>
> Additionally, practitioners join the Northwest General Practitioner's office every day. Their information is stored in a practitioner's information folder.
>
> A new practitioner must provide the following information:

Name
Social Security Number
Address
Home Telephone Number
Work or Mobile Telephone Number
Specialty (or list of specialties), if applicable
Hospital Affiliations, if applicable

© Springer-Verlag London Limited 2016
A.M. Langer, *Guide to Software Development*,
DOI 10.1007/978-1-4471-6799-0

Seven days before patients are due to come in for their appointments, the office begins to send reminder notices to them. There are three reminder notices sent. The first is sent seven days beforehand, the second is sent three days beforehand, and the third reminder takes place one day beforehand, via an automated phone call.

For those patients who are billed for services, a notice is mailed to them 30 days before payment is due.

Assignment:

1. Draw one data flow diagram depicting the logical equivalent for the above business process description.
2. Level the diagram to its functional primitives.
3. To the best of your ability, provide the data elements you will need for your data entities. **NOTE:** Pay particular attention to the patient medical history file, the physician information file, any file that keeps track of appointments, and, for extra credit, the invoice file.
4. Create an entity relational diagram depicting the relationship between your tables. **NOTE:** You should end up with at **least** eight entities, if not more.

Case Study created by Melanie Caffrey

Appendix C
Case Study: University Student Enrollment Database

The following enrollment form has been obtained from Southeast University's Computer Science program:

Student Enrollment Form	
Last Name:	_____
First Name:	_____
Social Security Number:	_____
Address Line 1:	_____
Address Line 2:	_____
City:	_____
State:	_____
Zipcode:	_____

Course #	Section #	Course Cost
_____	_____	_____
_____	_____	_____
_____	_____	_____
_____	_____	_____
_____	_____	_____
	Total Amount Due:	_____

© Springer-Verlag London Limited 2016
A.M. Langer, *Guide to Software Development*,
DOI 10.1007/978-1-4471-6799-0

The students are choosing their courses from the following Course List:

Course #	Course name	Section #	Section Time	Course Cost
QC2500	Intro to programming	1	9:00 A.M.	800.00
		2	10:30 A.M.	800.00
		3	3:15 P.M.	800.00
		4	6:00 P.M.	800.00
QC2625	Intro to analysis	1	11:00 P.M.	910.00
		2	4:00 P.M.	910.00
		3	5:30 P.M.	910.00
QC2790	Intro to web design	1	12:45 P.M.	725.00
		2	2:30 P.M.	725.00
		3	6:00 P.M.	725.00

Assignment: Using the above form, create a normalized ERD. Make sure you are in 3rd Normal Form.

HINT:
You should end up with at least four entities, possibly five.

Case Study created by Melanie Caffrey

Further Reading

Applegate, L. M., McFarlan, F. W., & McKenney, J. L. (1999). *Corporate information systems management: The challenges of managing in an information age*. New York: McGraw-Hill.

Berman, K., & Knight, J. (2008). *Finance intelligence for IT professionals*. Boston: Harvard Business Press.

Blackstaff, M. (1999). *Finance for technology decision makers: A practical handbook for buyers, sellers and managers*. New York: Springer.

Bolman, L., & Deal, T. (2003). *Reframing organizations: Artistry, choice, and leadership* (3rd ed.). San Francisco: Jossey-Bass.

Bysinger, B., & Knight, K. (1997). *Investing in information technology: A decision-making guide for business and technical managers*. New York: Wiley.

Carr, N. G. (2005). *Does IT matter? Information technology and the corrosion of competitive advantage*. Cambridge: Harvard Business School.

Chesbrough, H. (2003). *Open innovation: The new imperative for creating and profiting from technology*. Cambridge: Harvard Business School.

Chesbrough, H. (2006). *Open business models: How to thrive in the new innovation landscape*. Cambridge: Harvard Business School.

Cortada, J. W. (1997). *Best practices in information technology: How corporations get the most value from exploiting their digital investments*. Paramus: Prentice Hall.

Edwards, C., Ward, J., & Bytheway, A. (1996). *The essence of information systems* (2nd ed.). Upper Saddle River: Prentice Hall.

Gardner, C. (2000). *The valuation of information technology*. New York: Wiley.

Goonatilake, S., & Teleaven, P. (1995). *Intelligent systems for finance and business*. New York: Wiley.

Hogbin, G., & Thomas, D. (1994). *Investing in information technology: Managing the decision-making process*. New York: McGraw-Hill.

Langer, A. M. (2002). *Applied ecommerce: Analysis and engineering of ecommerce systems*. New York: Wiley.

Langer, A. M. (2004). *IT and organizational learning: Managing change through technology and education*. New York: Routledge.

Laudon, K. C., & Laudon, J. P. (1998). *Management information systems: New approaches to organization and technology*. Upper Saddle River: Prentice Hall.

Liebowitz, J., & Khosrowpour, M. (1997). *Cases on information technology management in modern organizations*. New York: Idea Group Publishing.

Lientz, B. P., & Larssen, L. (2004). *Manage IT as a business: How to achieve alignment and add value to the company*. Burlington: Elsevier Butterworth-Heinemann.

Lucas, H. C. (2005). *Information technology: Strategic decision making for managers*. New York: Wiley.

Marchand, D. A. (2000). *Competing with information: A manager's guide to creating business value with information content*. Wiley.

McCarthy, E. (1997). *The financial advisor's analytical toolbox*. New York: McGraw-Hill.

McDowell, R., & Simon, W. L. (2004). *In search of business value: Ensuring a return of your technology investment*. New York: Select Books, Inc.

Murphy, T. (2002). *Achieving business value from technology: A practical guide for today's executive*. Hoboken: Wiley.

Rapp, W. V. (2002). *Information technology strategies: How leading firms use IT to gain an advantage*. New York: Oxford University Press.

Remenyi, D., Sherwood-Smith, L., & White, T. (1997). *Achieving maximum value from information systems: A process approach*. New York: Wiley.

Speser, P. L. (2006). *The art and science of technology transfer*. Hoboken: Wiley.

Stenzel, J. (2007). *CIO best practices: Enabling strategic value with information technology*. Hoboken: Wiley.

Tushman, M., & Anderson, P. (1997). *Managing strategic innovation and change*. New York: Oxford University Press.

Von Stamm, B. (2003). *Managing innovation, design & creativity*. New York: Wiley.

Weill, P., & Ross, J. W. (2004). *IT governance*. Cambridge: Harvard Business School.

Willcocks, L. P., & Lacity, M. C. (1998). *Strategic sourcing of information systems: Perspectives and practices*. New York: Wiley.

Glossary

Acceptance Test Plans Set of tests that if passed will establish that the software can be used in production.

Alternate Key An attribute that uniquely identifies a row or occurrence in an entity. An alternate key cannot be the primary key.

Attribute A component of an entity or object. An attribute may or may not be an elementary data element.

Business Process Reengineering (BPR) A method to redesign existing applications.

Business Specification A document which reflects the overall requirements of a process or system written in a prose format. The focus of the business specification is to provide the user with enough information so they can authorize the development of the technical requirements.

Computer-Aided Software Engineering (CASE) Products which are used to automate and implement modeling tools and data repositories.

Case A format for developing application logic in a process specification.

Client An application that requests services from applications.

Crows Foot A method of showing the relationship or association between two entities.

CRUD Diagram An association matrix that matches the types of data access between entities and processes. CRUD represents create, read, update, and delete.

Data Dictionary (DD) A dictionary that defines data. A component of the data repository.

Data Flow Component of a data flow diagram that represents data entering or leaving a process, external or data store.

Data Flow Diagram (DFD) A tool that shows how data enters and leaves a process. A data flow diagram has four possible components: data flow, data store, external, and process.

Data Repository A robust data dictionary that contains information relating to data element behavior.

Data Store Component of a data flow diagram that represents data that can be accessed from a particular area or file. A data store is sometimes called "data at rest."

© Springer-Verlag London Limited 2016
A.M. Langer, *Guide to Software Development*,
DOI 10.1007/978-1-4471-6799-0

Data Warehousing A de-normalized database created to focus on decision support activities. Data warehouse holds historical information and cannot be used to update data.

Elementary Data Element A functionally decomposed data element.

Entity An object of interest about which data can be collected. Entities can consume a number of attributes.

Entity Relational Diagram (ERD) A diagram that depicts the relationships among the stored data.

Executive Sponsor An individual at an executive level who has responsibility for a business area. The executive sponsor is a defined role in JAD sessions.

External Component of a data flow diagram which represents a provider or user of data that is not part of the system. Externals are therefore boundaries of the system.

Facilitator An impartial individual responsible for controlling the flow of JAD sessions.

Functional Decomposition The process for finding the most basic parts of a system.

Functional Overview A subset view of a specification. The subset usually covers a particular function of the system.

Functional Primitive A functionally decomposed data flow diagram.

Gantt Chart A tool that depicts progress of tasks against time. The chart was developed by Henry L. Gantt in 1917.

ISO 9000 International Organization for Standardization, quality standard 9000.

Job Description Matrix The portion of an individual's job description that strictly focuses on the procedural and process aspects of the individual's position.

Joint Application Development (JAD) A method of developing the requirements for a system by focusing on group sessions. The sessions are typically under the direction of a facilitator.

Key An attribute of an entity or database that uniquely identifies a row, occurrence, or record.

Key Business Rules Business rules of key attributes that are enforced at the database level (as opposed to the application level).

Legacy System An existing automated system.

Leveling Functional decomposition of a data flow diagram. Each decomposition is called a "level."

Logical Data Modeling (LDM) A set of procedures that examines an entity to ensure that its component attributes should reside in that entity, rather than being stored in another or new entity.

Logical Equivalent An abstraction of the translation from physical requirements to software.

Long Division An abstraction of the relationship of arithmetic formulas to functional decomposition.

Metadata Data about the data being sent or received in a client/server network.

Normalization The elimination of redundancies from an entity.

Open Systems Standards in applications software that allow such software to run across multiple operating system environments.

Pre-Post Conditions A format for developing application logic in a process specification.

Primary Key A key attribute that will be used to identify connections to a particular entity. Normalization requires that every entity contains a primary key. Primary keys can be formed by the concatenation of many attributes.

Process A function in a data flow diagram in which data is transformed from one form to another.

Process Specification A document that contains all of the algorithms and information necessary to develop the logic of a process. Process specifications can be comprised of the business and programming requirement documents. Process specifications are sometimes called "minispecs."

Program or Technical Specification A technical algorithm of the requirements of a process or system.

Prototype A sample of a system that does not actually fully operate. Most software prototypes are visual depictions of screens and reports. Prototypes can vary in capability, with some prototypes having limited functional interfaces.

Pseudocode A generic or structured English representation of how real programming code must execute. Pseudocode is a method used in the development of process specifications.

Rapid Application Development (RAD) A method of application development that combines the analysis and design steps through the use of prototypes and CASE tools.

Reverse Engineering The process of analyzing existing applications and database code to create higher-level representations of the code.

Robust Software that operates intuitively and can handle unexpected events.

Scribe A person who is designated in a JAD session to record minutes and decisions made by the group. In certain situations scribes can also be responsible for data modeling.

Server An application that provides information to a requesting application.

Spiral Life Cycle Life cycle that focuses on the development of cohesive objects and classes. The spiral life cycle reflects a much larger allocation of time spent on design than the waterfall approach.

State Transition Diagram (STD) A modeling tool that depicts time-dependent and event-driven behavior.

Waterfall System Development Life Cycle A life cycle that is based on phased-dependent steps to complete the implementation of a system. Each step is dependent on the completion of the previous step.

Index

A

Acceptance test plans, 9, 16, 35, 212, 213, 292–294, 297, 312

Alternative keys, 146, 147, 149, 177

Architecture, 1, 8, 14, 15, 17, 39, 40, 72, 76–77, 89, 105, 145, 180, 192, 195, 199, 206–208, 216, 217, 224, 256, 258–263, 265, 282, 284, 285, 311, 312, 316, 318–321, 341–343, 345, 366, 369

Attributes, 141, 146–156, 158–165, 167, 173–176, 184, 187, 199, 204, 206, 216, 254, 255, 260, 269, 272–274, 284, 327, 330

B

BAA. *See* Business Area Analysis (BAA)

Balanced Scorecard, 92–97, 368–369

Batch, 197

BPR. *See* Business process re-engineering (BPR)

Budget, 7, 14, 79, 81–83, 89, 91–97, 212, 295–297, 301, 305, 306, 308–310, 315, 316, 325, 352, 368

Build *vs.* buy, vi, 11, 13, 37–47, 71, 368

Business Area Analysis (BAA), 34, 187, 194, 207, 217

Business process re-engineering (BPR), v, 11, 15, 17, 94, 184–189, 194, 207, 215–226

Business requirements, vi, 11–13, 21–36, 39, 118, 185, 215, 224, 265

Business specification, 54, 69, 70, 110, 111, 122, 297

C

CASE. *See* Computer-aided software engineering (CASE)

Chief information officer (CIO), 72, 215, 313, 333, 341, 367, 369

Client/Server, 23, 24, 174, 191, 194, 195, 209, 215–217, 221–225

Cloud, 44–47, 82, 84, 89, 90, 344

COBOL, 106–109, 112, 131, 179–183, 191, 216, 222

Combine user views, 146

Commercially-off-the-shelf (COTS), 3–4, 40, 41

Computer-aided software engineering (CASE), 22, 24, 32, 105–107, 109, 110, 133, 134, 187, 206, 219, 221, 258–259, 265, 268, 269, 274, 296, 318, 320

Concatenation, 127, 141, 150–152, 157, 158, 256

Concept of the logical equivalent, 99–103, 231

Confidentiality, 50, 358

Consulting costs, 91

COTS. *See* Commercially-off-the-shelf (COTS)

Creating, reading, updating, and deleting orders (CRUD), 189–191, 193, 195, 218, 219, 252

Critical tasks, 308

Crow's foot, 105, 142, 156–158, 166

CRUD. *See* Creating, reading, updating, and deleting orders (CRUD)

Custom modifications, 13, 39, 82, 91, 311, 358, 360, 365

© Springer-Verlag London Limited 2016
A.M. Langer, *Guide to Software Development*,
DOI 10.1007/978-1-4471-6799-0

Printed in the United States
By Bookmasters